Pacific-Asian Economic Policies and Regional Interdependence

Pacific-Asian Economic Policies and Regional Interdependence

EDITED BY
Robert A. Scalapino, Seizaburo Sato,
Jusuf Wanandi, and Sung-joo Han

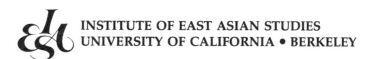

INSTITUTE OF EAST ASIAN STUDIES
UNIVERSITY OF CALIFORNIA • BERKELEY

A publication of the Institute of East Asian Studies, University of California, Berkeley. Although the Institute of East Asian Studies is responsible for the selection and acceptance of manuscripts in this series, responsibility for the opinions expressed and for the accuracy of statements rests with their authors.
Correspondence may be sent to:
Ms. Joanne Sandstrom, Editor
Institute of East Asian Studies
University of California
Berkeley, CA 94720

337.5

P119

The Research Papers and Policy Studies series is one of several publications series sponsored by the Institute of East Asian Studies in conjunction with its constituent units. The others include the China Research Monograph series, the Japan Research Monograph series, the Korea Research Monograph series, and the Indochina Research Monograph series. A list of recent publications appears at the back of the book.

113253

Contents

Abbreviations

ACP	Africa, Caribbean, and Pacific Countries
AIJV	ASEAN Industrial Joint Venture
ANZCERTA	See CER
APTQ	ASEAN Preferential Tariff Quota
ASEAN	Association of Southeast Asian Nations
AUI	ASEAN-U.S. Initiative
CBI	Caribbean Island Initiative
CER	Australia-New Zealand Closer Economic Relations Trade Agreement, or Closer Economic Relations
CMEA	See COMECON
COMECON	Council for Mutual Economic Assistance; also CMEA
DFI	direct foreign investment
EEC/EC	European Economic Community; European Community
FICs	Forum Island Countries
G-5	Group of Five
G-7	Group of Seven (U.S., France, West Germany, Japan, Britain, Italy, Canada)
GATT	General Agreement on Tariffs and Trade
GSP	Generalized System of Preferences
IBRD	International Bank for Reconstruction and Development (World Bank)
IDA	International Development Assistance (IMF)
IFC	International Finance Corporation (IMF)
IIF	Institute of International Finance
IGGI	Inter-Governmental Group for Indonesia
IMF	International Monetary Fund
IPR	intellectual property rights
JETRO	Japan External Trade Organization
MFA	Multi-Fiber Arrangement
MIC	middle-income country
MTN	multilateral trade negotiations
MOSS	Market-Oriented Sector Specific
NIC	newly industrialized country

OECD	Organization for Economic Cooperation and Development
OEM	original equipment marketing
OMA	orderly market arrangement marketing
OPIC	Overseas Private Investment Corporation
OPTAD	Organization for Pacific Trade and Development
PAFTA	Pacific Area Free Trade and Development
PAFTAD	Pacific (AF) Trade and Development (Conferences)
PATCRA	Papua-New Guinea–Australia Trade and Commercial Relations Agreement
PECC	Pacific Economic Cooperation Conference
PTA	Preferential Trading Agreement (ASEAN)
SITC	Standard International Trade Classification
SPARTECA	South Pacific Trade and Economic Cooperation Agreement
TNC	transnational corporation
UNCTC	United Nations Centre on Transnational Corporations
VER	voluntary export restraint

Introduction

ROBERT A. SCALAPINO

Since the macroeconomic policies of the two economic superpowers have had and will continue to have a profound effect upon most other nations, especially those in the Pacific-Asian region, it is appropriate that we commence our analysis of this collection of essays with the United States and Japan. The United States has lost its commanding economic position held after World War II—a position that was unnaturally accentuated, because other advanced industrial nations had exhausted themselves in recurrent wars. But with protracted peace and the acceleration of the great scientific-technological revolution, a greater balance in world economic power and growth has occurred. Unquestionably, a mix of policies, culture, and resource capacities—together with the international environment—has also determined which nations would advance rapidly, which would lag.

Despite the attendant problems accompanying its new position in the world economy, however, the United States remains an economic giant. Moreover, Lawrence Krause reminds us that we should not minimize the economic accomplishments of recent years: the creation of 15 million new jobs, bringing down the unemployment rate despite the rapid growth of the labor force; recovery from the 1980–1982 recession and the maintenance of the longest peacetime expansion in American history; and the effective management of inflation. At the same time, he points out the obverse: the massive budget and trade deficits creating the need for foreign borrowing on an unprecedented scale.

Meanwhile, structural changes in the American economy are occurring at an impressive rate. Earlier, because of high-priced dollars, consumption of goods rose relative to services, which increased imports. Furthermore, domestic savings fell for reasons not fully understood. One current question is whether, with a depreciation of the dollar against the world's major currencies, consumption of imported goods will fall and whether savings will return to usual levels. On another front, the share of service production has rapidly increased and not at the expense of manufacturing, either. Krause points out that although manufacturing did face a loss of international competitiveness prior to 1987 (before the value of the dollar dropped), the United States has not been deindustrializing. Labor productivity in manufacturing slowed down earlier, but in the 1980s, such productivity increased. This was

1

possibly because of the drive toward internationalization, a development some have labeled the "hollowing out" of American companies. Thus, a declining proportion of the American labor force has been employed in the manufacturing sector, leading in some quarters to the mistaken assumption of U.S. deindustrialization.

As Krause indicates, the policies of the Reagan administration have been critical to developments, favorable and unfavorable. Stressing supply side economic policies, the Reagan program encompassed tax decreases, heightened government expenditures, especially military, and a reduction of governmental regulation of the private sector. Business investment sparked the recovery. Yet savings rates did not increase since personal consumption took an ever larger share of income. Federal Reserve measures held inflation down, but interest rates rose. This attracted foreign investors and permitted the United States to borrow abroad. The loss of competitiveness stemmed from U.S. macroeconomic policies, and the combination of an easy fiscal policy and a tight monetary policy led to the two deficits.

Krause joins many specialist in believing that the position of the United States cannot be sustained. Current policies saddling future generations with huge debts run against the moral grain of the American people. They risk the rise of protectionist tides. Most important, they threaten a loss of confidence in the American economy abroad. He believes that a comprehensive program commencing with an assault on the budget deficit must be undertaken. The preliminary steps taken in this direction, together with the downward valuation of the dollar, are promising but insufficient. The years ahead will surely test both the will and the skill of those at the helm of the American government.

Meanwhile, American policies affect the other Pacific-Asian countries in certain vital respects, among them, monetary mechanisms, trade flows, and direct investment. The effects are not uniform. For example, Krause notes that earlier U.S. policies may have helped to cause a deterioration in the terms of trade for the natural resource-driven states, since the high real interest rates and the rising dollar worked against the rebuilding of inventories. On balance, however, the Pacific-Asian region gained greatly from U.S. policies, and no nation gained more than Japan. It surged forward, advancing market share in the United States and in the Third World, benefiting both from the rise of interest rates and the decline in world resource prices.

Assessing the U.S. future, Krause draws up a balance sheet. He sees many favorable signs: no shortage of industrial capacity; unemployment rates that, while relatively low, are still above labor shortage levels; further improvements in labor productivity; rising competitiveness leading to export expansion together with a drop in imports given the dollar adjustment; and no signs of serious inflation. The negative side is heavily laden with psychological and political factors regarding international confidence in the American economy and the will on the part of U.S. political leaders to undertake the necessary reforms, and in time. Will the protectionist waves rise as the United States seeks to promote exports and restrict imports? At a broader level, can collective responsibility for an international economic regime work? Or will Japan be prepared to play the role earlier assigned to the United States? Krause draws up optimistic and pessimistic scenarios, and notes in conclusion that change is inevitable, but that the process of that change will determine whether we shall have a destructive or harmonious international regime.

Yukio Noguchi's depiction of Japan's economic policies and their impact upon the Pacific-Asian region begins with an emphasis upon the rising influence of international factors, especially external pressures on Japanese domestic policies. Monetary policies have been determined by multilateral agreements on exchange rates. Fiscal policies have been strongly influenced by external demands for the expansion of domestic spending. And industrial policies have been increasingly guided by a need to forward an international division of labor despite concern for protecting employment at home. Even tax and land policies are now subject to external demands. In sum, in a situation where internal pressures for change have been relatively weak and often belated, Japanese economic policies have been essentially an accommodation to pressures and change relating to the external environment.

Increasingly, Japan has enlarged the focus of its attention from the United States and the other Organization for Economic Cooperation and Development (OECD) countries to the Asian NICs and ASEAN. Japan is now engaged in a major drive to shift from a vertical to a horizontal division of labor with these latter countries. Noguchi believes that the success or failure of this venture may well determine Japan's relations with the other dynamic Asian economies. He notes that exchange rate changes since the fall of 1985 have had a signal effect on this process, with Asian imports to Japan increasing and Japanese direct investment in NIC and ASEAN states growing rapidly, including investment from small and medium firms. He cites evidence to indicate that this latter trend will continue to flourish in the period ahead. Old economic relations based on other Asians exporting materials to Japan and importing Japanese manufactured goods is being transformed into a more complex horizontal division of labor. Economic relations between Japan and the NIC and ASEAN countries are increasingly characterized by product differentiation. (Japan exports high value-added products and imports relatively low value-added products). Cooperation in the supply of capital and technology is also occurring (whereby Japan supplies these needs via joint ventures, contributing to a sharing of products and markets). This trend is already well advanced in Japan-NIC relations. A similar development with ASEAN will be slower, but the NICs themselves may well pursue this strategy in Southeast Asia and elsewhere. Thus, prodded by U.S. pressure to rectify trade imbalances, Japan is at the head of a new interdependence within Asia. Noguchi notes that this trend will reduce the impact of Japan's short-run business cycle on other parts of the region while increasing the importance of long-run Japanese industrial and trade policies.

Noguchi notes that the factors shaping Japan's fiscal and monetary policies have been both external (notably, the budget deficit in the United States) and domestic (the closed Japanese market and the industrial structure as well as short-term macroeconomic policies). He cites strong evidence, however, to indicate that it is impossible to reduce Japan's surplus current account significantly merely through policies of fiscal expansion—although this would have a meaningful effect upon the Asian NICs. Fiscal management in Japan during the last decade has been directed principally toward the reduction of the budget deficit. Since efforts to enact a broadly based consumption tax have thus far failed, expenditure policy has been consistently tight during the 1980s. The government investment rate has been low. Even mounting external pressure did not produce substantial increases in public spending until 1987. Moreover, Noguchi indicates that policy differences remain within the Japanese decision-making structure as to whether expansionary polices are wise. This makes it unclear as to whether expanded public spending is temporary or signals a new trend. He himself is convinced that the public sector deficit is no longer a serious problem. However, he also insists that a substantial reduction in the current account surplus can only be realized by changing the basic structure of the Japanese economy. Hence, increased government expenditures should be directed to improve the social infrastructure and assist in the transformation of the industrial structure.

Japan's well-managed monetary policy was a key factor in its earlier strong economic performance. But it was primarily U.S. macroeconomic policies that kept the yen weak until mid-1985. Monetary policies have been eased since that time. Noguchi believes that further relaxation is unrealistic, however, since it might create future inflationary problems. This is another issue upon which opinions differ.

Desirable long-term structural policies have been sketched in the Maekawa Report with its emphasis on domestic demand-oriented policies. Noguchi feels that there is a broad consensus in Japan supportive of these policies. Moreover, he sees them supported by market forces, with offshore production one vital form of assistance. Yet, there are various factors serving as obstacles or restraints: wages lower than is desirable; excessive unemployment and underemployment; import restrictions; oligopolistic factors; government regulations; and corporate pricing strategies. In certain cases, governmental actions are necessary in testing the political will of the leadership and the capacity of the Japanese people to accept change, particularly, the liberalization of imports, especially of agricultural products; the rationalization of market structures; and the abolition of various regulations. Noguchi is convinced that Japanese agriculture must be transformed into an industry that can survive without heavy governmental subsidies and import restrictions, possibly by concentrating production into fewer hands. Budget reallocation must be aimed at providing a larger share of funds for the urban infrastructure. Land reform must be effectuated by raising the property tax despite the powerfully entrenched special interests in opposition. Tax reform is also essential, although its impact will be primarily domestic.

One of Noguchi's final points is that at some time in the twenty-first century, Japan's savings-investment balance will shift significantly, with the nation becoming a capital importer. A prominent reason for this change lies in the rapid aging of the Japanese population. In seeking a possible source for the needed capital, Noguchi finds the only logical place to be Asia, more particularly, the Asian NICs.

We turn next to the policies of the two massive socialist states and their regional impact. John Wong deals with the People's Republic of China (PCR). Understandably, China's initial economic ties were overwhelmingly (i.e., 80 percent of its trade) with the Soviet Union. Even after the break with the Russians at the end of the 1950s, the PRC had very limited economic relations with other Pacific-Asian countries except for Hong Kong and Singapore. Both its physical size and socialist economic system caused China to look inward, especially in the period when politics was in command.

The gradual modification of China's economic orientation began with the political events of the early 1970s. Yet, while the external sector of the Chinese economy expanded greatly, especially since the late 1970s, China's impact upon the regional economy remains modest. Its total trade turnover, for example, is smaller than that of Taiwan or Singapore. Nevertheless, the effects of China's opening are now being felt in diverse ways. China is a potential competitor as well as a possessor of an economy that can be complementary to others in many ways. And whatever the mix in these diverse factors, virtually all of Asia listens with rapt attention to various analyses of China's future. It is Wong's contention that the growing integration of the Chinese economy with that of other Pacific/Asian countries on balance will clearly enhance the region's overall growth potential.

Prior to examining more closely China's economic course, he paints the regional context. He divides the Pacific-Asian economies into three broad categories. The two global economies, the United States and Japan, will continue to serve as locomotives for the growth of other Pacific nations. The NICs, like Japan, have uniformly overcome natural resource deficiencies by cultivating their human resources, benefiting in the process from their Confucian heritage. The ASEAN community has also had impressive performers on balance, utilizing their rich natural resource base. Despite varying degrees of governmental involvement, each of these clusters has benefited from the extensive operation of market forces. Those forces have dictated a rapid growth of economic interdependence among the Pacific Basin countries. The very fact that each category of states is at a different stage in the developmental process makes economic complementarity possible. The pattern of shifting comparative advantage is the basis for the regionally based horizontal division of labor that is emerging.

The capacity of China to interact effectively with regional trends, Wong believes, hinges upon two interrelated questions: Will the Chinese economy maintain its capacity for high growth? And will Chinese leaders retain the open door policy? While indications were given as early as the mid-1970s that China wanted to alter Stalinist economics, political instability delayed actual change until the 1980s. The Five-Year Plan that was launched in 1981 inaugurated the era of basic reforms, commencing with the establishment of the family responsibility system in the rural areas. This radical development signaled the dismantling of agrarian collectivization. By late 1984, China was advancing to the more complicated task of urban reforms, an effort still in its preliminary stages.

Even in the Maoist era, China's growth record was respectable in statistical terms, largely due to very high domestic investment. Consumption was controlled, with the emphasis on heavy industry. Yet the economy was extremely inefficient and increases in productivity were negligible, seemingly inevitable by-products of the Stalinist strategy. With consumer goods scarce and living standards low, moreover, the regime could only seek to substitute ideological for material incentives— a losing proposition over time.

Wong believes that by pursuing the present decentralization and market-oriented policies, China can maintain its high growth rates despite its current difficulties. He also believes that whatever alterations may be made, the economic reforms cannot be reversed. Thus, while he asserts that it is entirely premature to describe China as an emerging economic power at this point, the potential is there, together with the likelihood of greater integration with other Pacific economies.

In exploring China's economic relations with the two economic superpowers, Wong is generally optimistic. China's market share in both countries has grown remarkably in recent years. Japan and the United States together with Hong Kong are the PRC's largest trading partners. Investment, especially American investment, has also grown despite various bottlenecks imposed by Chinese policies. The chief obstacles to intensified Sino-American economic intercourse are political and strategic, PRC relations with the USSR, Chinese military sales, and similar issues.

While political issues also exist between China and Japan, their principal problems are in the economic arena. The uncertainties of Beijing's economic course and extensive bureaucratic interference have troubled the Japanese private sector. For its part, the PRC has been unhappy about Japan's trade surplus and the low level of Japanese investment. Nonetheless, all signs point to the probability that Japan will continue to play a major role in China's future economic development.

The dynamic new element is the rapidly rising economic interaction between China and the NICs. Especially interesting is the upward spiral of economic relations between China and South Korea. This is happening despite the absence of diplomatic relations and also despite the PRC's supposedly close political and strategic ties with North Korea. In truth, China is following a two-Koreas policy today. Similarly, the absence of any government-to-government relations between Beijing and Taipei has not prevented a brisk trade growth, both indirect via Hong Kong and direct, and more recently, the advent of investment from Taiwan in Fujian and elsewhere. This development, combined with changes in the Taiwan government's attitudes toward visits to the mainland, augurs an unfolding China-Taiwan relationship of growing intensity. The NICs are natural economic partners with China if political factors do not intervene and if China can maintain its developmental momentum.

One situation that will naturally be watched with great interest and concern is the forthcoming incorporation of Hong Kong into the PRC. Wong is hopeful. Others are less certain, not because of any doubt that PRC officials want a strong, viable Hong Kong, but because they wonder if the bureaucracy and politicians of the mainland can keep their hands off the territory's affairs, economic as well as political. Only time will tell. Meanwhile, Singapore is in the process of making itself another "gateway" to China. At the same time, moreover, Chinese economic relations with the other ASEAN states are expanding, revealing both the complementary and competitive potentialities in this relationship. The competition most likely to grow lies in the drive for industrialization that marks both the ASEAN countries and China, especially as this relates to Third World markets. However, as Wong points out, the world market is not a zero-sum situation. Further, the ASEAN countries may need to upgrade their productivity to more capital-intensive activities as the NICs have done to meet the competition of all low labor cost countries. Meanwhile, the vast China market may become available to ASEAN producers as well as to others—assuming that market ultimately materializes to the degree that many hope. In sum, Wong's assessment is that China is destined to play an increasing and on balance, constructive role in Pacific-Asian economic growth.

Robert Campbell's assessment of the prospects for a greatly enhanced Soviet economic interaction with the region is considerably less sanguine. He notes that the USSR has not had a broadly gauged regional economic policy. With the exception of certain specific countries, its economic policies in the Pacific-Asian region have been unimportant, whatever Gorbachev's hopes for the future. As Campbell points out, economic interaction has often been at the mercy of political or military events. Thus, Sino-Soviet trade, which stood at 2 billion rubles in 1959, was a mere 42 million rubles in 1970; now again, it is climbing. Similarly, economic ties with India and Vietnam have been byproducts of strategic and political considerations, factors that can rapidly change.

Campbell notes that in global terms, the USSR has expanded its economic ties with nonsocialist states in the past, especially in the 1970s when an era of tension reduction was under way. He indicates that the USSR's share of trade with its socialist partners had fallen from 69 percent in 1965 to 53 percent in 1980. Moreover, Moscow did not accumulate a large debt as did most East European countries. Despite this development, however, Soviet trade with the Pacific-Asian region did not become significant, representing only 8 percent of total Soviet trade, mostly with the regional communist states together with Japan. In South Asia, on the other hand, the USSR was an important trading partner for India, with 13.6 percent of its trade with that nation. To late developing countries, the USSR exported relatively unsophisticated machinery and equipment, receiving in return raw materials and foodstuffs. China and India, however, exported finished consumer goods as well.

In recent years, Soviet economic aid has been confined primarily to Vietnam and North Korea insofar as the Pacific-Asian region is concerned. The same two communist states together with India have received Soviet arms, but Soviet arms shipments in this region run a weak second to the Middle East, according to Campbell. Similarly, industrial cooperation in the form of joint projects has been confined primarily to India and Vietnam, although a few projects in the USSR itself involve Japan.

Why has Soviet economic interaction with East Asia been so limited? Campbell cites three primary reasons. First, economic policies toward Siberia and other eastern portions of the Soviet Union have been tied to the nation's larger internal developmental needs. Second, political tension has reduced Soviet economic activity with certain states, for example, China. Third, for political and other reasons, the Soviet Union has elected to turn to West Europe and the United States rather than to Japan in its principal intercourse with advanced industrial nations.

Will this change under Gorbachev? After a careful analysis, Campbell is doubtful, although he is prepared to await various developments. The thrust of the new Soviet economic policies, he points out, is from extensive to intensive growth, with an emphasis on raising productivity. The old system required enormous capital, labor, and resource inputs. Yet at present, significant increases in the labor force are not to be expected, large gains in capital inputs are ever more difficult to achieve, and natural resources are being depleted. Thus, productivity increases must come from advances in technology, organizational improvements, the reduction of waste and inefficiency, and heightened material incentives. The premium is on economizing on imputs. This requires renovating the capital stock, with large investments in machinery and equipment replacements along with the development of new information technologies. Thus, the priority for investment in the eastern USSR is very likely to suffer, especially since in areas like Siberia, expensive infrastructural expenditures would be required.

Campbell points out that any effort to increase consumer goods challenges the need to replace obsolete capital and the necessity to accelerate investment now. He believes that in the final analysis, the success or failure of Gorbachev's efforts will hinge upon whether the institutional framework of the Soviet Union's economic decision-making processes can be changed to enable greater decentralization and permit more innovation. In any case, he believes that it is too early to expect the USSR to be extensively involved in the global economy. Under certain circumstances, Siberia might be able to take more local initiatives, and hence, develop closer regional ties with its Asian neighbors. However, basic decisions on such matters remain to be made. There is no evidence yet that regional independence is going to be given strong support, and the blunder surrounding the building of a second

Siberian rail line, the Baikal-Amur Mainline, is likely to engender caution.

In addition to the issue of Siberia, a number of other critical decisions lie ahead. Will the Soviet Union seek to increase its technical imports significantly? Gorbachev has indicated that such a development is not necessary. Could some of the Asian NICs, notably, South Korea, play an economic role in the Soviet Union as it has begun to do with respect to China? Will Japan, despite its decreased energy needs, agree to subsidize credit for the USSR at some point? Can Sino-Soviet trade continue to expand, going beyond the 3 billion ruble level projected for 1990? Campbell concludes by acknowledging that the Soviet Union feels frustrated by its inability to exert a strong influence in the Pacific-Asian region beyond that of being a foremost military power. However, he doubts that there is a basis for rapidly expanded economic activity in the Soviet East or in Soviet intercourse with Asia. Russia's natural economic partner, he concludes, is West Europe.

The essay by Dante Canlas reviews the recent industrialization policies of the four ASEAN members that are in the category of developing states. He draws from his data some conclusions about the prospects for greater ASEAN interdependence with the larger regional and global community. First, he presents data on ASEAN per capita GNP, growth rates, and sectoral distribution of the labor force, providing a brief comparison with similar data from the Asian NICs. He suggests that among the ASEAN developing states, the service sector is playing a more prominent role than in the developing societies of earlier times. This indicates some combination of an industrial and postindustrial stage. At the same time, rapid capital accumulation in the industrial sector is essential to alleviate the prolonged unemployment of surplus agrarian workers.

Canlas points out that all of the ASEAN developing states followed essentially the same strategy in their industrial policies. Initially, import substitution was pursued, with extensive governmental intervention as an accompaniment. The restraints on growth at that point in time were substantial, among them undeveloped human resources and high production costs. These problems led in turn to the necessity for protection. Chronic trade deficits and balance-of-payments problems, moreover, presented themselves as a product of the necessity to import capital goods that could not be produced locally. To address these problems, an export-oriented strategy was introduced to supplement import substitution, albeit, in varying degree. Beginning in the late 1960s, moreover, the advanced industrial states began to subcontract labor-intensive stages of production to manufacturers in the less developed societies, including the ASEAN four, providing modest but important assistance in alleviating unemployment.

A more detailed account of the recent policies of each of the four countries follows, with strengths and weaknesses noted. Canlas stresses the importance of handling balance-of-payments difficulties while moving forward with an outward-oriented strategy if the ASEAN countries are to interact effectively with the regional and global economies. Further trade liberalization, an emphasis on agribusiness for export, and various measures to attract foreign investment are necessary at this stage, in his opinion.

Our attention is next directed by Gustav Papanek to the economic policies of South Asia and the potentials here for a growth of economic intercourse both within this specific region and in the larger Pacific-Asian arena. Papanek highlights three critical developments pertaining to South Asia. First, each of the four countries on which he concentrates (India, Pakistan, Bangladesh, and Sri Lanka) are seeking to shift from the autarkic, inward-looking, import substitution strategy of the past to a more outward-looking strategy promoting exports. Second, because of the microelectronic revolution advancing automation, some labor-intensive manufactures will not be exportable in the future. This will reduce the number of nonautomated industries that can offer export opportunities. Finally, most of the countries of this region, including India, will be future exporters of food grains, a truly extraordinary development.

India will soon be home to 1 billion people, and in its sheer size, this nation possesses a huge reservoir of professionals, technicians, and skilled workers. Yet in the years 1960–80, the South Asian share of world trade in manufactured goods (in which India played a major role) declined. By the late 1970s, however, the four major countries of South Asia, with Pakistan taking the lead, were engaged in some degree of deregulation of their economies and promotion of exports. The least progress in deregulation has been made by India, yet Papanek asserts that in terms of the past record of this country, the change has been significant. A further asset for most of these countries has been foreign remittances; in addition to exporting goods, countries like Pakistan and India are exporting people. Yet the changes, especially in India, are still fragmentary and fragile and are strongly opposed by certain vested interests who regard themselves better served by the old protectionist policies.

Looking ahead, Papanek sees a limited future for regional trade within South Asia for both economic and political reasons. In looking at the Pacific-Asian region as a whole and the broader global scene, he draws up two scenarios. The pessimistic scenario is premised on rapid

automation in the United States and Japan; the potency of protectionism and demands for reciprocal concessions by the advanced nations;
intensified competition from the NICs; and the emergence of a new
competitor in China. The optimistic scenario is based on the creation of
a strong industrial base and the development of a strong domestic market. Key South Asian countries will take advantage of the combination
of low-cost labor and technical skills to become major suppliers of labor-
intensive and some skill-intensive goods while importing capital-
intensive and research-intensive products.

Sueo Sekiguchi's essay focuses on the role of direct foreign investment in Pacific-Asian regional interdependence. By injecting capital and
transferring technology, such investment makes a major contribution to
the industrialization of developing countries. At the same time, it may
raise nationalist reactions by increasing dependence on the investing
countries and limiting the host government's policy autonomy.

Sekiguchi first reviews investment trends and the major policy
issues stemming from these trends. He notes that while foreign investment has played a major role in the rapid progress of Asian industrialization, it has tended to exceed the capacity of the old industrial nations
to adjust to its consequences. Hence, serious trade friction has erupted.
In addition, direct foreign investment has become vastly more complex
in recent years. The NICs, as well as the old industrial countries, are
becoming important participants in such activities. Meanwhile, the
ASEAN states (excluding Singapore) have begun the process of slowly
integrating their markets. At the same time, they are taking over certain
industrial sectors from the NICs as wages in the latter societies rise,
causing them to move up the industrialization ladder.

A new and as yet uncertain factor is represented by the People's
Republic of China. Since the beginning of the 1980s, China has made
sustained efforts to attract investment and technology transfer. The
uncertainties of PRC economic policies and the daunting bureaucratic
structure that remains to be confronted, however, have induced caution
from foreign investors. Although results have thus far fallen short of
Chinese leaders' hopes, China's vast potential remains one of the
imponderables of the coming decades. Already, however, it has a number of ASEAN leaders worried.

Meanwhile, the phenomenon known as cross-hauling investment is
increasing in the advanced industrial societies as entrepreneurs there
undertake major adjustments to deal with declining sectors and seek
also to compete with other domestic producers. As Sekiguchi indicates
in examining investment trends by industry, the investment patterns are
being heavily influenced by the changes occuring in the division of
international labor. Labor-intensive industries are moving to the middle-

income countries and certain capital-intensive industries are establishing themselves in the NICs. A reshuffling of partnerships is taking place within the domestic as well as the international marketplace.

Sekiguchi then moves to the major policy issues, discussing first the framework within which such issues emerge. He outlines the policies that both investing countries and host countries pursue, dividing such countries into four basic categories. The governments of high-income countries are, in general, neutral, providing neither incentives nor disincentives for foreign investment, although local governments within them often do so. The NICs pursue industrial policies under strong governmental leadership. Recently, however, such policies have been extensively revised, especially in South Korea and Taiwan, with import barriers being reduced, the screening of foreign investment steadily relaxed, and greater protection provided for industrial property rights. Similar relaxation has characterized the policies of Singapore and Hong Kong. Meanwhile, all of the NICs, but especially the latter two, have been making their own foreign investments in ASEAN countries and in China in recent years.

The middle-income countries have combined incentives and performance requirements in an effort both to encourage investment and to protect their own interests. Similarly, China has strengthened its open door policies on the one hand, and sought to establish legal safeguards on the other. China's chief handicap, however, lies in the fact that under its socialist system, foreign enterprises cannot perform as efficiently and with the innovative capabilities possible in a market economy. Despite preferential treatment, therefore, many foreign entrepreneurs still regard the China market with skepticism or caution. Moreover, Council for Mutual Economic Assistance (COMECON) regulations and the concern of foreign suppliers about free copying have combined to place further restrictions on technology transfer.

Sekiguchi believes that governments interested in foreign investment can play important roles by improving the political climate, providing investment insurance, furnishing information services, and creating tax incentives or other forms of financial support to foreign investors. He proceeds to categorize the principal policy issues as North-South, East-West, and North-North. North-South issues include the debate over whether the technologies introduced are appropriate to the host country's stage of development; the effort of multinationals to restrict the use of a specific technology; and disputes over pricing and the unwillingness of foreign enterprises to introduce certain types of technology. So-called East-West issues encompass the guarantees of tenure for multinationals, the investment climate, and the extent of COMECON regulations. North-North issues relate primarily to specific cases involving such matters as disputes about patent coverage and appropriate norms for competition.

Sekiguchi concludes by drawing from his data certain implications for national policies that would forward regional cooperation. One of his interesting recommendations is the establishment of a Pacific center for education and training that would be located in one of the ASEAN countries, providing practical training for managers, engineers, and governmental officials.

Mingsarn Santikarn Kaosa-ard deals in considerable depth with technology transfer with the Pacific-Asian region in a contribution complementing that of Sekiguchi. She first provides an overview of the status of technology transactions currently taking place in the region. In so doing, she emphasizes the difficulties in presenting an accurate survey since technology transfer involves not merely the transfer of a production system but also the interaction of a host of related and essential factors including economic, social, and cultural requirements. Hence, no single index can measure the extent to which the process has been successfully completed. With this important reservation in mind, Mingsarn provides key data on technology trade and direct investment, indicating the respective roles of the chief exporters, the United States and Japan.

She then turns to the principal issues, amplifying Sekiguchi's analysis and presenting additional themes. She notes that the issues are shifting away from the emphasis on motivation, cost, and appropriateness toward questions relating to the acquisition and mastery process, namely, *how* technology is transferred. In this regard, she points out that the success or failure of the transfer depends to a considerable extent on the absorptive capacity, the awareness and the management ability possessed by the receiving enterprise, and on the appropriate choice of arrangement for transfer in accordance with the product, process, and characteristics of the local enterprises involved. These factors, she finds, are given less attention than is desirable by the recipient governments who tend to focus on issues of costs and controls.

Mingsarn divides the Pacific-Asian region into three groups of states in relation to technology transfer. The first group consists of countries allowing free flow of technology, and includes the United States, Japan, and Singapore, with South Korea approaching this status. The second group consists of countries that exercise controls, especially with regard to cost and restrictive clauses. In this group are Latin America, the Philippines, and India. Here, technology agreements must be screened and approved by regulatory agencies. The third group is represented by countries who impose fixed regulations on technology imports. Malaysia and Indonesia are included in this category.

Mingsarn concludes by noting that a number of Asian countries have been attracted to what she calls the Korean model. Namely, this is a policy of stimulating domestic research and development together with upgrading education as complements to the introduction of foreign technology. This enables the recipient country to take maximum advantage of the transfer. She insists, however, that whatever policies are followed, a country's technology policy must be integrated into its master plan for development.

Three essays follow that are devoted to trade friction and its impact both on domestic policies and regional relations. The first contribution by Ippei Yamazawa deals with the U.S.-Japan conflict. Yamazawa asserts that this bilateral conflict must be placed in a broader context. There are in reality three interrelated yet separate conflicts: that between the United States and Japan and those between developing Asia and the United States and Japan, respectively. Each of these conflicts is closely connected with what Yamazawa terms the three "structural elements" in the Pacific-Asian economy: policy discrepancies, catching-up industrialization, and integration. Regarding the first factor, he notes the long swing beginning in the late 1960s toward increases in commodity prices, the deflationary policies of the developed states in reaction, and the end of the cycle with the process resulting in a rising growth disparity. The second development was displayed in the continued growth of the Asian developing countries via the spread of industrialization through the introduction of advanced technology and strengthened by vigorous domestic demand. Japan began the process in the 1950s and 1960s, followed by the NICs, with the ASEAN countries now involved in a similar drive. These nations all had an essentially common strategy, i.e., outward-looking industrialization. While the global depression of the early 1980s hit the Asian developing countries severely, the basic process continues, recently with renewed vigor. The third structural element of importance has been the increased economic integration among the Pacific-Asian countries as a result of liberalized capital flows and the stepped-up direct investment of American and Japanese multinational firms. Despite the occasional destabilization caused by this development, it is a trend that cannot be reversed, according to Yamazawa. These three fundamental factors have provided a unique environment for the major economic conflicts taking place.

The U.S.-Japan trade conflict, Yamazawa asserts, had its origins in the process of Japan's catching up with the United States. The Japanese export structure changed dramatically and quickly when every new export was shipped to the U.S. market. American producers demanded protection, and the ensuing conflict was often concluded with voluntary restrictions. In the 1980s, however, the conflict expanded to include all of Japan's trade partners, with the policies of the Japanese government becoming the target of criticism at the international level. Japan responded with a series of trade liberalization measures. But since 1983, the U.S.-Japan conflict has been exacerbated by the rapid growth of huge imbalances, the results of the differences in the macroeconomic polices of the two countries.

From this, it follows that both nations must make major macroeconomic adjustments, a process that has begun. The imbalances, however, will not be corrected quickly. In addition to affecting corporate behavior at the microlevel, they have aggravated sectoral conflicts, leading to various measures in an effort to control these, with the requests or demands of both sides continuing.

Yamazawa next explores the impact of the U.S.-Japan conflict upon the Pacific-Asian region as a whole. He notes that due to U.S. policies, the Asian developing countries and the NICs both steadily increased their trade surplus with Japan, thereby expanding the arena of conflict. The United States clearly served as an agent of growth, providing a huge market for Asian industrial exports and at the same time, stimulating the relocation of American production overseas. But trade deficits soared, and various demands upon Asian NICs and ASEAN states followed, such as exchange rate appreciation; voluntary restraints on industrial exports; and faster trade liberalization. At home, meanwhile, protectionist pressures mounted. Yamazawa assumes that Asian exports to the United States must decline in the period ahead.

Japan also made its contributions to the growth of Asia's developing countries by being the foremost importer of their primary products. However, Japan's needs were reduced over time, both because of a slower growth rate and because of a reduced demand for such products. Regular trade deficits became major issues for both NICs and ASEAN members. Moreover, some ASEAN countries have requested Japanese cooperation in the restructuring of their economic strategy. These various demands reflect the catching up of industrialization in Asia. They also relate to the macroeconomic policy discrepancies between the United States and Japan. While the improvement of macroimbalances between these two countries would reduce the conflict, a coordination of policies between developing Asia and Japan is required for any basic resolution, in Yamazawa's opinion.

This leads to his final comment on the role of Japan in the region. Having begun to implement domestic market-oriented growth and to reduce exports to the United States, Japan must increase its imports from developing Asia. It must also accelerate the structural adjustment of the Japanese economy, and, until the imbalances are corrected, recycle its trade surplus.

The essay by Seung-Soo Han focuses on South Korean economic relations with the United States. In the course of his discussion, he exposes key elements of past and present ROK economic policies. He notes that there have been three broad phases in South Korea's economic relations with the United States: dependence (1945–60); the transitional era (1961–79); and rising interdependence (the 1980s).

With the latter era came major changes in Korean macroeconomic policies, notably the shift from tight fiscal/high interest rate policies to tight fiscal/low interest rate policies. In contrast to the United States, the South Korean government made strenuous efforts to curb government expenditures so as to contain inflation. Han then delineates the history of trade disputes with the United States, starting with textiles and footwear. The early disputes gradually broadened to include issues of market access by both parties, the opening of the ROK service market, the removal of South Korea from the Generalized System of Preferences (GSP), and exchange rate realignment. Han acknowledges that South Korea must accelerate changes in its economic policies to accommodate certain American requirements. However, he notes that Korea cannot by itself play a major role in reducing the U.S. trade deficit. He also remarks that it takes two hands to clap, indicating that more responsible U.S. economic policies are crucial to future ROK-U.S. economic cooperation.

Djisman Simandjuntak focuses on trade problems involving the ASEAN countries. He opens with a discussion of the factors that have led to friction. In the first half of the 1980s, ASEAN economies faced difficulties, largely as a result of low prices for primary commodities. Their balance-of-payments position deteriorated. The need for credit financing grew at a time when the international financial market was becoming averse to state borrowing. A difficult payment problem then faced the ASEAN countries due to the rapid increase in debt service costs. The gross inflow of direct foreign investment, moreover, suffered a downturn caused by declining growth performance. Despite these difficulties, the ASEAN countries generally succeeded in avoiding an increasingly protectionist course. Imports, however, declined as a result of contractionary fiscal and monetary policies. Manufactured exports were pushed despite the demands by countries like the United States for restraint. This was one important source of trade friction. A second, related factor, according to Simandjuntak, has been the tendency of advanced nations, especially the United States, to concentrate on bilateral trade balances rather than an overall balance, and beyond this, the trend to select specific trade sectors for emphasis. Thus, ASEAN countries suffer with negotiated protectionism in the form of voluntary export restraints.

A further cause of friction has been the refusal either to recognize what other countries have done in terms of market opening or to acknowledge the defects in one's own policies leading to a loss of competitiveness. Simandjuntak notes, without endorsing, other theories such as the loss of a hegemonic power that can enforce an international trade regime and the tightening of policies in anticipation of negotiations. But he underlines the critical importance of a final factor—the changing trade structure resulting from shifting comparative advantages and the difficulty in adjusting to such changes rapidly.

While the economic crisis confronting ASEAN countries in the early 1980s forced them to intensify exports, especially of manufactured products, Simandjuntak stresses that trade in primary commodities remains vitally important. Thus, the ASEAN states are demanding the inclusion of commodity-related issues into the agenda of trade talks. This request will undoubtedly provoke disagreement. Meanwhile, as the structure of ASEAN exports to the OECD countries changes, advanced states like the United States are prone to include these countries as targets in demands for reciprocity. Trade in services represents another area where friction is likely to grow, according to Simandjuntak.

Basically, he argues, the ASEAN stance to demands has been accommodative. Yet the ASEAN countries will be cautious in advancing trade liberalization. Protectionist sentiments are strong in certain quarters, since unemployment is a perennial problem, and there are also strategic considerations. Nevertheless, ASEAN members are as interested in a soft landing in the process of global structural readjustment as the developed nations. Progress in accepting interdependence is being made.

Thomas Layman deals with the critically important subject of financing development in Asia. He asserts that success in the region in the past two decades has occurred primarily because of high and rising investment rates and the judicious management of domestic policies. Further, although investment has been financed largely by domestic savings, foreign capital has played an important role.

Such capital can be divided into two basic categories, official and private. Official flows greatly exceeded private capital for most of the post-1945 period. However, beginning in the 1970s, deteriorating terms of trade for much of the developing world led to expanding current account deficits and rising balance of payments financing, Layman points out. This demand was met mainly by syndicated loans and credit arrangements through commercial banks. The other source of private finance was direct foreign investment.

Layman asserts that a country's development performance is essentially a function of its ability to generate sufficient financing and to utilize this finance in a productive fashion. He begins his detailed analysis by reviewing the growth performance of key Asian countries, paying attention to how policymakers utilized financial resources. The variations in growth, he notes, were great. NIC achievements, among the best, were mainly the result of the emphasis that policymakers placed on boosting domestic savings and pursuing a development strategy that focused on earning foreign exchange. The commodity-dependent economies of the ASEAN four were adversely affected in the early 1980s by the fall of oil and commodity prices, as noted by other authors. The South Asian nations, heavily dependent on agriculture despite efforts to improve industrial output, were disadvantaged, not by low investment or inadequate savings but by their relatively inefficient utilization of the capital available to them. Progress in economic liberalization and a reduction in governmental interference, if sustained, should result in improvements. Because of a lower dependence on trade than the NICs or the ASEAN countries, per capital real income growth in South Asia did better then the former states in the early 1980s. However, the route to sustained growth, in Layman's opinion, remains a market-oriented development strategy based on export promotion.

Next, he turns to the matter of domestic resource mobilization. Most Asian countries have succeeded in devoting a growing share of their national output to investment, especially the NICs, Malaysia, and China. Using various methods, the Asian countries have also caused savings rates to rise, Singapore and Taiwan being conspicuous examples.

The other source of financing, foreign inputs, also receives detailed attention from Layman. In the early post-1946 era, the U.S. government played a major role in providing bilateral assistance in cases where it had strategic interests, including South Korea, Taiwan, South Vietnam, and the Philippines. In a subsequent period, external financing came primarily from such official sources as the World Bank and the Asian Development Bank, mostly for specific investments. After the oil shock in 1973, private commercial banks began to play an important role. More recently, there has been a significant rise in nonbank private financing, primarily in the form of supplier's credits. By 1986, Japan had become the world's second largest development assistance donor, after the United States, and Japanese attention was heavily directed toward East Asia.

In the field of direct foreign investment, the United States established an early lead, but it has been overtaken by Japan. The concentration is in the skill-intensive, high-technology industries. Production for export to the United States and even to Japan has become more cost effective, since many of the developing Asian countries have aligned their currencies with the U.S. dollar, thereby benefiting from the reevaluation.

Layman points out that, in general, countries of the Pacific-Asian region have been able to secure sufficient financial resources from domestic and foreign sources to finance their growth. The main reason is that they have followed policies promoting domestic savings and stressing exports. Can this continue? Will the Asian countries be able to continue generating high levels of savings? Can export-oriented strategies remain feasible in the face of protectionist threats? Will the constraints existing on the growth of official finances and the increasing unwillingness of commercial banks to engage in international loaning as a result of the debt problem produce serious consequences? Layman optimistically believes that a combination of improving human resources and pragmatic policies will suffice to provide for economic growth, with an increasing share of financial capital for investment coming from within the region itself.

Hadi Soesastro and Miles Kahler conclude our studies with two essays devoted to the issues of Pacific-Asian economic cooperation, and more specifically, what, if any, institutional mechanisms are appropriate for such purposes.

Both authors sketch the background of institutional proposals, tracing their origins back to Kiyoshi Kojima's Pacific Area Free Trade Association, first put forth in 1965. This was intended to be the counterpart of the European Economic Community but garnered limited support. Many other ideas were subsequently advanced. It was always recognized that certain less sensitive functional areas such as energy, fisheries, forestry, and other resources lent themselves more readily to Pacific cooperation, according to Soesastro, but the truly high priority was on trade.

Soesastro points out that the development of subregional or bilateral trade structures can be clearly observed throughout the Pacific-Asian region today. ASEAN, the Australia-New Zealand free trade agreement, and the U.S.-Canada agreement are cited as the more prominent examples. But conspicuous by the lack of any similar accord is Northeast Asia, reflective of various historical and political divisions. Certain agreements of a bilateral or subregional type threaten to undermine the possibility of a general accord despite efforts to restore a generally applicable system presently going on via the Uruguay Round. The Pacific-Asian countries are engaged in particularistic efforts through a variety of regional conferences. Bilateralism concentrates on stability rather than equality of market access, a fundamental distinction that must be made.

After a detailed exploration of the various subregional trade structures that have emerged in the Pacific-Asian region, Soesastro looks at the models that have been proposed to link such structures into an integrated Pacific organization or system. He comes to three conclusions. First, the subregional arrangements that are being seriously pursued and developed reflect the different stages of economic development among countries of the region as well as the uncertainty of the international trading system. Second, the various subregional trade structures do recognize the need to maintain an outward orientation and relate themselves to the broader Pacific-Asian region. But integration does not seem en route; perhaps only a restoration of the international trading system can provide a framework for the movement of subregional arrangements into a more integrated structure. Finally, a subregional structure involving Japan is conspicuously missing. This suggests a role for Japan to facilitate a more integrated regional structure. This goal would be more feasible if it included more than trade, with recent ASEAN-Japan economic relations and Saburo Okita's proposal of a Japanese-style Marshall Plan being cited as examples.

Miles Kahler concludes our volume with a broadly gauged analysis of the problems and possibilities involved in a Pacific economic organization. At the outset, having distinguished between feasibility and desirability, he poses the central questions: What is the optimal political organization that will further economic cooperation in the Pacific and is that organization likely, given the present realities?

Outlining successive waves of earlier organizational efforts, Kahler notes a series of unresolved questions. First, what particular niche would any new organization fill? Second, what would be the membership and the specific institutional structure? Overwhelmed by problems such as these, the idea of organizing economic cooperation in the Pacific was progressively downgraded from integration, to consultation, to the current process, according to Kahler. In discussing the basic causes for this devolution, Kahler signals four principal factors. First, the international system has posed certain problems. Lurking behind most proposals have been security concerns, further complicating inclusiveness. Beyond this, the recent environment has been marked by the absence of a hegemonic power, a single leader. And whether one accepts this as a necessity, the scene has also been marked by the rising contention of the two economic superpowers, the United States and Japan, both of which must weigh the benefits and costs of regional leadership against their existing global interests.

A second factor set forth by Kahler is national interests. The two countries showing the greatest interest in a regional organization have been Japan and Australia. The United States has displayed a strong degree of ambivalence. The ASEAN community has been far less enthusiastic, fearing a dilution of their own somewhat fragile organization.

A third factor is that of elite attitudes. Here, Kahler distinguishes between governments in the aggregate and their component parts. It has been principally politicians, not bureaucrats, who have waxed enthusiastic about the concept. As for a second elite, the corporations, most large multinationals have a global outlook, whereas smaller firms frequently have a very parochial interest abroad; hence, there are few with distinctly regional outlooks. Academics, and especially economists, have been the most influential lobby for a Pacific regional organization, but alone they cannot play a truly crucial role.

A final factor lies in the ambiguity that has surrounded the regional organization concept. Here, Kahler discusses the problems of boundaries, alternatives, and modalities, indicating the cloudiness that has engulfed most proposals.

Kahler concludes his essay by sketching certain specific problem areas that might benefit from a regional approach, among them international financial issues, especially those dealing with private capital flows; the concept of a Pacific trade regime under certain circumstances, particularly if the General Agreement on Tariffs and Trade (GATT) negotiations stall and greater trade liberalization could be offered through a Pacific organization; codes governing direct foreign investment; and the commodity issue as it relates to North-South cooperation. He also indicates his views on the question of membership in such an organization.

In summarizing his rationale, he asserts that an important need for regional economic cooperation does exist, namely, in bridging issue areas that are separated at the global level as well as addressing aspects of other issues where global solutions are doubtful (trade) or nonexistent (commodities). But there must be an institutional structure designed to deal with such an agenda; consultation does not suffice. An intergovernmental organization is probably necessary.

Having set forth the purpose and the structure, however, Kahler regards the political feasibility of his proposal as virtually nil. The region does not face an economic crisis. Leadership is lacking. There is hesitation among more restrictive groups such as ASEAN, and they represent an alternative. Thus, the real needs are likely to remain unfulfilled.

As will be noted, the essays contained in this volume set forth the basic trends in Pacific-Asian economic policies and the degree to which they advance or retard regional interdependence. They also take account of those natural forces that are, at least, in some degree apart from governmental policies and yet exert a powerful influence on the economic scene. In this era of rapid, pervasive change, the central problem is to weigh and interrelate the many variables that shape the total picture. Our purpose was to advance that process.

1. Changing America and the Economy of the Pacific Basin

LAWRENCE B. KRAUSE

The U.S. economy has gone through a major structural change during the first half of the 1980s, and more changes are en route. This phenomenon has had a profound effect upon U.S. international economic policies. The United States now recognizes its greater dependence on the world economy and, most important, realizes that it has less room than before for independent action. One indicator of the change has been the elevation of the dollar in the foreign exchange market as a target of monetary policy.[1] A further demonstration was seen when instability in stock exchanges in all countries and the uncertainty of investors worldwide led to and in turn, was impacted by the U.S. stock market crash of October 19, 1987.

The United States is no longer uniquely strong in the world economy. One consequence of this fact is that even as they recognize that foreigners place constraints on U.S. economic policy, American policymakers are more amenable to actions they perceive to be in the narrow self-interest of the United States. Furthermore, the belief runs, the United States cannot afford to pay a price for system stability or regime support. The burden must now fall on other countries to pay for public goods; the United States, so this thinking goes, must look after itself. If this U.S. position persists, then either the maintenance of system stability must become a shared responsibility, or a single nation—possibly Japan—must be willing to take on the burden and/or opportunity by itself, or a period of international instability may be in the offing.

This essay addresses these issues by evaluating the current status of the U.S. economy and examining the mechanism that caused this condition. It poses these questions—Is the situation of the United States sustainable? What changes are likely to occur? What are the implications for the countries of the Pacific implied by these changes—and, finally, it attempts to speculate on the issue of system stability and change.

---

[1]U.S. Federal Reserve Board, *Federal Reserve Bulletin,* June 1987. Also testimony of Alan Greenspan before the House Ways and Means Committee, February 23, 1988.

The U.S. Economy in the Early 1980s

It is possible to advance an optimistic interpretation of the performance of the U.S. economy during the 1980s. After all, the United States almost single-handedly pulled the world economy out of the longest and deepest recession of the postwar period following the second oil shock. If it were not for the Reagan economic program enacted in 1981 and implemented in the following years, the downturn of 1980–82 might have been prolonged, possibly leading to a depression of the magnitude of the 1930s. Given the LDC debt crisis that appeared in August 1982, if the downturn had continued for just one more year we might have witnessed wholesale debt moratoriums, bank failures, and a possible downward spiral that would have been beyond the power of any country to reverse. This did not happen, thanks to the timely U.S. response to the Mexican crisis[2] and the sharp domestic economic recovery that began in November 1982.

This recovery from the 1980–82 recession became the longest peacetime expansion in American history. Although the hefty growth rates of GNP of 1983 and 1984 gave way to more modest achievements in subsequent years, the expansion progressed without interruption. By the end of 1987, the United States had created 15 million new jobs for its citizens (over a 14% increase in civilian employment), an achievement not even approached by any other advanced country.[3] Whereas European countries and Japan have seen their unemployment rates either rise or stay at remarkably high levels, the United States managed gradually to bring down its unemployment rate despite the rapid growth of its labor force. Thus, U.S. prosperity was widely shared within the country.

What also makes this recovery notable is that it was achieved while bringing down the rate of domestic price inflation. Of course, the beginning of the period was marked by high inflation propelled by the escalation of oil prices, and its abatement was aided by the decline of oil prices. Nevertheless, the moderate pace of wage increases was an indication that the country was also managing its domestic sources of inflation quite well. Thus, the Reagan administration along with the Federal Reserve gets very high marks for its success when measured by the growth of real output, the increase in employment, and the control of inflation. Unfortunately, there is more to the story.

In 1987, the United States had a deficit in its international trade of $159 billion—by far the greatest deficit ever recorded by any country.[4]

---

[2]Joseph Kraft, *The Mexican Rescue* (New York: Group of Thirty, 1984).
[3]*Economic Report of the President*, February 1988.
[4]Ibid.; *Federal Reserve Bulletin*, June 1987.

This eclipsed the record set by the United States of $144 billion in the previous year, which itself eclipsed the U.S. record of $122 billion in the year before that. The cumulative trade deficit of the United States from 1982 through 1987 amounted to the almost unbelievable sum of $600 billion. The cumulative deficit is significant because it had to be financed by borrowing from abroad. The need for foreign borrowing became so great that the United States shifted from being the world's largest creditor country to becoming its largest debtor. The implications of this fact are so profound that Hugh Patrick has likened it to a foreign policy mistake equivalent to the Vietnam War.[5] The negative consequences of the U.S. international imbalance certainly casts a shadow and may even outweigh the positive economic achievements of the Reagan administration.

Structural Changes in the U.S. Economy

Three separate concepts of structure need to be identified and distinguished because all three have changed in the United States in recent years, and they have different implications for the economy. These concepts are: structure of demand, structure of production, and structure of employment.

It has been established that the patterns of consumption respond to the broad movement of prices.[6] During the early 1980s, the price of goods in the United States declined relative to other prices in the economy, in part because of the rise of the dollar in the foreign exchange market (to be discussed subsequently). In response to this price change, households increased their purchases of goods and, along with the well-established trend of increasing services, significantly raised consumption as a share of output—in other words, private savings were sharply reduced.[7] Greater government expenditures on military hardware also worked in the same direction but were less important in the aggregate. With the subsequent fall in the value of the dollar and its expected consequence of raising the relative price of goods in the United States, this consumption trend will be reversed. A possible decline in military hardware expenditures will work in the same direction. One might expect that the pattern of production in the United States would conform to the shift in the structure of consumption, but this did not occur.

---

[5]Hugh Patrick, "The Management of the United States–Japan Trade Relationship and Its Implications for the Pacific Basin Economies," in *Japan-U.S. Relations and the Pacific Basin* (United States National Committee for Pacific Economic Cooperation, October 1987).

[6]Robert Lawrence, *Can America Compete?* (Washington, D.C.: Brookings Institution, 1984).

[7]*Survey of Current Business,* 1988; *Economic Report of the President.*

Table 1

Structure of U.S. Production
(by industry in 1982 US$billions, and as share of total)

	1970[a]	1980[b]	1985–86[c]	1970[a] Share	1980[b] Share	1985–86[c] Share
Total GNP	2,441.4	3,209.4	3,660.4	100.0	100.0	100.0
Agriculture, forestry, fishing	68.2	80.1	97.0	2.8	2.5	2.6
Mining	131.9	135.1	124.4	5.4	4.2	3.4
Construction	171.4	160.8	166.2	7.0	5.0	4.5
Manufacturing	519.7	679.5	801.2	21.3	21.2	21.9
Transportation, utilities	204.7	294.3	326.6	8.4	9.2	8.9
Wholesale trade	154.1	216.4⎱	628.4[d]	6.3	6.7⎱	17.2[d]
Retail trade	217.6	290.1⎰		8.9	9.0⎰	
Finance, insurance, real estate	323.5	465.9	537.4	13.3	14.5	14.7
Services	295.3	445.0	553.1	12.1	13.9	15.1
Government	339.9	131.4	402.2	13.9	11.9	11.0
Rest of world	18.3	55.5	32.9	0.7	1.7	0.9

[a] Average 1969–71.
[b] Average 1979–81.
[c] Average 1985–86.
[d] Sum of wholesale and retail trade.
SOURCES: U.S. Department of Commerce, Bureau of Economic Analysis, *Survey of Current Business*, April 1986, Table 4; *Economic Report of the President*, February 1988, Table B-11.

The change in the trends of production in the United States in the 1980s have often been mischaracterized. As Table 1 shows, the steady rise in the share of service production continued through 1985–86. This was not at the expense of manufacturing, however, which actually rose slightly. Rather, the rise in the share of service output was matched by a decline in mining, construction, and government production. Although each of the sectoral declines has various causes and implications, they certainly do not add up to a picture of a deindustrializing United States. Deindustrialization is generally thought to reflect a loss of total capacity to produce manufactured products, which could not have been the case here since manufacturing production continued to rise in line with total output.

Nevertheless, the manufacturing sector along with other producers of tradeable goods (agriculture and mining) was in a state of semicrisis created by a loss of international competitiveness. While manufacturing output expanded, manufacturing companies did not share in the prosperity of the mid-1980s. It was the international competitive position of the United States that kept the structure of production from changing in

Table 2

Year-over-Year Productivity Growth
(from quarterly data, actual values)

Quarters	Nonfarm Business	Manufacturing
1979:2–1980:2	− 1.32	− 1.58
1980:2–1981:2	1.72	3.14
1981:2–1982:2	− 0.80	1.44
1982:2–1983:2	3.67	6.36
1983:2–1984:2	1.64	5.14
1984:2–1985:2	0.38	3.26
1985:2–1986:2	1.14	1.87
1986:2–1987:2[a]	0.01	2.00
Average[b]	0.92	2.80

[a]Based on preliminary labor productivity number for 1987:1.
[b]Excluding 1986:1–1987:1.
SOURCE: U.S. Department of Commerce, Bureau of Labor Statistics, cyclical adjustments made by Martin Neil Baily.

response to the shift in domestic demand at that time. Indeed, not until the dollar had declined in 1987 did manufacturing become truly dynamic.

The third concept of structure relates to the pattern of employment. Patterns of employment result from the structure of production interacting with the pattern of labor productivity. Obviously, the greater the growth of labor productivity in a given sector, the fewer the workers that will be required to produce a given amount of output.

The American economy as a whole has had a slowdown in labor productivity in recent years for reasons that are not completely understood.[8] Some have suggested that there has been a deterioration in basic education. Others have pointed to the aging of the capital stock in both the private and public sector. Whatever the reason, the productivity slowdown explains why per capita incomes have grown so slowly in the United States. In the 1980s, however, as Table 2 shows, the remarkable statistic is how well American manufacturing has managed to increase its labor productivity. Of course, U.S. manufacturers were under tremendous pressure from foreign competitors to reduce costs. Some critics claim that they accomplished this by shifting production offshore and by buying essential components from producers in other countries

---

[8]Edward Denison, *Trends in American Growth 1929–82* (Washington, D.C.: Brookings Institution, 1985); and Martin Neil Baily and Alok K. Chakrabarti, "Innovation and Productivity in U.S. Industry," *Brookings Papers in Economic Activity* 2 (1985).

(the so-called "hollowing out" of American companies).[9] Nevertheless, American manufacturers did adjust to the competitive environment. However, the implication of a stable share of manufacturing in total output combined with a rapid increase in labor productivity in manufacturing is a declining share of manufacturing employment in total employment. Manufacturing employed 31 percent of the American labor force in 1960, 27.3 percent in 1970, and 22.4 percent in 1980. By 1987, that figure was only 18.7 percent.[10] Fewer workers were employed in manufacturing in 1987 than in 1980, despite the 15 million person growth in total employment. This statistic, which most observers cite when they describe the supposed deindustrialization of the United States, is in fact a characteristic of a mature stage of development. This trend will not be reversed even with the decline of the dollar. All advanced industrial countries have had a decline in manufacturing employment in the 1980s. Only in the NICs has manufacturing employment provided for a growing share of total employment, and not in all of them.[11]

Thus from 1980 through 1987, the structure of U.S. demand shifted toward the consumption of goods, but American production did not respond because of a lack of international competitiveness. Since labor productivity was rising relatively quickly in manufacturing (the most important producer of goods in the economy), the share of the labor force employed in the production of tradeable goods actually declined.

Causative Factors

Both the good and the bad features of the U.S. economy in 1987 can be traced to the economic program initiated by the Reagan administra-

---

[9]The argument is made that the way that American companies adjusted to foreign competition prevented them from increasing domestic production when their competitive position improved and new demand was created. The situation can be overcome only with significant new investment in manufacturing in the United States.

[10]*Economic Report of the President.*

[11]Although there are many reasons why comparative advantage in manufacturing (especially of labor-intensive products) is shifting to LDCs, one factor may be the structure of wages. Manufacturing in the NICs tends to be a low-wage occupation relative to others in the same economy. In Singapore, manufacturing wages are at the very bottom of the scale—below agriculture and fishing. In advanced countries, and the United States in particular, manufacturing wages tend to be elevated because it is the sector where labor unions have been most successful, and thus workers may be earning some monopsony rents. International trade tends to erode such rents.

tion when it came into office in 1981.[12] As already noted, the world economy was in difficult straits at the start of the decade. In response to the challenge, the Reagan administration designed a program emphasizing the supply side of the economy. When it emerged from the congressional process, the program had the following features: taxes were reduced sharply for both households and business; government expenditures for military purposes were greatly increased, especially for advanced hardware; the rate of growth of government expenditures for nonmilitary programs was slowed (and a few actually reduced); and government regulation of the private economy was selectively reduced.

The consequence of this program for the fiscal position of the government was dramatic. The actual fiscal deficit, which had been in the range of $50 to $70 billion in the late 1970s, expanded rapidly and began to exceed $200 billion by FY1983.[13] Measuring the deficit on a constant employment basis to correct for cyclical variations, the deficit expanded year by year through 1986. The stimulus to the economy peaked at 1.3 percent of GNP in 1983 and tapered down to 0.3 percent in 1986. Government consumption as a share of GNP rose from 19.5 percent in 1980 to 20.3 percent in 1986.[14]

Conventional wisdom now recognizes that the fiscal deficit became the major force shaping the economy.[15] The combination of the fiscal stimulus plus the favorable tax environment for business led to an initial rise in business plant and equipment investment, and the United States at first had an investment-led recovery. Most of the investment rise was in equipment—which can be imported—rather than in structures—which are produced almost exclusively from domestic resources. Whereas gross private fixed investment had been 14.1 percent of GNP in 1980, it rose to 18.1 percent in 1985, before moderating to 17.6 percent in 1986 and 17.9 percent in 1987.

---

[12]This discussion follows closely my earlier paper, "Economic Trends in the U.S. and Their Implications for ASEAN," in Tan Loong-Hoe and Narongchai Akrasanee, eds., *ASEAN-U.S. Economic Relations* (Singapore: Institute of Southeast Asian Studies, 1988), pp. 3–23.

[13]U.S. Department of Commerce, Bureau of Economic Analysis, "The Cyclically Adjusted Federal Budget and Federal Debt: Revised and Updated Estimates"; *Survey of Current Business*, March 1986; *Economic Report of the President*.

[14]Measurements of this kind over time have been done in constant 1982 dollars. Where a financial variable is involved, however, the measurement is generally in current dollars unless otherwise indicated.

[15]William H. Branson, "Causes of Appreciation and Volatility of the Dollar," in *The U.S. Dollar—Recent Developments, Outlook, and Policy Options* (Federal Reserve Bank of Kansas City, 1985); and Martin Feldstein, "Correcting the Trade Deficit," *Foreign Affairs* 66 (Spring 1987).

Though some believed that the program would encourage households to increase their rate of saving, in fact it had the opposite effect. The combination of higher after-tax incomes, stable product prices, and a rising stock and bond market convinced households to spend an even higher share of their current incomes. Personal consumption as a share of GNP rose from 62.6 percent in 1980 to 65.7 percent in the third quarter of 1987. Thus, the personal savings rate declined from 7.1 percent in 1980 to 3.2 percent in 1987. Ironically, the stock market crash may have returned the country to a more normal condition as the personal savings rate increased sharply subsequent to it.

The combination of the fiscal stimulus, the rise in fixed business investment, and the increase in personal consumption (decline in personal savings) led to the most rapid expansion of U.S. domestic demand in more than twenty years. Between 1981 and 1987, demand grew by 3.9 percent per year as compared to 2.9 percent during the previous fifteen years. Ex ante demand for investment rose, and ex ante supply of investable resources (savings) fell. There are three possibilities for reconciling this discrepancy ex post: domestic output could grow rapidly to permit actual savings to match ex ante investment; inflation could increase, which would result in forced savings and less real investment; or the United States could borrow from abroad. The actual outcome was mainly determined by monetary policy.

The Federal Reserve, under the chairmanship of Paul A. Volcker, took a strong stand against the reigniting of inflation. In its view, permitting inflation to rise again ran the risk of undermining both domestic and international financial markets. Thus it kept fairly close to its target for the growth of the money supply, despite the rise in the fiscal deficit and the lack of compensating increases in savings elsewhere in the economy. The result was a rise in both nominal and real interest rates, but inflation was contained. The rise in real interest rates, however, did limit the growth of the economy, and by pushing up the value of the dollar led to the third possibility—foreign borrowing.

Until 1986–87, the necessary increase in foreign borrowing required to make up for the shortfall of savings in the economy could be approximated roughly by the increase in the nominal fiscal deficit of the government. Though the financial transfer could be accomplished merely by selling U.S. government bonds to foreigners, the shortfall of resources could not be made up until the deficit on the current account in the U.S. balance of payments increased enough to match the financial transfer. As long as the financial transfer was greater than the current account deficit—that is, foreigners wanting to invest more dollars in the United States than they were earning from current operations—the dollar would be bid up in the foreign exchange market. When the dollar got high enough, U.S. exports would be discouraged and imports encouraged to the point that the real transfer could be made. Thus, a loss of competitiveness was a necessary consequence of macro policy choices of the United States.

When the equality of the two magnitudes (increase in fiscal deficit and increase in the current account deficit) was reached in 1984–85, the upward push of the dollar should have been ended. The value of the dollar (measured by two different indices: the Federal Reserve multilateral traded weighted index and the Morgan Guarantee bilaterally trade weighted index) is shown in Figure 1. The final upward spurt of the dollar—which may have been a speculative bubble—did in fact occur in the first quarter of 1985. As is well recognized, however, there is a time lag between a change in a currency value and its impact on trade volumes and an even longer lag until trade values record an improvement. This causes a delay in the adjustment process and may cause systemic overshooting in the foreign exchange market.

To recap the developments between 1980 and 1985, the process began when the United States adopted a highly stimulative fiscal policy. The subsequent deterioration in the fiscal position of the government led to a shortage of savings in the economy, to which the business sector did not adjust by reducing its investment, nor did the household sector through greater savings. The monetary authorities refused to monetize the deficit, so interest rates went up, the dollar rose in the foreign exchange market, and the savings shortfall was made up by borrowing abroad. This combination of easy fiscal policy and tight monetary policy led to two offsetting imbalances in the economy—the fiscal deficit of the government and the balance of payments deficit on current account.

Is the Position of the United States Sustainable?

It is possible to specify a model wherein a country maintains stability while perpetually borrowing net from abroad (Canada has been a net borrower for most of its existence). The United States, however, does not satisfy the conditions of the model. The necessary condition is that foreign borrowing be used to finance additional productive investment that will yield a flow of goods and services that can be sold to foreigners to service the growing foreign debt. As noted, from 1982 to 1985 foreign borrowing by the United States has been used to finance government consumption and subsequently private consumption.

The actual position of the United States is unlikely to be sustainable for three reasons. First, from a normative point of view this generation of Americans should not consume beyond its means by squandering the savings of previous generations, and at the expense of the welfare of

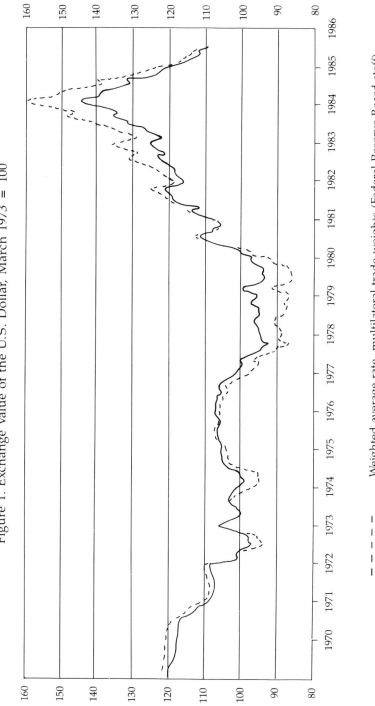

Figure 1. Exchange Value of the U.S. Dollar, March 1973 = 100

– – – – Weighted average rate, multilateral trade weights (Federal Reserve Board staff)
———— Weighted average rate, bilateral trade weights (Morgan Guarantee Trust Company)

future generations. This translates into a powerful domestic political argument. The American public is very uncomfortable with the huge government deficit, and resentful of so much foreign borrowing. Opinion polls indicate that the public believes that the federal deficit is the most serious economic problem of the country. Some political leader is bound to capitalize on this widespread sentiment and find a politically acceptable way to end both deficits.

Second, continuous borrowing from abroad requires a huge escalation of funding and refunding operations. They can be successful only if market confidence is sustained in the borrower. The very act of continuous borrowing to finance consumption, however, is a demonstration of irresponsibility, which will ultimately lead to a loss of confidence. The stock market crash of October 1987 (and the subsequent decline of the dollar) has been interpreted by some observers as a vote of no confidence in the way the U.S. economy has been managed.

In terms of portfolio balance theory, as the share of outstanding obligations of a borrower increases the willingness of investors to take an additional increment of its liabilities declines. Indeed, it is likely that private foreigners no longer were willing to buy U.S. bonds in 1987. Instead, all official debt financing of the U.S. external deficit in 1987 was provided by foreign central banks.

To entice foreigners to continue buying U.S. bonds, the interest rate being offered would have to be increased (to compensate for the rising risk associated with portfolio imbalance). Thus, the real burden to American taxpayers of servicing the foreign debt would rise exponentially and signal nonsustainability.[16]

This implies that the Federal Reserve would have to gear its interest rate decisions to the requirement of sustaining foreign confidence in the dollar rather than the needs of the domestic economy, which may well be in conflict. Over the long run, American policy makers would find such a constraint politically and economically intolerable. This condition is well known in Europe, where a currency crisis resulted when conflicts occurred between domestic and foreign needs.

Third, the huge rise in the value of the dollar and the even larger increase in the U.S. balance of trade deficit has led to protectionist pressures in the United States. The political system simply must respond when because of an overvalued currency, even the best-managed firms lose their international competitiveness and come to their government for relief. Of course, import-competing firms have their problems in

---

[16]Actually, the burden rises on all borrowers of dollars, including the heavily indebted developing countries.

meeting foreign competition magnified, and their cries for protection sound more welfare promoting. When decades of frustration over closed markets abroad are added in, the mixture becomes truly explosive. Though it is possible that Japan and some other countries would not react to new aggressive trade actions by the United States, some other countries—and especially the European Economic Community— might retaliate. This might set off a trade war that would threaten to end forty years of world prosperity. Thus, if the United States does not correct its two imbalances, the world economy is likely to suffer.

The Policy Corrective

There is no great mystery about what needs to be done to correct the two imbalances of the United States. Correcting the budget deficit is a necessary condition for correcting the trade deficit.[17] There was no consensus in the country, however, on how to reduce the budget deficit. Some, including President Reagan, wanted to do it by reducing nonmilitary expenditures. Others wanted to increase taxes. Still others wanted to reduce military spending. Practically all neutral observers have believed that federal revenues would have to be raised even with the most strenuous efforts at expenditure reductions.[18] What makes expenditures so hard to reduce is the deficit itself. In 1981, net interest payments of the federal government were $68.7 billion, which was 10.1 percent of expenditures and 2.1 percent of GNP. In 1986, however, net interest payments had reached $136.0 billion (despite the decline in interest rates), which was 13.7 percent of expenditures and 3.7 percent of GNP. Thus, discretionary government spending must be continually cut and/or revenues increased just to keep up with rising interest payments. To make a significant dent in the budget deficit, a comprehensive attack is necessary.

Progress has started. The Gramm-Rudman-Hollings Act was passed, but its enforcement mechanism was judged to be unconstitutional. Subsequently another version was passed that presumably is constitutional—with, however, a less demanding path of deficit reduction.[19] Nevertheless, a path toward correction has been defined and, even if not actually achieved, may well keep the momentum going

---

[17]Ronald McKinnon is of the belief that correcting the budget deficit is both the necessary and the sufficient condition for correcting the trade deficit. Indeed, he believes that the dollar has already declined too much in the foreign exchange market.

[18]Alice Rivlin and Associates, *Economic Choices 1984* (Washington, D.C.: Brookings Institution, 1984).

[19]It is noteworthy that even the stock market crash failed to energize the deficit reduction process. In future years this may be looked upon as a lost opportunity.

toward reduction (in the absence of a recession). The actual budget deficit in FY1986 was $221 billion; in FY1987, $150 billion. There was less real improvement than it appears, however, since much of the reduction was achieved by one-time expedients. The planned reductions for FY1988 and FY1989 that came out of the budget compromise of November 20, 1987 would do little more than keep the actual deficit at the $150 billion level, although in its absence this figure would have been significantly higher. Continual improvement, however, will require hard political decisions that have yet to be made.

A mixed government-private commission was appointed in 1988 to investigate the budget deficit. It was directed to make recommendations for its solution by March 1989 so that the new U.S. president taking office in that year would have the benefit of its wisdom. This duplicates the successful approach used in 1985 to solve the social security impasse.

The link between the budget deficit and the trade deficit suggests that the current account deficit can be cut if the savings in the budget are not absorbed by greater private consumption or investment.[20] Reducing the budget deficit makes room for an improvement in the current account deficit, but it will occur only if foreign markets are expanding and/or the United States improves its competitive position. The direct pass through of a budget deficit decline to trade improvement is only one-third.[21] (Only $1 of trade improvement comes directly from $3 of budget deficit reduction.) The competitive position of the United States can accommodate to the given rate of foreign expansion (within limits) by reductions in the value of the dollar. The dollar has declined considerably since its peak at the end of February 1985. In fact, by the end of 1987 it had retraced more than 90 percent of its rise from 1980.

Some observers have been concerned that the dollar devaluation is not working, given the scant improvement in the trade accounts. That concern is not warranted. In experiments sponsored by the Brookings Institution, several standard econometric models simulated what should have been U.S. trade results, given the actual movements in the dollar and world economic activity.[22] In fact, they tracked the actual trade performance fairly closely. Some discrepancy appears because for-

---

[20]Care must be taken to compare magnitudes in the same units, that is either current dollars or constant 1982 dollars. For convenience, this analysis is done in current dollars.
[21]Jeffrey Sachs, "Prospects for Global Trade Imbalances: A Simulation Approach," unpublished ms., January 1988.
[22]Ralph C. Bryant and Gerald Holtham, "The U.S. External Deficit: Diagnosis, Prognosis, and Cure," *Brookings Discussion Papers in International Economics* no. 55 (March 1987).

eign suppliers seem to be reducing the foreign currency price of their goods in order to hold down their dollar prices to sustain their market shares in the United States. Obviously this cannot continue without causing losses for foreign suppliers and violating U.S. anti-dumping laws. Actually, the trade balance measured in volume terms (constant prices) has improved sharply as U.S. exports have risen substantially (at a growth rate of 20 percent during 1987) because of their improved international competitiveness.

The exchange rate is working as well as it usually does—that is, with a considerable time lag. Thus, the current account improvement has not matched the budget deficit improvement because the decline in the value of the dollar did not start in time (and American consumption growth had not moderated sufficiently). In fact, the average value of the dollar was higher in 1985 than it had been in 1984. Hence significant improvement in the trade accounts should not have been expected until 1987 or later, and then only if the pace of world economic activity did not falter.

Further experiments with econometric models suggest that in order to reach equilibrium—defined as a zero balance in the current account— the U.S. dollar will have to sink below its 1980 level. If the dollar had stayed at the value agreed to by the Louvre Accords (the yen at between 140 and 150 per dollar and the deutsche mark between 1.8 and 1.9 to the dollar) and world economic activity had continued on its indicated path (industrial countries growing about 2.5 percent per year), then the improvement in the U.S. current account would have ceased around the end of 1988 at a level of deficit of almost $100 billion per year; after that point it would begin to worsen again.

Once more the problem is interest and other service payments on a rising foreign debt. In 1980, the United States could record a small current account surplus with a trade deficit of about $25 billion because it was a creditor nation earning more interest and dividends on its foreign investments than paying on its foreign debt. The situation is rapidly being reversed. In the future, the United States will have to earn a trade surplus just to come out even in its current account. Thus, the dollar will have to decline below its 1980 value to improve U.S. competitiveness to the point where the trade surplus can be achieved.

The U.S. Impact on Pacific Countries:
1981–85

There are three channels through which economic forces in the United States impacted on countries in the Pacific: monetary mechanisms, trade flows, and direct investment. Monetary conditions were impacted because, as previously noted, the Reagan program created a savings shortfall in the United States that forced up interest rates and appreciated the dollar. This in turn affected the rate of inflation, the terms of trade, and the interest burden/interest income of other countries. How individual countries were affected depended on their own economic structure and position and their own policy response to the international environment.

Countries whose currencies depreciated on average felt an inflationary impulse within their economies. It is also possible that they suffered a deterioration in their terms of trade, but since commodities were impacted differentially from manufactured goods, much depended on the composition of exports and imports. Countries that had more dollar liabilities than assets (especially if contracted on an adjustable interest rate basis) found their interest rate burden increasing. Countries that tied their currencies to the U.S. dollar and thereby appreciated along with the United States enjoyed the opposite effect.

Much of the impact of the United States on other countries was through the trade channel. U.S. imports increased rapidly both because demand was increasing and because the higher dollar improved the competitive position of foreign products. The value of U.S merchandise imports increased by $120 billion between 1980 and 1986, a 47.9 percent rise. At constant prices (volume), the increase was 56.9 percent. Of course, U.S. export competitiveness was also reduced as a result of the stronger dollar, which permitted other countries to gain market share at the expense of the United States, but there is no simple way to measure it. If U.S. exports had grown proportionally to world trade, however, they would have been $89 billion higher in 1986, or 40 percent more than they actually were. (This is just another way of reporting the rising trade deficit of the United States.)

The channel of impact through foreign direct investment is probably the least important of the three but also the hardest to verify empirically because it is almost impossible to specify the counterfactual alternative (what foreign investment would have been in the absence of the U.S. program).[23] It appears that the major beneficiaries of the high dollar–propelled investment were the NICs in both Asia and Latin America.

---

[23]The foreign investment decision seems to grow out of a two-stage process involving first a determination of whether it is a good time to invest, and then a decision as to where to place the investment. Historically, American firms increased their domestic and foreign investment together. Anecdotal evidence and common sense suggest that the rising dollar led many companies to make more foreign investment than they would have otherwise done, but a magnitude cannot be established without a fully specified econometric model. Such a reliable model does not yet exist.

The net result of all three channels differed sharply by region. German sensitivity to inflation may have made the net result contractionary for all of Europe for most of the period. While the dollar was appreciating through February 1985, the deutsche mark was depreciating. The Bundesbank was very conscious of the inflationary consequences of a depreciating DM and kept German interest rates relatively high (especially in real terms). The growth of central bank money—the best indicator of German monetary policy—was kept between 4 percent and 5 percent until 1986, when the period of a weak DM was clearly over. Meanwhile German fiscal policy was also contractionary during this period as measured by the OECD (for reasons that were unrelated to the U.S. program).[24] Thus the monetary channel was definitely contractionary for Germany.

Moreover, the direct trade linkage between Germany and the United States is rather modest. Only about 10 percent of German exports are usually sold in the United States, so Germany did not gain so much from the rise of U.S. imports. The main market for German goods are other countries in Europe who, along with Japan, are also Germany's main competitors. Since the currencies of all these countries moved more or less together, no significant competitive advantage was obtained by Germany while the dollar was rising. Thus, German growth of GNP was very subdued. There was a modest recovery in 1983 and 1984 from the recession of 1980–82, but unemployment continued to rise until mid-1985.

Germany is the critical country for the rest of Europe. When the German economy is sluggish, all of Europe is subdued. The French attempted to stimulate their economy independently of Germany at the start of the Mitterrand administration in 1981, and the experience was so painful for them that France—and the rest of Europe—will not attempt it again soon. The possible exceptions are the United Kingdom and Norway because of their position as oil exporters, but even their independence is circumscribed by the world energy market. Thus, since Germany failed to have a robust recovery in the early 1980s, all of Europe mirrored this experience. And Germany blamed its problems on high interest rates in the United States and the strong dollar.

The impact of the U.S. program on the Pacific-Asian region was quite different from its impact on Europe. It also differed, however, among the national resource countries (mainly ASEAN); the NICs, and Japan. All natural resource–driven countries suffered from a deteriora-

---

[24]Organization for Economic Cooperation and Development (OECD), *Economic Outlook*, various dates.

tion in their terms of trade from 1980 through 1986, and the U.S. program may have been partially responsible. The primary reason was the decline of prices of the natural resource products that these countries export, rather than the rise of prices of imported manufactured products. It was not unusual that the terms of trade of developing countries exporting primary commodities deteriorated in 1981–82 (by 13 percent per year) while the recession was in progress. Prices of natural resources have always been more variable than manufactures—falling more in recessions and rising more in recoveries. However, the fact that the deterioration continued through 1985 (by 9.5 percent per year) is unusual. Part of the explanation may be that the U.S.-led economic recovery, as already noted, was marked by high real interest rates and a rising dollar. High interest rates work against the holding or rebuilding of inventories—and prices of primary commodities are very sensitive to inventory change. Furthermore, since commodities are priced in terms of dollars, the rising dollar meant that commodities were not cheap to other countries whose currencies were depreciating relative to the dollar. This factor may also have held down demand for commodities.

The nonfuel exporters, the Philippines and Thailand, were impacted first, but Indonesia and Malaysia were impacted subsequently when oil prices dropped in 1985–86.[25] The manufacturing sectors of these economies, however, responded to rapid growth of demand in the United States for such products, and the industrialization of these countries was accelerated.

The Asian NICs, and especially South Korea and Taiwan, were impacted very positively by the U.S. program. They have been becoming increasingly competitive in both labor-intensive and medium-range technology manufactured goods, and their exports of such products to the United States grew enormously. Though South Korea, as other indebted countries, found the burden of its foreign debts rise as a result of higher dollar interest rates and also found its external credit being squeezed, the negative impact of these monetary factors was more than offset by the rising demand for its exports. Furthermore, the decline in world commodity prices—which the NICs import—helped restore price stability. For South Korea, it was the first expansion the country had managed with declining inflation. Moreover, the Asian NICs along with some Latin American countries may have been the recipients of some

---

[25]Singapore had a serious recession in 1985–86 that was partially related to the distress of its natural resource based trading partners in ASEAN. Lawrence B. Krause, Koh Ai Tee, and Lee (Tsao) Yuan, *The Singapore Economy Reconsidered* (Institute of Southeast Asian Studies, Singapore, 1987).

American direct investment fleeing the high dollar. More advanced technology than previously was embodied in these transfers, which may have been of significance to the recipients (more research will be required to establish this point).

It was Japan, however, that gained the most by the U.S. program. Indeed, the program was so favorable for Japan that one might have thought it was designed in Tokyo. Japanese exports were directly stimulated by the rise of demand in the United States. Japanese exports also gained market share in both the United States and in third markets at the expense of U.S. producers because of the rise in the value of the dollar—decline in the value of the yen. Furthermore, Japan benefited from the decline in world raw material prices since it is more dependent on imports of such products than any other industrial country. Finally, Japan gained from the rise of world real interest rates since it was a creditor country—soon to become the world's largest. Of course, Japan, like European countries, did encounter some inflationary pressures from a depreciating currency, but unlike Europe it evoked no policy response. Japanese policymakers are less concerned by inflation unless it signals a loss of international competitiveness, which cannot happen when generated by a depreciated currency.[26]

Thus, unlike Europe (and possibly Latin America and Africa), the Pacific-Asian region in general gained a great deal from the U.S. program. The countries in the Pacific Basin are more open to international trade, and are more dependent on the United States for markets, than other regions. Hence, when U.S. domestic demand is rising rapidly and especially when the United States is undermining its own competitive position by driving up the value of the dollar, the Pacific-Asian countries are bound to benefit.

The U.S. Economy in 1986–87 and Beyond

As already noted, the United States has made a start on correcting its twin deficits. The budget deficit has been modestly reduced and the dollar, which began its downward movement in February 1985, continued to depreciate into 1988. Although the trade deficit measured in current prices has just stabilized at a very high level of deficit, trade volumes since the third quarter of 1986 have shown the effect of devaluation as American exports for two years have been rising at a 9.3 percent

---

[26]It is possible to specify a model in which every inflationary impulse is magnified by domestic wage demands, which results in a loss of international competitiveness even when generated by a currency depreciation. Such a model must be considered pathological and certainly does not fit Japan.

annual rate (considerably above the 3.2 percent rate of all industrial countries).

Nevertheless, there is great uncertainty over the U.S. economic outlook for the rest of the 1980s. Economic fundamentals suggest the economy will continue to grow without interruption. None of the usual signs of an approaching recession are visible yet despite the unusual length of recovery. On the supply side, there is no evidence of widespread shortages of industrial capacity, for utilization rates have been rising very slowly and are only at a level of about 83 percent (although readings above 90 percent are not that unusual). If investment in new capacity in manufactures rises as fundamentals suggest, then further production increases are possible without raising the utilization rate. Unemployment rates have been declining but are still in the range of 5 percent to 6 percent (readings below 5 percent would be required to signal a general labor shortage). With improvement in labor productivity, unemployment need not be reduced below its natural rate.

On the demand side, improvements in U.S. competitiveness arising from the dollar's fall have generated an export-led expansion. Moreover, demand for imported goods should shift to domestic suppliers as import prices eventually reflect the depreciation. This should stimulate business investment even further to meet rising domestic and foreign demand—some by foreign investors attempting to safeguard their market shares. Finally, there are few signs of rapid escalation of prices from domestic sources that might force the monetary authorities to stomp on the monetary brakes in such a manner as to end the recovery. Import prices will continue to rise, but this is not an inflation concern unless magnified by domestic reactions.

On the other hand, confidence in the U.S. economy may have been lost both at home and abroad. The historic stock market crash of October 19, 1987 has raised the specter of the Great Depression of the 1930s. The meager reaction of the U.S. government in solving its most serious problem—the budget deficit—suggests that no political consensus now exists to deal forcefully with problems. The stock market crash, however, led to a rise in household savings. An increase in the personal savings rate is a necessary part of the adjustment process.

Even more damaging would be a loss of foreign confidence in the United States. As noted earlier, the United States is dependent on foreign savings. If new funds are not forthcoming, then the U.S. current account deficit must be corrected immediately. This could only happen with a collapse of the value of the dollar (the yen might rise to over 100 per dollar), which would have dire monetary consequences in the United States and real consequences abroad. In the United States, long-term interest rates would rise sharply because of the shock to inflation expectations even if the Federal Reserve attempted to hold down short-term rates. This would have a depressing effect on the economy, and the impact would be even greater abroad. Foreign suppliers to the United States would find their exports crumbling and a recession would start immediately in export industries. This is the scenario for a worldwide recession.

The external impact of the changing nature of the U.S. economy has been greatest on Japan because of the sharp rise of the value of the yen relative to the dollar. Japanese growth since 1973 (but not before then) has been export led. This necessarily had to come to an end, and the turnabout arrived in FY1986. The Japanese economy has become excessively dependent on exports and now must go through an extensive adjustment. In the past, the need for that adjustment has been denied by policymakers, but as Japanese growth stagnated under the pressure of the rising yen, sentiment turned. Prime Minister Nakasone initiated a domestic stimulative package that, if carried on, should sustain the current level of Japanese growth of between 2 percent and 3 percent, assuming that an external catastrophe does not occur elsewhere. Meanwhile real Japanese exports have begun to decline and imports to increase (especially of manufactures).[27]

The Asian NICs have been major beneficiaries of the rising value of the yen. In the main, they have kept their currencies pegged to the dollar and thus have had substantial improvement in their international competitiveness. They have witnessed an explosion of exports. Meanwhile the price of oil—which they import—has declined and at least South Korea has benefited from a decline in interest rates. These effects have been described as the "three blessings" in South Korea, and they have resulted in double digit growth without inflation.

For Taiwan, export-led growth has turned a large current account surplus into the largest relative surplus any nonoil country ever recorded—about 20 percent of GNP. It appears this surplus will be sustained for at least several years, a feat no oil country ever managed. For South Korea, the spurt of exports has turned a small current account deficit into a huge surplus. The currencies of both countries have begun to rise relative to the dollar, but not relative to the yen. Indeed, the exchange value of the New Taiwan dollar and the South Korean won will be a major focal point for international discussion for several years.

---

[27]Press reports indicate that less than half the rise of the yen has been passed along in lower prices to purchasers of imported products, which may explain the disappointing response of imports. It also suggests that Japan has a managed import regime.

The natural resource producers in ASEAN have been less impacted, although the declining dollar in time should improve their terms of trade—it has already had a decided impact on precious metal prices. Manufacturing, however, has been given a definite boost in these countries. For Thailand, the change has been truly remarkable, and manufactured exports may displace raw materials as its leading export before long. Furthermore, the rising yen may have reversed the decline of Japanese direct investment in ASEAN. It appears that Japanese firms are establishing export bases throughout the region to serve markets no longer profitably served from Japan. Thus the countries in the Pacific Basin seem to be able to receive positive stimulus no matter whether the growth leader is the United States or Japan.

How long the current state of affairs can continue is unknowable, although the analysis indicates that the status quo in the United States cannot be sustained. The same can be said for Japan, since it may have difficulty adjusting to an ever-rising value of the yen.

One scenario—the optimistic case—would have the world shake off the stock market crash as just the bursting of a speculative bubble and no more. The United States could deal with its budget deficit in an orderly fashion—say, annual reductions of about $40 billion per year through FY1991. This would permit the U.S current account to improve on a similar path and reach a zero balance by 1992. Achieving that result might well require further depreciation of the dollar, but much would depend on how much domestically oriented growth was generated in Japan and Germany and on how well the LDC debt crisis is handled. This scenario depicts a typical pattern of export-led growth that many countries have experienced, but it would be new to the United States.

Another scenario—the pessimistic case—has the stock market crash eventually leading to a worldwide recession. It hinges on the failure of the United States to accomplish fiscal consolidation. Foreign confidence would be lost in the United States, foreign buying of U.S bonds would cease, and the contraction would start. This is not a pretty picture, but it would also lead to a sharp improvement in the United States current account, as U.S. imports would be curtailed by both the recession and the weak dollar.

What such speculation suggests for the countries of the Pacific is that their market in the United States is going to be curtailed one way or another. Only the timing and the circumstances are uncertain.

U.S. Policy and the International Monetary Regime

As noted at the outset, U.S. economic policymakers have seen their leeway for independent action sharply reduced in recent years, especially in the monetary sphere. The United States had to reverse its previous position in September 1985 and seek the help of other advanced countries at the Plaza meeting of five industrial countries (the Group of Five, or G-5) to manage the foreign exchange value of the dollar. Before the Plaza Agreement, the United States was prepared to rely on its own policy and the workings of the market. The United States, however, realized that an unconstrained market risks a possible collapse of the dollar, and thus it endorsed cooperative management.

The Plaza Agreement marked a significant change in the international monetary regime. The floating exchange rate system was converted into a managed floating exchange rate system by it. It was explicitly recognized that the exchange rate is not separable from monetary policy and other macro policy instruments. Therefore, an agreement to manage exchange rates carries with it the implied willingness to coordinate all macroeconomic policy. The techniques for management were discussed at the Tokyo economic summit in 1986 (where Canada agreed to the G-5 formulation), were refined further at the annual IMF meeting in 1986 (when Italy also acceded), were refined still further at the Louvre Accord in February 1987, and were confirmed at the Venice Summit in 1987. How successful these techniques may be for achieving agreed upon goals is uncertain, and many observers are understandably skeptical.

Of course, techniques do not manage a system. Management comes from governments setting goals and implementing policy to reach those goals. How the goals are set and who has responsibility for implementing policy is a matter of political and economic power. The explicit goal set by the Plaza Agreement was an orderly devaluation of the dollar. Because this seemed to serve the needs of all five countries at the time, the ultimate power broker is hard to determine. Since the dollar had been declining for six months prior to the agreement, it may have been unnecessary for any new policy action to bring it about. Only Japan seemed to take an explicit action to help the dollar devalue when it briefly tightened monetary policy in November 1985, despite no obvious domestic need.

The pressure for agreement became clearer in October 1986, when the goal of the Plaza Agreement was changed as a result of a bilateral meeting of U.S. Secretary of the Treasury James A. Baker and Japanese Finance Minister Kiichi Miyazawa (the G-2). Despite the fact that the dollar was devaluing in an orderly fashion, the two countries agreed that the devaluation had gone far enough and that the then-existing exchange relationship was "consistent with fundamentals." Several of the other countries, and especially Germany, many have liked the decision, but it was taken by only the United States and Japan. The decision was ratified by the entire G-7 when it met in February 1987 and became the Louvre Accord.

On the face of it, the Baker-Miyazawa agreement seemed to serve the needs of Japan much more than the United States, suggesting that Japan is the ultimate power in operating the new managed floating exchange rate system. Japan was experiencing difficulty adjusting to the amount and the speed of the rise of the yen, and it is understandable why Japan wanted the yen stabilized. The United States, on the other hand, had not reached its objective of a current account moving decidedly toward balance.

In April 1987, the United States retaliated separately against a Japanese failure to live up to a trade agreement concerning computer chips, and Secretary Baker made a public statement suggesting that the Louvre Accord did not mean that the dollar could not decline at all. Immediately the dollar fell. Again the G-7 met and agreed that "it would not be desirable for the dollar to depreciate further." This time, U.S. policy was mobilized to support the goal. Secretary Baker joined Federal Reserve Chairman Volcker in strongly opposing further depreciation, and U.S. monetary policy was tightened.

The Louvre Accord, however, set an overvalued rate for the dollar that could not be sustained. Indeed, that agreement may have been the cause of the stock market crash.[28] Shortly after the crash, the dollar dropped further. Despite modest gains recently, econometric models suggest that the dollar still has to decline over the next several years for balance-of-payments equilibrium to be restored.[29] The question to ask is: How can that be accomplished while maintaining stability in world financial markets?

This interpretation of monetary events suggests that the international monetary regime is in the midst of a major change. Its character and performance characteristics are not yet settled.

The International Trade Regime

The international trade regime is also changing. Since World War II, the United States has been the principal defender of the liberal trade regime. The U.S. effort starting in 1982 to launch another round of GATT negotiations—the now agreed-upon Uruguay Round—may be the last expression of that policy.

---

[28]Lawrence B. Krause, "The Challenge of Japan's Financial Reach for the U.S. Economy," in *The Economic Outlook for 1988*, Thirty-Fifth Annual Conference on the Economic Outlook, November 19–20, 1987, Ann Arbor, Michigan.
[29]Bryant and Holtham, "The U.S. External Deficit."

The existence of the huge U.S. trade deficit has caused the change. The change can be seen in several ways. First, U.S. policymakers no longer feel that they have any leeway to offer further opening of the U.S. market in return for greater market access abroad. Instead, the United States is threatening market closure to obtain foreign market access. This suggests that the Uruguay Round is a high-risk venture and may fail. Second, the United States is more willing to take unilateral actions to protect American industry where previously bilateral negotiations ending up in so-called voluntary export restraints (VERs) were the rule. Though neither is desirable, it can be argued that VERs are less damaging to the existing international trade regime.[30] Furthermore, unilateral actions can lead to retaliation and open up the possibility of a damaging trade war.

In the future, American policymakers will recognize that U.S. economic prosperity is dependent on contracting the trade deficit. The post-Reagan era is likely to be characterized by an activist government in Washington, and such a government will look upon trade policy as a way to promote exports and restrain imports. This is the classical goal of mercantilist trade policy. Thus, U.S. trade policy is likely to become indistinguishable from that of many other deficit countries. While the stock market crash might constrain the most protectionist forces in Washington, it is unlikely to reverse the trend in policy.[31] Reciprocity and retaliation will be the guide for American policy, and the most-favored-nations principle may be discarded in the process.

Hence the international trade regime built around GATT is also in the process of change. Many have characterized the trend as moving toward a managed trade system. From the foregoing, it would appear that the United States is the catalyst for change, but it could well be that the larger role of Japan in the trading system is the more fundamental force for change. It is widely believed outside Japan (and possibly within) that Japan manages its trade and has maintained a relatively closed market. Unlike every other industrial country and every developing country making economic progress, import penetration did not rise

---

[30]From the viewpoint of national interest, the VER is the worst device to provide protection. It permits foreign producers to earn monopoly profits at the expense of domestic consumers while providing very little benefit to domestic producers.

[31]It is noteworthy that even after the crash, the United States indicated that it would retaliate against Brazil's closing of its computer software market by putting penalty duties on a wide variety of Brazilian products, when Brazil is one of the most indebted countries to American banks. Additionally, Representative Richard Gephardt based his U.S. presidential primary campaign in 1988 on thinly disguised protectionism. Despite his failure to win the nomination, it apparently hit a responsive cord.

in Japan from 1973 through 1986, although it did in 1987. As Japan took over larger shares of the world market, the stagnation of Japanese imports put tremendous pressure on the rest of the world and caused the reactive pressure for managed trade. Other countries may feel that they must manage their trade in order to obtain countervailing power to deal with Japan.

The other countries in the Pacific Basin may not welcome either change in international regimes. A managed flexible exchange rate system for non G-7 countries means that the other countries will be limited in their freedom to manage their own exchange rates. The IMF has often been the instrument for influencing deficit countries, but now attention is also being focused on surplus countries. As already noted, South Korea and Taiwan have been put under substantial pressure to appreciate their currencies as part of the managed correction of the overvalued dollar.

Changes in the international trade regime may be a matter of even deeper concern to the other countries, however. Protectionism is extremely damaging to outward-oriented countries. A trade war would be an unmitigated disaster for them. Furthermore, managed trade has little attraction to countries without much economic power. Thus, it would not be surprising if the ASEAN countries and the Asian NICs became the most fervent advocates of GATT and the liberal trade regime. Their support, however, may not be enough to save it.

Japan as the World's Economic Giant

If the United States is unwilling to manage the global economic system, and indeed may be incapable of doing so, what are the alternatives? Collective responsibility that would include the United States, Germany, Japan, and possibly others is one alternative. It is notoriously difficult, however, to supply public goods in a collective system without some instrument of compulsion. Without strong leadership from some country that is prepared to operate a system of rewards and penalties, it is hard to believe that the required supply of public goods needed to maintain regime stability will be forthcoming.

If the United States is not going to be the leader, then the only other candidate is Japan. Evidence is accumulating that Japan's economic strength is rising and may be surpassing that of the United States. When measured in a common currency, Japanese per capita income is already larger than in the United States, and the rising yen is increasing the gap. As already noted, Japan is the largest creditor nation in the world. Seven of the eight largest commercial banks in the world are Japanese. Three of the five largest insurance companies are Japanese, including the largest (Nippon Life). The largest brokerage firm is Japanese (Nomura). Japanese financial institutions are much more international than their American counterparts (although not more than some European financial firms). Japanese investors dominate many international markets, from the art auctions in London to the treasury bond market in New York. In 1987, the total value of equities in the Tokyo market exceeded that in New York even before the crash, and the drop was larger in New York than Tokyo. Other statistics could be mentioned to reinforce the point.

In the past, world economic leadership was inseparable from military might. If that is still an essential ingredient in economic leadership, then Japan is a long way from taking on that role, although Japan's military capability is usually underestimated. If the two dimensions of power can be separated, however, or indeed if economic power is furthered by minimizing military expenditures, then Japan might well be in a position to replace the United States.

How might the world be different with Japanese economic leadership? Much would depend on how willing Japan was to use its economic power to promote system stability, that is, invest in public goods. For example, Japan has the resources and the technical skill to solve the LDC debt problem by itself. Whether it chooses to do so is another matter. A country set on establishing its economic leadership might see this as an opportunity, but Japan has not played that kind of role in the international system in the past and may be reluctant to do so in the near future.

The difference between international regimes that reflect Japanese modalities rather than American ones may be less critical to the world economy than the process whereby the change occurs. Periods of transition from one leader to another have not been happy ones for the world economy. The last shift—from Great Britain to the United States—was associated with the Great Depression of the 1930s. History may not and need not repeat itself. The risks, however, are there.

Conclusion

The thrust of this essay is that major changes are taking place in the world economy with particular impact in the Pacific Basin because the two major players—the United States and Japan—are both Pacific powers. If one accepts the proposition that the budget and the trade deficits of the United States are not sustainable, then the finding of major change is inescapable.

Of course, the actual change may be different from the picture outlined here. The social and political forces that led to the present situation, however, are unlikely to be altered so quickly as to portend a totally different scenario. The Japanese are not likely to give up their proclivities toward hard work and savings, nor are Americans likely to reverse their habits of a different kind.

Economic reality does impinge on societal choice. In time, the United States and Japan will both make the required adjustments. The process by which this happens, however, can be either highly destructive or reasonably harmonious. The outcome can be affected by policy choices. The entire Pacific Basin has a stake in the path ultimately followed.

2. Japan's Economic Policies and Their Regional Impact

YUKIO NOGUCHI

As their interdependence increases, international considerations become more and more important in determining economic policies in many countries.[1] Japan is no exception. Rather, it is one of the countries in which this tendency is most clearly observed: Japanese monetary policy has been determined mainly by exchange rate considerations during recent years, especially since the Group of Five Plaza Agreement in September 1985. In spite of the strong opposition of fiscal authorities to increasing the budget deficit, fiscal policy is heavily influenced by external pressures demanding expansion of domestic spending. Greater emphasis is now being placed on such objectives as realization of international division of labor in determining the direction of industrial policy in spite of strong domestic concerns for preserving employment. Even the country's tax policy and land use policy, which have traditionally been regarded as purely domestic, have recently come to be strongly influenced by international considerations.

In the past, "international" in this context was almost synonymous with the relationship with the United States—or, at most, with the Organization for Economic Cooperation and Development (OECD) countries—and little consideration was given to relationships with Asian countries in spite of their geographical proximity. In a sense, this bias was unavoidable since the impact of Asian countries on Japan's economic activity was far smaller than that of the United States in quantitative terms.

The situation is rapidly changing. Japan's relationship with Asian countries is becoming increasingly important because a horizontal division of labor is being established between Japan and other Asian countries. Whether Japan will be able to transform its industrial structure to a more advanced one and to maintain harmonious relationships with other countries depends heavily on whether such division of labor can

---

[1] At the Venice Summit Conference, member countries agreed to implement strengthened arrangements for multilateral surveillance on the following indicators: economic growth rate, domestic demand, inflation rate, external current account balance, budget deficit, monetary indicators, and exchange rate.

be successfully realized. In this sense, taking into account regional impact becomes important even from Japan's own point of view.

In this essay, "Asian countries" will refer to the NICs and ASEAN countries. In most quantitative discussions I will refer to data from the NICs. This emphasis, however, results mainly from availability of data and does not imply neglect of the ASEAN countries. I will not treat China and other socialist countries in spite of their potential importance. First, I will review changing patterns of economic interdependence between Japan and other Asian countries during recent years and consider their implications for the international impact of Japan's economic policies. Here, the emphasis will be on the transformation of the relationship from vertical to horizontal division of labor. This has been accelerated by the recent exchange rate changes that have reduced relative importance of short-run demand-management policies and increased the importance of long-run supply-side policies. Next, I will examine fiscal and monetary policies and their international effects; I shall note that Japan's huge surplus in its external current account cannot be reduced significantly by Japan's macroeconomic policies alone. Whereas in the third section I focus on aggregate demand, in the following three sections, dealing with relatively long-term policies, I discuss the supply side. Then, I shall turn to relatively long-term policies, focusing on the first aggregate demand side then discussing the supply side. The basic transformation of industrial structure in Japan is from export oriented to domestic demand oriented. However, there are several areas in which explicit government actions are needed. Finally, I will analyze the long-term trend of Japan's capital accumulation and its effect on external balance, suggesting that in the long-run, Japan may become a capital importing country.

Changing Patterns of Economic Interdependence: The Regional Impact of Japan's Policies

There have been considerable changes in the exchange rates of Asian countries since September 1985.[2] Although the extent of change differs from country to country, the general direction has been: (1) relatively mild appreciation against the U.S. dollar, and (2) significant depreciation against the Japanese yen. The former has been brought about by the U.S. pressure aimed at reducing growing surpluses of

---

[2]Katsuhiko Suetsugu et al., "All Asia to NICs Through Division of Labor" [Bungyo susume Asia so-NICs ka he], *Nikkei Center Kaiho*, June 1, 1987.

these countries to the United States. The latter is, of course, the result of the significant appreciation of the yen against the U.S. dollar.

The second change has had a substantial impact on the economic relations between Japan and other Asian countries. First, exports from Asian countries to Japan have increased. This is particularly true for such NICs as South Korea and Taiwan. According to a recent Custom Survey, imports of electric appliances from NICs showed a remarkable increase in 1987. Import of color television increased by 16.2 times from the previous year; the corresponding figures were 9.1 for video tape recorders (VTR), 2.3 for electric fans and 2.0 for electric razors.

Second, direct investment from Japan to Asian countries has increased. Not only large corporations but also medium-and-small-sized firms are eager to shift production to abroad. This trend will continue in the future since the wage differential between Japan and these countries has grown so large. At present, Japanese firms' reliance on overseas production is not significantly high. According to a survey by the Ministry of International Trade and Industry, the ratio of overseas production was only 4.7 percent in March 1985. This is fairly low compared to that of other countries (19.3 percent for West Germany, 17.3 percent for the United States). This ratio, however, is expected to rise sharply in the future. According to the 1987 *White Paper on International Trade*, more than half of the firms surveyed forecast that the ratio will rise to 10 to 30 percent in ten years from now. A similar trend has been observed in a survey by the Toyo Keizai.[3]

These figures imply that the fundamental character of the economic relationships between Japan and other Asian countries is changing. In the past, the relationship consisted of the vertical division of labor—that is, Asian countries supplied raw materials to Japan and imported manufactured products. During recent years, this relationship, especially that with the NICs, has been transformed to the horizontal division of labor—that is, such new patterns as outsourcing and original equipment manufacturing (OEM) are increasing. According to a survey conducted by the Ministry of International Trade and Industry in January 1987, the percentage of firms importing parts and semiproducts was 58.7 percent in all manufacturing industries and 71.3 percent in assembling industries. The Asian region's share was 39.2 percent.[4] According to a survey by the Nomura Research Institute, the share of imported products from the NICs in total domestic sales in 1986 was 69 percent for radio-

---

[3]Toyo Keizai Shinposya, *Tokei Geppo*, May 1987.
[4]Ministry of International Trade and Industry, *White Paper on International Trade* [Tsusho Hakusho], 1987.

Table 1

Index of Intra-Industry Division of Labor Between Japan
and the NICs[a]

Industry	1980–81 (average %)	1985–86 (average %)
Iron and steel	75.1	55.5
Pottery and ceramics	49.7	36.6
Metal products	78.9	68.6
Noniron metals	85.5	77.1
Precision machinery	80.3	75.0
General machinery	93.3	88.9
Chemistry	63.1	61.0
Textiles	0.4	−0.4
Automobiles	100.0	99.6
Electric machinery	72.2	76.0

[a]The index is defined in text.
SOURCE: Ministry of International Trade and Industry, *White Paper on International Trade* [Tsusho Hakusho], 1987.

cassette tape recorders; 52 percent for radios; and 20 percent for record players, calculators, window-type air conditioners, electric fans, and vacuum cleaners.[5] The OEM of such advanced products as color television, refrigerators, and automobiles is also increasing. The role of off-shore production has also changed: in the past, it was aimed at satisfying demands in the host country or exports to third countries. In recent years, exports to Japan are growing.

The 1987 *White Paper on International Trade* calculates the index of intra-industry division of labor between Japan and Asian NICs. The index is defined by $(Xi-Mi)/(Xi+Mi)$, where Xi and Mi are export and import of the i-th industry. As division of labor proceeds, *both* import and export increase. Thus, the smaller value of the index represents a higher degree of division of labor. As shown in Table 1, the index has decreased in most industries during the period.

The 1986 *White Paper on Economic Cooperation* distinguishes four types of division of labor between Japan and other Asian countries:

1. *Value-added division of labor.* This is the traditional relationship. Japan imports raw materials from Asian countries and exports manufactured goods.

2. *Division of labor in production process.* Assembly is carried out in Asian countries using parts imported from Japan.

[5]*Nihon Keizai Shimbun*, June 21, 1987.

Table 2

Changing Pattern of Interdependence with NICs[a]

Year	Types of Interdependence			
	(1)	(2)	(3)	(4)
1980	56	11	10	20
1985	42	13	15	26
1990	31	14	23	28
1995	26	15	22	32

[a]Figures are percentage share of each type in total cases.

SOURCE: Ministry of International Trade and Industry, *White Paper on International Economic Cooperation* [Keizai Kyoryoku Hakusho], 1986.

3. *Product differentiation division of labor.* Japan concentrates on relatively high value–added products and imports relatively low value–added products.

4. *Cooperation in supply of capital and technology.* Japan supplies capital and technology through such means as joint ventures with firms in Asian countries and carries out a division of labor with regard to products and markets.[6]

At present, more than half the relationships belong to type 1. In the future, the White Paper projects, such traditional types will decrease and types 3 or 4 will increase, at least as far as Japan's relationship with the NICs are concerned (see Table 2).

It may take time before similar relationships are established between Japan and the ASEAN countries. There is a possibility, however, that the horizontal division of labor may be established between these countries and the NICs. In fact, the previously mentioned changes in the relationships between Japan and the NICs will cause the industrial structure of the NICs to become more advanced, and, as a result, part of the production presently carried out there will be shifted to ASEAN countries. In this way, a new interdependence is emerging in the East Asia region. This trend is accelerated by pressures from the United States to rectify trade imbalances.

These trends will affect the basic nature of the impact of Japan's economic policies on Asian countries. When the relationships were at the levels represented by type 1 (value-added division of labor), Japan's business cycle had an important impact on Asian countries, since changes in Japan's production level directly influenced Asian countries

---

[6]Ministry of International Trade and Industry, *White Paper on Economic Cooperation* [Keizai Kyoryoku Hakusho], 1986.

through changes in the quantity of raw material imports. Thus, it is the short-run stabilization policy that matters most.

As the relationship shifts to a higher level, however, the impact of Japan's short-run business cycle will diminish. In particular, if the relationship is type 4 (cooperation in capital and technology), the economic activities of Asian countries will become almost independent of Japan's business cycle. To this extent, the importance of short-run countercyclical policy will decrease.

On the other hand, the importance of long-run industrial or trade policies will increase. For example, if Japan resorts to protectionist measures for the sake of securing domestic employment in industries losing international competitiveness, the growing sophistication of the industrial structure in Asian countries will be seriously retarded. Other long-run policies have similar implications. Therefore, whether the new trend described here can in fact be realized depends to a large extent on Japan's long-term economic policies.[7]

Fiscal and Monetary Policies: Their Regional Impact

Many factors have caused Japan's huge surplus in its external current account. First, conditions in other countries, especially the budget deficit in the United States, are of great significance. Second, even if we confine ourselves to the Japanese side, such structural factors as the closed nature of markets or the industrial structure have important implications for the trade imbalance. It is also true that short-term macroeconomic policies have had a certain influence. Here I will review fiscal and monetary policies during recent years and discuss their international impact.

Fiscal Policy

According to the traditional analytical framework, the international effects of macroeconomic policies were supposed to work through income effect on imports—that is, if a country adopted an expansionary policy, income would increase through the multiplier process and imports accordingly increase. In time, this would raise the income of other countries.

This framework assumes a fixed exchange rate and ignores international movements of capital. In the present world, however, exchange

---

[7]Needless to say, the future course of the relationship depends also on the Asian countries' economic policies—in particular, on their liberalization of investment. I will not discuss this aspect of the problem in this essay, however.

rates are flexible and movements of capital are free. A basic framework for evaluating the effects of macroeconomic policies under such circumstances is provided by the Mundell-Fleming model.[8] According to this model, the effect of an expansionary fiscal policy is analyzed as follows: first, a tax cut or an increase in government spending will lead to an expansion of aggregate demand. If the money supply is kept unchanged, the interest rate tends to rise. This leads to an appreciation of the home currency because capital inflow is increased. Accordingly, the trade surplus is reduced and income is reduced to the original level. In this way, fiscal policy does not affect equilibrium output. Its effect is an appreciation of the currency and a reduction in trade surplus. In foreign countries, the trade balance will improve, income will rise, and the interest rate will rise.

This analysis assumes zero-interest-rate elasticity of demand for money (i.e., crowding out caused by fiscal expansion is perfect) and perfect substitutability between domestic currency–denominated assets and foreign currency–denominated assets (i.e., the international capital movement is perfectly free and the domestic interest rate cannot deviate from the world rate). In reality, however, things are more complicated, since these assumptions do not necessarily hold. Thus, income might rise. Also, there are uncertainties concerning the movement of exchange rates since demand for the home currency caused by increased capital inflow may be canceled by increased supply of the currency brought about by increased imports. Thus, the effect of fiscal policy on the exchange rate is an empirical matter. Although most econometric models predict appreciation of the home currency, some predict different results.[9]

Takenaka and colleagues (1987) constructed a world economy model and evaluated the effects of Japan's fiscal expansion.[10] The model is basically a Keynesian-type aggregate demand model and incorporates international capital flow and exchange rates as endogenous variables. Table 3 shows the result of a simulation for the case when government spending is increased by 1 percent of GDP (sustained change). The model predicts an increase in Japan's GDP, which is 1.4 percent of GDP

---

[8]A concise exposition of the Mundell-Fleming model is found in Rudiger Dornbush and Stanley Fischer, *Macroeconomics*, 4th ed. (New York: McGraw-Hill, 1987), ch. 6.

[9]Akira Sadahiro, "The Present State of World Economy Models" [Sekai Keizai Moderu no Genjou], *ESP* (Economy Society Policy) 170 (June 1986):28–35.

[10]Heizo Takenaka, Ryokichi Senda, Yutaka Hamano and Yoshida Yasushi, "Japan-U.S. Policy Coordination and the Pacific Region: A Simulation Analysis of a Sacks-Type World Model;" [Nichibei Seisaku Kyocho to Kantaiheiyo Keizai], *Financial Review* 3 (December 1986):70–93.

Table 3

Effects of Japan's Fiscal Expansion[a]

	United States	Japan	OECD	NICs[b]
GDP (%)	0.0	1.4	0.1	0.5
Interest rate (%)	0.3	7.1	0.4	1.1
Exchange rate (%)	—	0.6	0.4	0.1
Trade balance (US$ billion)	0.7	−2.2	1.1	0.2

[a]Figures are those of the second year after government expenditure is increased by 1 percent of GDP in Japan.
[b]NICs here implies Asian NICs: South Korea, Hong Kong, and Singapore (Taiwan is not included for statistical reasons); also in Table 5.

SOURCE: Heizo Takenaka et al., "Japan-U.S. Policy Coordination and the Pacific Region."

(i.e., the multiplier is 1.4) in the second year. This is a fairly large increase compared to the result of similar models. The reason is that the effect of fiscal expansion on the interest rate is small. The interest rate rises only by 7.1 percent (i.e., if the original interest rate is 5 percent, it rises to 5.35 percent) in the second year. The model predicts an appreciation of the yen. The magnitude, however, is small. The rate of appreciation is only 0.6 percent (i.e., if the original exchange rate is 150 yen per dollar, it becomes 149.1 yen) in the second year. This is because increased demand for yen caused by increased capital inflow is mitigated by an increased supply brought about by increased import.

Trade balance worsens by US$2.2 billion in the second year. This is a small effect compared to the original fiscal expansion, which is 1 percent of GDP, or about US$ 20 billion. Recall that according to the simple Mundell-Fleming model, the crowding out of net exports is equal to the original fiscal expansion. It is also very small compared with the total amount of the actual trade surplus, which was US$101 billion in FY1986. This indicates that it is impossible to reduce Japan's current account surplus significantly merely through that country's fiscal expansion. Japan's fiscal expansion has a negligible effect on the GDP of the United States and other OECD countries. Its effect is significant, however, on Asian NICs; the GDP of Asian NICs will increase by about 0.5 percent. Note, however, that the effects on trade balance are limited.

We now turn to examine the actual trend with respect to Japan's fiscal policies. The most important objective of fiscal management during the last decade has been the reduction of the budget deficit that increased significantly after the first oil crisis and was further enlarged by the expansionary policies of the late 1970s. To achieve this goal, the government once tried to introduce a new tax, called the "general con-

Table 4

Trends in GNP and Government Investment

| FY | Rate of Growth (%) | | | | Percentage Share IG[a]/GNP |
| | GNP | IG | GNP | IG | |
	(real terms)		(nominal terms)		(real)
1970	7.6	14.2	15.8	20.8	9.0
1971	5.0	22.4	10.2	26.8	10.2
1972	9.2	13.4	16.6	20.8	10.9
1973	4.5	− 6.3	20.9	11.6	9.8
1974	− 0.4	− 1.6	18.4	21.5	9.7
1975	3.9	3.8	10.2	9.0	9.7
1976	4.6	0.3	12.4	5.7	9.3
1977	5.3	14.7	11.0	19.6	10.1
1978	5.2	13.4	9.9	17.9	10.9
1979	5.3	− 2.4	8.0	6.0	10.1
1980	4.0	− 1.5	8.7	6.1	9.6
1981	3.3	0.8	5.9	2.6	9.3
1982	3.2	0.1	4.9	0.0	9.0
1983	3.7	− 2.2	4.3	− 2.8	8.5
1984	5.1	− 2.9	6.7	− 1.9	7.9
1985	4.3	− 6.4	5.9	− 6.6	7.1

[a]IG = government investment (including public enterprises).

SOURCE: Economic Planning Agency, *Yearbook of National Account Statistics* [Kokumin Keizai Keisan Nenpo], 1987.

sumption tax'' *(ippan shohi zei)*, a broadly based consumption tax similar to the value added tax (VAT) in European countries. This attempt failed, however, in fall 1979 because of political opposition, hence the government was forced to change its deficit reduction strategy to suppressing expenditures. Thus, fiscal policy during the 1980s has been consistently tight.

Table 4 shows the trend of government investment. Although it increased sharply during the years 1977–78 in response to international pressures represented by the so-called locomotive theory, the expansion was only temporary. The growth rate of real government investment became negative in FY1979 and has stayed at low levels up to the present. Even in nominal terms, the growth rate of government investment has turned negative since FY1983. Table 4 shows some interesting features: first, the expansionary policy during 1977–78, which aimed at raising the real economic growth rate to a 7 percent level, did not have significant effects on the actual growth rate. Second, in spite of the very low growth rate of government investment, economic growth rate returned from the 3 percent level to the 5 percent level in FY1984, as the adverse effect of the second oil crisis vanished.

During the last several years, external pressures for reducing the current account surplus have been strong. To respond to these pressures, the government launched "surplus reduction programs" almost every year. These programs, however, did not include a substantial increase in public spending until the Six Trillion Yen Emergency Economic Measure of 1987.[11]

Public works expenditures were increased rather significantly by this measure. It is still uncertain, however, whether this will lead to a sustained growth of government expenditures; in other words, it is not clear whether this is only a temporary measure or the beginning of a new era in which the basic stance of fiscal policy will be different than that of the past decade. The most important point is whether the "fiscal crisis" still exists. The view that it still exists and so fiscal austerity should be maintained is fairly common. In the remainder of this section, I will examine whether this view is supportable.

Several indices are used to represent "government deficit." The most frequently used are the bond dependence ratio (ratio of bond revenue to total revenue) and the annual amount of long-term government bond issues. The deficit represented by these indices has declined remarkably during the recent years. In the initial FY1987 budget, revenue from long-term bonds was 10,501 billion yen, or 19.4 percent of total revenue.[12] The reduction in the government deficit is more evident if we look at another index, the "savings-investment gap of the general government." This gap was reduced from 9,919 billion yen in FY1980 to 2,590 billion yen in FY1985.[13] If this trend continues, it is probable that the figure will turn positive in the near future, implying that the "fiscal crisis" has already been overcome.

Controversy exists, however, about whether the latter is a proper index of the "government deficit." The controversy arises because even though savings-investment gaps of the local government and the social security funds show significant improvement during recent years, that of the central government does not. The same trend is observed in sav-

---

[11]Reduction in the current account surplus by the Emergency Measure is estimated to be around US$5 to 6 billion.

[12]In the supplementary budget, the bond issue was increased by 1 trillion and 360 billion yen, and the bond dependence ratio rose from 19.4 percent in the initial budget to 21.1 percent. Outstanding debt at the end of FY1987 is 153 trillion and 300 billion yen. (Ministry of Finance, *Monetary and Financial Statistics* [Zaisei Kinyuu Tokei Geppo] April 1987.)

[13]Economic Planning Agency, *Yearbook of National Account Statistics* [Kokumin Keizai Keisan Nenpo], 1987.

ings figures: whereas those of the first two subsectors of the general government are positive and increasing, that of the central government is negative and shows no similar trend. The reason for this difference is not in the receipts; current central government receipts have grown at a rate exceeding those of the local government. The reason can be found in expenditures—in particular, in interest payments. Central government interest payments are growing rapidly, reflecting an increase in outstanding debt. Its share in the total current expenditure of the central government rose from 16.4 percent in FY1980 to 23.5 percent in FY1985.

This last fact is usually regarded as evidence of the seriousness of "fiscal crisis." In fact, however, it implies that the ratio of outstanding debt to GDP has reached a steady level. The reasoning is as follows: If the increase in outstanding debt is equal to the interest payment, its growth rate is equal to the rate of interest. It follows that if the rate of interest is equal to the economic growth rate, the outstanding debt grows at the same rate as the GDP, implying that its ratio to the GDP will remain constant. The same point can be made in the following way: In the past, expenditures other than interest payments were greater than current revenues. It was therefore necessary to raise greater amounts of revenue by bond issues than interest payment. In recent years, such an imbalance between expenditures and current revenues vanished, hence the amount necessary to be financed by bond reached a steady-state level.

This discussion leads to the conclusion that the public sector deficit is no longer a serious problem. Thus, there is now room for taking an expansionary policy. This does not, however, imply that Japan should increase its government expenditures solely for the purpose of correcting the international imbalance. As we have already seen, the amount of surplus that can be reduced by an expansionary policy is only marginal. Substantial reduction in the current account surplus can be realized only by changing the basic structure of the Japanese economy. Increased government expenditures should be used as measures to achieve this objective. Specifically, they must be used to improve the social infrastructure and to assist in the transformation of the industrial structure. This issue will be discussed further in a later section.

Monetary Policy

According to the Mundell-Fleming model, an increase in the money stock will lead to an increase in income and a depreciation of the currency. This conclusion is derived from the following analysis: first, monetary expansion lowers the interest rate. This leads to an increase in capital outflow, hence to a depreciation of the home currency. Accordingly, exports increase and income increases. This process continues as

Table 5

Effects of Japan's Monetary Expansion[a]

	United States	Japan	OECD	NICs
GDP (%)	−0.0	1.2	−0.0	−0.3
Interest rate (%)	−0.1	−8.6	−0.1	−0.6
Exchange rate (%)	—	−2.2	0.0	0.0
Trade balance (US$ billion)	−0.0	0.3	−0.1	−0.1

[a]Figures are those of the first year after the money supply is increased by 3 percent.

SOURCE: Heizo Takenaka et al., "Japan-U.S. Policy Coordination and the Pacific Region."

long as the domestic interest rate is lower than the world interest rate, if the international movement of capital is perfectly free. The effect on trade balance is uncertain because a currency depreciation improves the trade balance but an increase in income has the opposite effect. Effects on foreign countries are therefore uncertain and can be determined only by empirical studies.

The result of a simulation by Takenaka and colleagues is shown in Table 5. The figures represent the first year effect when Japan's money supply is increased by 3 percent (not three percentage points). Japan's interest rate is lowered by 8.6 percent, GDP increases by 1.2 percent, and the yen depreciates by 2.2 percent. The model predicts an improvement in Japan's trade balance, implying that the effect of currency depreciation is greater than the income effect. The magnitude, however, is very small: only US$0.3 billion in the first year and almost zero in the fourth year. Since Japan's trade balance has improved, the effect on other countries' income has been negative. Again, however, the magnitude is almost of negligible order.

Let us now review the actual trend of monetary policy during recent years. Monetary policy was tightly maintained after the second oil crisis. The growth rate of money stock has been kept at a fairly low level.[14] This contributed to preventing inflation that might otherwise have emerged as a result of the rise in oil prices. Indeed, a well-managed monetary policy is usually regarded as the key factor that made Japan's economic performance better than those of other OECD countries in the early 1980s.

As mentioned, a tighter monetary policy in Japan should theoretically lead to a stronger yen if other conditions remain unchanged. In

---

[14]Toyo Keizai, *Tokei Geppo*, June 1987.

actuality, however, the yen was fairly weak until mid-1985. The reason can be found in the U.S. macroeconomic policy: a highly expansionary fiscal policy and a highly restrictive monetary policy.

A significant change in Japan's monetary policy occurred in early 1986. In order to mitigate the adverse impact of the sharply rising yen on economic activity, the monetary authority was forced to relax its policy. The official discount rate, which was kept at 5 percent since October 1983, was lowered to 4.5 percent in January 1986. Since then, it was lowered in several steps to the present level of 2.5 percent, the lowest ever. The decline in the market rate was even steeper. Since interest rates in the United States began to rise, rate differentials between Japan and the United States enlarged to as much as 6 percent by May 1987.

The easing of monetary conditions can also be identified by the rate of increase of money stock. Since FY1985, the rate has risen continuously. In May 1987, it reached 10.2 percent, the highest level since March 1982. Marshall's k is also growing at a rate exceeding the trend line. Theoretically, the easing of monetary conditions in Japan should lead to capital outflows, hence to a depreciation of the yen, as mentioned before. At present, although capital outflow is continuing, the yen still continues to stay at a high level.

Although external pressures demand further relaxation of the monetary policy, it is unrealistic to expect significant easing. This would risk excessive liquidity, creating possible inflationary problems in the future. Increased lending for speculative transactions caused "stock inflation" in the stock and real estate markets. Also, since a number of interest rates are close to their "floor," further cuts would face serious institutional difficulties. Moreover, the effects of Japan's monetary expansion on the trade balance would be marginal, as was shown previously. Thus, monetary expansion is not desirable unless when fiscal policy turns expansionary.

Long-Term Structural Policies

The direction of Japan's long-term economic policies is best represented by the so-called Maekawa Report submitted to the prime minister in April 1986.[15] In April 1987, a new version of the Maekawa Report was published as a report of the Economic Council.[16] The basic stance of the reports is: (1) It is necessary to reduce the huge external surplus in

---

[15]Report of the Committee for Adjustment of Economic Structure for International Harmony, April 7, 1986.

[16]Report of the Special Committee for Adjustment of Economic Structure, April 23, 1987.

the current account for the sake of international harmony, and (2) to achieve this goal, Japan's industrial structure must be changed from an export-oriented to a domestic-demand-oriented type.

There seems to be a wide consensus among the Japanese people on these points. Also, some of the changes are already underway through market mechanisms, as mentioned earlier. In particular, the shift of production to Asian countries by way of establishing subsidiaries and affiliates is the most significant development.

This trend is desirable from several view points. First, it will contribute to the balanced growth of Asian countries. Increase in offshore production by Japanese firms in this region in such industries as steel, electronics, and machine parts will contribute to the increased sophistication of the industrial structure of these countries. Second, it will rectify trade imbalances between Japan and these countries. Japan used to be the most important supplier of capital goods to Asian countries. Although this greatly contributed to the industrialization of these countries, it resulted in the undesirable consequence of excessive reliance on Japan. Imports of capital goods have therefore become one of the major factors for the trade deficits of these countries with Japan. The need for capital goods in these countries will increase in the future as these countries succeed in industrialization. This might further increase imports and hence enlarge trade imbalances. If, however, offshore production is increased, the trade balance will be improved because the local supply of capital goods will replace imports. Although the changes will be achieved mainly by market forces, the process is not necessarily automatic, since there are several factors that prevent markets from functioning ideally. Thus, public policies will be necessary.

One factor that prevents changes in the industrial structure is the trend with respect to wages. The rate of wage increases in Japan has remained quite stable since the second oil crisis. Together with a tight monetary policy, this contributed to preventing inflation during the early 1980s. The problem is that the same trend continues up to the present in spite of the fact that the danger of inflation has virtually vanished.

If wage increases are restricted, the effects of exchange rate changes will be diminished. Japan's international competitiveness in the present industrial structure will remain high; hence the external surplus will not shrink. This may lead to further appreciation of the yen, and a vicious circle may occur. Thus, in order to realize a desirable international division of labor, wages must be increased at a steady pace. This is also necessary to produce increasing domestic demand for household consumption and housing investment.

Needless to say, the problem is unemployment. The unemployment rate in Japan used to be extremely low compared to that in other industrialized countries. Although this is still true, the rate has risen steadily during recent years and exceeded 3 percent in early 1987. Moreover, there is "hidden unemployment" within firms. According to the 1987 *White Paper on International Trade*, two out of three firms believe that "excessive employment" has increased because of the appreciation of the yen. The average ratio of "excessive employment" in the manufacturing industry was 11.6 percent. In order to cope with this problem, government action is necessary. Needless to say, the policy should aim at making the transformation easy and not at preventing the transformation itself.

There are other factors that prevent the smooth functioning of the market. They are: import restrictions, oligopolistic elements, government regulations, and corporate pricing strategy. Because of these factors, benefits derived from the appreciation of the yen are not necessarily transmitted to consumers.

A report by the Economic Planning Agency estimates that the total benefit arising from the fall in oil prices and appreciation of the yen amounted to 18 trillion, 170 billion yen during the period from October 1985 through December 1986.[17] Out of this, 10 trillion, 800 billion yen, or 59 percent, has been "returned" by way of reduction in prices. The distribution of the returned benefits was: household consumption, 5 trillion, 250 billion yen; corporate investment, 2 trillion, 840 billion yen; exports, 2 trillion, 710 billion yen. The report points out that there is room for further price reduction in such areas as transportation fees and agricultural product prices. It also states that some makers of electronic appliances and machinery use the savings derived from the fall in prices of materials to reduce export prices in order to maintain international competitiveness rather than using it to reduce product prices for domestic consumers.

To achieve the objective of completely passing on lower import prices to consumers, various measures should be taken, including liberalization of imports, especially of agricultural products; rationalization of market structures; and abolishment of regulations.

---

[17]Report submitted to the Budget Committee of the House of Counselors by the Economic Planning Agency on May 7, 1987.

Domestic Politics and the Direction of
Long-Term Economic Policies

I will now select some important policy areas and consider the direction of long-term policies by taking into account the effects of Japan's domestic politics.

Agricultural Policy

I argued in the previous section that liberalization of imports of agricultural products is necessary for passing on the benefit of currency appreciation to domestic consumers. It is also necessary in order to alleviate trade friction. Politically, however, this is far from an easy task, since farmers are more than proportionately represented in the domestic political system. Thus, although import restrictions will be lifted step by step as response to external pressures, complete import liberalization of such vital products as rice will not be realized in the near future.

In the long run, however, the number of farmers will steadily decline in the coming decades. This will bring a significant change in the basic orientation of agricultural policy even in the presence of the previously mentioned bias in the political process. In fact, this has already occurred in the allocation of the national budget, in which the share of agriculture-related expenditures has declined continuously in recent years.[18]

It is necessary to transform Japanese agriculture to an industry that can survive without heavy government subsidies and import restrictions. In theory, this can be achieved by concentrating farm lands in the hands of a small number of professional farmers. Although a considerable number of years may be required, this trend will be realized in the long run.

Budget Allocation Policy

To transform the economy to a "domestic-demand-oriented type," the public sector must play an important role. This is especially true in the construction of a social infrastructure in urban areas. It is generally believed that the budget deficit represents a serious constraint on the government in performing this task. As argued in an earlier section, however, this is no longer an essential constraint. In principle, it is possible to increase expenditures at a rate roughly equal to the economic growth rate. The real obstacles lie elsewhere. One is the rigidity in

---

[18]Yukio Noguchi, "Public Finance," in K. Yamamura and Y. Yasuba, eds., *The Political Economy of Japan*, vol. 1, *The Domestic Transformation* (Stanford: Stanford University Press, 1987).

budget allocation, especially that of public works. Because of incrementalism in the budget-making process, bureaucratic factionalism, and the tendency of avoiding explicit political conflicts among various interest groups, it is extremely difficult to change the status quo in the allocation of budget among different areas of public works and among different regions. Thus, agriculture-related public works still maintains a significant share, and investment in urban areas remains at an unsatisfactory level.

The necessity to change the present situation is widely recognized, however. There is a fairly general consensus that budget allocation should be changed so that more shares are given to such urban infrastructural needs as sewage, mass transit, parks and streets, and urban redevelopment programs. Recently, a new method has been introduced into the budget process in order to bring about the reshuffling of the existing shares.[19] Thus, it can be expected that in the long run this problem will be overcome.

The other obstacle is the land problem, which I will now discuss.

Land Policy

High and rapidly rising land prices are serious obstacles to improvement of housing and the general social infrastructure in urban areas. This problem has existed persistently since the end of the 1950s. During the last several years, the situation has become more serious, especially in the Tokyo Metropolitan Area, where land prices more than doubled in the single year 1986.

In spite of the fact that almost everybody talks about the necessity of solving the land problem, it is an extremely difficult task in actual politics. The fundamental reason is that landowners are in the majority; more than 60 percent of households own land in some form. Although most households own only tiny parcels of land, people are sensitive to any policy that might impair their property rights or impose additional burdens. Thus, no political party dares to propose such policies.

For example, one approach to solve the land problem in Japan would be to raise the effective rate of the property tax, because raising the rate would force intensive use of land, hence increase the supply of spaces. But since the immediate effect of this policy would be an increase in the burden of landowners, all political parties, including the Communist Party, are against it. On the contrary, they propose a reduction in the effective rate of the property tax in the face of rising land

---

[19]A part of the revenue from the sales of NTT shares is allocated to public works expenditures in a different manner from the traditional one.

prices. It seems, therefore, that the land problem will continue to be serious in the foreseeable future.

Tax Reform

A fundamental tax reform is underway in Japan.[20] The necessity for reform comes mainly from domestic considerations; hence the reform may have little direct implication for international relations. Nevertheless, it is important because it provides the basis for the long-term performance of the Japanese economy.

The basic orientation of this reform is to reduce the burden of both individual and corporate income taxes and to introduce a new broadly based indirect tax modeled after the VAT in European countries. This will remedy the present situation in which the income tax appears to impose relatively heavier burdens on salaried workers and will distribute tax burdens more evenly among different types of people. It will also reduce the burden of corporate income tax, which is heavy in comparison with international standards. Strong opposition arose, however, to the introduction of the new tax and the fundamental reform is still uncompleted. The opposition from small businesses is understandable. If the new indirect tax is introduced, the tax authority will be able to obtain detailed records of their transactions and may utilize them for strengthening tax collection. The opposition from the labor unions is incomprehensible, however, since in principle they are beneficiaries of the reform. It seems that there was considerable misunderstanding about the nature of the reform. If this situation is corrected, the probability that a new indirect tax will be introduced in the near future is fairly high.

Long-Term Trends in Japan's External Balance

It was stated earlier that macroeconomic policies will not significantly alter Japan's external balance. In the long run, however, there is a possibility that Japan's macroeconomic savings-investment balance will change significantly. This would make a fundamental impact on Japan's external performance. One of the most important factors that may cause such a change is the age structure of population. If the percentage of older people is small, the macroeconomic saving rate tends to be high,

---

[20]For further discussions on the tax reform, see the following articles: Yukio Noguchi, "Japan's Warped Tax Structure," *Japan Echo* 12(4) (Winter 1985); Yukio Noguchi, "Tax Reform: The Missing Rationale," *Japan Echo* 14(1) (Spring 1987); Yukio Noguchi, "In Defence of the Sales Tax," *Japan Echo* 14(2) (Summer 1987).

since the number of dissavers (retired persons) is small compared to that of savers (working people). Indeed, this is one of the major reasons for the high savings rate of present-day Japan. It is expected, however, that Japan's population will rapidly age in the future. According to a forecast by the Institute of Population Problems of the Ministry of Health and Welfare, the ratio of people over age sixty-five to the total population, presently about 10 percent, is expected to rise to about 17 percent by the beginning of the next century, and further to about 23.5 percent around the year 2020.[21] At that time the Japanese population will become one of the most aged in the world.

This will lower Japan's macroeconomic saving rate considerably. The 1985 *Economic White Paper* argued that because of population aging, the household savings rate will fall to around 10 percent at the beginning of the next century and, consequently, the macroeconomic savings-investment balance will change.[22] In particular, it suggested the possibility that Japan's surplus in the external current account will vanish and hence Japan will no longer be a capital-exporting country.

To examine this possibility from a different angle, this author constructed a long-term general equilibrium simulation model of an economy.[23] The model is an extension of an overlapping generations lifecycle model developed by A. J. Auerbach and L. J. Kotlikoff for a closed economy.[24] It consists of three sectors: household, production, and government. Each household makes rational consumption-savings decisions according to the life cycle theory of saving. The government manages a pay-as-you-go social security program. Assets accumulated in the household sector are used for production. Unlike the Auerbach-Kotlikoff model, a perfectly free international movement of capital is assumed in this model. Thus, if the rate of return of domestically accumulated assets is lower than the exogenously given world interest rate, capital flows out until the former becomes equal to the latter.

One of the important findings of the simulation is that the rate of capital accumulation is significantly influenced by the social security program. This is because people reduce savings if they believe that

---

[21]Institute of Population Problems, Ministry of Health and Welfare, *Estimation of Future Population* [Koseisho Jinko-Mondai Kenkyujo], 1986.

[22]Ministry of International Trade and Industry, *Economic White Paper* [Keizai Hakusho], 1985.

[23]Yukio Noguchi, "Future of Social Security and Japan's External Performance" [Koteki Nenkin no Shorai to Nihon no Taigai Pafomansu], *Financial Review* 4 (1987).

[24]A. J. Auerbach and L. J. Kotlikoff, "National Savings, Economic Welfare, and the Structure of Taxation," in M. Feldstein, ed., *Behavioral Simulation Methods in Tax Policy Analysis* (Chicago and London: University of Chicago Press, 1983).

Table 6

External Assets and Savings Rate
(simulation results: steady-state solutions)

	Tax on Labor Income				Tax on Consumption			
	RA[a] = 60		RA = 65		RA = 60		RA = 65	
RR	EA/Y	s (%)	EA/Y	s (%)	EA/Y	s (%)	EA/Y	s (%)
25.8	1.14	8.2	0.30	6.9	1.14	8.2	0.20	6.7
40.0	0.61	7.4	0.01	6.4	0.82	7.7	0.00	6.4
50.0	0.23	6.8	−0.20	6.1	0.59	7.3	−0.13	6.2
69.0	−0.47	5.7	−0.61	5.5	0.16	6.7	−0.40	5.8

[a]RA = retirement age; RR = replacement ratio (%); EA = external assets; Y = GDP; and
s = saving rate. Population growth rate is assumed to be 1.5 percent.

SOURCE: Noguchi, "Future of Social Security" (1987).

after-retirement life is supported by social security. The simulation analysis reveals that not only the replacement ratio of social security payments but also retirement age (which is assumed to be the same as the eligible age for social security benefit) and the method of financing have significant impacts.

Table 6 shows steady-state solutions, that is, solutions when the value of parameters is assumed to remain constant over time. The annual rate of population growth is assumed to be 1.5 percent. Various levels of replacement ratios and two cases for retirement age are assumed, as shown in the table. The revenue necessary for raising the replacement ratio from the present level of 25.8 percent to higher levels is assumed to be financed either by a tax on labor income or a tax on consumption. The savings rate falls to 8.2 percent even when the replacement ratio is fixed at the present level. This represents the effect of population aging. If the replacement ratio is raised, the savings rate falls further.

It is important to note that capital deepening, rather than shallowing, occurs as the population ages. This is because the number of asset holders (older people) increases relative to that of workers. Thus, external assets, as measured by the ratio to GDP, increase. The simulation shows that if the replacement ratio is kept at the present level, steady-state external assets become 1.14 times of GDP. If the replacement ratio is raised, however, the level falls and becomes negative if the replacement ratio reaches 69 percent.

Table 7

Trends in External Assets and Capital Exports
(simulation results: non-steady-state solution)

FY	Tax on Labor Income		Tax on Consumption	
	EA[a]/Y	KEX/Y	EA/Y	KEX/Y
1975	0.319	0.032	0.257	0.026
1980	0.476	0.040	0.396	0.038
1985	0.647	0.036	0.570	0.038
1990	0.794	0.032	0.730	0.035
1995	0.885	0.014	0.861	0.024
2000	0.907	0.005	0.963	0.026
2005	0.933	0.003	1.117	0.031
2010	0.992	0.007	1.336	0.039
2015	0.963	− 0.034	1.511	0.006
2020	0.677	− 0.075	1.440	− 0.034
2025	0.302	− 0.065	1.241	− 0.033
2030	0.095	− 0.026	1.154	− 0.006

[a]EA = external assets, KEX = capital export, Y = GDP.

SOURCE: Noguchi, "Future of Social Security" (1987).

If the retirement age is raised, the rate of saving and capital accumulation falls, because after-retirement life shortens. A tax on consumption eases the adverse effect on accumulation.

To disclose the time path of the external balance, non-steady-state solutions are calculated. In this simulation, it is assumed that the replacement ratio will be raised continuously from 25.8 percent in FY1973 to 69.0 percent in FY2005 and will be fixed at that level thereafter. The population structure is assumed to be changing according to the estimate by the Institute of Population Problems. The results are shown in Table 7.[25]

There are several important points to note in the results. First, Japan's capital export is high in terms of its ratio to GDP during the 1980s. This implies that an important part of the present surplus in the current account can be explained by such structural factors as demographic conditions and the social security system. Second, the ratio remains at fairly high levels for a considerable period of time. This is

---

[25]Actual net external assets at the end of 1986 were US$180.4 billion, or 9.2 percent of GDP calculated at 168 yen per dollar. Simulation results shown in Table 6 are thus fairly high. However, since the *level* is heavily affected by exogenous variables such as the world interest rate, *changes* in external assets (i.e., annual capital exports) are important.

especially true if tax on consumption is used. Third, Japan becomes a capital-importing country in the next century.

The last point has important implications for Japan's long-term economic policy. The issue here is where the capital will come from when Japan becomes a capital-importing country. Considering the stage of economic development, no country other than the Asian countries, especially the present NICs, can assume the role. It is not certain, however, if these countries can develop fast enough to carry the role of capital-exporting countries in the early stages of the next century. If it is considered to be difficult, Japan must continue to be a capital-exporting country. For that to happen, however, Japan must adopt long-term economic policies that help to maintain a high saving rate.

Conclusion

In this essay, I have examined changing patterns of economic interdependence in East Asia and discussed their relationship with Japan's economic policies. My main conclusions can be summarized as follows.

1. In determining Japan's economic policies, more attention should be paid to their regional impact. This is because relationships with Asian countries are of vital importance for Japan's future development in the sense that the establishment of the horizontal division of labor is necessary for the further advance of Japan's industrial structure and for reducing external surplus to a reasonable level.

2. The relative importance of Japan's short-term demand management policies will diminish as the traditional vertical division of labor relationship decreases. On the other hand, the importance of long-term structural policies will increase for several reasons. First, the possibility of establishing horizontal division of labor depends to a large extent on Japan's structural policies. Second, Japan's huge surplus in its external current account cannot be significantly reduced by short-run demand-management policies, and structural policies to transform the industrial structure to a domestic demand–oriented type are indispensable.

3. Japan may become a capital-importing country in the next century. To avoid this fate, its economic policies must be designed so as not to reduce the savings rate.

3. PRC Economic Policies and Their Regional Impact

JOHN WONG

China as a Regional Economic Power

After the formation of the People's Republic of China in 1949, the Beijing leadership immediately took steps to reorient the Chinese economy towards the Soviet bloc, which in the mid-1950s absorbed as much as 80 percent of China's total foreign trade, thus leaving little room for interaction with either the Western economies or China's neighboring countries in the Pacific region.

As the Chinese economy started to steer its orientation away from the Soviet bloc in the late 1950s following its ideological dispute with the Soviet Union, China's overall external economic impact, particularly on the Pacific countries, remained small. Only Hong Kong and Singapore, which have always operated an open trading system, managed to keep up a constant trade flow with China in spite of the obstacles posed by the Cold War. During this period, other Pacific economies either had only minimum commercial contact with China or prohibited any dealing with China altogether.

For its own part, the Chinese economy was then basically inward-looking in nature, a feature partly caused by its physical size and partly by its socialist economic system. A vast economy tends inherently to be more self-sufficient, hence less inclined to participate in the world economy. But central planning, with its penchant for autarky (or what Mao proudly referred to as "self-reliance") certainly intensified China's isolation from the world economic system. Consequently, China under Mao did not develop as an important trading nation. Its share in world trade was consistently below 1 percent, and its trade-GNP ratio was the lowest in the Pacific region.

With the advent of international détente in the early 1970s, China began to modify the orientation of its economy with a view toward entering into greater interaction with the world economy. When China first declared its open door economic policy in 1977, it immediately created a stir in the international economic community, giving rise to instant "China euphoria." China was seen as a large, untapped market or even a new frontier in global economic growth.

Today, some ten years later, the Chinese economy has indeed opened up further and it has also carried out many far-reaching economic and institutional reforms. But the actual external impact of resurgent China on the world economy remains minimal, even though the external sector of the Chinese economy has markedly expanded since 1977 (e.g., China's foreign trade has quadrupled during this period and its exports of goods and services have increased from 5 percent of GDP to 10 percent of GDP). In total terms, however, China's foreign trade turnovers are still smaller than Taiwan's or even Singapore's. To many world traders, the ''China market'' remains as elusive as ever.

Nonetheless, the effects of the opening up of China are already being strongly felt in the countries on the Pacific Rim. These effects are of both a competitive and a complementary nature. In aggregate terms, emerging China promises to create a profound impact on the Pacific Basin. It is well known that the Pacific Basin minus China has already become the world's most dynamic economic region. The growing integration of the Chinese economy with the other Pacific economies will clearly further enhance the region's overall growth potential. This enhanced potential will operate as a new factor in the global economy, likely to alter the international pattern of trade and resource flow.

China and the Pacific Basin

Even based on the relatively narrow definition used in this essay, the Pacific Basin constitutes a truly formidable economic region. It possesses all the necessary ingredients for high economic growth: capital, labor, raw materials, technology and markets. As can be seen in Table 1, the region accounts for the bulk of the world's land area and population as well as a large share of the world's GNP and trade. More significantly, it comprises countries or subregions that have experienced dynamic economic growth in the past and still hold strong potential for continuing high growth in future. Accordingly, the notion that global economic dynamism will gradually shift from the North Atlantic to the Pacific Basin is rapidly gaining currency.

The United States and Japan, the world's two economic superpowers, constitute the most developed component of the Pacific region. To be sure, they are more than Pacific economies because they are globally oriented. But both countries have been the locomotive for the economic growth of the other Pacific economies. Their role in this growth will not be diminished in the future, for the less developed Pacific economies will become even more integrated with them through extensive linkages of trade, finance, and technology.

The newly industrializing countries, namely, South Korea, Taiwan, Hong Kong, and Singapore, however, constitute the most dynamic com-

Table 1

Economic Potentials of the Pacific-Asian Region

| | Area (1,000 sq km) | Population 1985 (million) | GNP Per Capita 1985 (US$) | Total GDP 1985 ($US million) | Real GDP Growth (%) | | | | Per Capita Value-Added in Manufacturing, 1984 (US$) | Total 1985 ($US million) | Annual Growth Ratio (%), 1980-85 | |
					1965-80	1980-85	1985	1986			Exports	Imports
China	9,561	1,040	310	265,530	6.4	9.8	12.3	9.3	140	69,853	8.8	17.6
Japan	372	120	11,300	1,327,900	6.3	3.8	4.5	2.5	3,440	306,346	7.3	2.4
United States	9,363	239	16,690	3,946,600	1.7	6.1	2.6	2.8	2,725	574,771	-2.8	8.4
NICs												
South Korea	98	41	2,150	86,180	9.5	7.9	5.2	12.5	670	61,426	13.0	9.8
Taiwan	36	19	2,868	59,200	9.6	6.5	4.6	9.6	1,230	50,618	19.4	17.7
Hong Kong	1	5.4	6,230	30,730	8.5	5.9	0.9	8.5	1,290	59,889	9.4	7.7
Singapore[a]	1	2.6	7,420	17,470	10.2	6.5	-1.8	1.9	1,540	49,097	5.9	4.2
ASEAN												
Indonesia	1,919	162	530	86,470	7.9	3.5	1.0	1.8	80	30,659	1.1	4.9
Malaysia	330	16	2,000	31,270	7.3	5.5	-1.0	0.5	450	27,584	10.7	6.4
Philippines	300	55	580	32,590	5.9	-0.5	-4.0	0.2	160	10,080	-2.1	-5.9
Thailand	514	52	800	38,240	7.4	5.1	4.2	3.8	170	16,331	8.4	2.8
Brunei	6	0.2	21,000	—	—	—	—	—	—	—	—	—

[a]Singapore is also a member of ASEAN.

SOURCES: *World Development Report 1987*; FEER, *Asia 1987 Yearbook*; *Statistical Yearbook of the Republic of China, 1986*.

ponent of the region economically in the sense that these four economies have registered near double-digit rates of growth for a sustained
period spanning two decades. Generally speaking, these NICs are land
scarce and resource-poor economies. As city-states, Hong Kong and
Singapore have virtually no natural resources to speak of, except for
their geographical location. The only notable resource of South Korea
and Taiwan is their well-developed agricultural sector, which almost
from the beginning has served as an important precondition for their
industrial expansion. In any event, the past economic development of
these NICs, as with Japan, has not been hampered by their lack of
natural resources; in fact, they have all successfully overcome this constraint by intensifying the development of their human resources
through cultivating higher levels of skills, entrepreneurship, and industrial discipline. It has been argued that the mainstream cultural traditions of these East Asian NICs, as embodied in Confucianism, have also
produced positive effects on their economic development, much like
Protestant ethics in the Western capitalist counties.

As a result of their sustained economic growth over two decades,
these four Asian NICs are now clearly in the upper middle income
categories of the developing countries, with Singapore and Hong Kong
on the verge of crossing over to developed country status. Furthermore,
these open and outward-looking economies, heavily dependent on
dynamic export expansion for their economic growth, have begun to
make a significant impact on the world economy; their combined manufactured exports amounted to 60 percent of all the manufactured exports
from the developing world. Viewed in a different way, the total manufactured exports of these four small economies in 1983 were actually
equal to 52 percent of that of the United States or more than ten times
that of India.[1]

The third component of the region is made up of the ASEAN countries, which include Singapore. However, although Singapore is geographically and historically an integral part of Southeast Asia,
economically and socially it resembles the other NICs in East Asia more
closely because of its high per capita income and its similar economic
and social structures. By and large, the ASEAN economies, with their
long-term 6 percent growth rate, are still impressive growth performers.
In contrast to the resource-poor NICs, the ASEAN economies are

---

[1]For more detail, see John Wong, "The Asian NICs Towards Year 2000: Growth and
Adjustment," paper presented at the Beijing Conference on the Asian-Pacific Economy
Towards the Year 2000," November 12–15, 1986, Beijing. Proceedings will be published by
the Asian and Pacific Development Centre, Kuala Lumpur.

endowed with abundant natural agricultural and mineral resources, such as rubber, tin, palm oil, coconut products, sugar, rice, petroleum, and natural gas. The continuing export of these primary resources has been the main source of ASEAN's economic growth.[2] In recent years, ASEAN's economic growth has plummeted because of a prolonged slump in the world commodity markets. There can be no doubt that the ASEAN economies will resume their high growth once the international commodity markets begin to improve as now appears to be occuring.

The economies in all three sectors of the Pacific Basin have thrived on the free operation of market forces. This would seem to set China apart from the other Pacific economies because China is supposed to be a socialist economy operating on central planning. In reality, however, the economic and social distance between China and the other Pacific countries is being rapidly narrowed as China liberalizes its political and social institutions and rationalizes its economic structure through sweeping reforms. These reforms will make it easier for China to reshape its pattern of foreign economic relationship so as to interact more effectively with the Pacific economies.

From the standpoint of the Pacific Basin as a whole, the greater involvement of China with the various economic sectors of the region is a positive development in terms of both economic growth and regional integration. As noted, the Pacific Basin minus China has already developed into a dynamic economic entity. The addition of China, by virtue of its enormous size, huge population and resource base, and vast market potential, will obviously further expand the scope of economic growth for the whole Pacific region. Furthermore, the emergence of the Chinese economy will contribute to the greater economic integration of the Pacific Basin, which in turn can fuel added future growth.

Despite their inherent political, social, and economic diversity, the Pacific Basin countries have already developed a significant degree of economic interdependence. As can be seen from Table 2, the present intraregional trade is extremely high, with the Pacific economies being vitally important markets for one another: 47 percent for the United States, 68 percent for Japan, 75 percent for the NICs, 77 percent for ASEAN, and 69 percent for China.

This suggests that the various sectors of the Pacific Basin tend to have a high degree of economic complementarity with one another. The resource-based ASEAN economies certainly complement the manufacturing-based NICs, and both also complement the highly

---

[2]For more discussion of the economic structures of ASEAN, see John Wong, *ASEAN Economies in Perspective* (London: Macmillan, 1979).

Table 2

Export Matrix, Percentage Composition for 1985

From/To	PB5[a]	China	NICs2[b]	ASEAN6	South Pacific	Developing Pacific Basin	Total Pacific Basin	Rest of World	World (US$ million)
Australia	45	4	7	7	3	21	66	34	21,913
Canada	81	1	1	1	0	3	84	16	90,321
Japan	45	7	8	7	0	22	68	32	171,332
New Zealand	38	3	2	6	4	15	53	47	5,808
United States	36	2	4	4	0	10	47	53	208,454
PB5	48	4	5	4	0	13	61	39	497,828
PRC	33	0	26	10	0	36	69	31	27,230
Hong Kong	41	27	2	7	0	35	76	24	29,471
South Korea	57	1	5	4	0	10	68	32	28,911
Taiwan[c]	65	0	9	6	0	15	80	20	30,719
NICs	54	9	5	6	0	20	75	25	89,101
Brunei	70	0	7	22	0	29	99	1	2,489
Indonesia	74	1	5	8	0	14	88	12	18,014
Malaysia	41	1	7	26	0	35	76	24	15,061
Philippines	60	2	6	12	0	19	79	21	4,529
Singapore[d]	36	1	8	22	2	33	70	30	22,416
Thailand	36	4	6	15	0	25	61	39	7,056
ASEAN6	50	1	7	18	1	27	77	23	69,565
Fiji	28	2	0	8	17	28	56	44	229
Other Oceania	42	1	4	2	1	9	50	50	1,341
South Pacific	40	1	4	3	3	12	51	49	1,570
Developing Pacific Basin	49	5	9	11	0	25	74	26	187,466
Pacific Basin	48	4	6	6	0	17	65	35	685,294

[a]Pacific Basin 5: Australia, Canada, Japan, New Zealand, United States.
[b]NICs2 comprise Hong Kong and South Korea since trade with Taiwan is not separately recorded; NICs3 include Taiwan.
[c]The Taiwan trade data were converted into U.S. dollars using the current trade conversion factors.
[d]The Singapore trade data exclude trade with Indonesia.

Sources: International Monetary Fund, *Direction of Trade Statistics Yearbook*, 1986; Directorate-General of Budget, Accounting and Statistics, *Statistical Yearbook of the Republic of China*, 1986.

developed U.S. and Japanese economies. The huge potential of China promises to offer further opportunities for all.

Analytically speaking, the increases in the economic integration of the various sectors of the Pacific Basin were brought about by the dynamic forces associated with the evolution of international comparative advantage within the region. This came about because the United States, Japan, the NICs, ASEAN, and China happen to be at different stages of the industrialization process, in descending order. Japan, the first industrial state in Asia, initially relied on labor-intensive manufactured exports to spearhead its postwar economic recovery. In the 1960s and early 1970s, Japan moved into the more sophisticated capital-intensive activities, passing on the labor-intensive industries to the NICs, and the ASEAN counties were just about to begin industrialization in earnest. In the entire industrialization process of the Western Pacific region, Japan had a significant head start over the NICs, and the NICs over ASEAN and China. By the late 1970s, the NICs had overtaken Japan as the major exporters of labor-intensive goods such as textiles and clothing, shoes, plastic products, and some household electronic and electrical goods. Furthermore, the NICs were themselves forced to undertake the vigorous restructuring of their economies towards higher value-added and more capital-intensive activities in anticipation of more intensive competition in labor-intensive manufactured exports from latecomers such as ASEAN and particularly China, with its abundant low-cost labor.

Such a pattern of shifting comparative advantage is actually a classic form of regionally based horizontal division of labor. It facilitates the industrialization process of the respective country groups by allowing them to specialize in the production activities where they have strong comparative advantage as well as leading to a higher level of regional economic integration. Thus, the upgrading of the textiles industry in Hong Kong has led to more imports of intermediate products on the upstream from Japan such as ethyleneglycol, caprolactam, and acrylonitrile as well as automatic textile machinery. In the same way, the development of heavy industry in South Korea and Taiwan has led to more imports of new machines and tools from Japan. Meanwhile, the industrial adjustment of the NICs has also generated more import demand for raw materials such as rubber and timber from ASEAN as well also allowing the latter to fill in the slots in the export markets for certain labor-intensive items. In this way, these Pacific economies will also become vertically more integrated, laying down the basis for the further growth of intraregional trade.[3]

Another integrative force operating to draw the Pacific economies closer together is the increasing intraregional investment flow. It is well known that most Pacific economies are open and outward looking in terms of trade and foreign investment. In particular, the ASEAN economies have devised various forms of incentives to attract foreign investment, which is viewed not just as an additional source of capital but also as a vehicle of technology transfer and export market development.

Initially, American capital dominated the region. Since the mid-1970s, Japanese foreign investment has been catching up. By 1982, as shown in Table 3, the stock of Japanese direct investment in the region had surpassed direct investment. Obviously, this trend will continue. In recent years, the region has witnessed a new but significant development associated with more investment flowing from the NICs to ASEAN. The opening up of China has introduced yet another factor in the foreign investment pattern in the Pacific Basin because China is ready to absorb more foreign capital, not just from the United States and Japan but also from the NICs, to facilitate its economic modernization process. During the past nine years, China has signed and approved more than 8,000 contracts with foreign investors representing an investment commitment of more than US$17 billion, mainly from the Pacific countries. The flow of financial resources into China is an important force for integrating China into the Pacific Basin.

China's Transition to High Economic Growth

Whether or not the Chinese economy can interact with the other Asia-Pacific economies in a positive manner and to their mutual benefit in terms of enhancing each other's economic growth potential depends on two crucial conditions. First, can the Chinese economy maintain its capacity for high growth? Clearly, if the economy lags in dynamic growth, China cannot possibly interact with the other Asia-Pacific economies in a productive way. Second, will the present Chinese leadership in Beijing stand fast on its commitment to maintain an open door policy? Again clearly, without an outward orientation the Chinese economy will not be able to integrate itself further into the Asia-Pacific

---

[3]See Toshio Watanabe, "An Analysis of Economic Interdependence among the Asian NICs, the ASEAN Nations, and Japan," *The Developing Economies* (December 1980); also, Takuo Tanaka, "The Patterns of International Specialzation among Asian Countries and the Future of Japanese Industry," in the same issue.

Table 3

Distribution of Foreign Direct Investment Stock in Selected Asian Developing Countries or Areas, by Home Country/Region
(in US$ million)

Home Country/Region	1982						1978					
	United States	EEC	Japan	Other Asian	Others	Total	United States	EEC	Japan	Other Asian	Others	Total
Southeast Asia												
Indonesia	501.1	781.6	3444.5	1531.5	3264.0	9522.6	259.1	575.4	2398.5	1065.1	2022.8	6320.9
Malaysia	83.8	335.9	257.6	472.7	111.0	1261.0	73.7	199.5	169.4	360.4	110.7	913.7
Philippines	943.0	190.3	279.3	120.9	246.1	1779.6	450.8	58.6	164.2	45.3	133.2	852.1
Singapore	1252.6	1560.9	650.0	560.0	0.0	4023.5	208.2	267.1	364.7	342.5	26.4	1208.9
Thailand	51.3	45.1	87.2	34.4	33.7	251.7	32.7	28.2	79.5	42.2	8.8	191.4
East Asia												
Hong Kong	587.8	126.2	379.7	51.7	115.1	1260.5	197.0	68.0	83.0	36.5	33.6	440.0
Republic of Korea	417.9	163.0	675.9	46.0	133.6	1436.4	145.2	201.7	520.2	9.6	78.6	855.3

SOURCE: ESCAP/UNCTC Joint Unit on Transnational Corporations, *Asia-Pacific TNC Review* (June 1986).

region. These two conditions, however, are actually interrelated, and they must reinforce each other. Further growth of the Chinese economy on its present pattern will generate more pressures to open up the economy further in order to utilize the power of international capitalism on behalf of China's economic growth. At the same time, outward-looking strategies will expose a larger segment of the Chinese economy to the world market forces, forcing a reduction of its price distortions and hence increasing its overall efficiency.

After years of unfruitful experimentation with the ideologically motivated Maoist model of economic development, Chinese leaders finally came to realize that the old-fashioned economic growth strategy offers the best means of transforming China into a modern state. This sharp reversal of the fundamental development strategy coincided with the thawing of the Cold War in the region, touched off by Nixon's visit to Beijing in 1972. It took place, however, before China had settled the crucial problem of leadership succession.

In January 1975, at the Fourth National People's Congress, the late Premier Zhou Enlai called for a return to the essentially pragmatic and growth-oriented development strategy based on the "comprehensive modernization of agriculture, industry, national defense, and science and technology before the end of the century."[4] Such is the genesis of China's much-publicized Four Modernizations program. Meanwhile, Zhou's successor, Hua Guofeng, introduced the Ten-Year Plan for the transitional period in 1978, with very ambitious targets. Little progress, however, was made toward the implementation of the economic modernization program during the period when China was caught in a power struggle for succession. As soon as Mao Zedong died, Hua immediately took power and brought down the Gang of Four. Before Hua could consolidate his position, however, Deng Xiaoping returned to key posts in the middle of 1978, leading to additional political strife within the leadership. Political control eventually passed from Hua to Deng and Deng's proteges, Hu Yaobang and Zhao Ziyang.

The Deng group soon discovered to their dismay that the Chinese economy was seriously afflicted with grave "structural imbalance." On December 1, 1981, the Ten-Year Plan was officially superseded with the announcement of the Sixth Five-Year Plan, 1981–85, which emphasized "readjustment, restructuring, consolidation, and improvement."[5] This, in turn, opened the way for a more basic reform of the economic sys-

---

[4]Zhou Enlai, "Report on the Work of the Government," *Peking Review* [now *Beijing Review*] 4 (1975): 23.
[5]*Beijing Review,* May 23, 1983.

tems. Far-reaching economic reforms were first tried out in the rural areas with the introduction of the ''family responsibility system,'' which encouraged private initiative and market incentives. Success in the rural reforms was immediate, as manifested by several successive years of impressive gains in overall agricultural productivity. Beijing then moved in late 1984 to crack the bastion of central planning with the introduction of more complicated urban reforms. Meanwhile, more cities along the coastal areas were opened up for foreign trade and foreign investment by being designated Special Economic Zones. In this way, the open door policy was made an integral part of the overall economic reform process.

How has the Chinese economy actually performed during the past three decades? According to authoritative Western estimates, China has achieved an average annual growth rate of 4.4 percent at 1980 constant prices during 1953 76.[6] Such a long term growth record is quite respectable by the average standards of the Third World, though it obviously pales in comparison with that achieved by the high-performance economies of the NICs. From the World Bank figures as shown in Table 1, China had experienced 5 percent real growth during 1960–70 and 6.6 percent during 1973–84, with the latter generally comparable to the growth performance of the ASEAN economies though considerably below that of the NICs for the same period. This also serves to suggest that the Chinese economy for the whole period of Mao's rule was actually not performing too badly, despite its adherence to the main socialist economic strategies, which were not designed to maximize growth.

The major economic explanation of economic growth for China, as for the other Asia-Pacific economies, comes from its high domestic investment. As can be seen from Table 4, all Pacific-Asian economies tend to commit a large proportion of their gross domestic product to gross domestic investment, which is usually matched by an equally high proportion of gross domestic savings. In the case of some ASEAN economies with an open economic structure, their domestic investment can exceed domestic savings, with the resultant resource gap being filled by the inflow of external financial resources in the form of external borrowing or foreign investment. For China, with its closed door economy at the time of Mao, the high level of domestic investment could only be maintained by vigorous measures of controlling consumption. In fact, one typical feature of Soviet-type central planning (the so-called

[6]Dwight H. Perkins, *China: Asia's Next Economic Giant?* (Seattle: University of Washington Press, 1986); also *China: Long-Term Development Issues and Options*, World Bank Country Economic Report, 1986.

Table 4

Savings and Investment of the Pacific-Asian Economies

Country	Distribution of GDP (%)								Annual Growth Rate of Gross Domestic Investment (%)	
	Gross Domestic Investment				Gross Domestic Savings					
	1960	1965	1982	1985	1960	1965	1982	1985	1963–73	1973–84
China	24	25	28	38	24	25	30	34	12.9	8.0
Japan	33	32	30	28	33	33	31	32	14.1	3.0
NICs										
South Korea	11	30	26	30	1	30	24	31	19.7	8.8
Taiwan	20	23	36	21	13	20	33	34	16.5	6.0
Hong Kong	18	36	29	21	6	29	25	27	3.7	9.7
Singapore	11	22	46	43	-3	10	41	42	22.7	9.5
ASEAN										
Indonesia	8	7	23	30	8	6	19	32	17.5	11.3
Malaysia	14	18	34	28	27	23	25	33	9.1	11.4
Philippines	16	21	29	16	16	21	21	13	4.4	4.3
Thailand	16	20	21	23	14	19	21	21	7.6	5.3

SOURCES: *World Development Report*, 1984 and 1987; and *Statistical Yearbook of the Republic of China*, 1986.

"Stalinist model") lies in its concentration of resources for investment in industrial construction, particularly in the heavy industry sector, at the expense of the light industries or consumer goods industries. China followed this pattern of development closely, especially during its First Five-Year Plan period. In this sense, Chinese development strategies under Mao actually contained a built-in base for growth despite their manifested noneconomic objectives.

If the old system under Mao could deliver growth in reasonable terms, why then did the post-Mao leadership choose to change the system? The reasons are quite clear. First, the Chinese economy prior to 1976, though growing at a respectable pace, did not actually operate to maximize its real growth potential Given such high rates of domestic investment, the Chinese economy, if properly managed, should have grown much faster, or at least as rapidly, as those of the NICs. This means that the Chinese economy under the old form of rigid central planning was grossly inefficient. The major sources of China's economic growth during 1953–76 came from capital investment and the growth of the labor force, with productivity increases accounting for a very small share of the total growth.[7] This is in sharp contrast to the experience of Japan and the NICs, where high GDP growth was accompanied by high productivity growth.

Second, the old development strategies, though containing a strong safeguard for social equity, had generated a GNP with a low welfare content, as it tended to reflect the planners' preference for more steel products and machines, not the consumers' demand for more television sets and the like. In the other Asia-Pacific countries, economic growth has been accompanied by the steady increase in the level of living for its population through the trickle-down process. This effect in turn provides the incentive for the labor force to increase its productivity. In China, Mao had counted on the ideological incentive as a substitute for the material incentive, a motivation that was simply not tenable in the long run.

In short, the shift of policy in the post-Mao period from one based on the rigid system of central planning to one geared to greater decentralization of decision-making and more market incentives is economically and socially a rational move. It will allow the Chinese economy to realize its growth potential to a greater extent. Indeed, results from

---

[7]According to the growth accounting worked out by Dwight Perkins, the Chinese economy during 1953–76 experienced 4.4 percent growth in the net material product sense, with labor contributing to 1.8 percentage points. Productivity (or the residual), however, contributed to only 0.6 percentage points. See Perkins, *China: Asia's Next Economic Giant?*

recent economic liberalization have already appeared. With the onset of economic reforms, growth increased to an average rate of 8.3 percent a year during 1977–84, with productivity growth constituting the major source of total growth.[8] After 1984, as economic reforms were intensified to cover the urban sector, growth was further boosted through more efficient allocation of resources. Thus in 1985, China chalked up a hefty 12.3 percent growth, topping the Asia-Pacific region in growth performance. In 1986, China's 9.3 percent growth was still third highest in the region, after 12.5 percent for South Korea and 9.6 percent for Taiwan (Table 1). The Chinese economy has thus displayed high growth potential once mismanagement was reduced.

When China returned to the pro-growth development strategy in the late 1970s, Beijing set out its long-term growth target of quadrupling the gross value output of agriculture and industry between 1980 and 2000. This means an average of 7.2 percent growth per year for a period of twenty years. But China actually had an average of 11.3 percent growth during the first five years (1980–85), and so only a 5.8 percent average annual growth will be required for the remaining fifteen years. In 1986, China further achieved 9.3 percent growth, much more than the average rate of 6.7 percent called for by the Seventh Five-Year Plan, 1986–90. For 1991–2000, an average growth of only 5.4 percent will suffice to fulfill the target. Such a target is clearly well within the capacity of the Chinese economy to fulfill under the present mix of markets and central guidance (socialism with a Chinese character). If economic reforms were to be further intensified later, then the growth capacity of the Chinese could still expand further.

The next crucial question may then be posed: Will China continue to maintain its open door economic policy in order to allow the Chinese economy to interact more effectively with the other Asia-Pacific economies? The student unrest in December 1986, which led to the downfall of the Chinese Communist Party's General Secretary, Hu Yaobang, serves to point out all too clearly that both economic reforms and the open door policy rely completely on a supportive political environment. The new leadership that has emerged from the recent conclusion of the 13th Congress of the Chinese Communist Party has produced very encouraging signs both for a more stable political transition and for the continuation of the reform movement. Deng Xiaoping, along with a number of conservative Party elders, has now resigned from the Politburo in favor of the younger, technocratically inclined leaders, headed

---

[8]For this 8.3 percent aggregate growth, the contribution from productivity growth alone accounts for 5 percentage ponts. See ibid.

by the reform-minded Zhao Ziyang. this should boost the confidence of China's neighboring countries in the Chinese leadership's continuing commitment to reforms.

In China today the economic reforms have actually gone so far that it is not possible to reverse them. The tempo of reforms in the future may slow at times, but the course will not be changed. This is because both the reforms and the open door policy not only have met with positive results (which far exceed the negative spillovers), but also have been extended in such a way that more and more Chinese people have built up a stake in the new system. In other words, economic reforms can accelerate economic growth, and successful economic growth is the best bulwark for political stability.

It is entirely premature at this point to speak of China as an emerging economic power. The Chinese economy, however has a high growth potential, and such measures as economic reform and the open door policy are being used to mobilize this latent growth potential. A more outward-looking China with a stable economy is likely to become more integrated with the other Pacific economies.

China's Economic Interaction with the Pacific Region

The further integration of the Chinese economy into the Pacific Basin is bound to create a significant impact on all the other Pacific economies by virtue of China's enormous size. In the long run, such a process is undoubtedly beneficial to all because it can promote the faster growth of the region as a whole. But such a process is not likely to be without frictions. In the short run, it may well produce negative spillover effects for some developing Pacific economies, greatly depending on their individual economic structure and orientation.

A natural starting point to analyze the regional impact of China in the Pacific Basin is to look at the structure of China's exports in relation to those of the other Pacific economies. As shown in Table 5, China's export structure looks like something in between that of the NICs and that of ASEAN, as China exports both primary commodities (but not to the extent that ASEAN does) and manufactured exports (but not to the extent that the NICs do). Broadly speaking, China seems to be more complementary with the NICs and more competitive with ASEAN, whereas it does not pose any direct competition to the developed Pacific economies of the United States and Japan.

Since China and the other developing Pacific economies are still heavily dependent on the markets of the developed Pacific economies, the changes in the market shares of these developing Pacific economies in the industrial countries provide a good indication of their relative

Table 5

Structure of Merchandise Exports
(in percentages)

Country	Fuels, Minerals, Metals		Other Primary Commodities		Machinery and Transport Equipment		Other Manufactures		Textiles and Clothing	
	1965	1985	1965	1985	1965	1985	1965	1985	1965	1985
China	—	25	—	21	—	6	—	48	—	24
United States	8	8	27	1.7	37	48	28	27	3	2
Japan	2	1	7	1	31	62	60	36	17	3
NICs										
South Korea	15	4	25	5	3	36	56	55	27	23
Taiwan	0.4	1.8	57.9	7.5	4.3	27.9	37.4	62.8	26.2	19.7
Hong Kong	2	2	11	6	6	24	81	68	43	32
Singapore	21	29	44	12	10	32	24	26	6	4
ASEAN										
Indonesia	43	75	53	14	3	1	1	10	a	2
Malaysia	35	34	59	39	2	19	4	8	a	3
Philippines	11	13	84	36	a	5	6	46	1	7
Thailand	11	5	84	60	a	7	4	28	a	13

a Amount not significant.

SOURCES: *World Development Report 1987;* and *Statistical Yearbook of the Republic of China,* 1986.

competitiveness. NIC exports have already become well established in the U.S. market; and their market shares in 1985 ranged from 1.0 percent for Singapore to 4.5 percent for Taiwan. But the growth of China's market share in the United States from 0.1 percent in 1977 to 1.2 percent in 1985 has been staggering, especially in comparison with the shares for the ASEAN countries. During the same period, Indonesia's share in the U.S. market has actually declined from 2.4 percent to 1.4 percent while that for Thailand has remained at 0.2 percent. The growth of China's market share in Japan from 2.3 percent to 5.0 percent for the same period is equally impressive. Similarly, China's market share of 1.0 percent in the EEC, is the highest among the developing Pacific economies.[9] Based on this kind of "static" interpretation, the other developing Pacific countries would, quite rightly, be apprehensive of the emerging Chinese economy, whose forceful entry into the world market may have a displacement effect upon them. But a realistic evaluation should, of course, be based on dynamic considerations, and it is much more difficult to sort out the balance of net benefits and costs for the Pacific countries arising from the greater participation of the Chinese economy in the world market. Proper analysis needs to take into account the structure of the individual Pacific economies as well as their respective historical relationships with China.

China and the Developed Pacific Economies

Two salient features underlie China's overall economic relations with the developed Pacific economies of the United States and Japan. First, as full-fledged developed economies, both the United States and Japan are highly complementary with the developing Chinese economy. Individually or combined, these two countries can operate as the locomotives of Pacific Basin economic growth and the resultant prosperity in the region can spill over to China. More directly, both have the capacity to supply capital, finance, and technology to meet China's modernization needs. At the same time, both can provide important markets for China's exports.

Second, whereas China is still a regional economic power, the United States and Japan are clearly global economies, with their bilateral economic relationship with China governed by their global economic strategies. Hence their economic relations with China must be subordinated to larger issues of a global or regional nature. Japanese investment in China cannot be separated from Japan's worldwide

---

[9]International Monetary Fund, *Direction of Trade Statistics Yearbook, 1980, 1982, and 1985;* and *Statistical Yearbook of the Republic of China, 1986.*

investment pattern; the access of Chinese manufactured goods to the U.S. market must be subjected to the same conditions as goods from other developing countries. This implies that the structure of China's economic relations with the United States and Japan tends to be one of dependence for China. Lacking sufficient economic leverage, China has to be a "price taker" in its dealings with the United States and Japan, in much the same way that has characterized the economic relationship between the other developing Pacific economies and these two economic superpowers.

Unlike other developed countries such as Japan and members of the EEC, that generally followed a much more pragmatic approach in their commercial relations with socialist countries, the United States rigidly hewed to an ideological line of avoiding any direct or indirect commercial contact with China during the two bitter Cold War decades. Hence the two countries had no meaningful trade prior to Nixon's visit to Beijing in 1972. Even after the thaw began, commercial relations grew slowly because of the existence of many institutional barriers in the United States against the free flow of capital and technology to China. It took many years for the U.S. government to dismantle those anti-trade institutional barriers. Not until 1983, in fact, more than a decade after Nixon's trip to China, was China finally declared a "friendly, non-aligned" nation by President Reagan for the purpose of lifting high-technology export controls.

Nonetheless, Sino-U.S. trade began to grow rapidly once the two countries established formal diplomatic ties in 1979. Facilitated by their signing of a bilateral trade agreement in that year, and the subsequent U.S. granting of most favored nation status to China, two-way Sino-U.S. trade grew from US$2.3 billion in 1979 to $8.4 billion in 1986, representing an increase of some fourfold in the short span of seven years. From China's standpoint, this trade has increased from 8 percent of its total trade in 1979 to the current range of 11–13 percent, making the United States China's third largest trading partner after Japan and Hong Kong. The growth in volume has also been accompanied by a significant change in commodity composition. Formerly, U.S. exports to China were dominated by agricultural commodities; in recent years, however, they have become much more diversified to include a wide range of manufactured goods.

It should be stressed the the rapid expansion of Sino-U.S trade during this period was not merely caused by the relaxation of institutional conditions in the United States. Perhaps more important, trade growth was the consequence of even more drastic policy changes in China. In 1978, China began its open door policy, which was reinforced by sweeping economic reforms. As noted earlier, both the open door and reform policies have produced positive effects on the Chinese economy, doubling its GNP and quadrupling its foreign trade from 1979 to 1986. Hence China's trade with virtually every country has registered rapid growth during this period. In response to the opening up of the Chinese economy—for example, the setting up of the Special Economic Zones—foreign investment flowed into China. American investment in China, now amounting to US$2.2 billion, has also induced the growth of Sino-U.S. trade.

The prospects for the continued growth of Sino-U.S. trade look good, in part because the Chinese economic policy aims to continue high economic growth and the maintenance of the open door policy. In several areas relating to high technology and sophisticated equipment such as oil exploration facilities, power generation and telecommunications equipment, and electronics, the United States is either preeminent or highly competitive in the world market, so that China will continue to import these products from the United States. At the same time, the United States will continue to be a significant market for a wide range of low-tech and labor-intensive manufactured goods from China, despite rising domestic protectionist sentiments.

Although Sino-U.S. economic relations appear likely to grow rapidly in the future on the basis of favorable structural factors, there are potential obstacles. Both the United States and China are global powers in a political or strategic sense. The United States is particularly sensitive to the political underpinnings of Sino-U.S. economic relations. For instance, any drastic shift in China's relations with the Soviet Union could affect the American commitment to the Sino-U.S. relationship. The recent suspension of some high-tech American exports to China because of the Chinese sales of military equipment to Iran clearly demonstrates that the Sino-U.S. economic relationship is still subject to political intervention.

In contrast, the Sino-Japanese economic relationship is based on a different set of considerations. Since it is not a political superpower like the United States, Japan has been able to pursue its economic relations with China on a nonideological basis essentially governed by purely commercial motives. Thus Japan became China's top trading partner long before formal diplomatic relations between the two countries commenced in 1972. When Beijing first declared its open door policy, Japanese businessman were among the first to flock to China in search of new market opportunities.

Furthermore, Japan has always had an edge over the other developed countries in their commercial dealings with China because of Japan's cultural affinity, historical connections, and geographic proximity to China. The Japanese economy is also highly complementary with the Chinese economy. Japan can supply China with machines, capital equipment, and consumer durables in return for China's raw materials, coal, and petroleum, even though Chinese labor-intensive manufactured products have so far not been particularly successful in penetrating the Japanese domestic market. Not surprisingly, Japan now occupies the position of China's premier trading partner.

The inherent trading advantages Japan enjoys in relation to China are offset, however, by a number of long-term problems specific to the Sino-Japanese relationship. These two countries, historically and geographically so close, also have many old antagonisms that surface from time to time to mar their economic relations. Regional rivalries and suspicions are equally inevitable. For instance, the textbook issue brought back bitter memories in China of Japanese wartime atrocities. Beijing is also wary of potential Japanese ambitions regarding Taiwan. The Japanese formerly cultivated close relations with China in the person of Hu Yaobang. Hu's fall from his post as general secretary of the Chinese Community Party, however, has since deprived Japan of the type of Chinese leader both powerful and pragmatic enough to overcome the numerous diplomatic and bureaucratic hurdles inherent in the Sino-Japanese relationship.

Friction is also present on the economic front. Many Japanese industrialists were upset by what they called the unilateral suspension of contracts by the Chinese, amounting to US$2.5 billion in 1979. The Chinese, on the other hand, have grown increasingly concerned over their widening trade deficits with Japan. In addition, Beijing has also complained of the Japaneses reluctance to invest in China in recent years, despite Japan's dominant role in the China trade and its huge trade surplus. Japanese investment in China is currently estimated to be only about 2 percent of total foreign investment in China, which is plainly minuscule given Japan's worldwide surplus of capital.

These political and economic squabbles, however, do not seem to have produced much effect on the continuing growth of Sino-Japanese trade in recent years, which has increased from US$4.8 billion in 1978 to $16.4 billion in 1985. Meanwhile, Japan has signed a bilateral aid agreement with China through which Japanese soft loans can be extended to the PRC (e.g., a loan of 7.6 billion yen was advanced to China in 1983 for the construction of infrastructure required for the shipping of Chinese coal to Japan). In recent years, some Chinese state-run commercial organizations have also had access to the Tokyo market to float their bonds.

It is clear that, given Japan's growing economic preeminence, that country's economic influence in the Pacific Basin will continue to expand in a manner that could take over some of the roles formerly played by the United States, now in some degree of eclipse. Increasingly, Japan will become the focal point of economic growth in the Pacific Basin. This will indirectly affect China's domestic economic development as China becomes increasingly more integrated economically with the Pacific countries. At present, the level of Japan's direct economic involvement in China is still low and is clearly not commensurate with the capacity of the Japanese economy to interact with China to their mutual benefit. Should the Japanese economy in future become more oriented toward China, it would be a new significant factor in the economic growth of both China and the region.

China and the NICs

Economically speaking, strong integrative forces are already at work to draw the Chinese economy and the economies of the NICs closer together. The NICs, scarce in resources but highly industrialized, constitute natural economic partners with China, a massive country with a vast market. In response to the shift of international comparative advantage, the manufacturing sectors in the NICs are being rapidly restructured toward higher value-added and more skill-intensive activities, so that their manufactured exports are increasingly not in direct competition with the manufactured exports from China (which are largely labor-intensive) in third country markets.

Both South Korea and Taiwan have built up a strong industrial base, and the huge China market will be a potential outlet for a wide range of their manufactured exports once the political environment is further improved. In the future China can also resort to these countries for medium-level technology. As for Hong Kong and Singapore, these two entrepot trade centers in the region can additionally export economic and financial services to China to the mutual benefit of both sides.

In geopolitical terms, however, China as the dominant power in Asia has all the leverage in relation to the NICs. China alone holds the key to the political stability of the region, an indispensable precondition for the continuing economic growth of the NICs. China operates a powerful political lever directly on Hong Kong and Taiwan, and indirectly (via North Korea) on South Korea. Hence there is a strong tendency for both sides to upgrade their current level of economic interaction and develop it into a "special relationship."

South Korea at present has no diplomatic relations with China, but it has been trading with China, mainly indirectly through Hong Kong, since the middle of 1976. In recent years, their two-way trade has experienced a sharp increase. It was estimated that overall Chinese–South Korean trade for 1984 amounted to US$800 million, $1.8 billion for 1985 and $1.0 billion for 1986, with South Korea supplying steel products, ships, consumer electronics, and petrochemicals to China in return for Chinese raw materials and agricultural products.[10] Most of the trade is carried out in Hong Kong, where some forty to fifty Korean firms have been set up for this purpose. This flourishing but "illicit" trade relations culminated in the launching of a joint venture between Korea's Daewoo (one of South Korea's big *chaebol* or conglomerates) and China's Fujian province in early 1986.[11] Increasing numbers of South Korean businessmen have traveled to China, and many Chinese technicians have also visited South Korea for training. With the steady soaring of the Japanese yen, South Korea's manufactured exports have secured a strong comparative advantage, and the South Korean manufacturers are most eager to compete with the Japanese in the China market.

Officially Taiwan is not supposed to have any form of commercial dealing with the People's Republic of China on the basis of Taiwan's "Three No's" policy ("No contact, no talks, and no compromise"). But their two-way trade, again conducted mainly through Hong Kong but sometimes routed via Singapore and Tokyo, has been booming since 1979. Trade is estimated to have exceeded US$1 billion in 1985.[12] There has also been a thriving barter trade between Taiwanese fishermen and their Mainland counterparts off the coasts of Fujian and Guangdong provinces. Apart from traditional items like herbs, the Mainland supplies foodstuffs and industrial raw materials (e.g., cotton). In return, Taiwan exports a wide range of light industrial consumer goods such as television, bicycles, motorcycles, and watches to China. Recently, as Beijing clamped down on the import of consumer durables, Taiwan's exports shifted to chemicals, textile fabrics, and machinery. Trade has been consistently in Taiwan's favor.

Until the recent lifting of martial law, Chinese trading in Taiwan was punishable by death. But the Taiwan authorities turned a blind eye as long as trade was not conducted in a blatant manner. In July 1985, pressure from the private sector to legalize trade eventually forced Taiwan's Economic Minister, Li Ta-hai, to declare that the Taiwanese government has no control over the final destination of its exports, thereby effectively giving a limited official green light to this flourishing indirect trade. But pressures still mounted for opening up more contact with the mainland. In October 1987, the Kuomintang government made a momentous decision by allowing family visits to the mainland, thus

---

[10]*The Economist*, March 22, 1986; *Far Eastern Economic Review*, March 14, 1987.

[11]It was recently reported that Daewoo had withdrawn from this joint venture. *Far Eastern Economic Review*, May 7, 1987.

[12]*Asian Wall Street Journal*, July 25, 1985; *China Trade Report* (February 1986).

officially putting an end to its rigid "Three No's" policy with the main-land.[13] A very significant step towards normalization of relations with the mainland has thus been taken. Meanwhile, many forward-looking Taiwan industrialists are eyeing the lucrative mainland market for their wide range of medium-technology manufactured exports. In addition, Taiwan, as an important capital surplus economy, has much to contrib-ute to China's economic modernization efforts if political circumstances permit.

Of all the Asia-Pacific economies, Hong Kong has always enjoyed a special political and economic relationship with China—all the more so now, as Hong Kong is scheduled to return to China in 1997. From the outset, Hong Kong was developed as an entrepot trade center for South China. After the formation of the People's Republic of China in 1949, Hong Kong's entrepot trade role for China began to decline; it was reactivated in recent years, however, when China initiated its open door policy.[14] For years, Hong Kong has been a major source of foreign exchange earnings for China, amounting to between 25-30 percent of China's total export revenue.[15] In recent years, China has increased its economic stake in Hong Kong through direct investment. At the same time, most of the investment in China's Special Economic Zones has come from Hong Kong. In fact, Hong Kong is already being directly integrated into the Chinese economy. After the 1997 transition, Hong Kong will continue to carve a niche for itself in the growing Chinese economy. In the short run much depends, of course, on how the Chi-nese government handles the transition. A large number of profession-als are migrating to the advanced countries, but this exodus should not damage the prospects of the Hong Kong economy in a significant way. In the modern world, both capital and high-level manpower are highly mobile. So long as Hong Kong enjoys political stability and remains an open economy after 1997, it will continue to be a strong magnet for capital and additional resources from the other Pacific countries to fuel its economic growth.

---

[13]Recently the two largest newspapers in Taiwan, the *China Times* and the *United Daily,* called on the government to review the "Three-No's" policy and allow more contact between the people on both sides of the Taiwan Straits. *Lianhe Zaobao,* May 5, 1987, Singapore.

[14]For a good discussion of Hong Kong's recent entrepot trade role, see Yun-Wing Sung, "A Theoretical and Empirical Analysis of Entrepot Trade: Hong Kong, Singapore and Their Roles in China's Trade," paper presented at the 16th Pacific Trade and Development Conference held in Wellington, New Zealand, January 25-29, 1987.

[15]See A. J. Youngson, ed., *China and Hong Kong: The Economic Nexus* (Hong Kong: Oxford University Press, 1983).

Like Hong Kong, Singapore's economic relations with China began on the basis of entrepot trade for China in Southeast Asia. At present, Singapore has not yet established full diplomatic links with China, with both sides confining their relationship to the exchange of trade representatives. Uninhibited by political and ideological rigidity, Singapore has responded swiftly to the recent resurgence of the Chinese economy. Since 1984, the Singapore government has been taking measures to promote more economic involvement with China, and a number of government-controlled companies have gone into the China market. The recent economic recession in Singapore has also provided a "push" factor for the private sector to look to China for new opportunities. It has been reported that since 1979, Singapore has been involved in about 100 investment projects in China, amounting to some US$450 million.[16] Singapore, taking advantage of its cultural and linguistic affinity , is actively seeking to develop itself as another gateway to China after Hong Kong. This is the underlying motive of Singapore's Deputy Prime Minister Goh Chok-Tong's visit to China in May 1987.

China and ASEAN

China's relations with the ASEAN states to its south are extensive and deeply-rooted by virtue of history, geography and migration. After 1949, these relations assumed new dimensions, with complex ideological and political elements coming into play; and this gave rise to two decades of Cold War antagonism. In the early 1970s, with the advent of détente, individual ASEAN countries began to normalize relations with China: first Malaysia, then the Philippines, and finally Thailand.[17] Indonesia has not yet resumed its diplomatic link, severed in 1967, with China, but since July 1985, Jakarta has permitted direct trading with China.[18] Of all the ASEAN countries, Thailand currently enjoys the best relations with the PRC. As a front-line state facing expansionist Vietnam, Thailand happens to share China's similar strategic apprehension about Vietnam. Apart from supplying arms to Thailand, China has

---

[16]*Asian Wall Street Journal*, September 7, 1985; also *Straits Times* (Singapore), March 25, 1987.

[17]For a more detailed discussion of the historical background of China's economic relations with ASEAN, see John Wong, *The Political Economy of China's Changing Relations with Southeast Asia* (London: Macmillan, 1984).

[18]In June 1986, for the first time since breaking off diplomatic relations in 1967, China sent a large trade delegation to Jakarta to take part in Jakarta's annual trade fair. Jia Shia, head of the Chinese delegation, met a number of Indonesian high officials, including Cabinet Secretary Murdiono. Both sides agreed to increase their direct trade. *Sunday Times* (Singapore), June 21, 1987.

openly pledged to come to that nation's aid should it be attacked by Vietnam.[19]

From the economic perspective, the Sino-ASEAN relationship has both complementary and competitive aspects. Because the ASEAN economies are still heavily dependent upon primary exports for their economic growth, their external economic relations with any country are inevitably conditioned by trading in primary commodities. This explains why primary commodities figure so prominently in Sino-ASEAN trade, as shown in Table 6. For years, Malaysia's exports to China have consisted of virtually nothing but rubber. Sugar is an important item in exports from the Philippines and Thailand to China, and so on. On the other hand, China is also an important primary-exporting country (e.g., Chinese petroleum to the Philippines and Thailand; Chinese rice to Malaysia and Singapore). In general, Chinese exports of these primary commodities constitute no menace to ASEAN's own primary exports because ASEAN on the whole has a stronger comparative advantage over China in the natural resource area. In the future, China's further progress in industrialization should increase the Chinese demand for primary commodities from ASEAN. This trend has already developed. In recent years, China's imports from the ASEAN countries have become more diversified, not just with a greater variety of primary commodities but also containing more resource-based manufactured products.

ASEAN, however, is still apprehensive of the rising competitive pressures from China. Because both China and ASEAN are intent on carrying out their industrialization, the potential for competition in manufactured products, which are basically labor-intensive in nature, is likely to remain the most sensitive issue in evolving Sino-ASEAN economic relations. First, there are growing concerns in ASEAN over the possibility of China's flooding its low-priced manufactured exports into the ASEAN markets. This would present head-on competition to the nascent local industries in ASEAN, which have just emerged from the process of import substitution. A careful look at Table 7, however, reveals that such fears are more apparent than real, as China's market shares in the individual ASEAN countries remain generally stable and small—smaller than that of the NICs. Only Singapore in recent years has experienced a sharp increase in imports from China, mainly because of the influx of Chinese crude oil for refining in Singapore.

Second and perhaps more seriously, China is seen as a threat to ASEAN by competing indirectly in the third country market. Because

---

[19]"Pledge from China to defend Thailand," *Straits Times* (Singapore), January 19, 1987.

Table 6
Commodity Structure of China's Trade
with ASEAN Countries Showing Primary Product Concentration
(in percentages)

Imports from China

Indonesia's Imports from China	1974	1977	1978	1984
Rice	55.0	41.2	19.2	—
Sugar and honey	40.0	0.3	7.1	—
Oil seeds	—	—	—	16.8

Malaysia's Imports from China	1975	1978	1982	1984
Food (Rice)	47.2 (27.6)	49.7 (27.0)	38.3 (3.2)	40.4 (3.1)

Philippines' Imports from China	1976	1977	1982	1985
Petroleum	89.4	90.7	69.9	83.3

Singapore's Imports from China
1976 (highly diversified)

Thailand's Imports from China	1976	1977	1982	1985
Petroleum	38.3	64.2	36.7	33.9

Exports to China

Indonesia's Exports to China	1982	1983	1984
Coffee	99.3	96.3	4.0
Plywood	—	—	60.0
Rubber	—	—	25.0

Malaysia's Exports to China	1975	1978	1982	1984
Rubber	94.1	90.6	91.3	65.4

Philippines' Exports to China	1976	1977	1982	1985
Sugar	58.6	65.9	59.3	38.5

Singapore's Exports to China	1976	1980	1984	1985
Rubber	39.0	41.6	29.7	6.9

Thailand's Exports to China	1976	1979	1982	1985
Rice	47.7	29.0	36.7	—
Sugar	33.4	15.7	43.6	41.2
Rubber	—	—	—	15.9

SOURCES: For Indonesia, *Impor* and *Ekspor*; for Malaysia, *Perdagangan Luar*; for the Philippines, *Foreign Trade Statistics of the Philippines*; for Singapore, *Singapore Trade Statistics*; for Thailand, *Trade Statistics of Thailand*; all relevant years.

Table 7

ASEAN as Export Market for China, Japan, and the Asian NICs
(% distribution)

Imports from	Indonesia				Malaysia				Philippines				Singapore				Thailand			
	1977	1979	1981	1985	1977	1979	1981	1985	1977	1979	1981	1985	1977	1979	1981	1985	1977	1979	1981	1985
China	2.5	1.8	1.5	2.0	3.1	2.9	2.4	2.0	1.9	1.9	2.7	5.4	2.5	2.3	2.8	8.6	1.5	2.7	3.8	2.4
Japan	27.1	29.1	33.5	28.1	23.4	23.5	24.4	23.0	25.1	22.6	19.1	14.0	17.5	16.8	18.8	17.1	32.4	26.3	23.8	26.0
South Korea	0.9	1.6	3.0	2.1	0.7	1.5	1.4	2.2	1.0	1.5	1.4	4.0	1.0	1.1	1.1	1.6	1.0	1.5	1.7	2.0
Taiwan	2.5	2.5	1.9	2.9	0.8	0.8	0.8	1.0	1.0	1.3	1.3	4.5	2.5	2.6	2.7	3.4	1.1	1.2	0.9	2.6
Hong Kong	1.0	1.4	6.8	1.6	2.0	1.7	1.3	1.7	1.6	2.4	2.9	3.9	2.5	2.5	1.9	1.9	0.7	1.3	1.6	1.1
Other ASEAN Countries																				
Indonesia	—	—	—	—	1.0	0.9	0.6	1.1	3.7	3.0	2.7	3.6	n.a.[a]	n.a.	n.a.	n.a.	0.1	0.7	0.3	0.6
Malaysia	0.3	0.5	0.5	0.6	—	—	—	—	1.5	1.4	2.1	7.3	13.6	13.2	12.4	14.3	1.0	1.9	2.4	5.8
Philippines	0.3	0.7	1.5	0.2	0.6	0.9	0.8	1.9	—	—	—	—	0.6	0.4	0.4	0.8	0.1	0.3	0.5	0.6
Singapore	8.4	7.4	9.4	5.3	8.4	9.3	13.1	15.8	0.8	1.3	1.6	2.4	—	—	—	—	2.9	4.1	8.0	6.1
Thailand	5.3	3.0	1.2	0.6	4.6	3.6	3.4	3.5	0.3	0.2	0.3	1.0	2.2	2.7	1.7	2.1	—	—	—	—

[a]Not available.

SOURCES: International Monetary Fund, *Direction of Trade Statistics, 1980, 1983, and 1986*; for Taiwan, Executive Yuan, *Statistical Yearbook of the Republic of China, 1986*.

they are latecomers to industrialization, both tend to specialize in simple, labor-intensive manufactured products for exports and hence compete with each other in the slowly expanding or, in some cases, even contracting export markets, which are mainly the industrial countries. Attempts by China to enlarge its market shares for its manufactured exports in the industrial countries are likely, in the short run at least, to produce some displacement effect on ASEAN's own manufactured exports to those markets of such labor-intensive items as textiles, clothing, and footwear. Table 8 serves to show that ASEAN does have grounds for such a suspicion. China's large existing country and world shares in such leading labor-intensive manufactures as textiles and clothing appear formidable to the prospective exporters in ASEAN.[20]

This is, of course, a static way of interpreting competition. In a dynamic context, the world market is not a zero sum situation in which the expansion of China's exports is necessarily made at the expense of ASEAN's exports. In the long run, competition will drive industrialists in ASEAN to upgrade their production into more capital-intensive activities along the lines the NICs are developing. ASEAN has to come face to face with the scenario that if their chief competitor is not China, it may be India.

A balanced picture should also take into account some of the long-term positive effects. A prosperous China, with a market of 1 billion consumers, need not be exclusively exploited by the industrial countries or by the NICs. China's economic growth provides opportunities for all, and there is no reason why some ASEAN countries should not also strive to capture a share of the potential China market for their resource-based manufactured exports. Thus, in the long run, sufficient economic rationale exits for a viable relationship between China and ASEAN.

In sum, because of its successful economic reforms and open door policy, the Chinese economy has become increasingly integrated with the Pacific Basin, leading to the broadening and deepening of China's overall economic relationships with the various sectors of the region. If these trends continue, it is not difficult to envisage a future scenario in which all the Pacific economies, including China, develop a viable "economic symbiosis" with each other, which will further enhance the growth potential of the region as a whole.

---

[20]See Rodney Tyers, Prue Phillips, and Christopher Findlay, "ASEAN and China Exports of Labour-Intensive Manufactures: Performance and Prospects," *ASEAN Economic Bulletin* 3(3) (March 1987).

Table 8

Exports of Leading Labor-Intensive Manufactures,
by Pacific-Asian Economies, 1981

Country	Textiles, Yarn, Fabrics[a]			Clothing[b]			Footwear[c]		
	Amount (US$ million)	Country Share (%)	World Share (%)	Amount (US$ million)	Country Share (%)	World Share (%)	Amount (US$ million)	Country Share (%)	World Share (%)
China	3,079	14.3	7.2	2,093	9.7	5.8	259	1.2	2.2
NICs									
South Korea	2,139	10.1	5.0	3,732	17.6	10.4	1,024	4.8	9.0
Hong Kong	872	6.1	2.0	4,819	33.8	13.4	148	1.0	1.3
Singapore	309	1.5	0.7	469	2.2	1.3	41	0.2	0.4
ASEAN									
Indonesia	24	0.1	0.1	95	0.4	0.3	d	d	d
Malaysia	125	1.1	0.3	160	1.4	0.5	32	0.3	0.3
Philippines	25	0.4	0.1	347	6.1	1.0	73	1.3	0.6
Thailand	321	4.7	0.7	344	5.0	1.0	44	0.6	0.4

[a]Standard International Trade Classification (SITC), 651, 652, 656.
[b]SITC 841.
[c]SITC 851.
[d]Not significant.

SOURCES: For China, Directorate of Intelligence (CIA), *Handbook of Economic Statistics: China* (September 1983); for ASEAN and others, see UNCTAD, *Handbook of International Trade and Development Statistics, 1984 Supplement.*

4. Soviet Economic Policies and Their Impact on the Pacific-Asian Region

ROBERT W. CAMPBELL

Although the Pacific-Asian countries constitute one of the most dynamic regions in the world, with a rapidly growing significance in global affairs, the Soviet Union has not, in the past, been a very active economic player in this region. As one source puts it, "The Soviet economy, along with those of North Korea and Vietnam, are still largely closed and contribute little if anything to the economic dynamism of the Pacific Rim."[1] The nations of the region are highly diverse—in size, in their level of economic development, and in their relationship to the USSR. Some are large, others small—from China, with the world's largest population, to tiny Brunei, with a population of 7.5 million. Some are LDCs; some have moved from economic backwardness to the status of NICs; Japan is the epitome of a technologically advanced country. Some are communist, other as free market and enterprising as any in the world. Among the communist countries, only one—Vietnam—is a member of the Council for Mutual Economic Assistance (CMEA or COMECON), whereas the most important one—China—is not. The LDC members of the group have attracted a varied degree of interest from the USSR, some being totally ignored while one—India—numbers along the most important Soviet clients in the Third World.

The Soviet Union probably has no overarching economic policy regarding the region as a whole. Soviet policies in the area of international economic and political relations are more easily understood as falling under such headings as "policy toward the Third World," "goals and approaches to technology transfer," "policies on COMECON integration," and Soviet sensitivity or lack thereof to comparative advantage generally. Its policies under all those headings have an impact on the area, but as regards the past at least, it would be a mistake to assume that those various interactions could be meaningfully aggregated into an economic policy regarding the region as such.

---

[1]Philip West and Thomas Jackson, *The Pacific Rim and the Bottom Line*, briefing book for a conference on the Pacific Rim, Indiana University, April 22, 1987, p. 14.

Today the USSR is embarked on a new economic strategy, and one wonders how its new plans and policies may affect its involvement with Pacific-Asian development. There are strong hints that the Soviet Union may be moving toward a posture of increased interest and activism toward Asia, including a more active policy in the economic sphere. The task of this essay is to survey Soviet economic policies toward the Pacific-Asian region as they have emerged in the past and to assess possible implications of the general ferment in current Soviet economic policy for the USSR's relationship with the area. We begin by examining the background of previous Soviet interaction with Pacific-Asia.

Background

It will be useful to begin with a few reminders concerning the evolution of Soviet policies in the area of international economic relations generally over the last quarter century. The USSR has mostly favored autarkic policies, first for itself when it was the only socialist nation, and then for the newly established socialist bloc after World War II. Once the socialist bloc was formed, the USSR directed most of its trade toward the other socialist countries. At first China was an important partner in this trade, but as a result of the Sino-Soviet dispute at the end of the 1950s trade between China and the USSR fell drastically— from nearly 2 *billion* rubles in 1959 to a mere 42 *million* rubles in 1970.[2] In the mid-1950s, the USSR began to expand its economic ties with the Third World, using economic aid and arms sales as the entering wedge of a general economic presence. In the 1970s Soviet leaders embarked on a significant expansion of international trade in general. At the same time, Soviet trade was to some degree reoriented away from its COMECON partners toward a greater emphasis on trade with the industrialized West. The USSR permitted, and indeed encouraged, its socialist partners to make a similar shift. In the 1970s, Soviet foreign trade grew in real terms much faster than total output of the economy, at about 8 percent per year versus a little less than 3 percent per year for GNP.[3] At the same time, the share of its trade conducted with socialist partners fell from 69 percent in 1965 to 53 percent in 1980.[4]

---

[2]Ministerstvo Vneshnei Torgovli SSSR *Vneshniaia torgovlia SSSR* [Foreign Trade of the USSR], various years.

[3]Ministerstvo Vneshnei Torgovli SSSR, *Vneshniaia torgovlia SSSR v 1985 g.* [Foreign Trade of the USSR in 1985] (Moscow, 1986), p. 16; and CIA, *Handbook of Economic Statistics, 1986* (Washington, D.C., 1986), p. 65.

[4]Ministerstvo Vneshnei Torgovli SSSR, *Vneshniaia torgovlia SSSR*, various years.

The main motivation for this expansion of trade with the advanced market economies was to upgrade the technological level of the Soviet economy by importing sophisticated technology embodied in Western machinery. Subsequently, Soviet leaders also undertook massive grain imports from the nonsocialist economies to permit a rapid growth in livestock numbers and meat production. In contrast to the situation in Eastern Europe, the USSR did not go deeply into debt in the process of expanding its imports from the West. Rather, it was able to pay for the rapidly increasing imports from hard currency countries largely by expanding its exports of energy—mostly oil and gas. By the 1980s, hydrocarbon exports covered three-fourths of the USSR's hard currency earnings.

Under these general policies the USSR developed fairly extensive economic interaction with a number of countries in the Pacific-Asian region. Trade with Japan grew rapidly in the 1970s—at slightly over 15 percent per year between 1970 and 1980, driven to an appreciable extent by the Soviet need to import steel pipe and other inputs for the expanding Soviet gas industry.[5] Japanese trade was also stimulated by Japanese provision of credits for resource development projects in Siberia, especially in timber, and by the Soviet desire to acquire technology embodied in equipment. Imports from Japan were paid for in part by sales of oil and raw materials, some of it coming from joint development projects in fuels and raw materials. But the USSR has traditionally had a deficit in its trade with Japan, requiring the transfer of hard currency earned elsewhere to pay for Japanese imports.

The USSR has had quantitatively important economic ties with its allies China, North Korea, and later Vietnam though, as indicated, the ties with China collapsed after the disagreement at the end of the 1950s. In the early 1960s, it had a significant relationship with Indonesia as a friendly state for a short time. It developed the same kind of relationship with India on a much grander scale, and that tie has continued strong and has been carefully cultivated up to the present. For years India has ranked either first or second among the USSR's trading partners in the Pacific-Asian group.

Soviet economic relationships with these countries have three facets—trade, economic aid, and military aid. Trade is covered in Table 1, which shows the growth and distribution of Soviet trade with the

---

[5]Ministerstvo Vneshnei Torgovli SSSR, *Vneshniaia torgovlia SSSR*, various years.

Table 1

Soviet Trade with Pacific-Asian Countries
(exports plus imports)

Country	1970 MR[a]	1970 Percent	1980 MR	1980 Percent	1985 MR	1985 Percent	1985 Total[b]	1985 USSR Total
Communist	554	2.5	1,541	1.6	4,290	3.0	57,492	n.a.
China	42	0.2	317	0.3	1,605	1.1	57,492	2.8
North Korea	329	1.5	572	0.6	1,051	0.7	n.a.	n.a.[d]
Vietnam	183	0.8	612	0.7	1,446	1.0	n.a.	n.a.
Cambodia	neg.[c]	0.0	3	0.0	100	0.1	n.a.	n.a.
Laos	neg.	0.0	37	0.0	88	0.1	n.a.	n.a.
ASEAN	154	0.7	658	0.7	483	0.3	107,692	0.4
Malaysia	113	0.5	208	0.2	191	0.1	22,806	0.8
Indonesia	30	0.1	60	0.1	94	0.1	22,758	0.4
Philippines	neg.	0.0	134	0.1	40	0.0	8,262	0.5
Singapore	8	0.0	83	0.1	90	0.1	40,409	0.2
Thailand	3	0.0	173	0.2	68	0.0	13,458	0.5
Other	1,126	5.1	5,496	5.8	7,035	5.0	476,658	1.5
Japan	652	3.0	2,723	2.9	3,215	2.3	253,212	1.3
India	365	1.7	1,740	1.8	3,072	2.2	22,652	13.6
Australia	62	0.3	781	0.8	546	0.4	39,918	1.4
New Zealand	20	0.1	170	0.2	91	0.1	15,309	0.6
Burma	4	0.0	8	0.0	7	0.0	482	1.5
Sri Lanka	17	0.1	30	0.0	38	0.0	2,700	1.4
South Korea	neg.	0.0	10	0.0	n.a.	n.a.	48,560	n.a.
Taiwan	neg.	0.0	neg.	0.0	neg.	0.0	41,811	0.0
Brunei	neg.	0.0	neg.	0.0	neg.	0.0	2,716	0.0
Hong Kong	6	0.0	34	0.0	66	0.0	49,300	0.1
Total	1,834	8.3	7,695	8.2	11,808	8.3	641,843	1.8

[a]Million rubles. I have converted dollar values in the latter to rubles at the 1985 rate of exchange between the dollar and the transferable ruble, i.e., 1 ruble = 1.215 dollars.
[b]Total trade of the partner country.
[c]Negligible.
[d]Not available.
SOURCES: Data for Soviet trade with the countries shown are mostly from Ministerstvo Torgovli SSSR, *Vneshniaia torgovlia SSSR*, various years, while those for total trade of the partner countries are from standard U.N. sources.

Pacific-Asian countries,[6] and in Table 2, which shows the commodity composition of that trade for 1985, a year which is reasonably represent-ative of the picture generally. As Table 1 shows, the Pacific region has been relatively unimportant for the USSR's trade as a whole. The whole Pacific-Asian Basin accounts today for only about 8 percent of all Soviet trade, and of that total, most is accounted for by trade with communist partners and the single nation of Japan. Those five countries account for two-thirds of the Pacific-Asian total. Between 1970 and 1980, the area's share of all Soviet trade dropped slightly as the USSR directed its atten-tion to expanding trade with the advanced market economies. By 1985, however, the share was back to roughly the 1970 level. Viewed from the perspective of the Pacific-Asian countries, trade with the USSR is insig-nificant in their total trade activity. Japan's trade with the USSR, for example, is only about 1 percent of its total trade. India is rather an exception to this generalization, however, with 13.6 percent of its trade accounted for by trade with the USSR. For many years the USSR has been India's largest or second largest trading partner.

The composition of Soviet-Asian trade can be reasonably well described in a few generalizations that are generally consistent with broader Soviet trading patterns. Soviet exports to the LDC members of the group are dominated by machinery and equipment. Such nations provide a market in which the generally unsophisticated character of Soviet machinery is acceptable. If Japan is omitted, machinery accounts for 24 percent of the imports of the Pacific-Asian countries from the USSR, against just slightly over 2 percent in the flow of goods that advanced industrial countries import from the USSR. *From* the region (again omitting Japan) the USSR receives in return mostly raw materials and foodstuffs, with machinery accounting for only 6.6 percent, whereas from the industrialized West 28 percent of Soviet imports are machinery (these figures refer to 1985). Trade with Japan, however, fits the pattern of Soviet trade with other advanced industrial countries, with about 36 percent of Soviet imports from Japan consisting of

---

[6]The country coverage in this table does not fully reflect the prevailing concept of the Pacific-Asian group. India is not usually considered part of the group, but it is impossible to omit that nation in any view of Soviet interaction with the Asian economies generally. On the other hand, I did not include Afghanistan or Pakistan since they seem to have little interaction with the Pacific group. I have included some economically interesting mem-bers of the group even when the Soviet trade handbooks show no trade with them. The small islands of the South Pacific, despite the interest the Russians have recently shown in them, are probably too insignificant to be worth our attention when we are discussing the *economic* dimension of Soviet activity in Asia.

machinery, whereas Soviet exports to Japan consist mostly of raw materials, fuels, and other products of a low degree of fabrication.

India's trading relationship with the USSR, too, has a character slightly different from the overall pattern. India is not as good a customer as most LDCs for Soviet machinery and equipment, and in fact its exports to the USSR in this category exceed its imports. An interesting point to note about Indian-Soviet trade is that apart from the role of machinery, its commodity composition is quite similar to Chinese-Soviet trade. Both India and China rely heavily on exporting finished consumer goods to the USSR to pay for their imports. China and India may thus be seen as somewhat competitive with each other in Soviet trade policies.

This trade exhibits some characteristic imbalances. The USSR has a very large import surplus with Japan and, indeed, with most of the hard currency countries. It is unclear how much of the trade shown in Table 1 is hard currency trade, but if we take the countries whose trade is obviously in hard currency (Japan, Australia and New Zealand, Singapore, and Malaysia), the deficit in 1985 was 2.2 billion rubles, equal to about U.S.$2.7 billion. For the countries with which the USSR has trade and barter agreements, exports and imports are more nearly balanced.

With respect to economic aid, the Asian region has again played a relatively small role in overall Soviet international economic relationships. Considering the whole period since the mid-1950s, the area has accounted for a relatively small share of all Soviet extensions of economic aid. In the earliest period, China was an important recipient of Soviet aid, as was also Indonesia. That orientation ended relatively quickly as a result of the Soviet break with the Chinese and the Indonesian turn to China. Since the mid-1950s, when the Russians began to use trade and aid as a way of expanding their influence in the Third World, the USSR has extended a total of about U.S.$33 billion of economic aid to LDCs, of which a little over U.S.$13 billion has gone to the Pacific-Asian area.[7] Nearly all of that amount has gone to only three countries in the area—that is, India and two of the Soviet Union's communist allies, Vietnam and North Korea. India was the site of some of the Soviets' most spectacular aid projects in the 1950s and 1960s—the Bhilai and Bokaro steel plants, for example. This emphasis on economic

---

[7]The data sources on Soviet economic and military aid are highly complex in their conceptualizations and origins. They tend to be full of estimates and inconsistencies. Rather than trying to sort through all that in my discussion, I have relied heavily on the summaries produced by Abraham S. Becker in ''Soviet Union and the Third World: The Economic Dimension,'' *Soviet Economy* 2 (July–September 1986):240.

Table 2

Commodity Composition of Soviet Trade with Pacific-Asian Countries, 1985
(in thousands of rubles)

Country	Total	Machinery[b]	Fuels, Metals[b]	Chemicals, Timber, Lumber[b]	Textiles, Food[b]	Residuals[b]
			Exports			
Communist	2,769.1	833.1	836.6	211.2	167.6	720.6
China	778.8	245.6	176.4	119.6	8.8	228.4
North Korea	648.4	141.3	161.1	10.8	51.9	283.3
Vietnam	1,165.3	377.0	457.9	80.5	93.6	156.3
Cambodia	91.1	33.4	29.5	—	10.5	17.7
Laos	85.5	35.7	11.6	0.4	2.9	34.9
ASEAN	49.5	4.1	3.2	23.1	15.7	3.3
Malaysia	10.8	0.4	—	6.9	3.5	-0.1
Indonesia	3.7	2.2	—	0.6	0.9	0.0
Philippines	10.9	—	3.2	7.1	—	0.6
Singapore	10.7	0.1	0.0	—	9.2	1.3
Thailand	13.4	1.4	—	8.5	2.1	1.5
Other	2,453.9	223.7	1,223.5	362.2	106.5	538.0
Japan	928.0	8.8	333.3	284.7	99.2	201.9
India	1,499.6	210.2	883.0	68.0	2.5	335.9
Australia	13.7	3.2	7.2	2.2	1.5	-0.4
New Zealand	4.3	1.1	—	1.2	3.1	-1.0
Burma	0.0	0.0	—	—	0.0	0.0
Sri Lanka	8.3	0.3	—	6.0	0.2	1.7
South Korea	n.a.[c]	n.a.	n.a.	n.a.	n.a.	n.a.
Taiwan	n.a.	n.a.	n.a.	n.a.	n.a.	n.a.
Brunei	n.a.	n.a.	n.a.	n.a.	n.a.	n.a.
Hong Kong	n.a.	n.a.	n.a.	n.a.	n.a.	n.a.
Total	5,272.5	1,060.9	2,063.3	596.5	289.8	1,262.0
Percent of Total[a]	100.0	20.1	39.1	11.3	5.5	24.0
Total Without Japan	4,344.5	1,052.0	1,730.0	311.8	190.6	1,060.1
Percent of Total[a]	100.0	24.2	39.8	7.2	4.4	24.4

Table 2 (continued)

	Imports					
Communist	1,521.1	61.4	121.6	135.9	816.0	386.9
China	826.1	—	18.7	—	518.1	289.3
North Korea	402.8	61.4	101.3	99.0	97.3	43.9
Vietnam	280.8	—	—	28.3	200.2	52.3
Cambodia	9.1	—	—	8.6	—	0.5
Laos	2.3	—	1.0	0.0	0.5	0.8
ASEAN	433.8	0.0	73.2	97.0	208.3	55.3
Malaysia	180.4	—	7.8	69.7	84.0	18.9
Indonesia	90.5	—	—	27.4	34.9	28.2
Philippines	28.8	—	—	—	28.8	0.0
Singapore	79.6	—	62.9	—	10.0	6.8
Thailand	54.5	—	2.5	—	50.7	1.4
Other	4,441.6	1,026.0	756.9	274.8	1,917.7	466.3
Japan	2,286.9	815.8	742.7	226.4	249.6	252.4
India	1,499.6	210.2	13.8	48.4	1,057.0	170.2
Australia	532.1	—	—	—	499.9	32.2
New Zealand	86.6	—	—	—	81.4	5.2
Burma	6.6	—	0.4	—	6.1	0.0
Sri Lanka	29.8	—	—	—	23.7	6.1
South Korea	n.a.c	n.a.	n.a.	n.a.	n.a.	n.a.
Taiwan	n.a.	n.a.	n.a.	n.a.	n.a.	n.a.
Brunei	n.a.	n.a.	n.a.	n.a.	n.a.	n.a.
Hong Kong	n.a.	n.a.	n.a.	n.a.	n.a.	n.a.
Total	6,396.5	1,087.5	951.0	507.6	2,942.0	908.4
Percent of Total[a]	100.0	17.0	14.8	7.9	46.0	14.3
Total Without Japan	4,109.6	271.7	208.3	281.2	2,692.3	656.0
Percent of Total[a]	100.0	6.6	5.1	6.8	65.5	16.0

[a] Percent of trade falling in the various commodity groups (— indicates none or negligible).
[b] The values shown for the subcategories were obtained by summing whatever values are shown within broader categories according to the following scheme: machinery—codes 10-19; fuels and metals (including ores)—code 2; chemicals, timber, and lumber products—codes 3, 4, 50; textile materials and products, food commodities and products, and consumer goods—codes 51-98. The values indicated in the handbook under each of these broad headings do not exhaust the totals, so that the resulting residuals are of unknown, and probably variable, composition.
[c] Not available.

SOURCES: Compiled from Ministerstvo Torgovli SSSR, *Vneshniaia torgovlia SSSR, 1985*, Moscow, 1986.

Table 3

Soviet Arms Shipments to Countries in the Pacific-Asian Region
(in US$ millions, current prices)

Country	1967–74	1975–79	1979–83
Vietnam	2,481	1,300	5,200
North Korea	480	280	210
China	191	210	130
Laos	15	100	180
Kampuchea	5	20	170
India	1,323	1,800	3,400
Total	4,495	3,710	9,290

SOURCES: Compiled from U.S. Arms Control and Disarmament Agency, *World Military Expenditures and Arms Tranfers*, various editions. The concept is shipments of arms rather than agreements. Figures are only approximate.

development aid to India continued through the 1970s with various kinds of aid projects.[8] Today, a principal USSR Asian ally—Vietnam—is one of the most important recipients of Soviet economic aid. As Abraham Becker notes, "The most important, but least known fact, about Soviet aid is that the overwhelming majority of it is directed toward three communist allies—Cuba, Vietnam, and Mongolia."[9] The sources suggest that almost U.S.$10 billion of the U.S.$33 billion in aid cited has gone to Vietnam and North Korea.

Similarly, the Pacific-Asian region has not been at the top of Soviet priorities in arms shipments, ranking a weak second to the Middle East. Table 3 shows the main features of Soviet arms shipments to the area. The total of U.S.$17.494 billion shown in the table represents only 16 percent of all Soviet arms shipments (essentially all to LDCs) in the same period. The two major clients are India and Vietnam, which together account for about 90 percent of all Soviet arms transfers to the Pacific-Asian area. India has been an important recipient over many years, and for the Indians this arms trade has been extremely important. The Soviet Union is their biggest arms supplier, and the Indians produce some Soviet-designed equipment under license. Soviet arms shipments accounted for about 70 percent of all India's arms imports in

---

[8]For a characterization of Soviet aid to these countries, see H. Stephen Gardner, *Soviet International Economic Relations: Recent Trends in Policy and Performance*, California Seminar on International Security and Foreign Policy, discussion paper no. 90, February 1981, p. 62.

[9]Becker, "Soviet Union and the Third World," p. 240.

the period 1979–83, and about 80 percent in 1970–79.[10] North Korea has consistently received significant amounts of Soviet arms. As Table 3 shows, China has received significant amounts of arms from the USSR but currently receives virtually none.

The use of joint projects and industrial cooperation agreements as vehicles for stimulating trade have been limited mostly to the Soviet Union's interaction with Japan, the only member of the group that until recently, at least, has had the combination of capabilities, need, and willingness to provide credits for this kind of project. The USSR and Japan have had a variety of cooperation projects in Siberia and some compensation agreements, notably in timber and coal. But these have never been terribly successful, and the Japanese have become rather disillusioned about the prospects for this kind of interaction with the USSR. It will be argued later that the prospects for the rapid growth of Japanese-Soviet cooperative projects in the future are not encouraging.

The cases of Singapore, Hong Kong, and Malaysia are interesting. These are tiny countries, and one wonders if a significant part of the trade shown is not entrepot trade of some kind. Considering the large imbalance in that trade, these countries may be sources for acquiring Western goods in a setting where U.S. controls reach only weakly. If we take official Soviet statistics at face value, the USSR does not trade at all with Taiwan.

It has often been suggested that there is a natural trading relationship between the USSR and the Pacific Basin countries, founded on geography and a supposed economic complementarity. The eastern areas of the USSR have tremendous mineral wealth. This part of Soviet territory is large enough and so located that it might be considered almost a separate Asian nation; as a rapidly growing component of the world economy, the Asian region should attract Soviet trade just by its economic weight. But the fact is that until now the USSR and the other Asian members of the socialist camp have not participated to any extent in the rapid growth of the area. Even with its socialist partners in the region, the USSR's economic connections have been weak. Only Vietnam is a member of COMECON, and Soviet trade with the two longest-established communist countries in the group (China and North Korea) has been small. Trade with North Korea is tiny compared to trade with the other members of COMECON—less than with Vietnam, and only

---

[10]U.S. Arms Control and Disarmament Agency, *World Military Expenditures and Arms Transfers, 1985* (Washington, D.C., 1985), and an earlier edition of the same source covering the years 1970–79 (Washington, D.C., 1982), p. 130.

one-fourth as big as Soviet trade with Romania, the smallest of the European members.

To explain this anomalous situation, I would cite the following as the major factors: (1) Economic policy towards Siberia and the other eastern regions is tied to internal Soviet development needs; Siberia and the Far East have not been given independence to develop on their own in interaction with their geographically closer neighbors.[11] (2) Political disputes have minimized Soviet interaction with the biggest country in the area. (3) The USSR's needs for interaction with advanced countries for technology transfer are better met with ties with Western Europe and the United States than they are with Japan or the Pacific NICs.

Gorbachev's Economic Strategy

It is possible that the USSR's limited interaction with the Pacific-Asian region will change under the new attitudes and policies now being promulgated by the Gorbachev leadership. The current regime has not, however, provided any clearcut pronouncements on the implications it sees for itself in the dynamism of the Pacific region, or how it plans to interact with this region. The closest to an outline of ideas and attitudes on the matter is found in Gorbachev's statements when he visited the Soviet Far East at the end of July, 1986, and a fuller evaluation of his speech on that occasion will be provided later. Before taking up that topic, however, it will be useful to describe the overall strategy that appears to be guiding all Soviet economic policies under Gorbachev and consider what broad implications that strategy has for Soviet policy toward the economic development of the eastern regions and toward interaction with the Pacific-Asian region.

The driving preoccupation in Gorbachev's strategy is to get the Soviet economy moving again after the long period of deteriorating performance under weak leadership over the last fifteen years.[12] He sees the task as one of shifting the economy from the traditional "extensive growth" approach "onto the path of intensive growth," a formulation that has been repeated *ad nauseam* in the Soviet economic literature for the last several years. The traditional Soviet strategy for growth placed a

---

[11]Robert W. Campbell, "Prospects for Soviet Economic Development," in Donald S. Zagoria, *Soviet Policy in East Asia* (New Haven: Yale University Press, 1982), pp. 229–54; Leslie Dienes, *Soviet Asia: Economic Development and National Policy Choices* (Boulder: Westview Press, 1988).

[12]For a fuller description of Gorbachev's strategy, see Robert W. Campbell, "The Soviet Future: Gorbachev and the Economy," in Donald W. Treadgold and Lawrence Lerner, eds., *Gorbachev and the Soviet Future* (Boulder: Westview Press, 1988).

heavy emphasis on continually expanding the flow of inputs—labor, capital services, and natural resources—into production. Productivity growth—more output per unit of productive inputs used—has made relatively little contribution to Soviet economic expansion compared to its contribution in the growth experience of other countries. Indeed, beginning in the late 1970s, productivity change in the Soviet economy has actually been negative. That traditional strategy is no longer viable—the demographic situation is such that growth of the labor force will be virtually nonexistent, large net increments in capital inputs are increasingly hard to achieve, and the richest elements in the USSR's patrimony of natural resources have been severely depleted. If growth is to be accelerated in the current situation, the source will have to be productivity increases flowing from technological change, organizational improvements, reduction of waste and inefficiency, improvements in incentives, and so on.

The need for a transition to intensive growth had been acknowledged by the Soviet leadership for some time before Gorbachev, but little had been done to translate that recognition into a set of operational policies.[13] Gorbachev has added action to analysis. The central element in his approach in the Twelfth Five-Year Plan (covering the years 1986–90) is structural change. A novel element in the Gorbachevian interpretation of intensification is that productivity increments must be sought not only by saving capital and labor directly in each production process, but also by saving intermediate inputs, which in the Soviet economy are scandalously wasted. Any given Soviet machine contains more steel than its Western counterpart; Soviet trucks use much more fuel per unit of work than do Western models; the input of raw materials per unit of output in chemical production is much higher than in Western plants; similarly wasteful extravagance in use of intermediate inputs occurs in nearly every production process. The incentive structure of Soviet economic administration is weak in motivating producers to economize on inputs, including intermediate inputs. As one dramatic example, during the fifteen years after the price revolution in energy (roughly 1970–85), energy consumption in the United States remained constant while the output of the economy grew by nearly half. In the USSR during the same fifteen years, the growth of energy consumption was not checked at all—energy consumption grew as fast as national output.

This general inefficiency in use of inputs is reflected in a number of structural peculiarities of the Soviet economy, notably in an overempha-

---

[13]Robert Campbell, "The Economy," in Robert F. Byrnes, ed., *After Brezhnev: Sources of Soviet Conduct in the 1980s* (Bloomington: Indiana University Press, 1983).

sis on the sectors producing materials. Soviet steel output is huge, energy production and consumption are gargantuan. These primary product industries are very labor and capital intensive, and their continued expansion eats up investment and other primary resources that should be going into the production of final product. A shift in productivity, if achieved, will be accompanied by shifts in structure of output, of capital investment, and of labor force. Unfortunately, the economy is stuck with a huge stock of productive facilities, accumulated over the past years of extensive growth, that embody the old material-wasting technologies. The heart of the strategy must therefore be to renovate the capital stock, retiring old equipment and replacing it with more productive equipment. This implies a dramatic upward shift in scrappage rates, large amounts of new replacement investment, a shift in the allocation of investment among branches away from sectors producing intermediate goods, and a shift in the composition of investment away from construction in favor of machinery and equipment. The overall strategy, moreover, will work only if the new machinery is of a radically more modern design than that it replaces. Hence the first structural change has to be in machinery production itself, through modernizing the productive capital of the machinery industries and the mix of machinery produced.

This strategic shift inevitably means a strained machinery balance, both in terms of volume of machinery output and in terms of quality upgrading. The quantitative aspect will have to be dealt with by some combination of increases in output, shifts from military hardware to civilian machinery output, and imports of machinery. The qualitative aspect will have to be dealt with by some combination of domestic innovation and technology transfer, the latter either from abroad or from the high-tech military branches of domestic machinery production, utilizing the experience and resources of the defense industry to upgrade civilian machinery production.

Just how fast this restructuring can occur is not clear. But the Twelfth Five-Year Plan envisages a considerable acceleration of investment, a shift in machinery output from military hardware procurement to civilian investment goods, strong growth differentials among machinery sectors, favoring the kinds of machinery capable of transforming technology over a wide range of activities. Gorbachev has a formulaic listing of these as microelectronics, computers, the measuring and control instrumentation the Russians call *priborostroenie*, and the whole complex of information technologies.

This general strategy has several corollaries for the relationship of the Soviet Union to the Pacific-Asian region, explicitly noted in the commentaries of Soviet economists, or clearly implied. First, the emphasis on replacement of existing capital, and the policy favoring machinery over construction in investment outlays, mean allocating investment resources to those geographic areas where plant is already in place— and, by implication, a reduction of greenfield investment in big new projects in areas with expensive infrastructural requirements. Overall, I would predict that the relative priority of investment in the Asian regions of the USSR (i.e., the Far East, Siberia, and Central Asia) will suffer. The proponents of eastern development have already suffered one serious defeat in the rejection of the scheme, pushed for many years by the Eastern lobby, to divert the north-flowing rivers of Siberia southward to irrigate the deserts of Central Asia.[14]

A supplementary component of the strategy is emphasis on the human factor, with a focus on strengthening discipline and improving incentives. To the extent that this is a typical Soviet campaign, it might be discounted as likely to have limited, short-run effects. But Gorbachev appears to understand that this campaign must be backed up by a longer-run policy of enhancing the real return to effort. More differenti-ation is needed in money wages than exists at present. More important, differential money earnings must be translated into real rewards by pro-viding goods that are really desired and that are priced high enough that people will have to strive for increased earnings to obtain them. One of the best sources for high-quality goods that could provide real incentives for intensive effort is the world market. The Russians might be well advised to increase trade with Japan and the Asian NICs to obtain modern consumer goods, following the line the Chinese have used to some extent. Unfortunately, another corollary of the overall strategy is that Soviet consumption is likely to suffer in the short run. To undertake all that replacement of obsolete capital, it is necessary to accelerate investment *now*, before the productivity gains provide an increment in output. The Soviet premier, N. I. Ryzhkov, has acknowl-edged this clearly by stating that in the Twelfth Five-Year Plan the share of the accumulation fund in the national income will rise, implying that the share of consumption will fall.[15] This competition between invest-ment and consumption will be as sharp in import structure as in GNP as a whole, so that the prospects for early expansion of high-quality consumer goods imports are slight.

---

[14]In the summer of 1986, the Central Committee ordered that all work on this diversion cease (*Izvestiia*, August 20, 1986).

[15]This is in his speech to the 27th Party Congress on the Twelfth Five-Year Plan, available in *Ekonomicheskaia Gazeta* [The Economic Newspaper] (weekly) (1986):11, p. 29.

The leaders do intend to expand trade in the Twelfth Five-Year Plan, though no quantitative target has been revealed. Premier Ryzhkov did, however, outline the governing priorities in his report on the plan at the 27th Party Congress—"the determining factor [in expansion of international trade] . . . will be cooperation with the socialist countries . . . . Trade turnover with the Chinese People's Republic will expand significantly."[16] He has also said that the plan envisages wide development of trade with LDCs.[17] In general, however, it is difficult to find evidence of intent or capability to expand imports of high-quality consumer goods or any special priority for trade with Japan and the Asian NICs that might provide such goods.

The structural policies underlying the Gorbachev strategy probably depend for their success on institutional changes, but how far and how rapidly changes in the institutional basis of the Soviet economy will proceed is still unclear. Some institutional changes directly relevant to the present topic have, however, already been made. The most important are some measures restructuring the foreign trade mechanism, which in the past has insulated the Soviet economy from the example of, and competitive pressure from, the world market. Students of the Soviet economy generally agree that the volume of Soviet foreign trade in the past has been less than economically optimal, and that its composition and direction have suffered from too much centralization of control by the Ministry of Foreign Trade. The reformers under Gorbachev would like to change that. In particular, they hope to use the stimulus of foreign competition to bring Soviet products up to world quality standards. Beginning in January 1987, foreign trade activity was partially decentralized by giving some producing ministries and enterprises the right to conduct trade themselves rather than through the Ministry of Foreign Trade.[18] The producers will also receive the right to some of the hard currency they earn through these operations, which should give them both a motive to meet world quality standards and foreign currency resources that they can use to upgrade their technology by technology transfer. But this change is still in the stage of being organized, and most observers feel that it is bound to take some time before it will offer much stimulus to Soviet trade. It is important to remember, moreover, that the motivation for this reform is basically to stimulate sufficient quality improvements in Soviet machinery to make it competitive

---

[16]Ibid., p.29.
[17]Speech on the Twelfth Five-Year Plan, in *Ekonomicheskaia Gazeta* (1986):26, p. 14.
[18]"O merakh po sovershenstvovaniiu upravleniia vneshne-ekonomicheskimi sviazami" [On measures for improving the management of foreign economic ties], *Ekonomicheskaia Gazeta* (1987):4, pp. 34–35.

in the markets of the industrialized West. Success would undercut the traditional rationale for Soviet machinery exports to LDCs, namely, a match between their need for simple, not-at-the-frontier equipment, and the Soviet proclivity to produce such machinery.

The USSR has also passed new legislation permitting joint ventures with foreign capitalists. It is reported that these ventures will be allowed some degree of independence within the Soviet system of planning and will be offered some financial privileges, intended to make them attractive to foreign participants. Again, however, this change is so new that we can only speculate as to the likely response of foreign capitalists to it.

The program of *perestroika*, or restructuring, that Gorbachev initiated is still evolving, and what we see so far may not fully indicate what may happen over a longer period of time, especially in the Thirteenth Five-Year Plan after 1990. Most observers have expressed doubts that the kind of strategic reallocations and structural changes described here will be sufficient to attain the productivity acceleration implied in the growth targets for the Twelfth Five-Year Plan. Those structural changes will required significant changes in behavior of many different economic factors, which it is hard to imagine without significant changes in the institutional framework of Soviet economic decision making. The technical change component of the strategy, for example, is heavily dependent on innovation, a traditionally weak element in the Soviet system. In the opinion of outsiders, it is unlikely that the strategic redirection can be carried out without a great deal of decentralizing institutional change as well. Clearly, Gorbachev and his reform-minded allies have come increasingly to share this opinion, and the Plenum of the Central Committee in June 1987 endorsed a much more thoroughgoing set of reforms than had been accepted at the time of the 27th Party Congress.

There is thus a possibility of a continuous movement toward decentralization of the economy, with all that implies regarding local independence of decision, reliance on improved prices, and the profit yardstick to guide those decisions. If the economy *is* transformed in these fundamental ways, the consequences for foreign trade in general, and for the attractiveness of the USSR as a trading partner, may change radically. Giving the lower levels of the system more power in economic choices would help pave the way for eroding further the monopoly of foreign trade and for letting the scarcity relationships, potential gains from trade, and quality standards evident in the world market play a more influential role in local decisions. But it is surely premature at this point to assume that the premise for such expectations—achieving a radical transformation of the economic system—will come to pass.

Implications

Against the overall background sketched, what can we say that is more specific about particular items on a possible menu of Soviet economic expansion in Asia? I repeat that there is little in any of the pronouncements and actions of the recent past to tell us exactly what Gorbachev and the leadership plan for interaction with the world economy, with the Pacific-Asian region, or with individual countries and groups within it. We do not know much about the role that part of the world plays in their mind. We can, however, think about the prospects for Soviet interaction with economic development in the Pacific-Asian region in somewhat more concrete terms, and I now turn to that task. One can approach it both in terms of general functional issues and in terms of individual countries. The following discussion canvasses an inventory of possible developments.

1. What are the possibilities of deautarkizing the Soviet economy, increasing its general involvement in the world economy? The USSR has excited speculation on this score by expressing an interest in becoming a member of three institutions of the world market system—the World Bank, the International Monetary Fund, and the General Agreement on Tariffs and Trade (GATT). These overtures have been rather tentative, but most observers think that the Russians will persist in them. Membership in these groups would probably enhance Soviet interactiveness and competitiveness in world markets. Most observers, however, have suggested that the Soviet drive to become involved in these organizations is intended primarily to enhance Soviet ability to use economic issues in foreign policy, not to become a Western-style participant in the world economy. The Soviet leaders would like to have a voice in the discussions about the Third World debt problem. There may be possibilities for winning friends in what are likely to emerge as contentious debates over protectionist measures introduced by the leading industrial countries. It seems disingenuous to pretend, as does one Soviet spokesman, that they can really support the goals of GATT: "There is no doubt that if we acceded to GATT, the Soviet Union would fully observe the procedures and traditions of that organization just as it strictly observes all its international obligations."[19] Given the character of the Soviet economic system, there is no way that the USSR can honor the underlying purpose of GATT to remove trade barriers or that it can be pressured to do so through the functional means that the GATT machinery involves. So, overall, it is too early to predict that the Rus-

---

[19]M. Pankin, "SSSR i GATT: ''Perspektivy vzaimodeistviia'' [The USSR and GATT: Prospects for Interaction], *Ekonomicheskaia Gazeta* (1985):49, pp. 21.

sians are about to become more integrated into the world economy, responsive to scarcity relations in the world market and, because of their size, a generally influential participant in world economic development.

2. What is likely to happen to the regional development component of Soviet domestic policy—is there any chance that Siberia and the Far East will receive higher priority in Soviet economic priorities, with the corollary that this would enhance the role of Soviet involvement in Pacific Basin economic development? As noted earlier, Gorbachev used the occasion of his visit to Vladivostok to put forward some ideas about regional development policy and the USSR's relationship with the Pacific nations.[20] His statements were generally interpreted as a policy favoring an enhanced role in Asia. (The *Current Digest of the Soviet Press* titled its summary of his statements, "Gorbachev Accents Soviet Role in Asia.") One commentator has interpreted some of Gorbachev's remarks as indicating that he would like to open Vladivostok (currently a zone closed to foreigners) and create a Chinese-style enterprise zone around it.[21]

If we examine this speech carefully, however, it provides little support for the notion that the Soviet East will have an enhanced role in Soviet economic priorities. Gorbachev did say that "the Party has assigned a prominent place [in regional policy] to the priority development of the eastern regions . . . a great deal of work regarding planning the development of the Far East was done in the process of drafting the Twelfth Five-Year Plan . . . . However, this is just the beginning of the work to accelerate the development of the entire region." But he was remarkably vague about what would be done to encourage eastern development, and in laying blame and suggesting action to improve the situation he stated that much of the responsibility for languishing development in the east lies with local organizations. The more the Soviet leader said, the less it seemed that anything definite had been decided, or any commitments made: "We must look at the prospects for the Far East's economy, and this must be done quickly in view of the region's special significance. It is important to carry this out without delay, because the Far East's economy is developing more slowly than the

---

[20]The text of Gorbachev's speech in Vladivostok is available in *Ekonomicheskaia Gazeta* (1986):32, pp. 1–5, and (1986):33, pp. 1–4. For an English language version, see *Current Digest of the Soviet Press*, vol. 28, no. 30.

[21]Matthew Evangelista, "The New Soviet Approach to Security," *World Policy Journal* 3 (Fall 1986):575.

national economy as a whole . . . . The region's share in all-Union production . . . is actually decreasing." In particular, nothing was said about additional investments. The most concrete promise Gorbachev made was that the fishing industry in the Far East would be strengthened. He decidedly rejected the notion that the Far East should specialize in raw materials production; it should have instead a fully rounded economy taking in the whole cycle from materials to finished products. Although Gorbachev acknowledged that developing the region requires a solution to the social infrastructure problem, we cannot fail to observe that, given how tight investment is under the strategy described earlier, this task is likely to be neglected.

On the subject of trade, Gorbachev had the following to say:

> Possibilities for an export direction for the development of the Far East's economy will have to be fully used. At present, the region's share in the country's exports is extremely low and very far below its potential. What is needed here are cardinal changes and new approaches in order to invigorate coastal and border trade, to put into use progressive forms of economic ties with foreign countries, including cooperative production arrangements and joint enterprises, and to create a specialized export base.

This listing of desiderata is very much in the mode of exhortation common to all Gorbachev's speeches, and, as we know, his statement of goals generally reaches far beyond the policy changes and reforms he has thus far been able to accomplish.

In short, though Gorbachev notes the significance of the Pacific Basin as a rapidly changing region and reminds us that the Soviet Union is an Asian and a Pacific Ocean power, he is quite vague as to how a new line will be translated into new behavior. And indeed he seems to see the significance of the Asian direction more in terms of political and security issues and possible openings for Soviet influence than in terms of economic growth.

3. As an alternative to assigning priority to Asia as an aspect of *central* policy, the combination of some decentralizing elements in Soviet policy, including the steps that begin to undercut the foreign trade monopoly, might lead to some regional independence in economic development policy and more local initiative in foreign trade. There is a precedent for independent trade initiated and controlled on a regional basis in the Baltic area and in the Far East, that is, the so-called "border trade." In the Far East the instrumentality for this foreign trade is an

organization called Dal'intorg, which has some independence from the centralized foreign trade decision-making apparatus.[22] But this is a rather weak precedent, the degree of local independence having been heretofore quite limited. Dal'intorg has operated under very severe restrictions on the kind of goods in which it can trade and the areas in which it can operate, either in the USSR or abroad. It can only export goods produced in excess of plan assignments; it has no allocation of materials, no authorization for transport services. Its imports are limited to consumer goods. It has been authorized to deal with a highly circumscribed list of areas. These were originally Japan, North Korea and Australia, with China added in 1983. On the Soviet side it can operate only in a few border territories. As an indication of Dal'intorg's small role, in 1980 its turnover (then entirely with Japan) was only about 4 percent of the USSR's total trade with that country.

Dal'intorg's powers have been extended in conjunction with the Soviet policy of increasing trade with China.[23] These operations have expanded rapidly and reached 25 million rubles in 1985. But this is again a tiny fraction of the 1985 Sino-Soviet trade volume of 1,605 million rubles.

Still, the precedent is there, and if the policymakers want to do so, they could extend this kind of regional independence in trade, facilitating an expansion of Siberian interaction with Pacific countries. But I see no indication yet that anyone regards this as an important opportunity. It is significant that in the new foreign trade legislation of early 1987 Dal'intorg did not rate a single mention.

Rather more discouraging for accelerated development of the Asian USSR under reformed planning and decision making is the current discussion about the Baikal-Amur mainline. This project was to be a major stimulus to Siberian development, but it now appears that in reviewing the mistakes of the Brezhnev period many Soviet economic policymakers regard the BAM effort as a huge blunder. The BAM is now described as a poorly thought-out and administered project whose

---

[22]For a fuller description of Dal'intorg's operations in the past, see Elisa B. Miller, "Soviet Participation in the Emerging Pacific Basin Economy: The Role of 'Border Trade,'" *Asian Survey* 21(5) (May 1981):565–78.

[23]See, e.g., "SSSR–KNR: Dobrye traditsii prigranichnoi torgovli" [The USSR and the PRC: The good tradition of border trade], *Ekonomicheskaia Gazeta* (1986):47, p. 23. There is also an informative article on the role of Dal'intorg in Chinese trade in a recent issue of *Soviet Export*: "The Vast Opportunities Open to Dalintorg's Local Trade," *Soviet Export* (1987):2, pp. 58–61.

promise was greatly exaggerated.[24] It soaked up a disproportionate share of the investment resources allocated to the railroads; in trying to deal with the resulting transport bottlenecks, the railroad ministry is likely to shift its investment priorities toward renovating its other facilities and away from pouring more resources into BAM. There is now frequent commentary to the effect that under increased pressure to cover investments out of their own resources and to cut costs, many ministry-level planners will be even less interested than in the past in developing the Siberian infrastructure and production facilities that the BAM was supposed to encourage.[25]

4. To what extent can the Pacific-Asian economies play a role in the Soviet desire to import technology to upgrade Soviet productivity? Many believe that Gorbachev's goals for technological upgrading cannot be met without more technology transfer from abroad. On the other hand, it is quite clear that the current mood among the Soviet leadership is to turn away from Western technology imports. Gorbachev took the opportunity, during a speech at the Baikonur cosmodrome in the summer of 1987, to restate emphatically that the USSR does not need outside technical help. He praised the work of the space program as a completely indigenous technical achievement and added that "there is no need for us to go abroad, hat in hand" to obtain technology.[26] The new decree reorganizing the foreign trade institutions, along with its decentralizing goals, also makes it very clear that its drafters consider that the USSR has been importing a great deal of unnecessary equipment.[27]

To the extent that the Soviets will expand their technology imports, the most likely partner for the purpose among the Asian nations is Japan. Some of the Asian NICs might alternatively serve as partners in modernizing production methods. They exhibit a rapidly rising level of technical sophistication and expertise. If the USSR were to develop

---

[24]For example, an article in *Izvestiia*, August 21, 1987, excoriates the lack of any realistic forecast of the cost of the BAM (which has turned out to be twice what was estimated), of possible traffic (it today carries less than 1 million tons of freight per year versus the 35 million ton forecast used to justify the project), of where the funds would come from to build the production facilities that were supposed to generate traffic for it. A summary of the article is available in *Current Digest of the Soviet Press* 39(34) (1987):22.

[25]"BAM: problemy kompleksnogo osvoeniia" [The Baikal-Amur mainline: Problems of its complex mastery], *Ekonomicheskaia Gazeta* (1987):29, pp. 8-9. Another article along the same lines used the attention-getting title, "Why Are the Rails of the BAM Rusting?"

[26]*Ekonomicheskaia Gazeta* (1987):21, p. 1.

[27]*Ekonomicheskaia Gazeta* (1987):11, p. 29.

closer relations with South Korea, for example, this country might be a valid substitute for Japan in this role. What possibilities and signals can we detect regarding this possible stimulus to Asian trade? The Soviet modernization program could certainly benefit from Japanese experience, especially in automated production, which is one of the directions the current Soviet economic strategy heavily emphasizes. On the other hand, it is an area in which the Soviet leaders seem intent on developing this technology domestically. Moreover, it seems more and more evident that Japanese success in introducing robotics and flexible manufacturing systems flows as much from careful attention to production management, and from worker and management culture, as from technical wizardry. When U.S. firms have tried to implant the new techniques in our own country, we have learned that the toughest problems are found in the need to totally retrain workers and management, change the whole culture of production, and so on. It is very difficult to imagine the Russians introducing these kinds of changes in intimate interaction with, and under the guidance of, foreign partners.

As for the Soviet joint venture gambit, it seems more oriented toward the West than to Asia. In any case, most observers are skeptical about its chances of success. Successful cooptation of Western investment, technology, and managerial knowhow is too far out of line with everything we know about the habits, thoughts, and inclinations built into the Soviet industrial structure. Foreign businessmen who have looked at the idea carefully think that the Russians have been more sensitive than the Chinese to the need to allow the foreign partner to make profits by permitting joint ventures to hire labor at domestic prices (the Chinese make the joint venture pay external labor rates). But one observer notes that the law "calculates Western investment at the grossly distorted official ruble rate, which in effect means that outside firms will furnish most of the capital for less than 50 percent control."[28] The most discouraging feature is that joint venture production plants would have to operate in the standard Soviet framework, which means just too much frustration for the outside partner. Though the Soviet press reported toward the end of its first year that several hundred projects were under discussion, the program had generated only a handful of agreements. But it is reported that the Soviet officials conducting the negotiations seem to be willing to ease the rules to accommodate the concerns of potential Western partners, and over the long

---

[28]George Melloan, in *Wall Street Journal*, May 12, 1987, p. 29.

haul this program may become a serious avenue for bringing in advanced-country partners, including the Japanese.[29]

5. In joint projects involving resource development, foreign credits, and technology transfer under Soviet control (with compensation through exports of the output of the project), Japan is again the prime candidate for those who see growing Soviet interaction with Pacific-Asian economies. The experience of recent years, however, has led many commentators to believe that the prospects for Japanese trade in general, and this kind of joint development agreement in particular, are not encouraging. One author has put the case in the following way:

> The rapid expansion of trade between the USSR and Japan during the 1960s was the result of a special combination of factors that is highly unlikely to reoccur. The high level of commercial cooperation that existed between the two states was an exception rather than the rule. . . . The largest portion of Japanese-Soviet trade has been conducted under the umbrella of large goverment-to-government joint projects and funded with state supported credits.[30]

First, conditions have changed to make Japan much less interested in Siberian energy and mineral supplies than in the past, as a result of conservation and diversification of supplies. After the oil shock, Japan greatly reduced its needs for energy by undertaking conservation and structural changes. Between 1973 and 1985, energy consumption per unit of output was cut by almost 50 percent in machinery, 30 percent in steel, 35 percent in ceramics and cement, 40 percent in chemicals, and 50 percent in nonferrous metals.[31] In any case, Japanese experience with Soviet performance under the previous arrangements was sufficiently discouraging to leave them without much interest in getting into such arrangements again.

Second, the Japanese are not especially interested in expanding subsidized credit to the USSR. China probably represents a better field for such cultivation, and they have given ten times as much credit to China as to the USSR.

On the Soviet side as well, the motivations and conditions have changed. The Russians are today more interested in exporting finished products than raw materials. The current line in the Soviet press regard-

---

[29]According to the *Wall Street Journal*, October 27, 1987, p. 32, Western businessmen were told in the summer of 1987 that the rules are to be amended to remove some features that have discouraged Western interest.

[30]Gordon B. Smith, "Recent Trends in Japanese-Soviet Trade," *Problems of Communism* 36 (January–February 1987):56–64.

[31]Takao Tomitate, "Japan's Energy Issues for the Future," *Energy in Japan* (March 1987):6.

ing economic relations with Japan is that although trade has been declining, it could expand once again on a new basis. Soviet authors acknowledge that the Japanese are less interested in importing fuel and energy resources than in the past and are under U.S. domination in terms of export controls on high-technology equipment. (The Toshiba case would seem to suggest that important Japanese firms may well respond to the incentive of profits from high-tech sales evading export controls, but the subsequent reaction by the Japanese government suggests a significant strengthening of the barriers to such deals.) The proposed new basis for expanded trade consists of agreements in which the Japanese would help develop lines of production at intermediate levels of fabrication and technology and would take back part of the output in payment. They also see the Japanese as attractive partners in such efforts as modernizing the Soviet steel industry. It is difficult to see how the Japanese stand to benefit from any of these proposals. The Japanese would hardly want to buy back steel, which, after all, has been a major Japanese export to the USSR.[32]

6. Is there some role for consumer goods on the basis of the reasoning described earlier—that is, to raise the quality and variety of consumer goods to enhance worker incentives in the Soviet economy? If we think about the kind of consumer goods that could be imported to do this, imports from the Asian economies would be the fastest way to achieve dramatic results. It has always seemed to me that the Russians must envy the United States, which has the toiling masses of Asia producing fancy electronic goods, automobiles, clothing, and many other consumer goods to support the American way of life. Soviet ideology would no doubt describe this as imperialist exploitation, but the USSR seldom scruples to seek economic advantage for itself just because such actions are condemned in others. (It feels no embarrassment from its alignment with the OPEC cartel, with monopolistic diamond-marketing arrangements, and so on.)

So far, however, the USSR has denied itself these goodies from Japan and the NICs. It has imported a few personal computers from Japan, and this would seem to make good economic sense on a large scale, forgoing domestic production of this now-routine item. But the Russians are generally exceedingly reluctant to give up even a weak domestic development effort in any technical area. In any case, if they want to expand consumer goods imports, they would prefer to use Vietnam and China as sources to avoid further strain on their hard currency

---

[32]"SSSR–Iaponiia: Za dinamizatsiiu delovykh otnoshenii" [The USSR and Japan: For making business ties more dynamic], *Ekonomicheskaia Gazeta* (1986):43, p. 21.

balance of payments. Such development would not be inconsistent with the ambitions of the Chinese, who want to export consumer electronics, textiles, personal computers, and other modern consumer goods, especially as China feels increasing protectionist pressure from Western markets. The Soviet Union could also get more varied and better foodstuffs from China and could certainly use Chinese grain.

To sum up, there is probably a fundamental comparative advantage rationale for expanded imports of consumer goods from those Asian countries that are already modernized, or are moving in that direction. In the long run that is an encouraging possibility, but at the moment it conflicts with Soviet investment-consumption priorities.

7. The USSR's strongest economic tie in Asia is with India, and we may wonder how much room there is for expansion in that direction. USSR-Indian trade has expanded fitfully, but whenever its growth has languished some new development has been injected to keep it growing. Both the Russians and the Indians have political as well as economic motivations to cultivate this link. There has been a kind of natural trading relationship based on Indian needs for, and Soviet ability to provide, development assistance, arms, and an outlet for exports of foodstuffs and consumer goods. But changing conditions may be causing the old complementarity to diminish.[33] The Indians are having a difficult time meeting Soviet desires for rising quality in consumer goods and foodstuffs; on the other side, as Indian producers become more sophisticated, they are less eager to accept Soviet equipment in lieu of more modern Western equipment. Moreover, rather than depending on Soviet turnkey plants, they want to exercise an indigenous capability to create production facilities, using Western and domestically produced equipment as well as Soviet. They also want to expand their own machinery exports.

8. A central place in Gorbachev's new attitude toward Asia is accorded to China policy, and the USSR has undertaken some economic initiatives here.[34] A trade agreement covering the years of the Twelfth Five-Year Plan was signed in 1985. The agreement sets a goal of 12 billion rubles for total trade turnover in the Twelfth Five-Year Plan, growing from the level of 1,605 million rubles in 1985 to 3 billion rubles in 1990. The composition of this trade is not fully spelled out, but the

---

[33]This theme is developed in detail in Dilip Mukerjee, "Indio-Soviet Economic Ties," *Problems of Communism* 36 (January–February 1987):13–24.
[34]For a description of these initiatives, see E. Bavrin (Deputy Minister of Foreign Trade of the USSR), "SSSR-KNR: Perspektivy delovykh otnoshenii" [The USSR and the PRC: Prospects for business ties], *Ekonomicheskaia Gazeta* (1987):7, p. 20.

USSR will concentrate on exporting machinery, including machinery to reequip the plants it helped the Chinese build in the earlier era of economic assistance (seventeen such reequipment projects are envisaged, along with construction of seven new plants). The Chinese will send back largely agricultural products and consumer goods, plus some minerals, chemicals, and machinery. It seems reasonable to expect that considerable expansion of this trade can occur if political conditions permit it. Further expansion is likely to be along the lines of the structure already indicated. There are inhibitions, however. The Chinese will want to retain ties with the rest of the capitalist world and to avoid becoming excessively committed to the Russians. They were burned once by excessive economic dependence on the USSR, and that has left a very powerful memory. Also, as mentioned earlier, the Chinese-Soviet and the Indo-Soviet trading relationships are to some extent substitutes for each other, both in political terms and in comparative advantage terms. To the extent one flourishes, the other is likely to languish.

9. What possibilities for trade exist with those LDCs that have not heretofore figured prominently in Soviet economic and political activity in Asia? Specifically, what about the ASEAN countries? On the whole, these countries are anticommunist, but sometimes more anti-Chinese than anti-Soviet. Gorbachev specifically mentioned Pacific-Asian countries in his Vladivostok speech: ''We are prepared to expand ties with Indonesia, Australia, New Zealand, the Philippines, Thailand, Malaysia, Singapore, Sri Lanka, Nepal, Brunei, and the Republic of Maldives and with the youngest independent participants of the region's political life.''

The traditional Soviet approach to such countries has been the offer of economic development assistance and/or military aid. There have been many indications that the Soviet leaders have come to consider the burden of economic aid they have undertaken in the past as too large in relation to what they have gotten from it. Western writers have seen such economic aid as one element in the ''cost of empire'' that is thought to have burdened Soviet growth. In my view, however, we should not exaggerate that burden. One careful review of the Soviet experience with economic assistance concludes:

> It would be safe to predict that domestic economic limitations will constrain both the growth rate and the generosity of terms for Soviet economic aid. Unless Soviet economic prospects brighten considerably more than now seems likely, limited resources will probably continue to retard Soviet efforts in the Third World . . . [Nevertheless,] one might expect a continued Soviet search for the type of LDC project that also promises to contribute to Soviet development needs, and a hard-

ening of terms (hard currency repayments, better interest rate) where possible.[35]

If this kind of perspective is valid, it would certainly not rule out possible Soviet approaches to such countries as the Philippines or to Indonesia. There can always be instability, generating opportunities for the USSR. The Philippines, for example, is likely to have serious economic troubles and might be a tempting target for Soviet economic assistance and enhanced trade.

10. The South Pacific deserves at least a mention in this inventory of possible action areas. Diplomatically, and in terms of security relationships, the area could be important, but it has negligible relevance to Soviet economic involvement in the Pacific. An economic rationale for enhanced Soviet activity in the South Pacific is difficult to define.

Conclusions

The new Soviet leadership has certainly expressed an interest in playing a more important role in the Pacific. One might say that the USSR is now actively engaged in diplomatic initiatives with countries Gromyko did not even know existed. One cannot help but be impressed by the greatly enhanced emphasis on the region and its importance in the current Soviet economic press as well as in recent Soviet literature on external relations. Gorbachev and his advisors are sufficiently sensitive interpreters of world trends to know that this will be an increasingly important part of the world economy. The USSR is frustrated at its inability to exert a strong influence in the Pacific-Asian region, with its major instrument—military power—stymied by the various triangles in which it is caught up. Under Gorbachev, Soviet diplomacy in the region has become much more flexible and inviting. An expanded economic relationship with the region would be a powerful additional foreign policy instrument. Indeed, unless it can generate a more lively economic involvement, the USSR's isolation and impotence in Asia will increase.

Nevertheless, as we review the major themes of the Gorbachev economic strategy, focused as it is primarily on domestic targets and instruments, little room exists for radically expanded economic activity in the Soviet East, and on that basis an increased involvement in the Pacific economy. Despite the argument of geographic propinquity, the Pacific economy has not been a strongly interesting region for the USSR in the past, and the underlying conditions do not change rapidly. Despite his

---

[35] Abraham S. Becker, "Soviet Union and the Third World: The Economic Dimension," *Soviet Economy* (July–September 1986):2, pp. 248, 258.

political interest in the area, Gorbachev's priorities in economic affairs are likely to undermine rather than to enhance what complementarity there has been in the past. As one of the most knowledgeable geographers specializing on the USSR has put it, "If irreplaceable regional development programs, such as the oil and gas efforts in West Siberia, are taken out of the equation, the very essence of the Gorbachev economic policy, with its stress on improving the *existing* economic potential, implies a shift in orientation from vast, undeveloped open spaces of the east to the great centers of economic activity in the west."[36] The heartland of Soviet economic development lies in the European USSR, and much of Gorbachev's plans are focused on that area. To the extent his domestic strategy requires greater involvement in the world economy, Gorbachev will find that the natural partner is Western (and Eastern!) Europe rather than the Pacific-Asian countries.

---

[36]Theodore Shabad, quoted in Leslie Dienes, *Soviet Asia: Economic Development and National Policy Choices* (Boulder: Westview Press, 1987). This is a major theme in Dienes's own treatment of Siberian development and is related to a more general proposition of the book, namely, that in the USSR regional policy has always been subordinated to "metropolitan" concerns.

5. ASEAN as an Economic Region: Individual Policies for Greater Interdependence

DANTE B. CANLAS

In the 1970s, South Korea, Taiwan, Hong Kong, and Singapore emerged as newly industrializing countries, exporting manufactured products on a global scale. The three East Asian economies—South Korea, Taiwan, and Hong Kong—together with the Southeast Asian city state Singapore has since stirred the curiosity of many economists. The latter's attention has since been directed to the other countries in the Pacific-Asian basin, namely, the four other members of ASEAN: Malaysia, Thailand, the Philippines, and Indonesia.

Great interest has centered on extracting some generalizable results from the experience of the Asian NICs. A large body of work focuses on the question: Can the success of the four Asian NICs be duplicated? Alternatively, is there a blueprint for successful industrial development that the other developing economies in Southeast Asia can imitate?

In a search for possible answers to these questions, I assume that a major objective of the four developing ASEAN economies is to bring about a transformation from a predominantly agricultural economy to a modern industrial one.[1] In other words, the goal is industrialization. The speed of the transition is conditioned by several factors, including the manner in which production is initially organized and the availability of supportive institutions in and out of government.

By industrialization I have in mind what Harry Johnson once succinctly described:

> Industrialization, properly speaking, involves the organization of production in business enterprises characterized by specialization and division of labor both within and among themselves; this specialization is based on the application of technology and of mechanical and electrical power to supplement and replace human effort and motivated by the objectives of minimizing costs per unit and maximizing returns to

---

[1]This problem is treated in dual-economy models of growth; see, e.g., Dale W. Jorgenson, "The Development of a Dual Economy," *Economic Journal* (June 1961):307–34; and in Dale W. Jorgenson, "Surplus Agricultural Labor and the Development of a Dual Economy," *Oxford Economic Papers* (1967):288–312.

the enterprise. . . . So conceived, industrialization is an economy-wide phenomenon, applying to agriculture and the service trades as well as to manufacturing; the essence of it is not the production of the products typically considered as "industrial" but the rational approach to the production process that it embodies.[2]

To speed up transformation of the ASEAN economies it is requisite that the countries open themselves up and promote greater interdependence with the rest of the world through trade in goods, technologies, services, and securities. On this score, however, a diversity of opinions exists regarding the desirability of expanding international economic relations. These differing attitudes can be traced to a variety of economic, political, and traditional factors that influenced the design of economic policies at various points in time.

This essay has two interrelated objectives. First, I want to provide a brief review of the postwar industrialization policies of Malaysia, Thailand, Indonesia, and the Philippines while comparing or contrasting them with some policies of the Asian NICs—presented here as models of what is achievable in terms of successful industrialization. Second, I advance some conjectures on emerging policy shifts in the ASEAN countries and their possible impacts on fostering greater interdependence not just within the Pacific-Asian region but with the rest of the world.

My review of policies is selective in nature, limited to a body of rules that can be regarded as constituting a policy regime. This focus helps advance the analysis without miring it in discretionary or frequently changed actions of government economic authorities. Thus, inward orientation or import substitution with its high tariffs and quantitative restrictions is considered a policy regime, as is outward orientation with flexible exchange rates.

To set the stage for the twin objectives of this essay, the next section presents a development status report for the ASEAN countries and the Asian NICs followed by surveys of specific industrialization policies, prevailing macroeconomic policies, and emerging policy trends.

Some Characteristics of Developing and Transitional Economies

ASEAN Economies

As an approximate description of the state of economic development of the four ASEAN countries, I present here the levels and growth

---

[2]Harry G. Johnson, *Economic Policies Toward Less Developed Countries* (New York: Praeger, for Brookings Institution, 1967).

Table 1

Output and Growth Rates of Per Capita Income, 1985

Country	GDP (US$ millions)	GNP per Capita (US$)	Average Annual Growth Rate of GNP per Capita (%) 1965–85
Malaysia	31,270	2,000	4.4
Thailand	38,240	800	4.0
Philippines	32,590	580	2.3
Indonesia	86,470	530	4.8

SOURCE: World Bank, *World Development Report* (Washington, D.C., 1987).

rates of per capita income. These measures may be inadequate as indicators of economic development; they are useful, however, to the extent that reflecting on them opens up thoughts about other important issues, such as production capacity and population growth. The developmental role of the latter is widely acknowledged, but I will not be concerned with it here. Rather, my review is limited to the allocative and efficiency effects of some economic policies, the extent to which they might improve or impede the growth of a given economy's productive capacity.

Unless otherwise indicated, the figures in this section are all taken from the World Bank's *World Development Report* of 1987. Table 1 presents 1985 figures for real gross domestic product, real GNP per capita, and average annual growth rates of real per capita income. Malaysia, which has the smallest population base among the four, had the highest GNP per capita of $2,000. It was followed by Thailand with $800 and the Philippines with $580. Indonesia, the most populous among the four, had a per capita GNP of $530. Although Indonesia had the lowest per capita GNP, it posted the highest growth rate of GNP per capita, an average of 4.8 percent for the period 1965–85. Malaysia was the next fastest growing in the group with 4.4 percent, followed by Thailand with 4.0 percent. The Philippines, which experienced an output contraction of 11 percent in 1984 and 1985, could only post an average of 2.3 percent growth rate for the period. If these growth rates persist, Indonesia can hope to double its income in 14.3 years, Malaysia in 15.7 years, Thailand in 17.2 years, and the Philippines in 30 years.

All four countries still have a large portion of their labor force engaged in agriculture. In 1980, Thailand had 71 percent of its labor force in agriculture, followed by Indonesia and the Philippines with 57 percent and 52 percent, respectively. Malaysia still had 42 percent of its

Table 2

Output and Growth Rates of Per Capita Income, 1985

Country	GDP (US$ millions)	GNP per Capita (US$)	Average Annual Growth Rate of GNP per Capita (%) 1965–85
Hong Kong	30,730	6,230	6.1
Singapore	17,470	7,420	7.6
South Korea	86,180	2,150	6.6
Taiwan	53,814	2,830	5.7

SOURCES: World Bank, *World Development Report* (Washington, D.C., 1987). Taiwan's GDP and GNP per capita are for 1984; the growth rate is for 1965–84. These figures are taken from its *National Income Accounts* and Statistical Yearbooks.

labor force in agriculture. In terms of the share in gross domestic product, the agricultural sector accounted for 27 percent in the Philippines, 24 percent in Indonesia, 21 percent in Malaysia, and 17 percent in Thailand.

If we view industrial transition as the point at which the percentage of the labor force engaged in industry overtakes that engaged in agriculture, it can be argued that the four ASEAN economies are still confronted with the old problem of how an industrial sector can emerge from a predominantly agricultural economy. In terms of employment generation for workers released from the agricultural sector, the service trades appear to be picking up the slack. The ASEAN economies seem to be skipping a beat in their industrialization drives, moving from an agricultural to a postindustrial stage in which the service sector plays a prominent role in job creation. Unlike many modern postindustrial societies, however, the service-sector jobs in the developing ASEAN countries involve low-skill, low-wage personal services.

A major concern of the four ASEAN economies is to bring about a sufficiently rapid capital accumulation in the industrial sector. This is crucial so that workers released from agriculture are not rendered unemployed, except for a brief period of mandatory search and training when they make the transition from agriculture to industry.

Asian NICs

To demonstrate what is achievable in terms of successful industrialization, this section presents some development indicators for Hong Kong, Singapore, South Korea, and Taiwan. Table 2 presents figures for output and growth rates of per capita income for the four Asian NICs. In 1985, Singapore had the highest per capita real income of the four with $7,420, followed by Hong Kong with $6,230. In 1984, South Korea's per capita income level was $2,150; for Taiwan it was $2,830. There was also a diversity in average growth rates of real per capita income in 1965–85: 6.1 percent for Hong Kong, 7.6 percent for Singapore, and 6.6 percent for South Korea. Taiwan's average growth rate for 1965–84 was 5.7 percent. If these growth rates are maintained, Singapore's per capita income can double in 9 years, South Korea's in 10.4 years, Hong Kong's in 11.3 years, and Taiwan's in 12.1 years.

A Brief Survey of ASEAN Industrialization Policies

All the ASEAN countries, at the start of their industrialization drives, adopted essentially the same approach: import substitution or inward orientation. This strategy provided them with an opportunity to demonstrate their industrial expertise. Consumer products that were previously imported were manufactured locally; processing plants for some standardized intermediate products were established. At the time, it was believed that import substitution was a good way to conserve scarce foreign exchange.

A strong impetus to import substitution came from the surge in economic nationalism that followed the emergence of the ASEAN countries as politically independent nations or city-states (all except Thailand had been at one time or another under colonial rule). To demonstrate that they could be economically self-reliant, these countries shifted from importation to domestic production. This inward orientation, however, gave rise to some difficulties, bringing in their wake a host of interventionist moves from government, many of which could not pass the requirements of traditional public finance. Government intervention in many instances demonstrated uncertainty about what externalities or market failures had to be corrected; infant industry arguments were also used sparingly. In these ways, inefficiencies at the microeconomic level were bred.

When import substitution began, a number of production constraints had to be overcome. The ASEAN countries had limited supplies of skilled workers and managerial talents, and they were not capable of producing the capital goods needed to produce import substitutes. Given a low-quality human resource base, the shift from imports to local production meant higher production costs. The people behind the import-substituting enterprises asked for protection, and governments responded by setting up a maze of tariff and nontariff barriers designed to keep competing imports out.

The seeds of protectionism were nurtured at this stage, a trend accompanied by the institution of a strong activist role for government in planning industrial development. This is the origin of a phenomenon currently visible in all the ASEAN countries, namely, the prominent role played by investment and industrial planning boards in selecting the industries that can qualify for special fiscal incentives. The practice involves the replacement of private entrepreneurs by bureaucrat-managers in choosing industrial "winners." Usually, however, once these handpicked industries are subjected to strict cost-benefit tests, many fail.

The need to import capital goods ran into foreign-exchange constraints, thereby opening up government intervention in the allocation of foreign exchange. Local currencies were fixed and overvaluation became prevalent. This policy served to subsidize imports. In the process, however, incentives to export were damaged. Further, pure import-substitution strategy led to chronic trade deficits and balance-of-payments problems. Internally, the protected industries tended to be capital intensive, weak in providing employment for a growing labor force. These external and internal imbalances had to be confronted.

To address their external imbalances, the ASEAN countries realized that they had to temper import substitution with an outward-oriented or export-promoting strategy. This strategy they adopted to varying degrees. Those that pursued consistent trade and exchange-rate policies, giving equal incentives to import substitutes and exports, were more successful in handling their external imbalances than those that did not.[3] The outcome was expanded international trade relations. Meanwhile, the countries that maintained biases in favor of import substitutes experienced a worsening of their balance-of-payments problems. To ease temporary liquidity problems, they turned to the International Monetary Fund. When the problems persisted, however, they were forced to contend with the high conditionality practices prescribed by the IMF to client countries with fundamental balance-of-payments difficulties.

---

[3]The Asian NICs are prime examples of countries that adopted successful outward-oriented strategies. This success is due to the consistency of trade and exchange as well as rate policies, according to Bela Balassa, "Export Incentives and Export Performances in Developing Economies: A Comparative Analysis," *Westwirtschaftliches Archiv* 114 (1978); and Bela Balassa, "Policy Responses to Exogenous Shocks in Developing Countries," *American Economic Review* 76 (1982):1020–34. Supply-side policies by the Asian NIC governments, however—such as underpricing of investment goods relative to consumption and government goods—are regarded as the key factor by Colin Bradford, Jr., "Trade and Structural Change: NICs and Next Tier NICs as Transitional Economies," *World Development* 15 (1987):299–316.

As for correcting internal imbalances, opportunities for achieving full employment presented themselves in the late 1960s. Producers in the more developed countries of the world found it profitable to subcontract the labor-intensive stages of production to manufacturers in less developed countries. Precut garments from the United States, for example, were shipped to export-processing zones of some LDCs for sewing and packaging, then were reexported to the United States. Production arrangements like these helped some LDCs come close to their full employment goals. Those that managed to reach full employment experienced rising wages, a phenomenon that motivated them to extend labor subcontracting to more capital-using, downstream production processes, thus setting into motion mechanisms for sustained growth of output. Among the ASEAN countries, these developments in international trade helped somewhat in easing underemployment and unemployment problems, but the degree of success differed markedly.

We have noted in the previous section the diversity in levels and growth rates of real per capita incomes among the ASEAN economies. We have also pointed out the seemingly similar approaches to industrialization that were adopted. How, then, can we account for the variance in their current development status?

Focusing solely on production issues, it is helpful to examine the different policy responses these countries adopted during the supply-shocked years of the mid-1970s and early 1980s. This period saw a dramatic rise in the relative price of oil. Exporters of primary products, after a brief commodity boom, saw their terms of trade deteriorate. Oil-exporting developing countries, of course, were able to cushion the shocks. In the early 1980s, when the Third World debt crisis emerged openly, a major source of foreign financing contracted as commercial lending to sovereign borrowers by foreign banks dropped precipitously.

The LDCs responded to these shocks in different ways. The evidence seems to show that those that undertook deficit and inflationary financing went through some temporary growth of output, which then petered out. At the same time, countries that resisted depreciating their currencies also performed dismally. Among the oil-importing ASEAN countries, the Philippines exemplified the worst case. The government pegged the exchange value of the peso and racked up huge budget deficits, the financing of which led to high inflation rates. The recessions the country went through in 1984 and 1985 arose mainly from the inappropriate policy responses to the supply shocks. As a result, in terms of real per capita income growth rate it now lags behind the other countries in the ASEAN region.

Country Policies

Which of these four ASEAN countries will make the next industrial transition into the ranks of the NICs? Here I will briefly survey individual country strategies and their favored microeconomic policies. It is beyond the scope of this essay to isolate the effects of each policy; what I will do instead is focus on their macroeconomic outcomes to determine if any structural adjustment is indicated.

Malaysia

Malaysia's early efforts to industrialize took the form of special fiscal incentives granted under the Pioneer Industries Ordinance of 1958. Romeo Bautista, for instance, reported that Malaysia provided incentives to firms with pioneer status, giving exemptions from the 40 percent company income tax and providing subsidies for infrastructure services such as electricity, water, and transport in industrial estates.[4]

As a follow through to these initial efforts, the Malaysian Industrial Development Finance Berhad was created in 1960 to extend medium- and long-term loans and technical assistance to manufacturing enterprises. In 1965, the Federal Industrial Development Authority was established, taking over the task of industrialization. In 1968, the Investment Incentives Act was passed. In introducing a new set of fiscal incentives, it superseded the 1958 Pioneer Industries Ordinance of 1958. Export-oriented industries were accorded specific incentives, and free trade and export processing zones were set up in selected parts of Malaysia.

The industrialization efforts of Malaysia may be classified into three major thrusts: manufactured exports, agroindustrial processing, and heavy industry development. The manufacturing sector has been growing rapidly: during the periods 1971–75 and 1975–80, the sector grew at an average annual rate of 13.6 percent and 13.3 percent, respectively. For 1980, the share of manufacturing in total exports was 22 percent.[5] In 1970–74, Malaysia started with the development of labor-intensive manufactured exports. According to Ariff, Lim, and Lee, the sharp increase in exports of manufactured products during this period was mainly accounted for by four product groups: electrical machinery, footwear and clothing, textiles, and miscellaneous manufacturing. The establish-

---

[4]Romeo M. Bautista, "Industrial Policy and Development in the ASEAN Countries," monograph series no. 2, Philippine Institute for Development Studies, October 1983.
[5]Mohammed Ariff, Chee Peng Lim, and Donald Lee, "Export Incentives, Manufactured Exports, and Employment: Malaysia," discussion paper no. 84–09 (Quezon City, Philippines: Council for Asian Manpower Studies, December 1984).

ment of export-processing zones propelled the growth of exports in these industries. Multinational firms located in the zone subcontracted the labor-intensive stages of production—such as sewing of garments and mounting of semiconductor chips on a plane—and reexported these products later. The benefits to Malaysia came mostly from the earnings and employment generated by labor subcontracting.

Malaysia is a major exporter of primary products such as rubber, palm oil, and tin. Like other similarly situated exporters, Malaysia has found an agro- or resource-based industrial processing very appealing. Thus the Fourth Malaysia Plan of 1981–85 targeted further development of resource-based industrial projects, particularly in the processing of cocoa, palm oil, and crude petroleum, together with the manufacture of rubber- and wood-based products for both export and home consumption.[6]

More recently, the industrialization of Malaysia took on a heavy industry component. The government established the Heavy Industries Corporation of Malaysia in 1980 to plan, coordinate, and implement investment in heavy industries. Specific projects planned for implementation include basic metals and general engineering, transport equipment, other equipment and machinery, building materials, paper and paper products, and petrochemical products. The government has started a Malaysian car manufacturing program.

A centerpiece of Malaysia's development plan is greater *bumiputra* (Malay) participation in industries. Its New Economic Policy (NEP) envisions a restructuring of equity participation along ethnic lines. Thus, according to Ariff, Lim, and Lee, in 1980 the budget had a scheme whereby companies conforming to the NEP equity restructuring would have their income tax rates reduced from 40 percent to 35 percent.

The economic problem posed by the *bumiputra* is the extent to which it crowds out or bars the entry to key positions of non-*bumiputras*. To the extent that the latter are a complement rather than a substitute for *bumiputra*, the policy can lead to inefficient arrangements in which output is needlessly reduced. There is casual evidence that this may be the case. Hence, the Malaysian government does not now strictly enforce greater *bumiputra* participation in industries.

Reviewing the macroeconomic performance of Malaysia, we find that the average growth rate of real per capita income was 4.5 percent during the period 1965–85. The average annual rate of inflation was 3.1

---

[6]Bautista, "Industrial Policy," p. 13.

percent in 1980–85, down from 4.9 percent in 1965–80.[7] The moderation in inflation may be traced to the decline in the growth rate of nominal money holdings. For 1965–80, money growth rate was 21.5 percent. This decreased to 15.5 percent in 1980–85. Given Malaysia's prudent monetary policy, forces that tend to weaken the nominal exchange rate were held in check.

Turning to its balance of payments, we find that Malaysia had a current account deficit of US$723 million in 1985. Its gross international reserves stood at US$5.7 billion, equivalent to 3.7 months of imports. The country has a total long-term external debt of US$17.9 billion. Debt service as percentage of GNP was 16.9 percent, and as percentage of exports it was 27.5 percent in 1985.

Malaysia's ability to maintain a low inflation rate helped prevent undesirable macroeconomic fluctuations arising from inappropriate monetary policies even during the supply-shocked period of the mid-1970s and early 1980s. In 1985, however, the government budget deficit was 9.4 percent, which could be a problem area. If a deficit of this magnitude persists, a high inflation regime could be ushered in, a situation that could jeopardize long-term prospects for growth. Given the tightening of foreign commercial bank loans for development finance, a persistent current account deficit might also prove vexing to output and employment objectives.

Thailand

Thailand's drive for industrialization started in the 1960s with an import substitution strategy. It then adopted an outward-oriented approach in the 1970s with an eye towards increasing its exports of manufactured products. Government plans include as a next step the development of capital-intensive, heavy industries. The New Investment Promotion Act was introduced in 1962. Selected import-substituting industries were accorded special fiscal incentives—duty-free imports and tax exemptions, for example. Minimum plant sizes were stipulated, leading to the establishment of large-scale manufacturing.[8] The Export Promotion Act was passed in 1972, providing for tax rebates on imported inputs. Subsidized credit facilities were set up to provide financing to export-oriented industries. As reported by Bautista, the next stage of Thailand's industrialization is the development of basic industries, including iron and steel, soda ash, and newsprint.

---

[7]All figures are from World Bank, *World Development Report* (Washington, D.C., 1987).
[8]Bautista, "Industrial Policy," p. 23.

Thailand, which received a structural adjustment loan from the World Bank that was approved in 1982, is committed to introducing fundamental policy reforms in agriculture and industry. Macroeconomic policy reforms, designed to keep the government budget deficit and the current account deficit in the balance of payments manageable, form part of these commitments. According to Thailand's development plans, the agricultural sector's productivity is targeted to be raised over a longer time horizon, to be balanced by productivity growth in the industrial sector.

Thailand appears to have weathered the lure of low interest rates worldwide during the early part of the 1970s. Its debts were US$16.7 billion in 1984. This involves a debt-service ratio of 26 percent. This figure is higher than Indonesia's, but Thailand appears not heavily burdened by it. Thailand has maintained an average growth rate in real GNP of 4–5 percent. Some see Thailand as on the threshold of joining the ranks of the NICs, an optimism palpable in recent journalistic accounts.[9]

In an excellent survey of Thai economists writing in English, however, Peter G. Warr and Bandid Nijathaworn point out that a distinct contrast emerges between the work of foreign authors and Thai economists in their assessment of Thailand's long-term prospects.[10] Foreigners, they suggest, sometimes compare Thailand with the Asian NICs, whereas Thai writers tend to emphasize the structural problems of their economy.

Thailand's macroeconomic performance showed an average growth rate of 4.5 percent from 1965 to 1985. The country was able to weather the tumult of the mid-1970s and the early 1980s in the sense that it was not engulfed by a serious balance-of-payments crisis. This outcome has been attributed, among other factors, to the appropriateness of Thailand's exchange-rate adjustments. The baht, which is pegged to the dollar, was devalued by 10 percent in 1981 and by 15 percent in November 1984.

In any discussion of Thailand's economic performance by Thai economists the balance of payments looms large. A persistent current account deficit burdens the economy. In 1985, the deficit was equivalent to 5 percent of GDP. A modest surplus came about in 1986, but this was mainly the result of favorable oil prices. By 1985, Thailand's external

---

[9]Philip Bowring, "While Others Falter," *Far Eastern Economic Review*, June 25, 1987, pp. 68–74.
[10]Peter G. Warr and Bandid Nijathaworn, "Thai Economic Performance: Some Thai Perspectives," *Asian-Pacific Economic Literature* 1(1) (May 1987):60–74.

debt was US$17.5 billion. The long-term debt service as a ratio to exports rose from 17 percent in 1980 to 26 percent in 1985. Thailand is also plagued by a deficit in the national government budget, about 5 percent of GDP. Its tax structure and tax collection machinery, Thai writers stress, need to be improved. Warr and Nijathaworn sense that Thai economists feel little enthusiasm about reverting to the import substitution policies of the 1950s and 1960s. Still, they discern a protectionist element in some writings.

Thailand, no doubt, shares the problems of the other less developed countries. But it has shown itself capable of making the proper adjustments. This is the real basis, it seems to me, for the optimism about Thailand's prospects.

Indonesia

Among the five ASEAN countries, Indonesia is the most populous and largest in land area. These characteristics have provided the impetus for policymakers to opt strongly for import substitution, relying on the large size of the domestic sector to generate economic growth.

When Suharto came to power in 1966, he initiated a New Order in which public investment projects concentrated on the rehabilitation of the country's infrastructures. In 1967, a Foreign Investment Law was enacted to provide special fiscal incentives to foreign investors. A development plan, Repelita I 1969–74, was prepared. For the period 1970–79, the industrial sector grew by an average of 11.3 percent. Most of it came from import-substituting industries such as food processing, wheat flour, textiles, paper, and fertilizers. Indonesia set up an Investment Coordinating Board to oversee foreign investments and domestic industrial projects eligible for incentives. Some of the special incentives included tax exemptions, accelerated depreciation allowances, duty-free importation of raw materials, and capital equipment.

Because Indonesia is an oil-exporting country, with the oil-price shocks of 1973–74 and 1979–80 it was able to enjoy a boom. This windfall, however, worked against the development of an exporting manufacturing sector—a veritable Dutch disease problem. Indonesia also relies heavily on an agro- or resource-based industrialization strategy. Thus in 1985, it banned exports of logs to support investments in plywood, veneer, and furniture making. It also planned for investments in heavy industries: aluminum plants, smelters, and steel mills. It has an aeronautics industry project that is experiencing a scarcity of workers such as skilled engineers.

There is a developing consensus that Indonesia must expand its manufactured export sector and reduce its dependence on earnings from oil exports. In line with this thinking, Indonesia has adopted a policy package designed to increase the competitiveness of its products in world markets, including cheaper export credits, export credit insurance, and relaxation of some foreign exchange controls.[11]

Among the four ASEAN countries, Indonesia has turned in the highest average growth rate of real per capita income at 4.8 percent. Its average inflation rate for 1980–85 was 10.7 percent, on a money growth rate of 23.6 percent. For 1985, its current account deficit was US$1.8 billion, equivalent to 2 percent of GDP. Gross international reserves in 1985 was equivalent to 3.2 months worth of imports. Its long-term external debt stood at US$35.8 billion in 1985. Long-term debt service as percentage of exports was 25.1 percent.

Indonesia, like Malaysia and Thailand, seems to have made the appropriate policy responses that enabled it to avert the debt crisis that befell many LDCs in the early 1980s. In 1985, the government had a budget surplus of 1.5 percent of GNP. With oil prices firming up at about US$18 per barrel, Indonesia's prospects appear bright.

Even if Indonesia has committed some policy mistakes in the past, they have not been sufficiently damaging to the economy's performance in the long run. This is probably the main reason that a group of foreign bankers recently established a new loan facility for Indonesia even though the latter had not asked for it. The market fundamentals at this stage look acceptable.

The Philippines

The import substitution phase of Philippine industrialization began in the 1950s. Import and foreign exchange controls were set in place to support the import-substituting thrust. In the late 1950s, however, the import substitution strategy appeared to have lost steam, and by 1967, an Investment Incentives Act creating the Board of Investments (BOI) was enacted. BOI-registered firms were given special fiscal incentives similar to those the other ASEAN countries were granting.

In the late 1960s, the Philippines encountered a serious balance-of-payments problem that led to the Export Incentives Act of 1970, which was designed to stimulate the exports of nontraditional products. During the 1970s, and especially after the oil price shock of 1973, the Philippines resorted to expansionary fiscal policies that led to large government budget deficits. It succumbed to the low interest rates during the period, resorting to foreign borrowing to finance its budget and current account deficits. In 1983, the debt-service ratio rose to an intolerable level, and with a sluggish export sector the Philippines was forced

---

[11]Bautista, "Industrial Policy," p. 10.

to declare a moratorium on repayment of principal on its foreign debts. As of 1984, the external debts stood at US$28 billion, involving a debt-service ratio of about 30 percent. In 1986, the Aquino government came to power and began a return to constitutional democracy. The executive and judicial branches of government have recently been joined by a legislative body, with the recent conduct of a congressional election. Under this arrangement, economic policies will no longer emanate solely from the executive branch. Congress, via legislation, is expected to play an important role in the formulation of economic policies. And insofar as the judiciary may choose to interpret some legislation as unconstitutional, thereby setting a precedent for future decisions in the process, this branch of government also becomes an important source of public policy.

The Philippines, like Thailand, is the recipient of a structural adjustment loan from the World Bank. It is therefore committed to carry out macroeconomic, trade, and exchange-rate policy reforms. Because of its extensive exposure to high conditionality loans of the IMF, its domestic policies are constrained by IMF conditionality practices.

In 1986, the recession that began in 1984 was arrested. The growth rate of GNP was a very modest 1.5 percent. The price level declined by 0.3 percent. As far as macroeconomic performance is concerned, its balance of payments is still the major problem area. As noted, the Philippines went through a balance-of-payments crisis in 1983. The servicing of its external debt, which is currently about US$28 billion, requires massive improvements in the trade account. So far, however, little progress seems to have been made. In 1986, the trade deficit was US$202 million.

The persistence of the trade deficit can be traced to an inappropriate exchange rate policy. Focusing on the peso–dollar nominal exchange rate, we find that between December 1984 and 1985 the nominal exchange value of the peso declined by 3.7 percent. If we adjust the nominal exchange rate for differences in price movements in the Philippines and the United States, however, we note that the real exchange value of the peso in relation to the dollar increased by 8 percent. The strengthening of the real exchange rate largely explains the trade deficit for 1986. This was something that the economy could ill afford. The strengthening of the peso led to high nominal interest rates. Since investors did not expect the exchange rate to hold up, given the increasing trade deficits, they required a higher nominal rate to compensate them for the expected fall of the peso.

These expectations were revealed in the credit and financial markets. In early November 1987, one-year Treasury bills in the United States yielded 6.9 percent, whereas bills of the same maturity in the Philippines returned 15.3 percent to their holders. Since the interest-rate parity condition can be expected to hold approximately, we deduce that investors anticipated a fall in the value of the peso by 8.4 percent. Unless the peso is allowed to seek its free-market level, high nominal interest rates will persist in the Philippines. This has a dampening effect on investment that can adversely affect the long-term productive capacity of the economy. During the first three quarters of 1987, the economy grew by about 5.5 percent. A strong peso plus the income growth fueled the rise in the demand for imports. This was not accompanied by a rise in exports. As a result, the trade deficit became worse. The Philippines has made substantial progress in trimming the budget deficit and curbing inflation. The propensity to fix the nominal exchange rate, however, and to commit a fraction of the Central Bank's foreign reserves to its defense exposes the economy to balance-of-payments crises.

Emerging Policies for Greater Interdependence

The ability of the ASEAN countries to loosen the constraints imposed by their balance of payments can in the long run dictate the extent of interdependence that they can forge with the rest of the world.

I have noted how the ASIAN NICs became integrated with the world trading environment: by adopting an outward-oriented strategy and by avoiding an incentive structure heavily biased towards import substitutes. The ASEAN countries are working, in varying degrees, on some structural adjustment programs designed to usher in a more liberal trade regime.

Both Thailand and the Philippines, for example, are committed to some form of trade liberalization under existing structural adjustment loans with the World Bank. To promote labor-intensive manufactured exports, for instance, an import liberalization scheme has been initiated involving the removal of quantitative restrictions on imports of some intermediate goods and their replacement by more or less uniform tariffs. The list of imports to be liberalized include items like textile yarn, iron and steel products, and chemicals. The obstacles to import liberalization spring from the presence of some interest groups that benefit from the trade barriers. To the extent that these groups are able to lobby successfully within the existing political structure for maintenance of protection, import liberalization is bound to move very slowly.[12]

---

[12]For insights into the persistence of protection in the ASEAN countries, see the compendium of papers in Christopher Findlay and Ross Garnaut, eds., *The Political Economy of Manufacturing Protection: Experiences of ASEAN and Australia* (Sydney: Allen & Unwin, 1986).

In an effort to increase the value added dimension of their primary exports, ASEAN countries find agroindustrial processing for exports very appealing. Here they try to extend farther down the processing of agricultural raw materials, such as copra into coconut oil and coconut oil into fatty alcohol. One of the problems posed by agroindustrial processing is the foreign exchange requirements of imported capital equipment.

In the mid-1970s up to the early 1980s, many less developed countries liberalized the capital accounts in their balance of payments. This strategy was encouraged by the availability of excess petrodollars and low interest rates initially. When it was not accompanied by a liberalization of the trade account that stressed exports of manufactured goods, however, debt crises erupted. Given the external debt problems of many Third World countries today, a downsizing of commercial bank lending is to be expected in the remainder of this decade. To improve LDCs' capital accounts, the program has shifted to attracting direct foreign investments. ASEAN countries tend to favor incentive schemes for attracting foreign investors, though some countries like Indonesia are now downplaying such plans. Special fiscal incentives such as tax exemptions, duty-free importations, and interest rate subsidies are quite common.

One problem that arises from the granting of special fiscal incentives is this: the governments granting special fiscal incentives forgo revenues that can support public investment programs in roads, ports, telecommunication systems, and other social overhead capital. It is relevant to ask: What will serve the internal and external balance targets better—granting special fiscal incentives to foreign investors, or collecting the taxes and using these to fund worthy public investment projects?

In situations where the protective structure is maintained, the policy to attract foreign investors may not serve export-oriented objectives. Some multinational enterprises, for instance, are known to engage in tariff-jumping with the intention of selling solely in the local market. The incentives in place, along with the protection against competing imports, ensure that these enterprises realize a profit even if they sell only in the domestic market of the host country.

Although the ASEAN economies are indeed interested in foreign capital inflows through direct investments, some faintheartedness is still discernible among them. Foreign ownership normally involves ceilings on allowable shares—say, 40 percent of total. In adhering to ceilings, the ASEAN countries may be forgoing some benefits that emanate from different forms of industrial connections. Other ownership arrangements exist; either licensing or 100 percent foreign ownership through subsidiaries may deliver more benefits to the host country than joint ventures.[13]

In the case of joint ventures, the maintenance of local content protection to encourage the use of local materials is a popular strategy. Again, deadweight losses may accrue from this arrangement without the knowledge of the host country. Entrepreneurs who are adept at absorbing foreign technologies, if forced to observe local content requirements, end up with suboptimal and higher-priced outputs.[14]

Economic Cooperation

The emerging policy pattern invites questions about whether it can contribute to greater economic cooperation among the ASEAN economies. Economic cooperation has been much discussed in ministerial meetings, but so far these discussions have produced no tangible results.

Two of the most discussed areas for economic cooperation have been a plan for industrial complementation and preferential trading agreements.[15] The economic case advanced for industrial complementation rests on expected gains from the realization of scale economies and specialization. An infant-industry argument is being presented for preferential trading agreements. According to this thinking, intra-ASEAN trade with preferential tariff rates would be invoked initially to shield some industries from foreign competition.

Both these endeavors for enhancing economic cooperation have so far been limited in their implementation. There are several reasons for this outcome. First, the models of successful industrialization—the NICs—reached their present levels of development without resorting to industrial complementation and preferential trading agreements. But the deeper explanation probably lies in their varying endowments of human and physical capital, which affect the level and growth rates of per capita incomes in each country. This existing capacity serves to define the kind of trade that will emerge as a natural market response.

In the near term, as the developing ASEAN economies try to make headway with manufactured exports—whether through labor subcontracting or a more extended integration of production processes—trade liberalization within the region is not likely to occur. Trade will take

---

[13]See, e.g., Pranab K. Bardhan, "Imports, Domestic Production, and Transnational Vertical Integration: A Theoretical Note," *Journal of Political Economy* 90 (October 1982):1020–34.

[14]For a formal treatment of the allocative effects of local content protection, see Gene M. Grossman, "The Theory of Domestic Content Protection and Content Preference," *Quarterly Journal of Economics* (November 1981):583–603.

[15]Bautista, "Industrial Policy," pp. 32–35.

place with the more developed economies. With increasing per capita incomes, intra-ASEAN trade might open up to take advantage of transport cost savings. When this happens, the type of trade currently observed among developed industrial economies might begin to materialize—intraindustry trade with monopolistic competition.[16]

Conclusion

This essay has reviewed industrialization strategies and the emerging policy pattern among the four developing ASEAN economies. (The neglect of Singapore is deliberate, since I have focused on the drive for industrialization by the four countries using the Asian NICs, including Singapore, as models of dynamic economies in transition.) Based on this review, I have attempted to make some conjectures on the probable impact of these policies in promoting greater interdependence.

---

[16]Kelvin Lancaster, ''Intra-Industry Trade Under Monopolistic Competition,'' *Journal of International Economics* 10 (1980):151–75.

6. Economic Policies of the South Asian Countries and Their Impact on the Pacific-Asian Region

GUSTAV F. PAPANEK

Three major developments in South Asia and in the world economy during the last decade are having a considerable impact on South Asia's relations with the international trading system generally and especially with the Pacific-Asian region. They are:

1. For the first time in the forty years since most of the South Asian countries became independent, all are simultaneously trying to shift from an autarkic, inward-looking, import substitution strategy to a more outward-looking strategy that promotes manufactured exports. (South Asia includes India, Bangladesh, Pakistan, Sri Lanka, Nepal, Bhutan, and the Maldives, but this essay is limited to the first four countries, which account for about 99 percent of the region's economic activity.)

2. As a result of technological change in the OECD countries, especially the microelectronics revolution resulting in spreading automation, these countries will find themselves foreclosed from exporting some labor-intensive manufactures that have traditionally provided employment in the early stages of industrial export development. This will increase the pressure on them to move massively into activities that are not being successfully automated. Inevitably they will be competing even more vigorously with other countries in a limited number of industries.

3. While historically South Asia has been a major importer of food-grains, these countries have virtually ceased importing as a group and are likely to become net exporters in the not too distant future.

In analyzing these developments, one must distinguish between changes that have already taken place or are in progress, and those that remain probabilities. More important, these changes need to be analyzed in the context of similar changes taking place elsewhere, especially in other Pacific-Asian countries. That context will be discussed as each of the changes is examined in turn. Finally, the sheer size and potential of these countries need to be kept in mind. South Asia's population is about 1 billion. Some of the larger countries, especially India, have trained personnel—notably engineers and technicians—in numbers matched by only a very few other countries. (India alone is reck-

148

oned by the International Labor Organization [ILO] to have the second largest reservoir of professional, technical and related workers outside the centrally planned economies, eclipsed only by the United States.) In size and economic potential South Asia as a whole is quite comparable to China.

The Shift to an Export-Oriented Strategy

Although there were some exceptions—Pakistan in the 1960s, about which more later—historically South Asia has been *the* major area in the world whose manufactured exports, and nontraditional exports more generally, have remained far below its potential and have declined as a share of world trade. For most of their forty-year history after independence, these countries have pursued an inward-looking strategy. With an overvalued currency, the demand for imports generally far exceeded the availability of foreign exchange. Imports were restricted by import licenses. These were awarded by government (1) on the basis of past imports of a given commodity and by a given firm; (2) in relation to the presumed importance of a given good (more for such necessities as food and cloth, less for luxury goods, or inputs into such goods) and the availability of competing goods produced domestically; and (3) partly on the basis of political pressure, connections, and outright bribery. Producing for the domestic market behind high barriers to imports, which could reach hundreds and even thousands of percent,[1] could be highly profitable. Those able to get import licenses for especially scarce goods, or for the inputs needed to produce them, were virtually assured of phenomenal profits in most cases (e.g., in Pakistan, rates of return of 50–100 percent on industrial investment were not unusual in 1959, and they were even higher for importers).[2]

Exporters of nontraditional goods clearly faced heavy discrimination under such a system. For many years they were exporting at a rate of three to five rupees to the U.S. dollar. Simultaneously, those producing for the domestic market were in a much better position: they were competing with importers who paid 7 to 15 rupees per dollar of imports as a result of the protection provided by import licenses.

The consequences were predictable: South Asian exports declined steadily as a share of world trade, from 1.9 percent in the late 1950s to

---

[1]Gustav F. Papanek and Daniel Schydlowsky, "Shadow Prices: Comparative Advantage and Trade Policy for Bangladesh, Executive Summary," report prepared for the World Bank in 1980 (Boston: Center for Asian Development Studies, Boston University), unpublished.
[2]Gustav F. Papanek, *Pakistan's Development: Social Goals and Private Incentives* (Cambridge, Mass.: Harvard University Press, 1967).

Table 1

Total Exports from South Asia
(in billions of US$ and as % of world exports)

Year	Bangladesh[a]		India		Pakistan		Sri Lanka		South Asia		World
	$	%	$	%	$	%	$	%	$	%	$
1958	n.a.[b]	n.a.	1.2	1.2	0.3	0.3	0.4	0.4	1.9	1.9	100
1960	n.a.[b]	n.a.	1.3	1.1	0.4	0.3	0.4	0.3	2.1	1.7	118
1965	n.a.[b]	n.a.	1.7	1.0	0.5	0.3	0.4	0.2	2.6	1.5	170
1970	n.a.[b]	n.a.	2.0	0.7	0.7	0.3	0.3	0.1	3.1	1.1	286
1975	0.3[b]	0.04	4.4	0.5	1.0	0.1	0.6	0.1	6.3	0.8	812
1977	0.5[b]	0.04	6.4	0.6	1.2	0.1	0.8	0.1	8.7	0.8	1,047
1980	0.7[b]	0.04	8.4	0.4	2.6	0.1	1.0	0.1	12.7	0.7	1,883
1981	0.7[b]	0.04	8.4	0.5	2.9	0.2	1.0	0.1	13.0	0.7	1,851
1982	0.7[b]	0.04	8.8	0.5	2.4	0.1	1.0	0.1	12.9	0.8	1,716
1983	0.7[b]	0.05	8.7	0.5	3.1	0.2	1.1	0.1	13.6	0.8	1,666
1984	0.9[b]	0.06	8.5	0.5	2.6	0.1	1.4	0.1	13.4	0.8	1,763
1985	1.0[b]	0.06	9.9	0.6	2.7	0.2	1.3	0.1	15.0	0.8	1,783
1986	0.9[b]	0.04	9.4	0.5	3.4	0.2	1.2	0.1	14.9	0.7	1,989

[a]Since Bangladesh became independent only in 1971, and before then was East Pakistan, data for that country are included in the figures for Pakistan at least until 1971 in this, and subsequent, tables.
[b]Not available.

SOURCES: United Nations, _Yearbook of International Trade,_ various issues; International Monetary Fund, _International Financial Statistics Yearbook,_ 1986.

less than half that share from the mid-1970s on (see Table 1). With respect to manufactured goods, the decline was equally dramatic. Between 1960 and 1980, world trade in manufactures increased sixteenfold (in current prices), whereas Indian exports increased only sevenfold (see Table 2). The share of India in world trade of manufactured goods declined from 0.85 percent to 0.4 percent. The performances of Pakistan, Bangladesh, and Sri Lanka were stronger. But because of India's weight in the total, South Asia as a whole increased its manufactured exports only nine fold over the same twenty-year period, declining by a striking 50 percent from 0.9 percent to 0.6 percent of world trade.

But the potential of the region can be seen in the periods when policy was designed to encourage exports. In the 1960s, for instance, Pakistan adopted an export subsidy for nontraditional exports. As a result, manufactured exports increased fourfold, while for the world as a whole such exports increased less than threefold, a 15 percent annual growth rate for Pakistan and an 11 percent rate for the world. All four

Table 2

Manufactured Exports from South Asia
(in US$ billions and as % of world manufactured exports)

Year	Bangladesh[a] $	Bangladesh[a] %	India $	India %	Pakistan $	Pakistan %	Sri Lanka $	Sri Lanka %	South Asia $	South Asia %	World $
1958	n.a.[b]	n.a.	0.5	n.a.	n.a.	n.a.	neg.[c]	neg.	n.a.	n.a.	n.a.
1960	n.a.[b]	n.a.	0.6	0.85	0.1[a]	0.1[a]	neg.	neg.	0.7	0.9	70
1965	n.a.[b]	n.a.	0.8	0.75	0.2	0.2	neg.	neg.	1.0	0.9	109
1970	n.a.[b]	n.a.	1.0	0.5	0.4	0.2	neg.	neg.	1.5	0.7	202
1975	0.2[b]	0.03	2.2	0.4	0.6	0.1	0.02	.003	2.9	0.6	519
1977	0.2[b]	0.04	3.4	0.5	0.7	0.1	0.04	.006	4.4	0.7	672
1980	0.5[b]	0.04	4.4	0.4	1.3	0.1	0.17	.01	6.4	0.6	1,144
1981	0.4[b]	0.04	4.0	0.4	1.4	0.1	0.23	.02	6.1	0.5	1,125
1982	0.4[b]	0.04	5.1	0.5	1.4	0.1	0.27	.02	7.2	0.7	1,080
1983	0.5[b]	0.04	5.0	0.5	2.0	0.2	0.30	.03	7.7	0.7	1,088
1984	0.6[b]	n.a.	5.4	n.a.	1.8	n.a.	0.39	n.a.	8.2	n.a.	n.a.
1985	0.7[b]	n.a.	6.0	n.a.	1.3	n.a.	0.42	n.a.	8.0	n.a.	n.a.
1986	n.a.[b]	n.a.	n.a.	n.a.	1.9	n.a.	0.56	n.a.	n.a.	n.a.	n.a.

[a]For Pakistan, 1960 figures are for 1961.
[b]Not available.
[c]Negligible; less than US$0.5 million.

SOURCES: United Nations, *Handbook of International Trade and Development Statistics*, 1983; United Nations, *International Trade Statistical Yearbook*, various issues; International Monetary Fund, *International Financial Statistical Yearbook*, 1986; Indian Ministry of Finance, *Economic Survey*, 1986–87; Bangladesh Bureau of Statistics, *Monthly Statistical Bulletin of Bangladesh*, October 1986.

countries began to push exports in the late 1970s or early 1980s, sometimes with dramatic results. Bangladesh, in part by a rapid devaluation of the currency, achieved a 13 percent rate of growth in manufactured exports in 1977–85 and increased such exports in the 1980s by about 50 percent. The most far-reaching policy changes came in Sri Lanka after 1977, when a sharp devaluation was accompanied by a decline in controls and the encouragement of foreign private investment. A 37 percent per annum rate of growth in manufactured exports was reached by 1984, albeit on a small base, involving small absolute amounts and highly concentrated in garments. But even when the base was larger, the increase in manufactured exports in Sri Lanka was more than threefold in 1980–86. Pakistan nearly tripled its total exports in the period 1977–83. These declined slightly in 1983–85, as booming remittances along with rising aid following the Afghanistan conflict resulted in sharply rising domestic demand. As other sources stagnated, however, another push increased exports again in 1986. Even India achieved a 50 percent increase in the 1980s while world trade in manufactures stagnated. All of South Asia saw a 25 percent increase in manufactures between the average for 1980/81 and that for 1984/85.

Garment exports were the big success story for much of South Asia in the 1980s (see Table 3). Even in the late 1970s, South Asia was a negligible factor in world garment trade, with exports totaling less than US$300 million. In 1987, Indian garment exports alone were expected to reach at least $1.3 billion. Bangladesh was exporting half that, and even small Sri Lanka was exporting about the same amount as all of South Asia a decade earlier. Garment exports had increased about tenfold in a dozen years at current prices.

What is more, the rapid growth in manufactured exports occurred in South Asia during the 1980s, when world trade in manufactures essentially stagnated. That growth was the result of deliberate policy: beginning in the late 1970s, all four deregulated their economies and shifted to an emphasis on promoting exports, especially manufactured exports, by improving their relative prices. While Pakistan (then including the present Bangladesh) had partially adopted such a strategy in the 1960s, that decade had been one of stagnant manufactured exports (in real terms) for both India and Sri Lanka. The late 1970s were the only time in postcolonial history when all four countries moved deliberately towards greater reliance on the market, and especially the world market. The change was least and most hesitant for India, but in terms of Indian history, which had been determinedly inward looking for thirty years, the change was significant.

In the last decade the South Asian countries have also become major exporters of people. Before the sharp decline in oil prices, official and unofficial remittances to Pakistan from those working abroad reached an estimated US$5-6 billion a year and were by far the largest source of foreign exchange. Official remittances to India have also grown rapidly and reached about US$2.5 billion, with smaller but significant amounts to Bangladesh and Sri Lanka.

These countries have, however, only begun to compete in the world market for services. In bidding for contracts—for example, to take responsibility for major construction projects rather than simply supplying labor to contractors—South Asian firms have been handicapped by government controls, just as they have been handicapped in exporting nontraditional goods. They became major suppliers of labor when specific governments changed their policies from controlling to encouraging labor exports (e.g., in Sri Lanka after 1977). If policies were similarly to encourage the organized export of services—as policies in South Korea do, for example—then some of the South Asian countries have

Table 3

Major Manufactured Exports, South Asia

(in millions of US$ and % of total manufactured exports from each country)

	India											
	Clothing		Textiles		Machinery and Transport Equipment		Chemicals		Other Basic Manufactures[a]		Miscellaneous	
Year	$	%	$	%	$	%	$	%	$	%	$	%
1957	n.a.[b]	n.a.	424	70	4	1	12	2	146	24	21	3
1960	2	neg.[c]	465	78	8	1	15	3	87	15	23	4
1965	13	2	581	76	22	3	23	3	140	17	32	4
1970	36	3	461	43	106	10	47	4	355	33	63	6
1975	195	9	600	28	322	15	116	5	802	37	127	6
1977	430	13	882	26	375	11	147	4	1,515	44	100	3
1980	590	13	1,145	26	622	14	315	7	1,417	32	343	8
1981	593	15	1,053	26	613	15	332	8	1,097	27	335	8
1982[d]	466	9	947	19	n.a.	n.a.	386	8	n.a.	n.a.	n.a.	n.a.
1983	542	11	1,226	25	n.a.	n.a.	344	7	n.a.	n.a.	n.a.	n.a.
1984	610	11	1,052	20	n.a.	n.a.	289	5	n.a.	n.a.	n.a.	n.a.
1985	744	13	1,480	27	n.a.	n.a.	391	7	n.a.	n.a.	n.a.	n.a.
1986	768											

[a]Includes such major items as leather, metal manufactures, lumber manufactures, iron and steel, nonferrous metals, paper and paperboard, etc.

[b]Not available.

[c]Negligible.

[d]Figures for 1982–86 were obtained from Indian Ministry of Finance, *Economic Survey*, 1986–87.

SOURCE: United Nations, *Yearbook of International Trade*, various issues.

Table 3 (continued)

Major Manufactured Exports, South Asia
(in millions of US$ and % of total manufactured exports from each country)

Bangladesh

Year	Clothing $	%	Textiles $	%	Machinery and Transport Equipment $	%	Chemicals $	%	Other Basic Manufactures $	%	Miscellaneous $	%
1975	neg.c	neg.	158	88	1	neg.	2	1	18	10	2	1
1976	neg.	neg.	182	82	neg.	neg.	2	1	34	16	2	1
1977	neg.	neg.	187	75	2	1	2	1	58	24	1	neg.
1978	neg.	neg.	274	81	3	1	2	1	59	18	1	neg.
1979	neg.	neg.	326	76	3	1	neg.	neg.	97	23	1	neg.
1980	neg.	neg.	414	83	10	2	10	2	64	13	2	neg.
1981	5	1	366	83	4	1	4	1	63	14	2	1
1982	11	3	306	74	24	6	7	2	62	15	2	neg.
1983	21	4	354	74	19	4	10	2	75	16	2	neg.
1984	77	13	431	72	3	1	1	neg.	87	15	1	neg.
1985a	14	22	392	60	11	2	2	neg.	50	8	1	neg.
1986b	125	25	283	57	2	neg.	5	1	84	17	1	neg.

a1985 figures were obtained from Bangladesh Bureau of Statistics, *Monthly Statistical Bulletin of Bangladesh*, October 1986.
bData for 1986 from Export Promotion Bureau of Bangladesh, *Statement on Monthly Exports*.
cNegligible.

SOURCE: United Nations, *Yearbook of International Trade*, various issues.

Pakistan

1961	neg.c	neg.	91	84	4	3	1	1	7	7	6	6
1965	2	1	151	80	5	2	4	2	17	9	11	6
1970	5	1	320	75	30	7	6	1	38	9	26	6
1975	31	5	378	66	15	3	12	2	75	13	61	11
1977	54	8	457	67	27	4	13	2	70	10	64	10
1980	103	8	876	69	61	5	21	2	126	10	90	7
1981	136	9	976	68	57	4	22	2	143	10	110	7
1982	144	10	929	67	58	4	14	1	144	10	98	7
1983	226	12	1,316	68	35	2	30	2	192	10	131	7
1984	245	14	1,001	57	66	4	60	3	234	14	155	9
1985a	n.a.d	n.a.	866	65	n.a.	n.a.	n.a.	n.a.	n.a.	n.a.	n.a.	n.a.
1986b	245	13	769	41	69	4	57	3	401	21	340	18

a1985 data from *Pakistan Monthly Statistical Bulletin*, March 1987.
b1986 from *Pakistan Economic Survey*, 1987.
cNegligible.
dNot available.

Source: United Nations, *Yearbook of International Trade Statistics*, various issues.

Table 3 (continued)

Major Manufactured Exports, South Asia
(in millions of US$ and % of total manufactured exports from each country)

Sri Lanka

Year	Clothing		Textiles		Machinery and Transport Equipment		Chemicals		Other Basic Manufactures		Miscellaneous	
	$	%	$	%	$	%	$	%	$	%	$	%
1955	neg.[a]	neg.	neg.	neg.	neg.	neg.	2	61	7	19	neg.	2
1960	neg.	neg.	neg.	neg.	neg.	neg.	2	51	2	48	neg.	1
1965	neg.	neg.	neg.	neg.	neg.	neg.	1	37	2	44	1	17
1970	1	27	neg.	neg.	neg.	neg.	1	23	2	40	1	10
1975	3	17	neg.	neg.	neg.	neg.	10	52	5	24	2	8
1977	16	37	neg.	neg.	neg.	neg.	19	43	7	15	2	5
1980	109	64	3	2	7	4	6	3	42	24	4	2
1981	153	67	6	3	27	12	5	2	31	14	6	3
1982	166	62	5	2	21	8	12	4	53	20	10	4
1983	202	67	6	2	15	5	6	2	57	19	13	5
1984	294	75	10	3	21	5	7	2	42	11	19	5
1985	281	54	9	2	17	3	13	2	166	32	36	7
1986	325	58	13	2	24	4	16	3	159	28	19	3

[a]Negligible.

SOURCES: United Nations, *Yearbook of International Trade*, various issues; Central Bank of Sri Lanka, *Annual Report, 1985, 1986*.

South Asia

1961	2	neg.[b]	566	78	12	2	18	3	99	14	26	4
1965	15	2	732	73	27	3	29	3	159	16	43	4
1970	43	3	781	52	135	9	54	4	395	26	88	6
1975	229	8	1,135	39	337	12	140	5	900	31	191	7
1977	500	11	1,526	34	404	9	180	4	1,650	37	166	4
1980	804	13	2,439	38	700	11	351	6	1,649	26	438	7
1981	886	14	2,400	39	701	11	364	6	1,333	22	453	7
1982	787	11	2,187	30	n.a.	n.a.	419	6	n.a.	n.a.	n.a.	n.a.
1983	991	13	2,902	38	n.a.	n.a.	390	5	n.a.	n.a.	n.a.	n.a.
1984	1,224	15	2,494	30	n.a.	n.a.	357	4	n.a.	n.a.	n.a.	n.a.
1985	1,437[a]	18	2,750[a]	35	n.a.	n.a.	n.a.	n.a.	n.a.	n.a.	n.a.	n.a.
1986	1,464	n.a.[c]	n.a.	n.a.	n.a.	n.a.	n.a.	n.a.	n.a.	n.a.	n.a.	n.a.

[a]Estimated.
[b]Negligible.
[c]Not available.

SOURCES: Compiled from data in United Nations, *Yearbook of International Trade*, various issues; Indian Ministry of Finance, *Economic Survey, 1986–87*; Bangladesh Bureau of Statistics, *Monthly Statistical Bulletin of Bangladesh*, October 1986; Export Promotion Bureau of Bangladesh, *Statement on Monthly Exports*; *Pakistan Monthly Statistical Bulletin*, March 1987; *Pakistan Economic Survey*, 1987; Central Bank of Sri Lanka, *Annual Report*, 1985, 1986.

sufficiently experienced management organizations to become serious competitors in the services field as well. They also have such a large number of very low-cost high school and college graduates, and of skilled technicians in such fields as computer programming, that they have considerable potential as major exporters of such services as data entry, programming and software development, and some aspects of design. To some degree, that potential is already being realized in the 1980s, especially in India.

In short, when the countries of South Asia adopted appropriate policies, primarily more favorable prices, and less onerous regulations, they were able to achieve growth rates of 10–15 percent per annum in manufactured exports, even when world trade in such goods was essentially stagnant, and even more impressive growth in the export of people.

If higher prices in domestic currency had been accompanied by other steps to facilitate and encourage exports, an even higher export growth rate could have been achieved. All of the countries continued to maintain a very cumbersome system of direct controls over investors and a distorted system of prices. With a more thoroughgoing decontrol, combined with more deliberate government support and intervention to help exporters—as in East Asia—these countries clearly are major potential exporters of manufactured goods.

On the other hand, the fragile and preliminary nature of the policy changes so far adopted, especially in India, needs to be emphasized. It is obvious that a protectionist regime that fosters import substitution builds up powerful vested interests in government, politics, and business who strongly resist losing the power and income this strategy has conferred on them. And when such a regime has been followed unremittingly for thirty years, changes are difficult to bring about, especially in a democracy.

Continued reform will be especially difficult because the short-term benefits may prove disappointing. All four countries are near or at their garment and textile quotas in their major markets. Those exports that registered the fastest growth (see Table 3) are therefore likely to expand more slowly in the future. Continued rapid growth in some other lines may also encounter rising protection. But the main problem is likely to be stagnant or slowly growing world trade, combined with the increasingly effective automation of some previously labor-intensive industries in the OECD countries (see later).

In addition, a truly rapid expansion of manufactured exports would doubtless also require a solid underpinning in terms of an efficient infrastructure, and access to technology and marketing knowledge. But the history of rapid expansion of manufactured exports in South Asia

Table 4

Manufactured Exports for Some Countries with Rapid Increases
(in billions of US$ and as a % of world manufactured exports)

Year	Korea $	Korea %	Hong Kong $	Hong Kong %	Brazil $	Brazil %	Thailand $	Thailand %	ASEAN $	ASEAN %
1955	n.a.[a]	n.a.	0.3	0.7	n.a.	n.a.	0.01	0.01	n.a.	n.a.
1958	neg.[b]	neg.	0.4	n.a.	0.02	n.a.	neg.	neg.	n.a.	n.a.
1960	neg.	neg.	0.6	0.8	0.10	neg.	0.01	0.01	n.a.	n.a.
1965	0.1	0.1	1.0	0.9	0.10	0.1	0.03	0.03	n.a.	n.a.
1970	0.7	0.3	2.3	1.2	0.40	0.2	0.10	0.06	1.1	0.6
1975	4.1	0.8	5.6	1.1	2.20	0.4	0.45	0.09	4.3	0.8
1977	8.6	1.3	9.0	1.3	3.10	0.5	0.80	0.12	6.9	1.0
1980	15.8	1.4	18.1	1.6	7.60	0.7	2.30	0.20	17.6	1.5
1981	19.2	1.7	20.1	1.8	9.20	0.8	2.20	0.20	17.5	1.6
1982	20.0	1.9	19.3	1.8	7.80	0.7	2.20	0.21	17.4	1.6
1983	22.3	2.1	20.1	1.9	9.20	0.8	2.20	0.20	17.2	n.a.
1984	26.8	n.a.	26.1	n.a.	n.a.	n.a.	2.70	n.a.	n.a.	n.a.
1985	n.a.	n.a.	n.a.	n.a.	n.a.	n.a.	2.80	n.a.	n.a.	n.a.
1987	46.2[c]									

[a]Not available.
[b]Negligible; less than US$5 million.
[c]Total exports according to newspaper reports; almost all manufactures.

SOURCES: United Nations, *Handbook of International Trade and Development Statistics*, 1983; International Monetary Fund, *International Financial Statistical Yearbook*, 1986; Bank of Thailand, *Quarterly Bulletin* 26(2) (June 1986); Singapore Department of Statistics, *Monthly Digest of Statistics*, February 1987.

during some periods, and in East Asia for twenty-five years, suggests that these are not insurmountable obstacles if governments are determined to expand exports. When trade policy changed, even Bangladesh, whose infrastructure has always been exceedingly weak and which suffered extensive destruction in the early 1970s from war (and from floods intermittently thereafter), was able to expand industrial exports by more than 10 percent annually. In South Asia, India is at the other extreme in this respect: it had a strong physical and institutional infrastructure even at the time of Independence.

If South Asian countries manage to overcome the obstacles to further changes in policy, as East Asia and some other countries have, then they would rapidly become major participants in the world trade for some industrial products. The scope for further expansion can be seen from the magnitude of manufactured exports by other countries and the speed with which they grew (see Table 4). Note that South Asia, with a billion people, has manufactured exports of less than a third those of

South Korea or Hong Kong that have a tiny fraction of its population. Indeed, South Asia's *total* manufactured exports in 1985 were less than the *increase* in South Korean exports in 1987. The potential of South Asia, even if manufactured exports never approached East Asia's on a per capita basis, is therefore enormous. That all South Asian countries will change their policies to achieve that potential is unlikely. That none will is equally unlikely. Given the size of three of the South Asian economies and their low labor costs, even one would be a formidable competitor in some labor-intensive industries.

Automation and the Concentration of Exports

Moreover, as Table 3 makes clear and as one might expect, industrial exports are highly concentrated. Textiles and clothing are nearly 90 percent of Bangladesh's total manufactured exports, nearly 80 percent for Sri Lanka's, and usually about 40 percent even for highly diversified India. These figures epitomize the labor-intensive sector of industry, and South Asia is *the* major world region (with the possible exception of China) possessing abundant, low-cost labor. It has tens of millions of unskilled workers available to industry at a dollar per day (or less, in some cases). The only other major known supply of labor at comparable cost is on the island of Java. Wage costs in some parts of China may be also comparable, but apparently are higher. South Asia's competitive (and comparative) advantage inevitably therefore is, and will remain, in labor-intensive industries.

But for some of the traditionally labor-intensive industries, the lowest-cost methods of production are changing, at least in part, to a far more capital-intensive technology. Garments are the best example. With current tariffs in place, and ignoring the effect of quotas, it is already cheaper to carry out some stages of garment production in the United States with automated equipment that is now available than in a country with wages of US$1–1.50 a day.[3] The country for which the analysis was carried out happens to be Indonesia, not one of the South Asian countries, but the conclusions can readily be applied to them as well. Indeed, for all six garments studied in detail (e.g., standard men's dress shirts, women's high-quality dresses and skirts), the lowest-cost option was to combine U.S. robotic techniques for some stages in the production process—fabric preparation and other presewing steps—with other

---

[3] Ashoka Mody and David Wheeler, "Towards a Vanishing Middle: Competition in the World Garment Industry," Discussion Paper No. 34 (Boston: Center for Asian Development Studies, Boston University, 1986).

stages (generally sewing) in low labor cost countries, either Indonesia or the Caribbean.

Two other points need to be noted about this study: (1) the shift from semiautomatic processes to fully automated reduces U.S. costs by 25 percent to 50 percent (depending on the product), and (2) the lowest-cost production partnerships involve a production process of 35–95 days (depending on whether the partner for the United States is Jamaica or Indonesia) as against ten days for integrated production in the United States. In short, as the cost of automated production declines with the development of better machinery, and as the importance of quick delivery increases because of more rapid changes in fashion, some of the activities in which low-wage countries are now competitive will move back to automated factories in the OECD countries. (The closure of a Fairchild electronics plant in Indonesia and the shift of some of its activities to the state of Maine in the United States is a small example of this trend.)

The same study also shows that even in a low labor cost country like Indonesia the lowest-cost method of production will be semiautomated in the near future. That technology will reduce the requirement for unskilled labor by half while slightly increasing the number of skilled, professional, and technical people required. Note that contrary to the belief of advocates of "appropriate technology," the study shows that, at least in some previously labor-intensive fields, the lowest-cost technology—the only one that is competitive in world markets—is less labor intensive than the currently used method of production. No doubt there are some activities where new technology is labor using rather than labor saving, but this study of six major industries did not encounter such a case.

Finally, there is evidence that learning curves, technological change, and taste changes have all accelerated, in part as the result of more rapid and cheaper communications. An extreme example is microchips. Costs for a new generation have been found to drop from about 18 U.S. cents to a fraction of a cent in the course of only two years, largely as the result of learning by doing. By that time, technological development means that a new generation of chips is ready to take over the market. Any firm that trails six months or more behind the leader is likely to lose money. Although other products may not show such extremely short learning curves and rapid technological change, the phenomenon is widespread.

Moreover, in such industries as garments there are rapid changes in tastes or fashions with respect to many products. This is due in part to the greater proportion of income now devoted to discretionary purchases than in the past. For such goods, whose utility and durability is of less importance, fashion and changes in fashion are more important. Forty years ago, only a small number of consumers could afford to discard perfectly serviceable goods simply because fashion changed or because some minor improvements had become available. Now such discretionary purchases are commonplace for hundreds of millions of consumers. The result is to put a high premium on the ability to respond quickly and flexibly, to be near markets and near the sources of technology, and to move into new lines and activities as early as possible.

The exact numbers produced by the study are obviously subject to error and to change as production processes evolve and as new equipment is developed, and the changes described will differ among industries and activities, but the major conclusions have been confirmed by analysis of several other industries and countries (the industries also include textiles, automobile parts, consumer electronics, and microchips; the countries include Japan, South Korea, the Philippines, and India). For the purposes of this chapter, the most relevant conclusions are:

1. The low-wage countries will no longer be the low-cost producers for at least some manufactured exports and at least some stages in the production of other goods, several of which have been a mainstay of early, outward-looking industrialization. These activities will gradually move back to the OECD countries. South Asia, just moving into such activities and with its principal advantage a large pool of low-cost labor, will be particularly hard hit by this development.

2. Location will become a crucial consideration for those goods in which some stages in the production process can be automated at low cost; for other stages, labor-intensive technology will remain the lowest-cost option. The closer the physical proximity between the country carrying out the automated stage and the country producing the labor-intensive stage, the easier, cheaper, and less time consuming the whole production process will be. South Asia is obviously poorly situated in that respect, further away from the United States, Japan, and the European Economic Community than other countries with low labor costs.

3. Labor-abundant countries will also find it increasingly difficult to generate productive employment for their large labor force because of the spread of semiautomated production processes even to activities that remain relatively labor intensive. This will force them to expand very rapidly in lines where productive jobs can still be generated and to sell large quantities in the world market, at the best prices they can obtain. The South Asian countries with the largest underemployed labor pool, with the possible exception of China, will again be most affected.

4. The speed of change will increase the pressure for decentralization of decisions, which means greater reliance on the market. Any country that wants to remain competitive in the world market, important in reaping the benefits of comparative advantage in order to achieve rapid growth, will therefore have to rely heavily on market forces and incentives. South Asia will have much further to go than most Pacific nations, except for China and the Indochinese countries, in achieving needed flexibility. It is therefore quite likely that only some of the South Asian countries will make the rather far-reaching policy adjustments that will prove to be necessary for continued expansion of manufactured exports.

As a consequence of the rapid technological changes sketched here, it is very likely that those South Asian countries that decide to fully participate in the race will become fierce competitors in a limited range of industrial activities. For instance, in garments they are likely to concentrate in the production of medium fashion items, with short production runs, and within that process in the sewing operation specifically. The labor-abundant countries are already no longer competitive in some garments that are produced in large quantities, with little change due to fashion (some men's trousers), because these lines are being successfully automated, and they cannot compete in genuinely high-fashion items because they are too far from designers and customers.

South Asian countries that develop economies sufficiently open and flexible to be competitive in the world market may also attract industries producing items that require relatively short production runs—some measuring and testing equipment, for instance—or that require much hand labor—some automobile wiring. Goods that have both short production runs and manual labor are likely to concentrate in the region if their transportation costs are not too high. Finally, South Asian countries, and especially India, should be able to compete in industries that require large numbers of technical and professional personnel but relatively little capital, such as software development, data entry, and other information processing that cannot be automated; some design work; and some metalworking.

But note that while some South Asian countries, most notably India, are so well supplied with low-cost skilled and professional personnel that they can compete on the world market in some high-tech fields where other less developed countries have little chance, this is unlikely to diminish significantly their need to push aggressively into activities that principally employ unskilled labor. For example, the study previously cited suggests that India could be competitive in the production of microchips in highly automated factories. The employment created for unskilled workers in these activities, however, will generally be quite small, even if one takes into account indirect effects. But India needs to provide productive employment for several tens of millions of unskilled workers, as well as for hundreds of thousands of technically and professionally trained ones. The unskilled can be employed only if industries that are labor intensive in the traditional sense are also developed. And if India does not create productive jobs for them, the social and political tensions from which the country suffers are likely to become unbearable before long.

South Asia's future competitive position obviously also depends a great deal on the policies China ultimately adopts with respect to industrial exports. At the moment it clearly lags behind South Asia in creating conditions to compete effectively in the world market for many manufactured goods. But it has a system ideally suited for subsidizing nontraditional exports and can price labor at levels needed to be competitive in the world market for labor intensive goods. China's highly centralized and authoritarian decision-making process also facilitates a quick and radical change in policy compared to a country like India, where interest groups can more effectively influence decisions through a more decentralized and democratic process. Given these advantages, China could become a formidable rival to South Asia in labor-intensive exports if it overcomes ideological and vested interest group opposition to radical change.

Among the five populous countries—China, India, Bangladesh, Pakistan, and the labor-abundant parts of Indonesia—there will almost certainly be some whose governments will move effectively to take advantage of their factor endowment, that is, their low-cost labor. They will then become major exporters in the increasingly narrow range of goods where low costs of unskilled labor are a decisive advantage. The countries whose wages have always been high, such as the United States and Japan, or have become relatively high, such as South Korea, Singapore, and Malaysia, need to plan now to adjust to this probable development.

Approaching Self-Sufficiency in Foodgrains

The third new development is the rapid expansion of foodgrain production in South Asia. That region, unlike a number of African countries for a number of years, has rarely featured in headlines or the television news as an area of outright starvation in the postwar world. Indeed, with the exception of Bangladesh in 1974, one of the great achievements of governments in the region has been the avoidance of famines since the great Bengal famine in the 1940s.

But the region has traditionally been both hungry and foodshort. By virtue of its size—sub-Saharan Africa has a population of about 400 million; South Asia, nearly 1 billion—South Asia has been an important importer of foodgrains, taking more than 10 percent of total world imports in the mid-1960s. More important, its net foodgrain imports grew at almost 10 percent a year in real terms from 1959 to 1967 (see Table 5), doubling every eight years and threatening the development of import needs that would prove difficult to satisfy in another decade or two.[4]

Extrapolating the needs of South Asia was a major factor in predictions some twenty-five years ago that the world faced widespread famine in the near future, with the United States in position to decide the literally life-and-death issue of who would survive and who would not under a global triage process. Looked at from the perspective of foodgrain exporters, these countries promised to provide a large market for the exports of the United States, Australia, and Thailand and for the surpluses of the EEC and Japan, as long as means could be found of financing their imports.

Indonesia was not a major factor at the time in the world food market because it simply did not have the foreign exchange, or the generous donors, to finance large-scale imports. It was then in desperate economic straits and its recorded foodgrain imports were smaller than those of Sri Lanka, although its people needed additional food far more.

The dire predictions about South Asia's food needs did not materialize. By the late 1960s, the Green Revolution was beginning to take hold in South Asia. As a result, the region has confounded the pessimists and by 1980 net foodgrain imports in real terms had shrunk to one-quarter of what they had been some thirteen years earlier. In the late 1970s, the pessimists—in terms of the world food situation, though to some of the food exporters they sounded more like optimists—again predicted that the Green Revolution was running out of steam. They also pointed out that increased food imports by Indonesia were partly replacing declining needs in South Asia. Net recorded imports for Indonesia rose by nearly 10 percent a year from 1967 to 1980, as rising demand outraced rapidly increasing production. But even combining South Asia and Indonesia, by 1980 net imports were only half of what they had been earlier.

---

[4]Agricultural output, of course, fluctuates sharply from year to year and trade, as a residual, tends to fluctuate even more. Therefore all the data used here are synthetic figures. They are the estimated trade, based on regression analysis that smoothes out these fluctuations. They are also at constant 1985 prices, so that they are the equivalent of physical quantities and the conclusions are not affected by price change.

Table 5

Cereals Trade, South Asia and Indonesia
(estimated data)[a]

Country	Millions of US$ in Constant (1985) Prices				Annual Growth Rate (%)	
	1959	1967	1980	1985	1959–67	1967–85
India						
Imports	605	1,556	413	170	12.5	–11.6
Exports	–0.2	1.8	113	156	neg.[b]	28.5
Balance	–603	–1,554	–300	–14	12.6	–23.1
Pakistan and Bangladesh						
Imports	216	306	370	365	1.7	1.0
Exports	25	74	295	383	14.5	9.6
Balance	–191	–233	–76	18	2.5	–8.3[c]
Sri Lanka						
Imports	150	198	159	135	3.5	–2.1
Exports	0.8	0	0.8	0.9	neg.	neg.
Balance	–149	–198	–158	–134	3.6	–2.2
Total South Asia						
Imports	971	2,060	942	669	9.9	–6.0
Exports	26	75	409	540	14.2	11.6
Balance	–945	–1,985	–533	–129	9.7	–14.1

					Annual Growth Rate (%)		
					1959–67	1965–80	1976–85
Indonesia							
Imports	296	136	553	334	–9.3	11.6	–7.5
Exports	0	6	7	28	Inf.	–11.4	
Balance	–296	–130	–546	–306	–9.8	12.3	–8.4

[a]With one exception, the trade balance for all countries has always been negative. A positive growth rate therefore implies a worsening in the negative balance and increased imports. A negative growth rate implies a decline in imports.
[b]Negligible.
[c]Annual growth rate 1967–80.

SOURCE: Figures were estimated by using regression technique based on data from *FAO Trade Yearbook*, various issues.

The 1980s proved the pessimists wrong again. Net imports into South Asia continued to decline as output increased rapidly. By the middle of the decade the region was virtually self-sufficient, for net imports declined an average of nearly 10 percent a year in real terms in

1967–85. All major countries shared in the improvement. Because of its size, the improvement in India was the most important. In 1985 prices, imports declined from US$1.5 billion in 1967 to nothing in 1985. Pakistan, which was barely self-sufficient in the early 1970s, exported (net) an average of US$300 million in the 1980s. Bangladesh, whose net imports had been US$400 million in the mid-1970s, declined to less than US$100 million a decade later.

Moreover, by the end of the 1970s the situation in Indonesia had also begun to turn around. Net imports declined at over 8 percent annually to the mid-1980s. At one time the largest importer of rice in the world, a decade later Indonesia witnessed its officials talking of self-sufficiency and worrying about the possibility of a high-priced surplus.

For the exporting countries—Thailand, the United States, Canada, Australia, and even Japan—the improvement in these countries' situation naturally presented some problems. Real prices declined and the expected serious world deficit turned into a glut, in some part because of the changed situation in India and, to a lesser extent, Pakistan and Indonesia.

Moreover, the prospects for the exporters are not promising. Some agricultural technicians argue that with current technology Pakistan could become a major exporter of foodgrains at competitive prices, rivaling countries like Argentina and Australia, and second only to the United States. Yields in most Indian states are far below those in the most successful areas. Bangladesh has one of the best agroclimatic conditions for rice growing in the world and has by no means fully developed its potential. Its yields should be among the highest in the world and are among the lowest. *If* these three countries continue to pursue appropriate policies, their expansion of foodgrain production could continue. And the history of the last twenty years has been that all three are quite capable of carrying out such policies. Though substantial—in some cases, radical—changes in policies are needed for manufactured exports from South Asia to grow rapidly, relatively smaller changes will be enough to keep agricultural output growing. Considerable potential also exists in Indonesia, especially with respect to crops other than rice.

At present growth rates of per capita income and agricultural outputs, the South Asian countries (and Indonesia) should not again become major importers. Indirectly they will therefore contribute to the world glut in foodgrains and consequent pressure on prices. But it must also be remembered that there are tens of millions—indeed, several hundred million people—in South Asia who are underfed and even larger numbers who are poorly nourished. Their consumption is restricted by low, and slowly rising, incomes. Therefore the grain balance could change radically if the commitment to more effective economic policies were to persist despite short-term political costs at home and rising protectionism abroad, and per capita income grew not at the 1–2 percent traditional for most of South Asia much of the time, but at the 3–4 percent that Pakistan achieved during two periods.

With higher incomes, grain consumption would sharply increase. To bring Indian and Bangladesh caloric levels to those of Sri Lanka would require roughly a 10 percent and 25 percent increase in consumption. More important would be a shift to greater consumption of animal products with rising incomes, requiring far greater amounts of grains for livestock feed. What happened in Indonesia is an indication of what would happen in South Asia. Although agricultural output grew at the very respectable rate of nearly 5 percent a year between 1965 and 1973, substantially above the rate for South Asia, Indonesia imported about 2 million tons of cereals a year in the mid-1970s because demand grew even more rapidly. In short, the impact of South Asia on world trade in cereals depends very much on the region's per capita growth rate: it could either become a net exporter, contributing to world glut and the policy problems of the OECD countries and the major exporters like Thailand, or it could return to the ranks of net importers as a region.

The poor worldwide harvests due to unusually bad climatic conditions have not changed the long-term relative position of South Asia. The drought in the United States and the floods in Bangladesh, the most severe of the climatic effects, were both unprecedented and are unlikely to change the basic trends.

The discussion so far has ignored other agricultural products because the impact of South Asia on the rest of the world is far more important with respect to grains than other agricultural products. But output of fruits, vegetables, and cotton, among others, is also growing in the area, and the potential for increased output of tea and a few other tree crops is considerable. Again, how rapidly output increases depends very much on whether some trends in policy reforms are continued. The extent to which greater production spills into the world market depends very much on domestic demand determined by per capita income growth.

The Future

Not surprisingly, future economic relations between South Asia and the rest of the Pacific region depend very much on a complex interaction between the policies adopted in South Asia and in the rest of the world. It is possible to sketch either a vicious or a beneficent cycle, with substantial effects on the Pacific-Asia region, or various alternatives in between. Before examining these alternatives, however, it is necessary to deal with the possibility that the dominant trend will be intraregional trade, with little impact on the rest of the world.

The Potential for Intraregional Trade

That trade within the South Asia region has a very great potential has long been argued by some in all these countries. They have seen intraregional trade as providing an alternative to competing on the world market, which is viewed as increasingly protectionist.

Indeed, there are some important and obvious complementarities within the region that could be exploited. India's more developed industrial sector could become a major supplier of capital goods, some consumer durables (automobiles), chemicals, and metal products to the other countries in the region. It also is a potential exporter of iron ore and coking coal, essentially missing elsewhere. Bangladesh can produce raw jute more cheaply than India and could become a major supplier to that country, just as it now supplies Pakistan. It could also supply natural gas to its neighbor, either in its raw form, or as such chemicals as fertilizer. Sri Lanka is the largest and cheapest producer of several tree crops in the region. Pakistan is the logical exporter of cotton, wheat, and other crops to Bangladesh and Sri Lanka. In the industrial field, complementarity in production and trade would permit economies of scale that could help all countries.

Some of the intraregional trade potential is now being exploited. The South Asian Association for Regional Cooperation (SAARC) set up to develop this possibility further, has had only very limited success, and actual trade is a fraction of its potential. This is likely to continue. The first and obvious problem is political. India, the dominant political influence in the region, has been in conflict with all of its neighbors in South Asia at one time or another. As a result, the other countries are leery of much closer trade relationships, which India is likely to dominate.

Economic factors also mitigate against greater regional trade. The most important is that in many activities, especially in manufacturing, the economies are essentially competitive, not complementary. All four of the major South Asian economies need, and want, to export labor-intensive goods, especially those intensive in relatively unskilled labor. Their natural trading partners in this endeavor are the OECD countries having high wages; to an increasing extent, the East Asian and other NICs, whose wages have been rising rapidly; and those natural-resource exporting countries with high labor costs (especially the West Asian economies).

The three non-Indian countries also want to increase the skill mix of their industrial sector. They aspire to produce many of the more technologically complex goods that India is now producing. This is partly for nationalist reasons, partly to provide employment and keep their more highly trained personnel at home, partly because only through learning-by-doing can they reach the levels of industrial development to which they aspire. They are therefore reluctant, or unwilling, to enter into a trading relationship that will slow, or even foreclose, their own production of some capital goods, intermediates, and consumer durables that India now produces more cheaply. In upgrading their technology, gaining access to world markets, and attracting outside capital, it is again the OECD countries, the NICs, and the capital-rich West Asian economies who are seen as the natural partners of the non-Indian South Asian countries. India, even more than the other three, seeks the cooperation of the OECD countries—to the extent that its political, technical, or business leaders think they need to cooperate with anyone—in gaining access to technology and markets.

There is no doubt that all of the South Asian countries could be economically better off, especially in the short term, by far greater economic cooperation than now exists. Even if their resource endowment leads all the South Asian countries to emphasize similar labor-intensive industries, the existence of economies of scale would justify major efforts over the next ten to thirty years to reach agreement on specialization: one country to assemble automobiles for the region, others to produce various parts; one to produce TV tubes, another textile machinery, a third specific chemicals or steel. But even ASEAN, set up more than a decade ago to promote such economic cooperation and composed of countries that have not recently been involved in violent conflict, has had quite limited (economically negligible) results in evolving such complementary development. It is therefore not surprising that South Asia, whose two largest economies have been involved in three wars and have come close to armed conflict several more times, is not even attempting an ambitious program of complementary economic development.

At least for the next decade, one can predict with a good deal of confidence that these countries will look outside the region for their principal trade partners. Increasing trade within the region is unlikely to be a major element in the future economic scenario. How extraregional economic relationships will evolve, with the world market in general and the Pacific-Asian region in particular, is far more difficult to predict.

A Pessimistic Scenario

The most pessimistic scenario for South Asia's economic future runs something like this:

1. The OECD countries, and especially the United States and Japan, automate rapidly, thereby sharply reducing costs in some of the activities that have traditionally been labor intensive. Their imports of these labor-intensive goods drop or rise much more slowly than in the 1960–80 period.

2. This effect is aggravated by rising protectionism and reciprocal concessions excluding the less developed countries, since the OECD countries are under increasing pressure to deal with levels of unemployment that have remained at unprecedented levels for a nondepression period.

3. The NICs in East Asia (and in Latin America, facing unprecedented debt burdens) determine to maintain their markets: they take full advantage of their historical quotas and their position as major trading partners of the OECD countries as well as their ability to subsidize their exports through both hidden direct subsidies and an undervalued currency. They remain the major suppliers of goods that are not successfully automated (fashion garments) and capture an increasing share of those that are only partially automated (automobile parts and assembly).

4. China becomes a major exporter of labor-intensive goods, relying both on subsidies its system makes easy to hide (losses on public enterprises, cheap inputs for exporters) and on its bargaining power as a major potential market whose imports are directly controlled by government.

5. As a result, the South Asian countries find that their shift to a more open, export-oriented policy is costing more and gaining them less than they expected. For these countries to compete, their exports have to be sold at very low prices, if they can be sold at all, given trade barriers, lower costs in the major OECD markets, and competition from the NICs. As the economic costs of "liberalization" rise, so do political costs. South Asia again turns inward. In India this trend is accelerated by the vindication of the Gandhians, the communists, and the populist nationalists, who have always argued that the world market is unreliable and implies an exploitative relationship and that a lower growth rate with self-reliance is a preferable strategy. South Asia's growth, constrained by the traditional foreign exchange problem, slows to a rate of 3–4 percent per annum.

The net result for other countries in the trading system, and especially in the Pacific-Asian region, is that South Asia remains a minor market for capital and high-technology goods. Indeed, its imports decline as its agricultural output increases and as it moves into new areas of import substitution behind higher and rising trade barriers.

The Optimistic Scenario

The opposite scenario is one in which South Asia grows at a rate comparable to that of Southeast Asia (ASEAN) or even approaching the rates of East Asia—that is, at an annual rate of 4–7 percent per capita, 7–9 percent in absolute income. There are two reasons for skepticism about this outcome: (1) There has been a history of per capita growth rates of less than one-quarter that figure, which has persisted for about thirty years for the largest and best endowed among them, India. One can justifiably question why much higher rates should suddenly be possible. (2) Given the size of the countries involved, how can the world market absorb the resulting exports, especially since they are likely to be highly concentrated in a few industries? To make a simpleminded comparison: for South Asia to employ the same proportion of its population in exports as South Korea, it would need to export nearly US$800 billion of goods and services, assuming a similar economic structure, compared with total exports of about US$400 billion from *all* low and middle income countries in 1984. On the same assumptions, nearly US$200 billion of South Asia's exports would be in the form of textiles and clothing, compared with less than US$40 billion from all low- and middle-income countries at present. These seem fairly impossible magnitudes.

But the situation is by no means this bleak. First, with respect to the growth rate: both Pakistan (in the 1960s) and Sri Lanka (1977–83) achieved *per capita* growth rates of 4 percent with just modest improvements in the policy regimes and in capital inflows. India's potential is, in fact, quite awesome among low-income countries in terms of trained personnel; a strong industrial base; experienced entrepreneurs, managers, and civil servants; and an extensive infrastructure. Several of these countries have a very low-cost labor force, not only in unskilled labor, but also in engineers, technicians, and professionals of various kinds. (A well-trained engineer in India costs less than one-quarter his South Korean counterpart.) With essentially minor changes in policy, India raised its per capita growth rate in the 1980s to 3 percent from the traditional 1.5 percent. What needs to be done is reasonably clear to most economists. With significant policy reform, a per capita growth rate of 4–5 percent should not be too difficult to achieve.

Second, there is no reason that these countries would need to achieve export rates, much less manufactured export rates, comparable to those of South Korea. Their internal market is much greater than South Korea's was at comparable stages of development. They have a far better agricultural base and India a much better minerals endowment, further increasing the potential for internal sales of manufactured goods and for the export of primary products. Moreover, their present exports are so low that there is scope for considerable increase before their levels would be such as to create real economic problems of absorption. After all, even India, by far the largest among them, has exports only half those of China or Brazil. Both these countries have expanded exports at nearly 10 percent a year in the recent past. India could achieve the same growth for seven years and only reach the magnitudes of current Brazilian or Chinese exports.

There are further reasons for optimism. China achieved high rates of growth with moderate economic change. Yet compared to China, South Asia would be far easier to integrate into the world trading system. The knowledge of English is widespread, as is the knowledge of Western markets and technology. All the South Asian countries have a large group of expatriates who have become highly successful entrepreneurs in other countries. They are thoroughly familiar with practices abroad. Even though South Asian economies suffer from severe distortions in the price and allocation system, they are mixed economies with prices that bear some relationship to world prices for most goods and factors of production. China is moving in that direction, but has very far to go before it reaches South Asia's current position in the use of market forces in industry and trade.

But the main reason for optimism, and the major point of this speculative discussion, is to sketch the consequences of rapid growth in South Asia for the whole Pacific area. If South Asia, with its 1 billion people, were to grow rapidly, with relatively open economies, the impact on trade and growth throughout the Pacific region would be considerable. South Asian exports would expand rapidly, but so would its imports. India, even more than China, has the potential of becoming the most important supplier of goods that are intensive in both skilled and unskilled labor, including not only textiles and clothing, but also some metal products, machinery, and vehicles.

A rapidly growing South Asia would become a major supplier of labor-intensive and some skill-intensive goods, a major importer of capitals and research-intensive goods. The East Asian NICs became major actors in world trade in fifteen to twenty years, although their combined population is less than that of Pakistan. Within ten years South Asia could be as important as they are now, if it achieved a growth rate well within its grasp by adopting a reform package whose economic dimensions are clear, even if its political feasibility remains murky.

If one or two of the three large South Asian countries manage to carry out thoroughgoing policy reform, they will be formidable competitors in some exports, but at the same time they will provide a rapidly growing market for other goods and services. That India, Pakistan, or

Bangladesh could pose a competitive threat to East Asia or the United States may seem farfetched now. But in the early 1950s most economists saw India as the most promising of the less developed countries and considered the economic prospects of South Korea, Taiwan, Hong Kong, and Singapore to be dim. Now the perceptions are reversed. But the potential remains. The other countries in South Asia do not have India's depth of trained people, developed industrial base, or strong institutional infrastructure, but several have carried policy reform further and they have other assets. That all of South Asia will achieve rapid economic growth is unlikely, but it is equally unlikely that none of the countries will do so.

7. Joint Ventures and Multinational Activities in the Pacific Region

SUEO SEKIGUCHI

Economic interdependence in the Pacific region has increased not only through expanded trade in goods but also through growing investment, which aims at the operation of joint ventures and foreign subsidiaries. Direct foreign investment is a typical form of corporate penetration across national borders. On one hand, direct foreign investment contributes to the industrialization of a host developing country, through transfer of technology as well as through injection of capital. On the other hand, direct foreign investment may enhance the economic dependence of LDCs on investing countries, as some argue, and may hurt the host government's autonomy of policy making as well as decision making of businesses in LDCs. This is because a subsidiary of a multinational corporation is naturally subject to division of labor within the parent company's global strategy.

Some more complicated aspects of interdependence can be cited: A multinational corporation often constructs production bases to supply parts and components for the head office, which reduces the cost of the final products, but protectionist pressures emerge from domestic producers who seek to compete with these overseas bases, demanding import restrictions that conflict with the multinational corporation's interests. A product labelled "made in a LDC" is in reality often made by a company of the importing nation.

Before examining this subject, it seems useful to clarify several concepts I will use in this essay. First, *direct foreign investment* means international reallocation of managerial resources, which consist of technology of production, marketing, and management. Regardless of the percentage of ownership, we define it as direct foreign investment if the investor participates in management, including 100 percent controlled subsidiaries and joint ventures. The game is played by three major actors: multinational corporations, host governments, and governments of investing countries. Obviously, depending on the matter at issue, other actors participate, including joint ventures partners, workers employed by a multinational corporation, and so on.

Next, *Pacific region* refers to nations located on the Pacific coast of the two American continents as well as Oceania and East Asia (which consists of Southeast and Northeast Asia). A convenient concept of the Pacific region is that adopted by the Pacific Economic Cooperation Conference (PECC) in 1980, though some nations are still excluded from membership despite the fact that they are located in the region.[1] When I refer to *Asia*, I include the countries west of Thailand, including Thailand itself. The USSR, Vietnam, and North Korea will not be discussed here because information is limited, even though these countries recently declared that they would invite direct foreign investment.

The time horizon I cover spans the decades from the 1950s to the 1980s. The focus however, is on recent years, when new trends in direct foreign investment emerged. Direct foreign investment has been diversified as an increasing number of countries started investing abroad, whereas in the 1950s the investor was almost solely the United States.

A multinational corporation tries to maximize long-run profit by operating factories in various host countries as well as in its home country. It is assumed that the government concerned seeks to maximize its national economic welfare, and the policies adopted toward multinational corporations or their subsidiaries are usually taken from this standpoint. Obviously, such policies also affect the welfare of the other countries, similar to the trade policies of a large country. What is unique with direct foreign investment is that these policies directly influence employment and other critical economic variables. The issues become more specific than trade policies because some of a multinational corporation's overseas activities contradict the interests of other domestic producers and workers in the same field whereas trade policies treat producers of a given sector as a group. Rivalry among same-sector producers is central to investment issues.

This essay intends to review direct foreign investment trends and major policy issues in the Pacific region and clarify the implications of national policies for the economic welfare of both investing and host nations in the new complicated situation of increased multi-directional foreign investment. After this introductory section, general direct foreign investment trends in the Pacific region will be reviewed. Then the evolution of policy within the designated countries both for investing and receiving nations will be discussed. As some policies can only be developed through multinational consultation, the possibilities of

---

[1] This organization held its fifth conference in 1986 in Vancouver, Canada. As of now, most Latin American countries still remain as observers, but China and China Taipei joined as full members.

regional cooperation for policy improvement will be explored in the final section.

Direct Foreign Investment Trends in the Pacific Region

Direct foreign investment in the Pacific region has expanded rapidly in the past two and a half decades, but with a significant change in composition. In the 1950s and 1960s, the United States dominated such investment in the region as well as worldwide. Since the 1970s, however, new investors have emerged, including Japan as well as the Western European nations. Furthermore, newly industrialized countries have become the latest actors in direct foreign investment in various aspects.[2]

The success in industrialization that Asian developing countries have experienced—which in itself has been a contribution of direct foreign investment and/or technology transfer through multinational corporations, if not the sole cause—has brought with it new problems. A rapid expansion in exports of industrial goods by NICs, though it benefits consumers of old industrialized countries (OICs), tends to exceed the speed of industrial adjustment in the latter states. The speed of technology transfer exceeds the development of new technology, which makes it more difficult for those who are displaced in the declining sectors in OICs to find new jobs in other activities. Here lies the critical source of trade friction between OICs and NICs.

In the face of import restriction on the side of OICs, sometimes in the name of voluntary export restraint (VER), NICs initiated direct foreign investment in the industrial countries to penetrate these markets. In labor-intensive industries, NICs could no longer compete with lower-income countries as wage rates as well as exchange rates were substantially appreciated, which in turn induced their investment in LDCs. The NICs' increasing need for raw industrial materials added another stimulus for direct foreign investment in mining and other sectors. Thus NICs are becoming important new participants in making such investments.

Following the NICs, the so-called middle-income countries (MICs)—the ASEAN five excluding Singapore, for example—are promoting their industrialization, with the slower but steady integration of their own markets. It is true that market integration in such forms as tariff unions

---

[2]That NICs were becoming investors was suggested by this author in the 1983 ''Report for the PECC'' (Pacific Economic Cooperation Conference), given in Bali, Indonesia. See *Issues for Pacific Economic Cooperation* (Jakarta: Center for Strategic and International Studies, November 1983).

or free trade areas has not been realized,[3] but institutions that make mutual trade and investment easier have been or are being created. Frequent consultations by ministers of the ASEAN member countries now attract more attention from the industrial nations. Negotiations as a group with industrial countries have strengthened the bargaining power of the individual ASEAN countries against others. Furthermore, NICs as new investors now compete with OICs in investment in MICs, thus improving their bargaining position.

Meanwhile, the MICs' division of international labor has entered into a phase whereby they can take over some NIC industrial sectors as increased NIC wage rates facilitate transplantation of labor-intensive industries to the MICs. The multinational corporations of the older industrial states are also transferring some technology to the MICs to reduce production costs of high-tech machine components, as evidenced by the increased production of integrated circuits in the ASEAN countries.

A potentially significant change in the market for direct foreign investments in the Pacific region is the emergence of the People's Republic of China as a large host nation. It is true that China's politico-economic system tends to limit the inflow of direct foreign investment from Western market economies because Western firms are cautious about making a serious commitment in a socialist country. China's domestic politics also provide evidence that there have been continuous political struggles between the "conservatives" and "revisionists" in the Chinese Communist Party. Moreover, while the economic reforms include more incentives for improving productivity, the awesome bureaucratic structure hinders efficiency. So real progress in the PRC is yet to come.

Despite these difficulties, however, China has made steady efforts to encourage direct foreign investment and technology transfer since the early 1980s. To give more definite signals and to advance economic incentives, the State Council published its "22 Articles Resolution" in October 1986. Special Economic Zones have been increased in numbers, and export promotion and the importation of high technology to encourage import substitution industries have been given the highest priority.

Although direct foreign investment and technology transfer have increased rapidly in China measured against East European standards,

---

[3]The term "middle-income country" does not refer to industrialization phases; it has become popular among economists since the World Bank's *World Development Report* first coined it.

they are still much less than the government hoped to have, at least up until 1988. This partly reflects the fact that Western investors have not been attracted by the investment climate in China. In addition, the Chinese government has become more selective in inviting direct foreign investment by shifting emphasis from service to "productive" activities. Because most potential investors are interested in selling in China's potentially large local market, investment having its primary goal exports from China as Beijing wants, has limited appeal.

Nonetheless, many ASEAN leaders are gravely concerned that China may absorb a disproportionately large share of direct foreign investment and technology transfer from Western industrial countries. Thus, lower middle-income nations such as Indonesia perceived China as a formidable competitor in labor-intensive industries, whereas many NICs believe that they are not in direct competition with China and that they will find an attractive market in that country for their products.[4]

As for OICs, cross-hauling direct foreign investment has increased. The United States has become a large host country, partly because of its import restrictions. To expand employment and further regional development, many state governments invite direct foreign investment, as do provincial governments in many other high-income countries. Most OICs and high-income nations such as Australia and Canada face major industrial adjustment tasks in absorbing those who are displaced in the declining sectors. Cross-hauling investment has also been promoted by oligopolist producers, establishing a technological partnership with producers in foreign countries in order to compete with other domestic producer groups.

Although adjustment assistance is a task for national governments, private enterprises try to adapt more rapidly to changing environments on their own account. This may aggravate adjustment difficulties with respect to domestic employment. When domestic production becomes less competitive, firms invest abroad to survive, shifting their production bases to more cost-advantageous countries. Such a producer, from the home country's viewpoint, now plays the role of importer. Employment must shift from the manufacturing to the distribution sector. Increasing original equipment manufacturing arrangements (OEM), in which a producer produces goods sold with the importer's brand in the

---

[4]For a more detailed account, see Sueo Sekiguchi and Makito Noda, "China-Japan Economic Relations: Implications for ASEAN-Japan Relations," paper presented at the Asian Dialogue conference held in Hakone on October 26–28, 1986. At this conference and at an interim workshop held in February 1986 in Hong Kong, some ASEAN representatives expressed grave concern about competition with China.

importing market, are now combined with technological partnership and joint venture operations.

Now let us broadly review direct foreign investment trends by industry. As already mentioned, some labor-intensive industries, formerly important export sectors in the NICs, have shifted their location to the MICs. Some capital-intensive industries, such as steel and other heavy industries, declined in the OICs and became competitive in the NICs, though direct foreign investment did not play as important a role as technology importation and capital borrowing.

In technology-intensive industries, however, direct foreign investment has been an engine of industrial relocation among nations. By this means machine and chemical industries as well as technology imports increased in NICs. The more important the technology element becomes, the more difficult for technology-importing countries to purchase this technology separately; the pharmaceutical industry provides an example of this effect. In electric and electronic industries and automobile sectors, direct foreign investment promoted technology transfer and these transplanted industries became exportable sectors in the NICs; here again, original equipment manufacturing arrangements played an important role. In some cases, such as the automobile industry, large multinational corporations established solid technical partnership groups of manufacturers across national boarders. In other cases, such as the computer industry where technological progress is rapid, such a partnership seems as yet to be unstable as producers try to outdistance future rivals in technological competition.

Thus, reshufflings of partnerships take place within domestic as well as international marketplaces. When basic systems and software play a critical role in the sales of products, as in the case of large and personal computers, making a system widely accepted by users ahead of other competitors is of primary importance. Such competition creates collusions among late comers and early arrivals so as to deter the emergence of threatening competitors. Sometimes advanced producers try to forge partnerships in order to establish market dominance, but sometimes they also try to defer the growth of potential rivals.

Notwithstanding these business struggles, the oligopolists still transfer technology to the NICs and MICs. To expand the use of their basic systems, they need to cultivate customers and so they invest in other industrial countries including the NICs. At the same time, a cautious multinational corporation sticks to 100 percent ownership in making direct foreign investment so as to protect advanced technology.[5]

---

[5]As for appropriability, see S. P. Magee, "The Appropriability Theory of the Multinational Corporation," *The Annals* (November 1981):123–35.

As in the case of original equipment manufacturing, multinational corporations that import products from foreign partners function as assemblers and sometimes as pure distributors who sell the imported final products. In the latter case, marketing capability with established distribution networks plays a most important role. Though OEM does not necessarily accompany capital participation and technology licensing, when it is arranged among industrial countries it often involves these in the case of North-South contracts. Here the suppliers of goods are presumed to have purchased the multinational corporations' technology and marketing ability, including brands, goodwill, and distribution network services.

Whether or not this phase continues depends on each individual case: Enterprises in a LDC or in a NIC may prefer being specialized in production, saving investment in marketing. But some may prefer that their own marketing not depend on multinational corporations, thereby reducing the uncertainty caused by changes in the strategies of foreign distributors. In the latter case, producers will soon or later invest in marketing activities in industrial countries. Thus, the NICs have begun investing in OICs in such fields as well as in repairing services. The NICs' investment in finance and monitoring in OIC high-tech industries is also rapidly increasing.

Major Policy Issues

First, I will briefly discuss the framework in which policy issues are to be investigated. As stated earlier, the national governments are assumed to maximize national income and/or the real consumption of the nation. In reality, many other specific policy targets affect the conduct of multinational corporations and their subsidiaries.[6] The basic goals of economic policies, however, can be summarized as above.

Looking at the subject from this viewpoint, a host government will try to maximize the net gain from direct foreign investment, which consists of net income increases after paying the stipulated return to foreign production factors. Because domestic factors must be mobilized for income gain, a most important short-run benefit is labor income accrued to workers employed by joint ventures and foreign subsidiaries. If local capital is also mobilized by more efficient production opportuni-

---

[6]An example of such a specific target is the U.S. regulations on conduct by MNC affiliates to prevent corruption in host countries, as evidenced in the Foreign Corrupt Practices Act. See Lawrence B. Krause, *U.S. Economic Policies Toward the Association of Southeast Asian Nations: Meeting the Japanese Challenge* (Washington, D.C.: Brookings Institution, 1982).

ties caused by direct foreign investment, this adds to the net benefit.[7] A portion of the fruit of improved efficiency must be paid for foreign technology and management, but income sharing here is unclear.

In the long run, however, net gain will increase through the diffusion of technology and skills in the host economy. I call this *externality of industrialization*. The mechanism allowing this phenomenon to take place is the turnover of engineers and workers in the host country. *Learning by watching* by local firms can be another channel. There may be *pecuniary externality*, by which we mean that reduced cost of production in a given sector benefits those sectors that use such products as input. All such benefits from externality belong to the host nation. Thus promotion of technology transfer and diffusion, from the host government's viewpoint, is worth being assigned a top priority.

For the government of an investing country, similar arguments also apply. If the economy is maintaining full employment and if capital together with technology flows out for more favorable opportunities, this benefits the investing nation. The higher return to capital and technology will add to the national income. If the country is large, there is also a terms of trade effect. If the terms of trade become favorable because of direct foreign investment in the importables sectors, the investing national can save the cost of import, which increases real consumption.

Domestic unemployment is the factor that makes benefits complicated, though unemployment itself mostly has its own causes, such as rigidity of wage rates. Thus, although there were once regulations or taxation of outgoing investment in the United States, most governments of investing countries seem to maintain a neutral policy toward direct foreign investment except for national security and social reasons.[8]

If direct foreign investment promotes technology transfer and accelerates changes in trade patterns, promotion of industrial adjustment is what the governments of investing countries must pursue. In this connection, promotion of research and development for expanding new

---

[7]This is a simple truth based on the following reasoning: If only capital comes in and claims the market rate of return in a full employment small economy (prices of goods remaining constant), there is no net benefit unless the host government levies taxes on the income accrued to foreign capital (this refers to a standard trade model of small country with two goods). If a tax is imposed, however, foreign capital will not flow in.

[8]When invention and technology transfer are treated as product innovation, the welfare consequences of these two are different in terms of trade effects. Faster invention favors inventing nations; if the speed of transfer exceeds that of invention, recipient nations benefit. Paul Krugman, "A Model of Innovation, Technology Transfer, and World Distribution of Income," *Journal of Political Economy* 87(2) (April 1979). The policy implication, however, is not to restrict transfer, but to promote both innovation and transfer.

industrial frontiers is also needed. Innovation and improved profit opportunities will, in fact, attract more investment in OICs. Such evidence is observed in deregulation that is intended to induce foreign investment in developed industrial countries.

The game multinational corporations play in such circumstances is to seek long-run profit maximization by reallocating their managerial resources among countries. If a government offers more favorable opportunities, a multinational corporation would invest more in that country. One question remains: Does a multinational corporation maximize profit after taxes in home currency, and in what time horizon?

If all profits are transferred to the home country and are double-taxed by both governments because of the absence of a tax treaty, foreign investment to lower tax countries increases. Even though double taxation is avoided by a tax treaty, tax policies can be non-neutral for investment allocation. Taxation is neutral if the taxation system of a country taxes that portion over the home tax rate, but there is also compensation for overpaid taxes in the host country when its tax rate is higher. In reality, however, taxation is asymmetrical in the sense that the home government does not compensate for overpayment of taxes abroad whereas it does impose home taxes when host countries' tax rates are lower.

Various tax incentives provided by the host governments may or may not work, depending on the home country's tax situation. When a tax treaty exists and the home country allows tax credits given by the host country to apply, then the incentives function; they do not if the home country's tax policy cancels them out. Transfer pricing, though often exaggerated, is a multinational corporation's tax saving response. If corporate firms can accumulate retained earnings for one reason or another, a multinational corporation can establish a paper company in a so-called ''tax haven'' country.

When a multinational corporation transfers technology to a subsidiary, it can claim the imputed price from the subsidiary for the use of a specific technology, but it does not necessarily do so because technology fees can be collected in the form of profit. Though a subsidiary is subject to the host country's jurisdiction, its function nevertheless becomes nothing more than that of a branch of a multinational corporation. Therefore, transactions between branch factories and the head office are considered to be internal transactions within the company. This creates a conflict with the policies of a host government. When foreign affiliates are joint ventures, there are plural parties in a firm, which makes decision making more complicated.

Many other factors affect the behavior of a multinational corporation and its affiliates. Obviously, variations in exchange rates affect their behavior when they evaluate their after-tax income in terms of home country currency. Because the rate of return to investment depends more on fundamentals in the case of direct foreign investment, however, the influence of expected changes in exchange rate is considered to be less than with portfolio investment.

Keeping these factors in mind, I will now review the government policies of host and investing countries. At the same time, the background of these policies and some important policy debates must be examined. First, let us sketch the policies of the governments that receive direct foreign investment.

Policies of Recipient Countries

It is useful to classify Pacific Basin countries into several categories and some subcategories. First are the high-income countries, which consist of large industrial countries (the United States and Japan) along with those countries with a relatively small proportion of manufacturing industries (Canada, Australia, and New Zealand). Second are the NICs, which may be divided into two subcategories, namely, relatively large economies (South Korea, Taiwan, Mexico, and others) and city states or small economies (Hong Kong, Singapore, and Panama). Third are the MICs with market economies, and fourth the central planning countries (China and others).[9]

The Policies of High-Income Countries. Large industrial economies in general are neutral with no incentives and disincentives, even though local governments often provide incentives. Government intervention is seldom except for national security and some social reasons. Those nations with a high income but relatively small industrial sectors formerly had screening mechanisms in pursuit of their industrial policies; direct foreign investment in mining in some national districts was directly regulated by the government. Banking was another area in which regulations exist. In the deregulation trend of recent years, however, the governments in general removed regulations and became more neutral. Provincial governments are now eager to receive direct foreign investment for regional development purposes. As the industrial composition tends to be dominated by competitive primary industry sectors, these governments maintain policies to develop manufacturing sectors by var-

---

[9]Although many other countries could be included, most of the Central and South American countries will not be covered in the following discussion because they still do not belong to PECC. North Korea and Vietnam and even the USSR can potentially become members, but because of the unavailability of information, they also will be excluded from this discussion.

ious policy instruments. Industrial policies, though not directly addressed to policies toward investment, will affect DFI in such countries.

Policies of NICs. For political as well as economic reasons, the relatively large NICs have maintained their own industrial policies with strong government leadership. Direct foreign investment in general had to obtain approval by the government. Because of the size of their economies, these governments tried to keep a certain composition in the industrial sectors. As they occasionally faced balance-of-payment difficulties, the governments intervened in foreign exchange outflows. When the governments invited foreign investment in high-tech sectors, they provided tax incentives but kept strict controls because such investment was regarded as competing with small domestic enterprises.

As the situation changed drastically, however, policies have been rapidly revised, especially in South Korea and Taiwan. An increasing surplus in the current overseas account led to appreciation of their currencies; import barriers have been reduced year by year. Screening of foreign investment has been steadily relaxed. In South Korea the "positive list formula" was switched to the "negative list formula" which meant that an approval for receiving direct foreign investment was required only when the sector was explicitly listed by the government.

Because of entry into some high-tech industries, these governments accepted the Paris Convention's stricter protection of industrial property rights that they formerly opposed. On the other hand, they increased their own direct foreign investment.

City states have also adopted freer policies toward incoming direct foreign investment. They have had, after all, no option but to adapt to changing international market trends, and it has worked well in the end. Hong Kong has been more oriented to laissez-faire policies, with generally favorable tax treatment. In recent years, however, some economists have argued that Hong Kong should pursue some industrial policies, though it is unclear how effective these can be; the government does prepare industrial sites to attract electronic industries. In the case of Singapore, even though the basic policy stance is that of promoting freer competition, the government has raised wage rates with the intention of constructing an economy emphasizing high-skills. With the cooperation of multinational corporations, it has also been active in establishing and operating a training center.

Because of higher wage rates and limited space, these city states had started making their own foreign investment much earlier than the larger NICs. In fact, Hong Kong and Singapore have been important investors in the ASEAN countries and China in recent years.

Policies of Middle-Income Countries. Most MICs face a serious dilemma: They need direct foreign investment for employment promotion, economic growth, creating entrepreneurs, and promoting industrialization. This in itself highlights their dismay that because of a lack of modern domestic enterprise, direct foreign investment may dominate their domestic industries. Such investment is assigned various targets together with other investment: export promotion, regional development, employment expansion, ownership regulations, required local content, technological development, and in a few countries, more equal opportunities for some ethnic groups.[10]

As the number of policy instruments are limited in contrast to their many targets, these governments have provided "incentives and performance requirements." To attract more direct foreign investment, they had to give pecuniary incentives by such means as tax holidays, restriction on entry of other producers, and protection from import competition. All these incentives raised the cost of receiving these investments. On the other hand, joint ventures and the subsidiaries of multinational corporations are subject to various performance requirements.

Thus, government policies become exceedingly complicated as a reflection of their dilemma. To encourage new industries, they give them special preferential treatment such as that for "promoted firms" in Thailand and "pioneer firms" in the Philippines.

China's Policies. After Beijing established four "Special Economic Zones," mostly in southeast China, in July 1979, the government continued to strengthen its open door policy by adding "Open Economic Districts" for three delta areas in 1981 and then fourteen "special cities" in coastal regions. At the same time, legal safeguards have been established including enactment of the "Law on China–Foreign Joint Venture Operations," laws on income tax, and others.

As explained earlier, these policies reflect the desire of government leaders to promote technical progress, improve efficiency, and expand employment. Direct foreign investment is expected to achieve two goals: efficiency improvement and relaxation of foreign exchange constraints. But there are opponents of such a strategy; in addition it is unclear to what extent government leaders share a common understanding of direct foreign investment with Western economists and business circles.

---

[10]Because most of these targets are well known, we will skip an explanation of the details. The ethnic problem is protection of the *bumiputra* in Malaysia and the *pribumi* in Indonesia.

China is handicapped in inviting Western enterprises because the limited power of enterprises under the socialist system does not allow foreign subsidiaries to perform efficient and innovative activities in the same way they can in an economy where private enterprise and the market mechanism are the central mode of economic activities. Furthermore, such infrastructure as telecommunications, transportation, and harbor facilities as well as energy supply are not yet highly enough developed for China to induce foreign investment. To compensate for this handicap, Beijing provides various tax incentives and some privileges to foreign subsidiaries, as the announcement of the State Council of October 1986 made clear.

Though preferential treatment includes tax reduction and discount of land rent, reducing the shared cost of social security, and even exemption from the obligation to earn foreign exchange, the attractiveness of the China market is only slowly rising. Cumbersome procedures for obtaining approvals from the local as well as the central government, most of which are legally or administratively required, make potential investors hesitant.[11]

Some additional political factors may also make it difficult for China to prepare a truly favorable business climate for foreign investment. From the economic viewpoint alone, however, many difficulties remain. Nonetheless, the recent record of direct foreign investment in China seems to have exceeded that of East European nations.[12]

Beijing endeavors to promote technology transfer, not only through direct foreign investment but through direct imports as well. The basic policy stance was stated in May 1985, soon after China joined the Paris Convention on industrial property rights, in the "Legislation on Management of Contracts of Technology Importation." This clarified the type of technology that could be imported under certain basic conditions, emphasizing quality improvement, environmental protection, foreign exchange earnings, and improvement of efficiency as goals. On the other hand, it warned that unfair and too restrictive clauses should not be accepted.

---

[11]Interesting evidence of the abuse of administrative powers is indicated by Article 16 of the resolution by the State Council of October 1986, which states that the district and administrative sectors should not impose arbitrary surcharges on foreign subsidiaries and joint ventures. That such an article was needed points to activities that were taking place.

[12]Our judgement here is based on the comparison of China's performance with Carl H. McMillan's review of DFI in East Europe, "Trends in Direct Investment and the Transfer of Technology," in Bela Csikos-Nagy and David Young, eds., *East-West Economic Relations in the Changing Global Environment* (London: Macmillan, 1986), ch. 14.

There are two major problems in technology transfer. One is that a stricter control based on COCOM regulations hampers technology transfer to China. Delay in concluding and implementing contracts creates unfavorable effects on China's import of technology, as most Chinese officials argue. Second, if China wants to diffuse imported technology to enjoy a spillover effect on domestic innovation, Western suppliers may be concerned about the free copying of technology being exported to a single producer in China, although this can be handled through the wording of the contract.

Policies of Investing Countries

Generally speaking, the governments of investing countries in the Pacific region are neutral on the issue of country distribution of investment abroad, except for very close neighbors. Canada and the United States have special arrangements relating to mutual direct foreign investment, and Australia has an explicit arrangement to encourage direct foreign investment in Papua New Guinea and South Pacific countries.

A critical role that must be played by government is to improve the political climate for foreign investment, namely to conclude agreements with host countries to protect DFI from political risks. One means is to conclude investment guarantee treaties. Obviously, there is a limit to such arrangements because the treaty loses its effectiveness if the governments involved are overthrown by a revolution. Most high-income countries in the Pacific region, in fact, had not concluded such bilateral agreements by 1981. When South Korea started investing abroad, however, the government did conclude treaties with nine countries, including some outside the region.[13]

A second important governmental task in this context is to provide a unilateral arrangement for guaranteeing direct foreign investment by means of investment insurance. This kind of insurance by the government or governmental organizations exists in almost all investing countries, including South Korea. Though private insurance is able to cover some investment risks, government involvement may be necessary to reduce the type of risks associated with political relations.

A third governmental task is to provide information services to actual and potential investors about the host country. In the case of the United States, the Overseas Private Investment Corporation (OPIC) provides feasibility studies. In Japan, the Japan External Trade Organization (JETRO) and its trade centers in various countries provide

---

[13]The source for this discussion is Sekiguchi, "Report for the PECC."

information services. Australia has its Development Assistance Bureau in the Department of Trade; in South Korea, the Chamber of Commerce and the Bank of Korea provide some information. Here again, it is possible for the private consultant business to take over the job, but most governments seem to consider that information as a public good should be supplied by the government directly or by connected governmental organizations.

Finally, many governments provide tax incentives or financial support to their foreign investors. The Australian government provides such tax incentives to its investors in Papua New Guinea. The Export Import Bank of Korea and Japan have special arrangements to support investment finance, though their effectiveness is unclear because of no significantly attractive terms attached to them as compared with market interest rates. Japan has a scheme called the "Special Reserve Fund for Losses from DFI," which allows postponement of the payment of corporate income taxes. Companies that invest abroad can accumulate for some years a certain percentage of investment as a reserve fund, which is regarded as a loss for tax purposes; after some years, the fund must be used up. Canada and Japan have a "tax-sparing system" in which, when a subsidiary is given a tax credit for a specific investment in a host country, the head office in the home country is counted as already having paid the credit equivalent tax. This system is intended to keep effective some tax incentives that are given by a host government to Canadian or Japanese subsidiaries.

As mentioned earlier, there are only a very few regulations on actions of foreign subsidiaries by the governments of investing countries. The U.S. Foreign Corrupt Practices Act, unfavorable taxation on American income abroad, and overseas application of the Anti-Trust Law are pointed to as examples of such disincentives.[14]

Policy Issues and Debates

Although the economic policies of most nations share common goals, the specific objectives of these policies may vary at various times, as we have seen. For example, a LDC government places great importance on creating its own entrepreneurs and establishing its own new industries, whereas many industrial countries do not pay great attention to such objectives. The latter may be more cosmopolitan in that citizens do not care about the nationality or ethnicity of those involved in entreprenurial activities or the industrial labor force.

---

[14]See Krause, *U.S. Economic Policies Toward ASEAN.*

When a Western company makes a direct foreign investment in China, it will be a serious ideological issue whether or not the socialist government allows private ownership of the means of production, in the Marxian sense. Put another way, since "anarchy of production" was attacked by Marx and many socialist thinkers after him, at many points it comes as no surprise that the Chinese government intervenes in production activities. When Beijing introduced direct foreign investment from Western countries, it had to first of all place a time limit on foreign ownership. It was further required to control all operations by foreign subsidiaries and joint ventures in its territory. Thus, between China and its foreign investors, policy issues differ radically from those between OICs and LDCs in market economies.

In this section, I will classify direct foreign investment policy issues into three categories: North-South, East-West, and North-North. Because certain features distinguish issues in these regions from those debated in the global context, we will focus on major regional issues, not those debated at UNCTAD.

North-South Issues

In the 1960s and 1970s, many economists in ASEAN criticized the multinational corporations for introducing "inappropriate" technologies into their countries. In the narrowest sense, this meant that the multinational corporations adopted more capital-intensive techniques than were optimal because their techniques had worked in capital-abundant countries. This is not necessarily true, however; if a multinational corporation adopts an unsuitable technique in a LDC, then it will lose out against its competitors. Furthermore, it was often counterargued that because wage rates in efficiency units were not as low as they appeared in a LDC, it was rational for a multinational corporation to use a more capital-intensive technique than that best fitting the apparent wage-rental ratio.

Arguments were then expanded to cover other aspects of the issue: The new technologies tended to destroy the environment in LDCs, whose environmental regulations were less strict; multinational corporations introduced management techniques that forced drastic changes in the structure of LDCs. As the speed of changes exceeded that of social adjustment, social disorder took place.

Counter arguments contended that the government of a host country was responsible for environmental regulations and that if pollution was increased as a result of direct foreign investment, it was because of the host government's loose regulations.

It should be noted that some confusion exists regarding issues of "appropriate technology": sometimes "appropriate industries" refer to those not yet introduced and other times to those already in an industrial sector. If a LDC tries to establish capital-intensive industries, then it is inevitable that capital-labor ratios will be raised, affecting employment.

A second issue, the solution of which is still not yet clear, relates to "restrictive business practices." It is not surprising that a multinational corporation tries to confine the use of a specific technology by explicitly restricting the conduct of joint ventures and/or technology importers. Basically, this is a matter of private contracts, unless the laws of both investing and host countries have been broken. Restrictive practices include: restriction on overseas marketing; limitation of the use of techniques; unduly unequal treatment of techniques revised by the importer; and restrictions on the purchasing of equipment and of raw and intermediate materials for production.

Despite these issues, however, the facts themselves remain unclear in many Southeast Asian countries, partly because multinational corporations and joint ventures naturally do not want to disclose contracts and partly because antitrust laws and the government agencies that supervise business conduct are not established and/or do not function well.[15]

If we examine current Japanese contracts with foreign suppliers of technologies, we find a number of restrictive clauses, especially in the area of overseas marketing. From this fact we may surmise that restrictive practices have not decreased but rather increased, because technology is transferred to LDCs in a package with management controls. Although the appropriate policy response for a LDC is to strengthen antitrust regulations, their effectiveness may be limited; if regulations are too strict, the multinational corporations will search for another market in which to make investment or transfer technology.

A third issue concerns the attitude of multinational corporations toward technology transfer and protection of industrial property in a host country. Many LDCs accuse multinational corporations of exploiting them by overpricing technology; multinational corporations, they charge, are reluctant to transfer so-called high-tech. From the multinational corporations' perspective, the weak protection of industrial property in LDCs appears unfavorable to technology suppliers. This is a

---

[15]In a joint study on Japanese DFI in Southeast Asia, some country papers referred to restrictive practices. Because the reported case stated that "the joint venture will import intermediate goods from the technology supplier in case the terms are equal to or more favorable than those of other suppliers," it did not appear to be restrictive. For more details, see Sueo Sekiguchi, ed., *ASEAN-Japan Relations: Investment* (Singapore: ISEAS, 1983).

factor that prompts multinational corporations to claim a higher patent fee and makes them reluctant to bring in high tech. It also depends on whether a LDC allows multinational corporations to have wholly owned subsidiaries, because if "appropriability" is better guaranteed, a MNC will be more willing to transfer such high technologies.

In fact, whether or not multinational corporations are reluctant to transfer technology is open to debate. Because of competition among multinational corporations, a MNC will lose if it fails to transfer technology for improving efficiency. The bargaining power of MNCs may have been exaggerated in direct foreign investment and technology transfer negotiations, because the government intervention in a host country strengthens the position of local partners and technology importers.

East-West Issues

From China's viewpoint, direct foreign investment and technology transfers are needed to relax foreign exchange constraints for domestic investment in the short run and to accelerate industrialization in the long run. Here industrialization includes such individual targets as efficiency improvement, export promotion for financing domestic investment, and introduction of new industries.

A first issue is of the most fundamental nature: when China invites foreign enterprises, how long will multinational corporations and their subsidiaries be allowed to stay as resident companies? No one knows the answer, though Beijing has guaranteed a certain number of years; most investors then have to adjust themselves to a limited time horizon in investment planning. What status is guaranteed investors? At the moment, foreign subsidiaries and joint ventures are given some guest privileges with tax incentives. Naturally, they must accept administrative guidance for these benefits.

All incentives reflect China's present handicaps. It is rational for potential investors to expect that incentives will be removed after the investment has reached a target size. What status can these firms enjoy then? Because Beijing refuses to give national treatment to foreign subsidiaries, their status after these goals have been achieved looks quite uncertain.[16]

This also applies to other socialist nations in the region, who are reportedly anxious to invite direct foreign investment for the purpose of promoting industrialization.

---

[16]A key issue that blocked the conclusion of the Japan-China Investment Guarantee Treaty was reportedly Beijing's refusal to provide national treatment to Japanese subsidiaries and joint ventures. However in August 1988, the treaty was concluded; it included a clause for national treatment.

Second, assuming that it allows foreign enterprises to operate for several decades, it will be of crucial importance for China to improve the investment climate. This includes simplification of administrative procedures for obtaining approvals, or the removal of these procedures, thereby making it easier for firms to procure input materials through the market, letting prices reflect more market trends, improving communication and transportation, and so on. One point to add: policy instruments that indirectly stabilize economic activities must be developed; otherwise, government policies fluctuate wildly to counter business fluctuations. Direct controls by government tend to damage foreign subsidiaries because they leave too much room for bureaucratic arbitration.

Too many targets assigned to foreign investment such as foreign exchange earnings from the early period of investment or requirements that the investor earn his own foreign exchange make potential investors hesitant. Although exceptions are granted to firms that develop import substitution through new technology, it is reported that administrative procedures to obtain such privileges are too cumbersome.

Third, COCOM regulations on technology exports to socialist counties can create serious problems even though China is given favorable treatment among socialist counties. The state of affairs, however, seems fragile. If COCOM intends to prohibit the export of technology that can be applied to the development of military capability, it should prevent the transfer of such technology through whatever channels. Otherwise, how can one expect that transfer to the USSR through a third country, including China, is effectively prevented? In this sense, there is a contradiction between the strict application of COCOM toward the USSR and its loose application to China.

Issues in the North

Generally speaking, issues here seem more related to individual cases than in other regions. The remaining restrictions on direct foreign investment exist as security and social matters. As mentioned earliers, disputes about incoming direct foreign investment become more and more case specific because of the varying interests of different groups. Although DFI generally benefits the workers of a host nation, competing producers try to exclude new entrants from abroad. This is because workers who are employed in a competing enterprise tend to oppose foreign investment. The position of labor unions, who are assumed to protect their members, becomes ambiguous, depending on what portion of their membership they try to protect.

More generally, production factors that can freely move across national borders benefit from greater access to markets. Thus managers, capital owners, and even inventors of new technology favor freer treatment by all national governments.[17] It will be increasingly important for governments to offer reciprocal treatment because of intensified competition among producers in home and foreign markets.

On the other hand, if we assume that immigration will not be liberalized in the foreseeable future, those who own internationally immobile factors such as labor and land will be highly sensitive to the rewards paid to them in the home country. Naturally, they cannot be as cosmopolitan as the owners of internationally mobile factors. As income transfer to those damaged will never be enough to fully compensate, national policies will be constrained by the interests of internationally immobile factors.

Let us now examine specific policy issues.

First, more severe competition in innovation and invention creates more intensified legal disputes about patent coverage. This is applicable not only to international but to domestic competition as well. Difficulties in the international realm are mostly caused by the lack of a common standard of regulation. In this context, more intensive consultations among national governments on patent treatment, industrial property in general, and intellectual property are badly needed.

Similarly, more standardization of the appropriate norms for competition or regulations under antitrust laws are required, because the conduct of multinational corporations and their subsidiaries can violate the laws in a host country despite the fact that they may be legal in the home country. As governmental cooperation and coordination lag behind the actual evolution of foreign investment, national laws are often applied over jurisdictional borders, which in turn becomes another source of international dispute. All these issues do not remain simply those of OICs but spill over into their relations with NICs.

Implications for National Policies and Regional Cooperation

First, let us remember our assumptions with regard to the policy goals of each national government in dealing with direct foreign investment and technology transfer. We assume that national governments try to maximize national income and/or real consumption. Although the roles of governments differ among nations in the Pacific-Asian region depending on their stage of economic development, political system, and other reasons, basic goals can be identified. A host government tries to maximize the direct and indirect benefits of direct foreign invest-

---

[17]Here we assume that a factory owner makes inconsistent arguments in that he or she claims freer access to foreign markets while demanding protection in the home market.

ment and technology transfer, a policy that may conflict with interests of investor countries. Taxation is one of the policy instruments that manipulates shares of income generated by direct foreign investment. When retaliation is taken into account, however, a seemingly optimal policy can never be optimal in isolation. A similar argument applies to the policies of investor countries. If a government restricts direct foreign investment and technology transfer for the sake of its labor income, the country not only loses opportunities for a higher return on capital and technology but also misses expanded markets for its exportables. Retaliation could further worsen the situation.

In this sense, governments will pursue policies based on broader and longer-term perspectives. It follows, then, that the governments of OICs should promote technological development so that their economies can expand production opportunities for which those who are displaced in declining sectors are recruited. Under such circumstances, technology transfer does not reduce national income. On the contrary, such income grows along with real consumption, because the prices of importables will decline by the use of less expensive labor in NICs and LDCs.

Generally, the governments will stay neutral toward both incoming and outgoing direct foreign investment, allowing investors to find the best investment opportunities. If the governments of OICs take more active steps, they can make the investment climate better by concluding intergovernmental agreements for investment guarantees and providing information services. One area worth exploring is common action to transfer resources to LDCs for economic cooperation, a step that eventually improves investment climate in host developing countries. "Tax-sparing" measures that make the tax incentives provided by a host government more effective can also be adopted by all OIC governments in the Pacific region.[18]

Major tasks for governments of MICs and low-income countries still remain those of improving the domestic environment; developing entrepreneurs, engineers, and middle management classes; and improving the skills of workers. Investing in infrastructure is another important task. Most of these jobs depend heavily on the host governments' initiatives. It is true that economic cooperation is needed until the market mechanism works favorably for these LDCs to induce pri-

---

[18]Here we do not refer explicitly to NIC policies, because the NICs' position is rapidly approaching that of the OICs, except that NICs may still need some reservations pertaining to equal access to mutual markets. In most other respects, it seems that NICs can be treated like "North" countries.

vate investment. Thus, intergovernmental cooperation for infrastructure building remains an important goal for all governments in the region.

On the other hand, it should be emphasized that complicated regulations and erratic government policies that induce the flight of local capital must be changed so that domestic capital can be more effectively used in the host countries; otherwise, it will be far more difficult to attract foreign capital. NICs have been successful in this respect and it is now time for market forces to favor investment in NICs without the necessity for government encouragement.

Economic evaluation of the benefits of direct foreign investment and technology transfer, as indicated earlier, suggests that the host government should reduce tax incentives and protection for direct foreign investment by means of high tariffs on competing imports and entry restrictions. On this point many host governments argue that, because of competition among host countries, they cannot remove these costly incentives. This reasoning is understandable. Further, it seems difficult for these governments to cooperate in unifying incentive systems because of the varying situations in each country. The evidence suggests however, that a more stable investment climate with fewer incentives attracts more direct foreign investment than a host country with more incentives but less stable and less transparent policies.

China, and possibly other socialist countries as well who encourage direct foreign investment and technology transfer from Western countries, will have to undertake significant adjustments to facilitate these activities effectively. As this discussion makes clear, the incentives these socialist countries provide are not as strong as they seem to believe. If incentives are a compensation for the stricter controls required by domestic politics, their effectiveness is inherently limited. Some incentives, such as a government guarantee for the procurement of electricity and water, are not effective at all when investors evaluate them from an international perspective.

Despite all these difficulties, the market economies of the Pacific Basin should welcome China and other socialist countries as investment partners to the extent that this stabilizes political relations in the region.[19] Trade and investment games are not zero-sum. New participants will expand opportunities for enlarged transactions out of which everyone obtains a net positive gain, even though for some, competition may seem to outweigh complementarity. Drastic changes, however, will be regarded as threatening by competing economies.

---

[19]There may be conflicting views regarding specific countries, but we argue a general principle here.

Taking into consideration the fact that the countries of the region are diverse in a great variety of respects—resource endowment, stage of economic development, political and economic systems as well as social and cultural differences—regional cooperation in the area of direct foreign investment and technology transfer will remain modest. A feasible task is to improve the investment climate and avoid unexpected shocks by means of frequent consultation on policies. Policy coordination seems to be difficult even among the countries of the same category. Perhaps economic cooperation by which OICs can help MICs and low-income countries to improve their investment climate and absorptive capacity for technology in general is most reasonable and useful.

As most important actors, multinational corporations play active roles in promoting both foreign capital and technology in developing countries. They invest in education and training for their own interest. In what industries and in what form multinational corporations invest depends on the policies of host governments to which they respond. Therefore, the main actor who determines whether it makes the best use of DFI and technology transfer is the host government. The governments of investing countries play only a supplementary role in keeping the policies of host countries effective.

As we have already discussed, the most important net benefit of direct foreign investment to a host developing country lies in the external effects of industrialization and technology transfer, including diffusion. From a multinational corporation's view point, however, technology diffusion has two sides. To the extent that it contributes to the improved efficiency of its own subsidiaries, a multinational corporation gains net benefits, but externality to other rivals is not desirable. Thus, investment in education and training by a MNC will be limited as long as the turnover of employees benefits others.

It is in this context that I propose that Pacific countries contribute to the establishment of a Pacific Center for Education and Training to promote direct foreign investment and technology transfer. Contributions to the fund could be income progressive, with high-income countries subscribing more. The center would provide training in practical management and engineering for those sent by member countries as well as from OICs.[20] The reason that trainees from developed countries should participate is because the center could provide sound orientation for

---

[20]To distinguish these activities from those of universities, the center will not provide instruction in basic science and technology but will focus on strengthening the capability of middle-level engineers and mangers as well as government officials.

those potential managers and engineers who may be engaged in investment in LDCs in the region.

Such a center could also provide training for government officials who are engaged in direct foreign investment screening and technology transfer promotion in LDCs as well as other countries. Exchanges of views and experiences by middle-level officials would facilitate smoother implementation of policies and even policy improvement, thereby reducing the shocks caused by abrupt changes in policies and regulations. The most significant effects that I would expect from this activity are that government officials of socialist countries could learn much from the experiences of other countries.

The location of the center should be somewhere in the ASEAN countries so that ASEAN could play an active role. The center should also maintain close cooperation with the Asian Development Bank because improving the investment climate should be within the goals of the ADB as it contributes to expansion of investment opportunities. Such an activity is in line with ADB policy.

To avoid duplicating the activities of existing institutions, the proposed center should be clearly be differentiated from universities, though academics as well as business and government officials could be invited as lecturers and coordinators of programs. Expert consultants could also be mobilized for the programs according to subject. It is true that some multinational corporations actively promote on-the-job training and education at their head offices; these programs would continue to be separately promoted by individual companies. Bilateral intergovernmental programs would also proceed by themselves. The goals of the center would be to fill the gap between the private benefit and the social benefit of education and training within the region. A regional center would have the advantage of providing an international perspective on a manageable scale.

Let us provisionally divide the center's activities into two major course categories: business and policy. Because practical training in engineering requires an enormous investment in facilities, the business courses should start with management classes in the first stage. Later they could be expanded to cover engineering, but might use private companies on contract for training sites. Policy courses should cover taxation, antitrust regulations, antipollution policies, screening and administrative guidance, and other topics.

Policy improvement, together with more transparency of policy implementation and improved skill in management, will enhance the attractiveness of Pacific markets for investment and technology transfer. This in turn will promote the industrialization of developing countries, and eventually a virtuous circle will develop.

8. Technology Transfer Within the Pacific-Asian Region

MINGSARN SANTIKARN KAOSA-ARD

Technological change has been accepted as a part of an indispensable set of conditions required for national economic growth, if not the actual vehicle of growth itself. Studies conducted in the United States suggest technological change as a major source of economic expansion. The rapid growth of relatively resource-scarce countries such as Japan and South Korea have further provided concrete evidence that technology is a necessary input for development. Consequently, the issue of technology transfer has attracted attention at government, corporate and academic levels.

Technology transfer activities can be broadly divided into two categories: transfer of commercial and noncommercial assets. The former involves the transfer of assets that are not commonly available in the public domain. Commercial technologies are either legally owned by a commercial enterprise or are system specific, that is, they are technologies developed as a result of a combination of resources within an enterprise. Therefore, commercial transfers require compensations for their costs. Noncommercial transfers generally involve technologies that are publicly available. The benefits arising from their use cannot be fully acquired by monetary expenditures. The most important mechanism of noncommercial transfers consists of education and publications.

This essay aims to summarize issues related to technology transfer from developed to developing countries. First I will broadly examine the technology transactions now occurring within the Pacific-Asian region. I will investigate conventional debates regarding technology transfer, describe emerging issues, and, finally, discuss policy issues and directions.

The State of Technology Transfer Within the Pacific-Asian Region

We cannot easily gauge the extent of technology exchange currently taking place within the Pacific Asian region because the process involves a variety of externalities. Technology transfer is not simply a matter of moving machines from one location to another. It involves not only the transfer of a production system, but also the interaction of new and old work ethics as well as engineering, economic, social, and culture-related attitudes. Technology is transferred when communication between transfer and transferee is effective and complete. Because technology transfer is ultimately a part of the process of human resource development of the recipient countries, no single index effectively measures the extent to which the process has been successfully completed.

Bearing in mind this definition, statistics can be employed only as a rough approximation of technology transfer activities. These statistics include international investment and technological services, which are only partial indicators. Moreover, these two indicators are not mutually exclusive. They are, nevertheless, the only available starting points. In this essay, we will examine only trade in technical services and international investment.

Trade in Technical Services

Within the Pacific-Asian region, the United States has been the only net exporter of technology, earning US$8,305 million worth of technical services in 1985 (see Table 1). Japan has been a net importer, but its receipts from technology export are growing faster than its payments.

Information on technology payments of developing Asian countries is available only for a few countries. On the basis of the three-year average of technology fees between 1979 and 1981, the total annual technology imports of the ASEAN countries excluding Brunei were estimated at US$456 million.[1] In the same period, the size of South Korea's technical imports was US$102.75 million.

A remarkable feature of technology trade in this region is that it is growing very rapidly. As Table 1 shows, U.S. technology receipts increased 5.6 times from US$1.5 billion in 1965 to US$8.5 billion in 1985. Japan shows an even more rapidly increasing trend from US$27 million in 1965 to US$1 billion in 1983, an increase of thirty-sevenfold. Between 1965 and 1985, the annual compound growth rate of U.S. technology payments was 2.2 percent and the rate of receipt was 8.9 percent. For Japan, the annual compound growth rate between 1965 and 1983 was 19.9 percent for technology receipts and 11.5 percent for technology payments.

On the recipient side, payments from the countries in the region tended to rise rapidly. Between 1972 and 1985, technology imports into Thailand increased more than elevenfold, from US$6.8 million to

---

[1]ESCAP/UNCTC Joint Unit on TNCs, *Cost and Conditions of Technology Transfer Through Transnational Corporations*, ESCAP/UNCTC publication series B, no. 3 (Bangkok, 1984).

Table 1

Technology Trade of Selected Developed Countries with the Pacific-Asian Region, 1965–85[a]
(in US$ millions)

	United States[b]		United Kingdom		France[b]		Federal Republic of Germany		Japan		Five-Country Total	
	1965	1985	1965	1984	1965	1984	1965	1985	1965	1983	1965	Latest Year
Receipts	1,534	8,512	138	1,194	169	4,804	75	545	27	1,014	1,943	16,069
Payments	135	207	131	845	215	2,872	166	995	133	1,176	780	6,095
Total trade	1,669	8,719	263	2,039	384	7,676	241	1,540	160	2,190	2,273	22,164
Balance	1,399	8,305	7	349	-46	1,932	-91	-450	-106	-162	1,163	9,974

[a]The data for 1983–85 are drawn from U.S. Department of Commerce, *Survey of Current Business* (Washington, D.C., March 1986); United Kingdom, Central Statistical Office, *Balance of Payments* (London, 1985); *Monthly Report of the Deutsche Bundesbank*, May 1986; Ministère de l'Economie, des Finances et du Budget, *La Balance des Paiement de la France 1984* (Paris: Statistique et Etudes Financieres, 1985); Japan Statistics Bureau, *Kagaku Gijutsu Kenkyu Chosa Hokoku* (Tokyo, 1984).
[b]For France and the United States, includes all fees and royalties; for all other countries, includes royalties and license fees.

SOURCE: UNCTC, "Transnational Corporations and Technology Transfer: Effects and Policy Issues" (New York: United Nations, 1987).

US$75.2 million. The same trend has also been observed in Malaysia. From 1975 to 1978, Malaysia's outflow of payments related to technology increased by 116 percent.[2] For the Philippines, technology payments increased sixfold, from US$5.81 million in 1972 to US$37.2 million in 1981.[3]

The pattern of technology trade of the two major exporting countries, the United States and Japan, varied substantially. Whereas the United States received only about 20 percent of technology payments from developing countries, 60 percent of Japan's receipt from technical services came from developing countries (see Table 2).

Trade statistics also suggest that a substantial amount of technology trade is intrafirm. About 80 percent of U.S. exports of technology were intrafirm (see Table 2). In Thailand, 57 percent of the total technology fees in 1981 were remitted by firms with more than 50 percent foreign equity share. Intrafirm or intragroup transactions in technology services are also prevalent in other ASEAN countries. Although remittance values of royalties classified by buyer-seller relationship are not available for Malaysia and the Philippines, existing information suggests an association between foreign investment and trade technology services. In Malaysia, 79.6 percent of total sampled technology contracts were concluded between multinational corporations and their fully owned subsidiaries. In the Philippines, 306 out of 634 contracts (48 percent) filed at the Technology Transfer Board between 1978 and 1985 were concluded with equity-related companies; forty-nine were contracts of foreign subsidiaries or foreign majority-owned companies.

In Southeast and East Asia, Japan is by far the most prominent supplier except for the Philippines, where the United States accounted for 46 percent of the total number of technology agreements,[4] and South Korea, where the United States accounted for 43 percent and Japan accounted for 30.7 percent of the value of technology imports between 1962 and 1985. In terms of the number of agreements, however, the share of Japanese technical services supplied to South Korea was higher (45.16 percent). Japan is the contracting party in 32 percent of technology agreements concluded by the private sector in Malaysia. Between 1982 and 1985, an average of 37.6 percent of Thailand's payments for

---

[2]Kamaruddin Nordin, "The Implementation of Proposals of Technology Transfer: Malaysia's Experience," paper presented at the meeting of the Malaysia-Japan Economic Association, Kuala Lumpur, December 14, 1979, cited by the ESCAP/UNCTC Joint Unit on TNCs, *Cost and Conditions of Technology Transfer.*

[3]ESCAP/UNCTC Joint Unit on TNCs, *Cost and Conditions of Technology Transfer.*

[4]Technology Transfer Centre, "Status of Imports of Foreign Technology," 2509/001 (Bangkok, 1986) [in Thai].

Table 2

Selected Developed Countries: Technology Receipts
from Developing Countries
(in US$ millions)

	United States			Japan	
	Total Receipts from Developing Countries	Percentage of Total Receipts	Percentage of Receipts from Affiliates	Total Receipts from Developing Countries	Percentage of Total Receipts
1970	557	22.3	88.2	—	—
1971	601	21.6	89.4	—	—
1972	644	20.9	88.8	—	—
1973	593	18.4	87.5	—	—
1974	724	18.9	87.0	—	—
1975	824	19.2	87.6	123	55.1
1976	806	18.5	85.1	159	56.6
1977	834	17.4	84.4	199	57.1
1978	1,039	18.0	84.3	402	69.4
1979	1,187	19.5	84.9	290	64.2
1980	1,442	20.7	85.1	434	61.6
1981	1,591	21.9	83.7	454	57.2
1982	1,492	20.9	78.6	404	54.4
1983	1,598	20.3	80.0	592	58.4
1984	1,501	18.6	81.3	—	—
1985	1,546	18.2	81.0	—	—

SOURCES: U.S. Department of Commerce, *Survey of Current Business*, various issues. Japan Statistics Bureau, *Kagaku Gijutsu Kenkyu Chosa Hokoku* (Tokyo, 1984), cited by UNCTC, "Transnational Corporations."

technology were made to Japan, whereas 25.5 percent of the same went to the United States.[5]

Direct Foreign Investment

Statistics on direct foreign investments further confirm that the United States is by far the largest exporter of technology. In 1984, U.S. investments amounted to $223,412 million (see Table 3), about three times the size of total direct investment made by Japan between 1951 and 1984 (see Table 4). Whereas 44.2 percent of U.S. investments were in Asia and the Pacific (Table 3), nearly 70 percent of Japan's direct investments were in this region (Table 4).

These two major countries show a number of interesting features. First, within Asia and the Pacific Rim, direct U.S. investment tended to

---

[5]Technology Transfer Centre, "Status of Imports of Foreign Technology."

Table 3

Balance of U.S. Direct Investment in the Pacific Economic Community
(in US$ millions)

	1970		1975		1980		1983		1984	
	Amount	%	Amount	%	Amount	%	Amount	%	Amount	%
PEC	35,083	(44.9) 100.0	52,337	(42.1) 100.0	80,077	(37.1) 100.0	92,553	(40.8) 100.0	98,680	(44.2) 100.0
Advanced countries	27,761	79.1	39,807	76.1	59,461	74.3	64,950	70.2	68,553	69.5
Australia	3,304	9.4	5,065	9.7	7,662	9.6	8,756	9.5	9,188	9.3
Canada	22,790	65.0	31,038	59.3	44,978	56.2	47,553	51.4	50,468	51.1
Japan	1,483	4.2	3,339	6.4	6,243	7.8	8,063	8.7	8,374	8.5
New Zealand	184	0.5	365	0.7	578	0.7	578	0.6	523	0.5
Asian NICs	—	—	—	—	3,151	3.9	4,661	5.0	5,450	5.5
Hong Kong	—	—	—	—	2,078	2.6	3,310	3.6	3,799	3.8
South Korea	—	—	—	—	575	0.7	650	0.7	823	0.8
Taiwan	—	—	—	—	498	0.6	701	0.8	828	0.8
ASEAN countries	701	2.0	2,325	4.4	4,770	6.0	8,140	8.8	9,946	10.1
Brunei	—	—	—	—	—	—	—	—	—	—
Indonesia	—	—	1,587	3.0	1,314	1.6	3,213	3.5	4,409	4.5
Malaysia	—	—	—	—	632	0.8	1,121	1.2	1,153	1.2
Philippines	701	2.0	738	1.4	1,259	1.6	1,107	1.2	1,185	1.2
Singapore	—	—	—	—	1,204	1.5	1,969	2.1	2,232	2.3
Thailand	—	—	—	—	361	0.5	370	0.8	967	1.0
Island countries	—	—	—	—	—	—	—	—	—	—
Fiji	—	—	—	—	—	—	—	—	—	—
French Polynesia	—	—	—	—	—	—	—	—	—	—
Papua New Guinea	—	—	—	—	—	—	—	—	—	—
Vanuatu	—	—	—	—	—	—	—	—	—	—
Solomon Islands	—	—	—	—	—	—	—	—	—	—
Western Samoa	—	—	—	—	—	—	—	—	—	—
Others	—	—	—	—	—	—	—	—	—	—

Table 3 (continued)

	1970		1975		1980		1983		1984	
	Amount	%	Amount	%	Amount	%	Amount	%	Amount	%
Latin America	5,171	14.7	7,150	13.7	12,695	15.3	14,802	16.0	14,731	14.0
Chile	748	2.1	174	0.3	536	0.71	627	0.7	601	0.1
Colombia	698	2.0	648	1.2	1,012	1.3	1,894	2.0	2,103	2.0
Costa Rica	—	—	—	—	—	—	—	—	—	—
Ecuador	—	—	—	—	322	0.4	437	0.5	356	0.0
El Salvador	—	—	—	—	—	—	—	—	—	—
Guatemala	—	—	—	—	—	—	—	—	—	—
Honduras	—	—	—	—	—	—	—	—	—	—
Mexico	1,786	5.1	3,200	6.1	5,989	7.5	5,006	5.4	5,380	5.0
Nicaragua	—	—	—	—	—	—	—	—	—	—
Panama	1,251	3.6	1,907	3.6	3,171	4.0	4,519	4.9	4,061	1.0
Peru	688	2.0	1,221	2.3	1,665	2.1	2,319	2.5	2,220	—
Other Asia and Pacific	1,450	4.1	3,055	5.8	—	—	—	—	—	—
China	—	(—)	—	(—)	—	(—)	—	(—)	—	(—)
World total	70,166	(100.0)	124,212	(100.0)	215,598	(100.0)	26,962	(100.0)	223,412	(100.0)

SOURCE: *Survey of Current Business, 1970–1985*, U.S. Department of Commerce, cited in Pacific Basin Economic Council, *Pacific Economic Community Statistics, 1986* (Tokyo: Japan Member Committee, May 1986).

Table 4

Direct investment by Japan in the Pacific Economic Community
(in US$ millions)

	1980		1981		1982		1983		84		1951–84	
	Amount	%	Amount	%	Amount	%	Amount	%	Amount	%	Amount	%
PEC	3,528	(75.2) 100.0	6,943	(77.7) 100.0	5,748	(74.6) 100.0	6,008	(73.8) 100.0	6,955	(68.6) 100.0	49,821	(69.7) 100.0
Advanced countries	2,035	57.5	2,925	42.1	3,306	57.5	2,878	47.9	3,653	52.6	24,860	49.9
Australia	431	12.2	348	5.0	370	6.4	166	2.8	135	1.5	3,153	6.3
Canada	112	3.2	167	2.4	167	2.9	136	2.3	131	2.6	1,575	3.2
Japan												
New Zealand	8	0.2	56	0.8	31	0.5	11	0.2	15	0.2	238	0.5
United States	1,484	42.1	2,354	33.9	2,738	47.6	2,565	42.7	3,359	48.2	19,894	39.9
Asian NICs	238	6.7	456	6.6	558	9.7	795	13.2	534	8.4	4,991	10.0
Hong Kong	156	4.4	329	4.7	400	7.0	563	9.4	412	5.9	2,799	5.6
South Korea	35	1.0	73	1.1	103	1.8	129	2.1	107	1.5	1,548	3.1
Taiwan	47	1.3	54	0.8	55	1.0	103	1.7	65	0.9	647	1.3
ASEAN countries	926	26.2	2,839	40.9	801	13.9	975	16.2	911	13.1	12,641	25.4
Brunei	—	—	5	0.1	—	—	2	—	5	0.1	107	0.2
Indonesia	529	15.0	2,434	35.1	410	7.1	374	6.2	354	5.4	8,015	16.1
Malaysia	146	4.1	31	0.4	83	1.4	140	2.3	142	2.0	1,046	2.1
Philippines	78	2.2	72	1.0	34	0.6	65	1.1	46	0.7	832	0.7
Singapore	140	4.0	266	3.8	180	3.1	322	5.4	225	3.2	1,980	3.9
Thailand	33	0.9	31	0.4	94	1.6	72	1.2	119	1.7	711	1.4

Table 4 (continued)

	1980		1981		1982		1983		1984		1951–84	
	Amount	%	Amount	%	Amount	%	Amount	%	Amount	%	Amount	%
Island countries	10	0.3	20	0.3	20	0.3	13	0.2	37	0.5	326	0.0
Fiji	—	—	—	—	—	—	—	—	—	—	—	—
French Polynesia	—	—	—	—	—	—	—	—	—	—	—	—
Papua New Guinea	—	—	—	—	—	—	—	—	—	—	—	—
Vanuatu	—	—	—	—	—	—	—	—	—	—	—	—
Solomon Islands	—	—	—	—	—	—	—	—	—	—	—	—
Western Samoa	—	—	—	—	—	—	—	—	—	—	—	—
Others	—	—	—	—	—	—	—	—	—	—	—	—
Latin America	319	9.0	703	10.1	1,063	18.5	1,347	22.4	1,770	25.4	7,000	14.1
Chile	9	0.3	3	0.0	13	0.2	3	0.0	37	0.5	179	0.4
Colombia	—	—	—	—	—	—	—	—	—	—	—	—
Costa Rica	—	—	—	—	—	—	—	—	—	—	—	—
Ecuador	—	—	—	—	—	—	—	—	—	—	—	—
El Salvador	—	—	—	—	—	—	—	—	—	—	—	—
Guatemala	—	—	—	—	—	—	—	—	—	—	—	—
Honduras	—	—	—	—	—	—	—	—	—	—	—	—
Mexico	85	2.4	82	1.2	143	2.5	121	2.0	56	0.8	1,220	2.4
Nicaragua	—	—	—	—	—	—	—	—	—	—	—	—
Panama	222	6.3	614	8.8	722	12.6	1,223	20.4	1,671	24.0	4,916	9.9
Peru	3	0.1	4	0.1	185	3.2	—	—	6	0.1	685	1.4
China	12	(0.3)	26	(0.3)	18	(0.2)	3	(0.0)	114	(1.1)	187	(0.3)
World total	4,693	(100.0)	8,931	(100.0)	7,703	(100.0)	8,145	(100.0)	10,155	(100.0)	71,431	100.0

SOURCE: Overseas Private Investment Division, International Finance Bureau, Japan Ministry of Finance.

be concentrated in the more developed countries (70 percent); about 50 percent of Japanese investments went to developed countries. Second, the United States alone accounted for 40 percent of Japan's direct investment in Pacific areas (Table 4), whereas the bulk of the U.S. direct investment was in Canada (51 percent). Third, the investment pattern of the two countries shows some similarities. For instance, direct investments of both countries were twice as large (or more) in the ASEAN region than in the Asian NICs. The investments in Latin America show approximately the same proportion—that is, 14 percent—reflecting analogous push and pull factors.

The Conventional Issues

Although the discussions about technological change and growth began in the 1950s, it was not until the 1970s that the issue of technology transfer became widely scrutinized. Earlier studies of technology issues emphasized technology as a source of growth. Although estimates of the extent of the contribution of technology to growth varied from study to study, developing countries are more interested in issues of how and at what cost technology should be transferred. The following discussion briefly outlines the major issues related to international transfer of technology that are of particular interest to developing countries.

The Choice of Technology and Its Appropriateness

It was soon noted that technology generated to suit the consumption patterns, environment, and factor endowments of advanced countries may create social conflicts and waste, accelerate deterioration of the environment, and increase unemployment when it is applied to developing countries. Moreover, the technological gap between rich and poor nations is widening. The use of many modern techniques is thought to have a substantial labor displacement effect. At the same time, the population in developing nations is growing at an alarming rate because of better public health and medical services. Low income from agricultural production has caused a rural-to-urban drift transforming part of rural underemployment into urban unemployment.

These facts have led to a call for "appropriate technology," a concept defined by David Morawetz as a

> set of techniques which makes optimum use of available resources in a given environment. For each product or process, it is the technology which maximizes social welfare if factors and products are shadow priced.[6]

---

[6]David Morawetz, "Implications of Industrialization in Developing Countries: A Survey," *Economic Journal* 84 (1974):517.

In relation to labor-abundant LDCs, the concept has become loosely connected with labor-intensive techniques.

Debates on the appropriate choice of technology have centered around substitutability, both in products and inputs. Supporters of employment objectives believe that if potential rather than current production functions are considered, the range of production techniques will be substantially widened. If sufficient research and development effort is invested in adapting past innovations and developing new ones, the conflict between maximum output and maximum employment can be alleviated. Moreover, since the social cost of unemployment—including the affront to human dignity—is so great, the optimum strategy is to select a labor-intensive product mix and relative labor-intensive techniques.

On the other hand, other economists argue that the elasticity of substitution between capital and labor in manufacturing industries is lower than commonly assumed, especially when skill constraints in LDCs are taken into account.[7] They believe labor-intensive products that do not require inputs of a scarce skill are quite limited and confined to certain traditional cottage industries and those differentiated products with a high income elasticity of demand, such as high fashion goods, furniture, and so on. Moreover, once products are chosen, there is little scope for variation in factor proportions unless the product specifications are altered. Handwoven and machine-woven textiles, for example, belong in the same product group but, strictly speaking, have different specifications and are produced for different markets. Even in product lines where a fairly wide selection of techniques is possible, modern techniques may be preferable to reach certain specifications in international markets.

The empirical evidence for both sides of the argument is inconclusive.[8] Without entering this debate, I believe three points should be borne in mind. The first is this: a strategy of industrialization based on modern large-scale manufacturing and imported technology designed for growth objectives is in itself an inappropriate strategy for the achievement of employment objectives. Such a strategy is unlikely to provide appropriate technologies for recipient countries for several rea-

---

[7]Kenneth J. Arrow et al., "Capital-Labour Substitution and Economic Efficiency," *Review of Economics and Statistics* 43 (1961):225–50; C. St. J. O'Herlihy, "Capital-Labour Substitution and the Developing Countries: A Problem of Measurement, *Bulletin of the Oxford University Institute of Economics and Statistics* 34 (1972).

[8]For a good review of this issue, see Frederick T. Moore, "Technology Change and Industrial Development: Issues and Opportunities," World Bank Staff Working Papers no. 613 (1983).

sons. First, the bulk of research and development activities are centralized in the activities of multinational corporations, the competitive edge of which depends on their technological lead. Second, the LDCs demand for labor-intensive technology is not sufficiently strong to induce economic production of such technology.[9] Last, the cost of searching for "appropriate technology" from an "international technology shelf" could prove to be a considerable strain on the meager capital resources of LDC entrepreneurs.

The second point to bear in mind is that urban unemployment and rural underemployment are the result of numerous factors besides simply the wrong choice of techniques. The problems of unemployment should be considered within a macro rather than a micro framework. Within the macro framework, different sectors may be allowed to play different roles using different techniques with different factor proportions while making sure that the overall balance will not leave abundant resources idle.

The third point is, as Frederick Moore has noted,[10] that the discussion of technology choice has generally avoided certain dynamic aspects of the process, namely, the relationship between factor proportion on one hand and adaptation, innovation, and growth on the other.

Despite the fact that the majority of the academic literature related to technology transfer is devoted to the issue of appropriate technologies, this subject has never raised commensurate concern among the governments affected. Nor has it been a cause of conflict between the transferring and the recipient countries. In contrast, the issue of the appropriate cost of technology transfer—to be discussed in the next section—has attracted much more debate in the international arena.

The Cost

In earlier days, it was argued that because the marginal cost of using technology was zero, technology should be transferred free of charge. It has been increasingly recognized, however, that although commercial technologies do have certain public good characteristics, the transfer of right of use to a second party may generate a certain opportunity cost to technology owners or decrease the value of expected return to the first party's technological assets and to other assets used in conjunction with the technological assets. In addition, there are also costs associated with the transfer activities, such as duplications of blue-

---

[9]Howard Pack and Michael P. Todara, "Technological Transfer, Labour Absorption, and Economic Development," *Oxford Economic Papers* 21 (1969): 395–403.
[10]Moore, "Technology Change and Industrial Development."

prints, preparation of manuals, and so on. Concern over the financial costs of technology has thus shifted to the issue of whether the technology recipients have received a "fair" price or whether technology sellers are discriminating monopolies. The price is considered "fair" if other recipients have been charged similar prices. From intrafirm sales, attention is given to whether or not an abuse of transfer price has occurred. Apart from financial cost, concern has been expressed over the implicit costs found in restrictive clauses, such as export bans, tie-in purchases, extraterritoriality, and so on.

Empirical findings on technology pricing vary substantially in their methodology and results. Studies focusing on suppliers' behavior suggest that suppliers cannot extract the maximum rent and can obtain only one-third to one-half their rent, and that their average royalty ranged between 3 to 4 percent of sales.[11]

Empirical evidence based on studies in developing countries, however, suggest the contrary. For example, a study on the financial cost of technology transfer in Thailand indicates that the range of the prices of imported technologies is relatively wide, exceeding 5 percent of gross sales in four industries and 5 percent of net sales in two other industries.[12] Thirty-eight (out of a total of 388) contracts for which fees exceeded 5 percent of sales accounted for approximately 10 percent of total remittances in 1981. Moreover, suppliers from Japan and developing countries (i.e., technology emulators) tended to charge fees that fell in the lower ranges compared with the United States and European countries.

Other studies indicated that the range of fees in Malaysia and the Philippines was narrower than those prevailing in Thailand. The fact that the range of fees in Thailand (where no regulatory agency exists) is relatively high tends to support the hypothesis of discriminating monopolistic practice.

The difficulty arising from research on the cost issue is that markets for some technologies are imperfect and no bench mark prices are readily available. Moreover, each package of technology may differ in both content and quality. Therefore, most of these empirical studies have provided only ranges of technology fees.

Empirical findings relating to restrictive conditions are more conclusive and confirm that restrictive practices are widespread. Approxi-

---

[11]Richard E. Caves, Harold Crookell, and J. Peter Kelling, "The Imperfect Market for Technology Licenses," discussion paper no. 903, Harvard Institute of Economic Research, June 1982.
[12]ESCAP/UNCTC Joint Unit on TNCs, *Cost and Conditions of Technology Transfer.*

mately 25 percent of contracts concluded by Japanese enterprises with foreign technology suppliers in 1981 contained some restriction on exports.[13] The situation is similar in Korea and Thailand and even more prevalent in Malaysia (30.4 percent). It appears that technology suppliers have attached greatest importance to export conditions. Even when regulatory mechanisms exist, as in Malaysia, export restriction is no less pervasive. Other relatively common restrictive conditions include tied-in purchase and restrictions on the use of expertise after expiration of contracts.

Thus far, research has not been able to indicate a "fair" price for technology transfer. Nor can a best method of payment for an industry be indicated, because each solution is unique depending on the sophistication of the technology acquired and the absorptive capacity of the recipient firm. The final price depends a great deal on the bargaining strength of the recipient, which is likely to be strongest in the areas of mature technology where the technology market is expanding and weakest when the technology market is monopolized.

Appropriate Mechanisms of Transfer

In the past, international transfer of technology through multinational corporations has been accomplished by direct foreign investment in a host country. More recently, however, there has been a proliferation of alternative arrangements for technology transfer that include a range of contractual agreements for the transfer of specific elements of technologies. The issue of interest here is whether the effectiveness of transfer varies according to type of arrangement.

Case studies on the effectiveness of technology transfer through different arrangements suggest that the promotion of local technological capacity is more effective in firms that are predominantly locally owned than in firms with significant foreign equity.[14] In the former, local participation in management positions opens more opportunities for actual involvement by local staff in critical production areas and in project execution.

The case studies also suggest that although firms with significant foreign equity are relatively efficient, they tend to transfer mainly capital-embodied and peripheral or auxiliary technology and highly capital-embodied technology such as papermaking. The core technol-

---

[13]ESCAP/UNCTC, *Cost and Conditions of Technology Transfer*, Table 7.
[14]UNCTC, "Transnational Corporations and Technology Transfer: Effects and Policy Issues" (New York: United Nations, 1987); "Technology Acquisition Under Alternative Arrangements with Transnational Corporations: Selected Industrial Case Studies in Thailand," St/CTC/SERA/6 (New York, 1987).

ogy is generally under foreign control, rendering the absorption process slow and incomplete. Several cases studies, however, indicate that the transfer of auxiliary processes provided by the foreign partners has been effective and substantial.

The second area of concern is whether multinational corporations, especially those from developed countries, are the appropriate agent for transferring technology to the capital-scarce, labor-abundant developing countries. Studies in this area generally compared multinational corporation affiliates with local firms, and results are inconclusive as to whether these affiliates were relatively capital intensive.[15] One conclusion, however, can be made: capital intensity is positively related to the size of firms regardless of nationality of ownership.

The emergence of multinational corporations from developing countries and small developed countries has been proposed as a means of alleviating these problems to a certain extent.[16] Multinational corporations from newly industrializing countries specialize in transferring the processing activities of the products at the tail end of Vernon's product cycle. Multinational corporations from developing countries are thought to engage in "two-step" transfer, that is, they may have, through their own experience, adapted Western technologies to suit their own needs, which are more similar to those prevailing in the developing countries. Multinational corporations from small developed countries may also have scaled down the plants aiming at producing smaller lots, more suited to the quantity demanded in developing economies.

Emerging Issues

Studies on technology transfer have slowly shifted away from an emphasis on motivation, cost, and appropriateness toward the acquisition and mastery process, that is, how technology is transferred. By shifting the focus from the technology-pricing behavior of multinational companies to studies on absorptive capacities and domestic science and technology policies of developing countries, the pressure to scrutinize multinational firms has lessened.

---

[15]Robert Hal Mason, "The Transfer of Technology and Factor Proportions Problem: The Philippines and Mexico," UNITAR Research Report no. 10 (New York, 1971); L. T. Wells, Jr., "Economic Man and Engineering Man: Choice of Technology in a Low-Wage Country," *Public Policy* 11 (1973): 319–42; Mingsarn Santikarn, *Technology Transfer: A Case Study* (Singapore: Singapore University Press, 1981); Waranya Pancharoen, *Multinational Corporations and Host Country Technology: A Case Study of Thailand* (Quezon City: Council for Asian Manpower Studies, University of the Philippines, 1980).

[16]D. C. Lecraw, "Direct Investment by Firms from Less Developed Countries," *Oxford Economic Papers* 29 (1977).

Case studies in the acquisition of technological capabilities confirm that the success or failure of technology transfer depends to a significant extent on the absorptive capacity, awareness, and management ability possessed by the recipient enterprise and on an appropriate choice of arrangement for transfer according to the product, process, and the characteristics of the local enterprises involved.[17] An appropriate selection of supplier is imperative. An individual specialist, for example, is generally most successful if he is asked to supervise a narrow range of products, or when the product is relatively standardized, or when the scale of the business is relatively small. Similarly, suppliers from developing countries may be best suited to transferring standardized, single-product and relatively small-scale production technology. A turnkey arrangement is an appropriate choice when the local concern has some industrial experience. For an industry whose technology is continuously changing, an advanced technology supplier with R&D facilities may be more appropriate.

Another area of investigation is the impact of demand for final product on the process of transfer. A study on technological acquisition in the rice milling industry of Thailand suggests that the change in the characteristics of the demand for the final product is a catalyst for technological change.[18] Policies that seek to reduce such constraints as lack of credit and managerial resources and that neglect to give due attention to the market factor may fail to promote technology transfer in the desired direction, as the change in technology may imply changes in market. This finding has an important implication for international trade in technological services. The demand for the technical services of advanced countries depends on the degree of free trade allowed in the developed markets.

Frances Stewart has pointed out that international technology transfer necessarily involves the discussion of not only sale of knowledge but also sale of marketing rights and market access.[19] The latter refers to the sale of trademarks and brand names. Previously, the issues of sale of

---

[17]UNCTC, "Technology Acquisition."

[18]See, e.g., Carl J. Dahlman, Bruce Ross-Larson, and Larry E. Westphal, *Managing Technological Development*, World Staff Working Papers no. 717, 1985. See also the fourteen case studies conducted by Mingsarn Santikarn Kaosa-ard, "Local Technological Capabilities Under Alternative Arrangements for Technology Transfer" (ESCAP/UNCTC Joint Unit on TNCs, 1987); and the same author, "Technological Acquisition in the Thai Rice Milling and Related Capital Goods Industries," World Employment Programme Research Working Papers (Geneva: ILO, March 1986).

[19]Frances Stewart, "International Technology Transfer: Issues and Policy Options," in Paul Streeton and Richard Jolly, eds., *Recent Issues in World Development* (Oxford: Pergamon Press, 1981).

knowledge and marketing rights have been raised by developing countries. I have already discussed the first point, that is, the cost associated with the sale of technology. The second point deals with the packaged nature of knowledge and the marketing rights of certain technologies. It is agreed that "while knowledge itself may be worth acquiring from a national point of view, marketing rights may not be."[20] Earlier suggestions in this regard have been: to buy the knowledge (i.e., patent rights) and to buy marketing rights (trademarks and brand names) only if the owner has invested resources in capturing the market that the buyer intends to share.[21] Ownership of trademarks does not necessarily imply ownership of market.

The United States has reintroduced this issue from the angle of property owners and has been pressing its trading partners, especially those in East and Southeast Asia, to protect its intellectual property rights (IPR) so that returns from these industrial assets could be fully appropriated.

The U.S. government has hinted to the Thai government that the Generalized System of Preferences (GSP) privileges provided to certain Thai exports might be terminated and that the supply of the U.S. technology could be disrupted, if an agreement on IPR is not reached. Only the first threat, however, carries weight with some government agencies, although it is generally felt that GSP has been intended as a short-term, unilateral gift that would be self-terminating once a certain export level to the United States is achieved. Moreover, IPR laws are considered economic laws and should be applied in accordance with the stage of development current in Thailand. As for technology supplies, the United States is unlikely to be the only seller of the range of technologies Thailand requires. The technology market in Thailand is not one seller's market; Japan, South Korea, and Taiwan and others have proven to be more competitive sources of technology than the United States.

The extent of the economic gain the U.S. private sector will reap through its government's forceful position regarding IPR might not be substantial considering that 86.5 percent of U.S. firms in Thailand (surveyed by the American Chamber of Commerce in March, 1987) indicated that the current laws governing the protection of intellectual property rights in Thailand have no quantifiable impact on their operations. The political cost of the U.S. "IPR phobia" is likely to be high,

---

[20]Ibid.

[21]Mingsarn Santikarn Kaosa-ard, "Technology Transfer," and "Technological Acquisition in the Thai Rice Milling and Related Capital Goods Industries."

however. In Thailand, the issue has already shaken the stability of the coalition government. It is interesting to note that Japan, which has much to gain from property right protection, has adopted a low-profile approach to the same issue.

Although the competition of Japan and the United States in technology markets in the third countries will improve the bargaining strength of the economically more successful ASEAN countries, it may create yet another source of tension between the two major economic powers. To the extent that the countries who are technology recipients prefer sources that offer market access, Japan is likely to be in a more advantageous position. The United States may threaten to close its market, but to take away what has already been given is more difficult (or damaging) than to offer hitherto closed markets. With the rapidly increasing value of the yen, Japan also needs to establish external production capacities. The important implication is that if this trend develops, future trade conflicts will not be simply bilateral matters—that is, the United States versus Japan or the United States or Japan versus an LDC—but rather the United States versus Japan and her LDC associates.

Policy Issues and Directions

Essentially, the issues discussed in the essay are related to policy issues on which a government decision is to be made regarding the international transfer of technology. First, for example, the decision to control or not to control technology imports depends on the advantages and disadvantages of allowing a free flow of technology. Second, the policy on direct foreign investment must take into account the costs and benefits of technology transfer under different modes or channels of transfer—that is, whether direct foreign investment is a more effective mode and a less costly means than alternative arrangements. If the difference in costs and benefits arising from alternative modes is significant, policies may have to be designed to promote the preferred modes for a specific sector. Third, what kind of policies are needed to enhance technology transfer? Is a policy on technology imports a sufficiently effective mechanism to ensure the fulfillment of national objectives? What are the policies that may have indirect but effective impact in determining technology inflow?

Among the academic issues discussed earlier, technology import costs and controls have tended to attract most attention from the governments of the developing countries with the issue of appropriate technology receiving only lip-service. Governments in the Pacific-Asian region are more preoccupied with subsidizing the use of capital in the large-scale modern sector and are disturbed by imports of what they regard as outdated and secondhand technology. In the area of technology imports, countries in the Pacific-Asian region can be broadly divided into three groups. The first group consists of those countries that allow free flows of technology, such as the United States (except defense-related technology), Japan, Thailand, and Singapore. South Korea is in the final stage of totally liberalizing its technology imports from an approval system to a reporting system. Since 1984, firms paying technology fees below 10 percent of sales have been allowed to import technology (excluding trademarks and "outdated" technology) freely. Since the latter half of 1986, South Korea has planned to abandon the restricted entry of trademarks and outdated technology.

The second group consists of countries that exercise control on technology imports, especially with regard to financial cost and restrictive clauses. These are mainly Latin American countries, the Philippines, and India. In these countries technology agreements must be screened and approved by regulatory agencies; their main concern focuses on the foreign exchange impact of technology imports and technological dependence on external sources. In recent years, however, some countries in this group—for example, India—have relaxed their regulations. Therefore, their major negotiation issues are the rates and the size of payments and restrictive clauses contained in technology contracts.

The third group consists of countries with some regulations on technology imports. Malaysia and Indonesia appear to belong to this group. Malysia tends to exert a higher degree of regulation than Indonesia and has set up a Technology Transfer Unit to examine technology contracts. Malaysia, however, does not impose foreign exchange control on payments of technology. In Indonesia, high-technology fees are allowed but have to be calculated on the basis of profits rather than sales.

Compared with technology imports, policies on foreign investments of most countries in the region have been more liberal, especially foreign investments in high-tech industries. As more developing Pacific-Asian countries adopt an export-led growth strategy, buying more technologies implies exporting more goods. A technology supplier who can also offer a market will be preferred.

Finally, a number of countries in this region have been impressed by the "Korean model" of stimulating domestic research, development, and education activities to enhance technology transfer. Fewer countries have noted that planning for technology transfer and development requires not only the establishment of a specific microeconomic policy on the regulation of imported technology but also an understanding of the country's existing quantitative and qualitative factor endowments. In addition, intelligent planning requires an assessment of the country's dynamic comparative advantage and its position in the international market. Both technology import policy and science and technology policy, in fact, must be related and integrated into every Pacific-Asian country's master plan for development.

9. Japan-U.S. Economic Conflicts and Their Impact on the Pacific-Asian Region

IPPEI YAMAZAWA

Current Issues for the Pacific-Asian Economies

Throughout the 1970s, the Pacific-Asian developing countries achieved rapid economic growth, and their potential for continued future growth gave substantial momentum to the prospects for Pacific economic cooperation. In the 1980s, however, this expansion has slowed, with serious setbacks in 1982 and 1985. ASEAN countries in particular experienced a downturn to slow or minus growth, resulting in a "hollowing" of economic growth in Asia and the Pacific. On the other hand, South Korea and Taiwan suffered less in 1985 but the nature of their economic expansion has changed from the 1970s. Both Asian NICs and ASEAN countries resumed higher growth rates in 1986 and 1987 but the stock exchange market turbulence of October 1987 together with uncertainties relating to the U.S. economy has cast a shadow on the future.

The depression affecting the ASEAN economies was caused mainly by such global trends as the rapid decline of prices of petroleum and other primary products as well as the stagnant growth and protectionist policies in developed countries. The economic conflict between the United States and Japan was especially important. Furthermore, economic conflicts prevalent in the region caused a deterioration of the trading environment and aggravated preexisting difficulties. Two other economic conflicts have emerged in the area, one between the United States and developing Asia, and the other between developing Asia and Japan. Both are characterized by persistent bilateral trade imbalances, and they are often regarded as a mere spillover of the similar and larger U.S.-Japan conflict. This is not correct. Developing Asia has never been only a bystander, but has been actively involved in the U.S.-Japan conflict. The industrial catching up process in these countries is closely interrelated with the United States and Japan.

The purpose of this essay is first to analyze the three economic conflicts in the region and to understand the forces affecting them. Since the Pacific-Asian region is open to the outside world, its current difficulties should be understood in the context of fluctuations in the world economy. We are now in the final phase of a long swing that began with the rapid price increase of petroleum and other primary products in the late 1960s and early 1970s and is ending with the recent rapid decline of those products, a swing that was exaggerated by the ill-managed policy response of developed countries to these price increases. Large imbalances and economic conflicts still remain among the trading partners and the economic difficulties of Pacific-Asian countries have been aggravated by all three conflicts. Furthermore, these economies have become closely interrelated through direct investments and liberalized financial flows, circumstances that have complicated each economic conflict and its relationship to the others.

The second purpose of this essay is to discuss the role that Japan is expected to play in resolving these conflicts and restoring the vitality of the region's economies. I will first identify three current structural elements of the region's economies: policy discrepancies, catching-up industrialization, and integration. Then, with the assistance of these structural elements I will examine in turn the three economic conflicts in the region. I conclude, finally, with Japan's role in regional solutions of the current difficulties.

The Structure of the Pacific-Asian Economic Conflicts

The present state of the Pacific-Asian economies should be understood in the broader context of the worldwide economic fluctuations since the late 1960s that characterize the first structural element of our current economic order.

Growth Disparity Between Developed and Asian Developing Countries

Let me start with a quick review of the growth performance of individual countries in Asia and the Pacific. In the 1970s, especially after the first oil price hike, most developed countries experienced continued slow growth after their rapid growth during the 1950s and 1960s (see Table 1). Japan's real GDP growth rate has never exceeded 6 percent since 1974, in contrast to its more than 10 percent growth, on average, in the 1960s. The United States continued its 2–3 percent growth in the 1970s and experienced repeated ups and downs, ranging from − 2 to 6 percent. Many EEC member countries recorded 2–5 percent growth during this period.

In contrast, developing countries in East Asia achieved high growth throughout the 1970s. Asian NICs experienced 8–10 percent growth, and ASEAN countries (other than Singapore) experienced 6–8 percent growth on average. In the 1980s, however, their growth performance

Table 1

Growth Performance of Asian-Pacific Countries[a]

Country	1961–70	1971–80	1981	1982	1983	1984	1985	1986
Japan	11.8	4.7	3.7	3.1	3.2	5.0	4.5	2.8
United States	3.3	2.4	2.3	−1.9	5.0	6.2	2.8	3.2
South Korea	9.6	8.2	6.9	5.6	9.4	8.0	5.1	10.4
Singapore	9.6	9.1	9.9	6.3	7.9	8.1	−1.9	1.9
Thailand	7.9	6.9	6.3	4.1	5.2	6.1	3.2	3.8
Indonesia	4.2	8.0	7.9	2.1	4.2	5.1	1.9	0.5
Malaysia		8.1	7.1	5.7	5.9	7.3	−1.0	0.4
Philippines	5.1	6.0	3.9	2.9	1.1	−4.5	−3.9	0.5

[a]Percentage of annual growth rates of real GDP.

SOURCE: International Monetary Fund, *International Financial Statistics,* 1986 annual.

has showed a tendency to deteriorate. Both Asian NICs and ASEAN countries experienced setback in their growth in 1982 and 1985. In particular, ASEAN countries—except Thailand—experienced very low growth rates of 2 to −2 percent in 1985 and 1986.

Exports of Asian developing countries expanded more rapidly than their GDP and were shipped mainly to developed country markets, which grew at much slower rates. These countries rapidly increased their shares in the developed country markets but caused conflicts with domestic producers there. On the other hand, the import demand of developing countries expanded equally in excess of their GDP and their major supply sources were developed countries. Thus, developing countries contributed to the growth of developed countries through their imports from the latter. The growth disparity provided both conflicts and stimuli for the world economy.

Increase in Commodity Prices and Policy Response by Developed Countries

What is the mechanism underlying the worldwide fluctuation and growth disparity described here? It is a long swing that started with a large price increase for petroleum and other primary products in the late 1960s and early 1970s, proceeded with running inflation and the threat of unemployment in the latter half of the 1970s, was eventually countered with deflationary policies instituted by developed country governments in the early 1980s, and is now ending with a rapid decline in commodity prices. Let us review the individual stages of this swing in chronological order.

A quadruple increase in petroleum prices from October 1973 to early 1974 finally ended the rapid growth of developed countries that had continued since the mid-1950s. Other commodity prices, however, had started to increase since the late 1960s. Labor wage rates continued to increase in most developed countries throughout the 1960s as well. All these effects resulted from an excess demand for productive resources at the end of rapid growth and accelerated inflationary pressure. International monetary disturbances in the late 1960s added an excess supply of international liquidity and aggravated the trend.

The oil crisis in 1973 simultaneously caused rapid inflation, a large trade imbalance, heavy deflationary pressures, and negative growth in major developed countries. Governments tried to restore the level of output and employment by means of active fiscal expansion. Medium economic growth was restored in the latter part of the 1970s, but inflation was built in and further accelerated by the second oil crisis in 1979.

Deflationary response by governments came in 1979 to curb inflation. In the United States, the Federal Reserve tightened its money supply, which led to much higher interest rates than planned. The higher interest rate invited a heavy flow of money to the United States and the U.S. dollar appreciated as a result. Japan and the EEC countries followed the United States in tightening their monetary policies, partly to curb their own inflation at home and partly to discourage the outflow of money and stop the depreciation of their currencies, a source of imported inflation. Very high interest rates and the strong dollar resulted from these actions, and most developed countries have suffered from accumulated fiscal deficits since the oil crisis.

A disparity appeared among developed countries in the process of the deflationary response. The United States continued a fiscal expansion and accumulated twin deficits in both current accounts and fiscal budgets. Japan, on the other hand, adopted an austere fiscal policy and succeeded in reducing its fiscal deficits. Japan's production was oriented toward the export market under conditions of stagnant domestic demand, which resulted in a huge trade balance surplus and slower growth. The undervaluation of the yen still continued because of persistent capital flow to the dollar market. The EEC fell between Japan and the United States, but West Germany and some other member countries remained closer to the Japanese situation.

The Group of Five agreement in September 1985, however, has changed this trend. High interest rates and the overvaluation of the U.S. dollar have been adjusted for the last two years. The downward adjustment of interest rates started earlier as inflation slowed and tight monetary policies were eased in major developed countries. The price index of other primary products reached its peak in 1980 and turned down since then, reflecting the slackened demand for raw materials in developed countries. The decline of oil prices came more drastically. It began with a small decrease in 1983 but dropped sharply after December 1985.

The long swing is now finishing its final phase, although large imbalances between developed economies still remain unresolved.

Continued Growth of Asian Developing Countries

The second structural element is the catching-up industrialization of Asian developing countries. Japan's rapid growth in the 1950s and 1960s can be regarded as its predecessor and provides a typical example of the "spread of industrialization," to use Alexander Gerschenkron's terminology.[1]

Late-starting countries introduce the most advanced technology and, helped by the vigorous increase in domestic demand, expand their plants and equipment and improve their competitiveness. Their products are exported to developed country markets and compete with domestic producers there, which leads to protection demands in the developed countries. Japan's rapid growth in the 1950s and 1960s was a typical example of this catching-up industrialization. The NICs followed Japan; South Korea and Taiwan took their best advantage and were able to overcome the oil shock in the 1970s. ASEAN countries followed Asian NICs and started industrialization in the late 1960s, which provided the basis for the recent spurt of manufactured exports.

These Asian countries have a common strategy, namely, outward-looking industrialization, compared to the inward-looking strategy of their Latin American counterparts. Asian NICs succeeded in their export-led growth, partly benefiting from the unprecedented expansion of world trade before the oil crisis. The growth of the ASEAN countries, on the other hand, came later but benefited from the favorable prices of their main exports, petroleum and other primary products. They implemented ambitious development programs and continued rapid growth throughout the 1970s.

The worldwide depression of the early 1980s, however, hit Asian developing countries hard for the first time. As their exports to developed country markets stagnated and their export earnings decreased drastically, their imports for development continued to grow and they incurred large trade deficits. To avoid further accumulation of foreign debts, many countries reduced their development programs. The ASEAN countries exporting primary products have thus been trapped in a serious depression. On the other hand, South Korea and Taiwan have not been adversely affected during this final phase, partly because of decreased payments for energy and raw material imports, and partly

---

[1]Alexander Gerschenkron, *Economic Backwardness in Historical Perspective* (Cambridge: Belknap Press of Harvard University, 1966).

because of accelerated exports caused by their undervalued currencies due to exchange rate alignment. Thailand, with less reliance on primary product exports, has been less affected by stagnant commodity markets and has maintained a medium growth.

The third structural element is the increased interdependence or economic integration among Pacific-Asian countries, through liberalized capital flow and activated direct investment by American and Japanese multinational firms. These factors, however, also occasionally destabilize the regional market, but the trend cannot be reversed. Interacting with each other, these three elements have yielded a unique type of economic environment. This environment is the framework for the three major economic conflicts now taking place in the region.

Economic Conflicts Between Japan and the United States

The current U.S.-Japan economic conflict has been complicated both by economic logic and by political maneuvering. The interaction of the three structural elements needs to be clarified in order to reveal the economic reasoning behind this conflict. A clear cause-and-effect explanation requires a distinction between sectoral and overall conflict.

From Sectoral to Overall Conflict

The U.S.-Japan trade conflict has its origin in the process of Japan's catching up with the United States. Japan's export structure changed drastically during her rapid growth period. Every new export was shipped to the U.S. market and competed with American producers. American producers demanded protection, and the conflict was often concluded with voluntary restrictions placed on Japanese exporters. Textiles are a classic example,[2] followed by iron and steel, television sets, cars, machinery, and semiconductors. Most of these products have still been held under voluntary export restriction; they represent the conflict between Japanese exporters and American producers in individual sectors.

In the 1980s, however, a conflict emerged in the overall trade relationship between Japan and her major trading partners. Not only the export behavior of Japanese firms but also the trade and industrial pol-

---

[2]The trade dispute over textiles between the United States and Japan in 1969–71 was spread to similar disputes between the United States and South Korea, Taiwan, and Hong Kong and was finally concluded with the full-fledged framework of managed trade in textiles, the Multi-Fiber Arrangement, in 1974. See I. M. Destler, H. Fukui, and H. Sato, *The Textile Wrangle: Conflict in Japanese-American Relations, 1969–1971* (Ithaca: Cornell University Press, 1979).

icy of the Japanese government began to be a target of criticism on such occasions as summit meetings and OECD ministerial meetings. In 1981, the Japanese government received in succession requests from the EEC committee (September), the United Kingdom (October), and the United States (December) with all parties complaining about their persistent trade deficits with Japan and demanding market liberalization and import expansion. Japan's increasing conflicts with its developed country partners reflects the catching-up process just mentioned.

Japan responded with a series of trade liberalization programs. Complaints were also heard about the complicated distribution procedures of the Japanese market and commercial practices that prevent access by foreign exporters. In July 1985, the Japanese government announced the Action Program to further reduce those barriers and promote imports, the seventh in the series of trade liberalizations since 1972. The Action Program included the reduction or elimination of tariffs on over 1,800 items from January 1986, a package of liberalization and simplification measures in standards and certification procedures, and government procurement procedures. This program departed from previous trade liberalization programs in its principle and scale, and it is expected to increase imports and reduce trade surplus in the long run.

Since 1983, however, the overall conflict between the United States and Japan has been seriously aggravated, reflecting the rapid expansion of the bilateral trade and current account imbalances between the two countries. Japan's trade surplus with the United States was around US$12 to $13 billion in 1981–82, but it increased rapidly up to US$51.4 billion in 1986. The United States strengthened its request for further liberalization of the Japanese market and the reduction of bilateral imbalance down to a tolerable level.

Macroeconomic Imbalances

Bilateral trade imbalance, though recorded in the trade between Japan and the United States, reflects the fundamentally individual overall imbalances of the two countries. Japan's overall trade surplus expanded from around US$20 billion in 1981–82 to US$93 billion in 1986, whereas the overall U.S. trade deficit expanded from $28 billion in 1981 to $148 billion in 1986 (see Table 2). The U.S. statistics show a slightly larger trade deficit of $156 billion. Increasing bilateral imbalance between the two countries simply reflects their increasing overall imbalances. That is, a large total import demand from the United States has created a large import from competitive Japan, and a small total import demand from Japan has resulted in a small U.S. export to Japan. The United States has similar imbalances with West Germany and other EEC member countries. The U.S. trade deficit, partly offset by the sur-

Table 2

Balance of Trade of United States, Japan,
and Developing Asian Countries
(US$ millions)

Country		1981	1982	1983	1984	1985	1986
United States	B/T[a]	− 27,978	− 36,444	− 67,080	−112,522	−124,439	− 14,700
	X (f.o.b.)[b]	237,085	211,198	201,820	219,900	214,424	221,750
	M (f.o.b.)[c]	265,063	247,642	268,900	332,422	338,863	369,450
Japan	B/T	19,967	18,079	31,454	44,257	55,986	92,959
	X (f.o.b.)	149,522	137,663	145,468	168,290	174,015	205,558
	M (f.o.b.)	129,555	119,584	114,014	124,033	118,029	112,899
	B/T w U.S.	13,312	12,151	18,182	33,075	39,485	51,402
	X (f.o.b.)	38,609	36,330	42,829	59,937	65,278	80,456
	M (c.i.f.)	25,297	24,179	24,647	26,862	25,793	29,054
South Korea	B/T	− 3,628	− 2,859	− 1,764	− 1,036	− 19	4,206
	X (f.o.b.)	20,671	20,879	23,204	26,335	26,442	33,913
	M (f.o.b.)	24,299	23,474	24,967	27,371	26,461	29,707
	B/T w U.S.	− 389	− 287	1,971	3,603	4,265	7,335
	X (f.o.b.)	5,661	6,243	8,245	10,479	10,754	13,880
	M (c.i.f.)	6,050	5,956	6,274	6,876	6,489	6,545
	B/T w Japan	− 2,871	− 1,917	− 2,834	− 3,038	− 3,017	− 5,183
	X (f.o.b.)	3,503	3,388	3,404	4,602	4,543	5,292
	M (c.i.f.)	6,374	5,305	6,238	7,640	7,560	10,475
Taiwan	B/T	1,825	3,646	6,268	9,233	11,170	15,609
	X (f.o.b.)	22,408	21,776	25,028	30,185	30,466	39,785
	M (f.o.b.)	20,583	18,130	18,760	20,952	19,296	24,176
	B/T w U.S.	3,469	4,681	6,996	9,924	10,099	13,578
	X (f.o.b.)	8,091	9,047	11,292	14,735	14,652	18,994
	M (c.i.f.)	4,622	4,366	4,296	4,811	4,553	5,416
	B/T w Japan	− 3,324	− 2,135	− 2,698	− 3,136	− 1,894	− 3,161
	X (f.o.b.)	2,434	2,441	2,468	3,009	3,432	4,691
	M (c.i.f.)	5,758	4,576	5,166	6,145	5,326	7,852
China	B/T	− 155	− 2,135	− 783	− 1,129	− 15,205	− 8,386
	X (f.o.b.)	21,476	21,865	22,096	24,824	27,329	31,472
	M (f.o.b.)	21,631	18,920	21,313	25,953	42,534	39,858
	B/T w U.S.	− 3,177	− 2,540	− 1,040	− 1,524	− 2,863	1,662
	X (f.o.b.)	1,505	1,765	1,713	2,313	2,336	4,771
	M (c.i.f.)	6,183	3,902	5,495	8,057	15,178	9,856
	B/T w Japan	− 1,436	− 904	− 978	− 2,902	− 9,087	− 4,204
	X (f.o.b.)	4,747	4,806	4,517	5,155	6,091	5,652
	M (c.i.f.)	6,183	3,902	5,495	8,057	15,178	9,856

Table 2 (continued)

Country		1981	1982	1983	1984	1985	1986
Singapore	B/T	−6,716	−7,564	−6,276	−4,497	−3,629	−2,328
	X (f.o.b.)	21,314	21,087	21,700	23,572	23,838	21,300
	M (f.o.b.)	28,030	28,651	27,976	28,069	27,467	23,628
	B/T w U.S.	−726	−1,035	−297	628	876	3,131
	X (f.o.b.)	2,814	2,652	3,937	4,725	5,045	11,447
	M (c.i.f.)	3,540	3,687	4,234	4,097	4,169	8,317
	B/T w Japan	−3,132	−2,820	−3,047	−2,944	−2,446	−3,114
	X (f.o.b.)	2,141	2,297	1,995	2,207	2,243	1,463
	M (c.i.f.)	5,273	5,117	5,042	5,151	4,689	4,577
Thailand	B/T	−2,924	−1,604	−3,919	−2,985	−2,121	−507
	X	7,031	6,945	6,368	7,413	7,121	8,758
	M	9,955	8,549	10,287	10,398	9,242	8,251
	B/T w U.S.	−380	−260	−340	−109	353	349
	X	907	880	951	1,273	1,399	1,402
	M	1,287	1,140	1,291	1,382	1,046	1,053
	B/T w Japan	−1,400	−1,049	−1,855	−1,789	−1,501	−639
	X	994	954	960	963	950	1,391
	M	2,394	2,003	2,815	2,752	2,451	2,030
Malaysia	B/T	220	−388	842	2,433	3,141	3,369
	X	11,770	12,030	14,104	16,484	15,443	13,719
	M	11,550	12,418	13,262	14,051	12,302	10,350
	B/T w U.S.	815	254	537	−64	89	724
	X	2,272	1,959	2,205	2,231	1,970	2,420
	M	1,457	1,705	1,668	2,295	1,881	1,696
	B/T w Japan	503	508	360	1,537	2,162	2,138
	X	2,927	3,010	3,131	4,412	4,330	3,846
	M	2,424	2,502	2,502	2,875	2,168	1,708
Indonesia	B/T	8,988	5,434	4,800	8,020	8,331	5,249
	X	22,260	22,293	21,152	21,902	18,590	14,824
	M	13,272	16,859	16,352	13,882	10,259	9,575
	B/T w U.S.	2,565	1,129	1,733	1,945	2,827	2,374
	X	4,360	3,546	4,267	4,505	4,168	3,312
	M	1,795	2,417	2,534	2,560	1,341	938
	B/T w Japan	7,427	6,914	5,885	7,045	6,388	4,649
	X	11,416	11,193	9,678	10,353	9,007	7,733
	M	3,989	4,279	3,793	3,308	2,619	2,662

(Continued)

Table 2 (continued)

Country		1981	1982	1983	1984	1985	1986
Philippines	B/T	− 2,759	− 3,243	− 2,974	− 1,037	− 482	− 202
	X	5,720	5,021	5,005	5,391	4,629	4,842
	M	8,479	8,263	7,979	6,428	5,111	5,044
	B/T w U.S.	− 160	28	− 38	318	314	623
	X	1,771	1,889	1,793	2,032	1,658	1,972
	M	1,931	1,861	1,831	1,714	1,344	1,349
	B/T w Japan	− 355	− 513	− 358	183	306	133
	X	1,254	1,149	984	1,034	1,243	1,221
	M	1,609	1,662	1,342	851	937	1,088

[a]Overall balance of trade (B/T) is compiled from balance-of-payments statistics so that both exports and imports are recorded on an f.o.b. basis. Bilateral balance-of-trade figures are computed from trade statistics on a customs clearance basis (exports in f.o.b. and imports in c.i.f.). 1986 balance-of-trade figures for Korea through Philippines with Japan obtained from Japanese customs data so that exports are Japan's imports (c.i.f.) and imports are Japan's exports (f.o.b.). The 1981–85 figures for Malaysia's balance of trade with Japan are also compiled from the latter data. There are some discrepancies between figures from the two sources, but they do not distort our major findings.
[b]X = exports; freight on board.
[c]M = imports; costs, insurance, freight.

SOURCE: Bank of Japan, *Gaikoku Keizai Tokei Nempo* [Foreign Economic Statistics Annual], for 1985, October 1986, compiled originally from individual country statistics and supplemented by Japan's foreign trade statistics.

plus in service account, resulted in a current account deficit of $141 billion in 1986. This persistent deficit has been financed by capital inflow, half of which came from Japan. The United States became a net debtor country in 1985, and its net external debt balance amounted to $264 billion by the end of 1986.

Japan's huge surplus and the United States' huge deficit have directly resulted from different policy responses by the two countries over the long term. Japan, under strict administrative reform, reduced its fiscal deficit from 4.0 percent of GDP to 1.7 percent between 1981 and 1985, whereas the United States expanded its fiscal deficit (relying mainly on a tight monetary policy) from 2.8 to 5.2 percent during the same period. Japan expanded exports, overcoming stagnant domestic demand, and experienced slow growth and a huge trade surplus. In contrast, the United States implemented a tax cut and increased expenditures, thus experiencing a boom in 1983 and 1984 but also incurring huge twin deficits.

Cooperation for Macroeconomic Adjustment

Both American and Japanese economists agree that their bilateral trade imbalance, the symbol of their economic conflict, resulted from the discrepancy of their macroeconomic policies and can only be resolved through macroeconomic adjustment.[3] Two types of macroeconomic adjustment have been identified: (1) aggregate expenditure adjustment through fiscal and monetary measures, and (2) exchange rate adjustment.

What have Japan and the United States done so far for their aggregate expenditure adjustment? The Bank of Japan reduced the official rediscount rate four times in 1986 from 5.0 to 4.5 percent in January, to 4.0 percent in March, to 3.5 percent in April, to the record low of 3.0 percent in November, and further to 2.5 percent after the second G-5 meeting in February 1987.[4] In the Overall Economic Measure announced last September, the Japanese government also implemented a policy package, including a public investment program of 3 trillion yen, in order to boost domestic demand and to achieve a 4 percent growth target. The growth rate of real GDP, however, turned out to be as low as 2.6 percent for the year 1986, and even down to zero growth for April-June 1987, picking up thereafter. In May 1987, before the Venice Summit Meeting, the government implemented an additional expenditure of 6 trillion yen (about US$40 billion) in order to boost domestic demand. It succeeded in boosting private housing investment and producing an 8.3 percent growth (annual converted rate) in the July-September quarter 1987, assuring a 3.5 percent growth for the 1987 fiscal year.

On the other hand, in 1985 the U.S. Congress enacted the Gramm-Rudmann-Hollings Act, which obliged the government to eliminate fiscal deficits by 1991. The scheduled budget cut has been difficult, because of conflict between defense and social security demands, and the tax revenue has fallen short of the expected amount. Money supply has been eased to lower interest rates and stimulate investment in productive capacity. The real GDP grew at 2.3 percent for the past year (until September 1986). Economic growth has accelerated in 1987 even to the extent that inflationary pressures were felt, while the twin deficits still continued.

---

[3]C. Fred Bergsten and W. R. Cline, *The United States–Japan Economic Problem,* Institute for International Economics, revised January 1987; and C. Fred Bergsten, ''Economic Imbalances and World Politics,'' *Foreign Affairs 66* (Spring 1987).

[4]*Nippon Keizai Shimbun* [Japan Economic Journal], January 14, 1987.

Adjustment of Exchange Rates

The two countries resorted to an exchange rate adjustment at the G-5 meeting in September 1985. The U.S. dollar had been overvalued for 1981–85, resulting from very high interest rates and capital inflow to the United States. This weakened the competitiveness of American products and aggravated the country's trade imbalance. In contrast, Japan was annoyed by the undervalued yen and welcomed the appreciation of the yen up to 190–200 yen per dollar, although no target zone was agreed upon at the G-5 meeting. The appreciation of the yen proceeded further than expected, however: in March 1986, when the yen fell short of 180 yen per dollar, the Bank of Japan intervened by reverse transaction—that is, by selling yen and buying dollars—but the appreciation did not stop and the yen fell short of 160 yen per dollar by August. It stayed at the 160 yen level for three months after the Miyazawa-Baker agreement in November 1986, but it started to rise rapidly again after the middle of January. The dollar depreciated rapidly against the deutsch mark as well, down to a record low. Through repeated rapid declines interspersed with a month or two of limited change, the U.S. dollar depreciated in comparison with the yen and the mark, down to 132 yen and 1.63 marks per dollar by the end of November 1987.

In spite of the drastic exchange rate adjustment, however, the trade imbalance has been adjusted only slowly. As for the adjustment on the Japanese side, Japanese export volume turned downward after the middle of 1986 although the trade surplus did not decrease in terms of the dollar until April 1987. This was because of the J-curve effect. Also, the import value did not increase because of the decline of the price of petroleum. The Japanese current account however, has decreased consecutively since May and the trade surplus since July 1987. Thus, only a small increase was recorded for the current account surplus for the 1987 calender year in comparison with 1986.[5]

On the other hand, the exchange rate adjustment has significantly affected corporate behavior at the micro level. Manufactured imports have increased in both amount and variety. New imports such as cameras and personal computers began, and imports of textiles and standardized steel products continued to increase. Manufactured imports made up 44 percent of Japan's total imports for the first nine months of 1987.[6] In such heavy industries as shipbuilding, steel, and petrochemicals, a large proportion of existing capacities and equipment have been abolished and workers laid off or shifted to other jobs. Such exporting

[5]*Nippon Keizai Shimbun* [Japan Economic Journal], December 1, 1987.
[6]Ibid., December 2, 1987.

industries as automobiles and electronics either relocated production abroad through direct foreign investment or developed new products for the domestic market and increased their share of domestic sales. Small- and medium-sized firms have become more active in direct foreign investment. Direct investment by Japanese firms began in response to trade conflicts or exchange rate appreciation. Now these firms engage in business cooperation with American and other Asian firms and are developing a multinational strategy so that the past trend will not be reversed even if the conflict is resolved and exchange rate adjustment is reversed. These developments will lead to a drastic long-term change in the trade and production structure of the Pacific-Asian region.

The adjustment of the U.S. trade deficit, in contrast, lagged behind. The trade deficit continued to increase until the summer of 1987. The U.S. export volume began to increase after October–December 1986, but the import increase tended to exceed it. Only in November 1987 did a consecutive improvement of the trade balance begin, but it was feared that the slow policy responses had already discouraged the market to continue its confidence in dollar.

Indeed, the delayed implementation of aggregate expenditure policies has tended to accelerate the adjustment of exchange rates. But the fear has begun to arise that further depreciation of the dollar, if not accompanied by the increased competitiveness of American exporters and offset by inflation, may endanger the international monetary order. It was reported that the target zones of 140–160 yen and 1.70–1.90 mark per dollar were implicitly agreed upon at the second G-5 meeting in Paris in February 1987. This target, however, was abandoned after the turbulence in the stock and foreign exchange markets in late October 1987.[7]

Aggravated Sectoral Conflicts

The prolonged macroeconomic imbalances of the United States and Japan have aggravated sectoral conflicts between the two countries. Trade negotiation has continued on sectoral problems. Existing agreements on voluntary export restraints have been renegotiated (textiles, steel, television sets, working machinery, automobiles, and semicon-

---

[7]At the Second Group of Five meeting in Paris (February 21–22, 1987), five finance ministers agreed on a package of macroeconomic policy coordination to maintain their currency exchange rates at the present range. This package includes the reduction of the Bank of Japan's rediscount rate (down to 2.5 percent) and further stimulation of domestic demand through fiscal expansion by Japan, stimulation of domestic demand through tax reduction by West Germany, and improvement of balance of payments through the reduction of fiscal deficit by the United States (*Nippon Keizai Shimbun*, February 23, 1987).

ductors). Although the undesirable effects of VERs have been criticized by both American and Japanese economists, they cannot be easily disconnected, as demonstrated by the seven-year VER for automobiles, whose export performance has fallen short of the quota.

In addition, a new approach was introduced for semiconductors. This resulted from the rapid export expansion of Japanese chips (semiconductors) to the United States and anti-dumping suits by the U.S. producers. As a compromise solution, an agreement in August 1986 was made by the U.S. and Japanese governments that the anti-dumping suits would be dropped in exchange for the application of price surveillances on Japanese producers. In March 1987, the U.S. government invoked Article 301 of the U.S. Trade Act because of an alleged violation of the anti-dumping accord by a Japanese producer and prohibitive tariffs were imposed on the imports of related Japanese products.

Market-Oriented Sector Specific (MOSS) talks were also introduced for the liberalization of the Japanese market. The talks started with four new sectors (telecommunications, medicine and medical equipment, electronics, and forest products). They now include such services as equal access for American construction companies to the Kansai new international airport project.

The American request for Japanese market liberalization has been most insistent with respect to agricultural products. The United States criticized Japan's residual import restrictions on twelve agricultural products and submitted its complaint to the GATT panel, which decided that Japan violated the GATT rule on ten of the twelve products. The issue is yet to be finalized, but domestic producers resist it strenuously. This ruling, however, provides the impetus to promote import liberalization to the Japanese market.

Serious resistance has also greeted the demand for the liberalization of rice imports. The U.S. Rice Millers Association denounced Japan's policy of rice self-sufficiency and demanded the start of rice imports. Rice has long been a sanctuary for agricultural protection in Japan, and Japanese rice farmers protested the U.S. demand. Backed by consumer criticism of long-lasting rice protection and very high rice prices, the Japanese government has begun modifying its rice policy and reducing governmental subsidies to rice farmers.

The U.S. Request for Reciprocity

Many requests for Japanese market liberalization are well founded, and Japan should respond to them for its own sake. Both the Action Program and the Maekawa Report are consistent in this respect. The conflict, however, has tended to become aggravated by the American way of making its requests with the condition that American products actually be allowed to increase their share in the Japanese market, as was included in the Omnibus Trade Act. This may appear to be consistent with the request for reciprocity, but import performance is affected by the policy discrepancies as well as protectionism. Even if the market is liberalized, import expansion will not be realized if appropriate macroeconomic policies do not accompany such measures.

Furthermore, the request for market liberalization on the basis of revealed import performance has evoked an undesirable response from the Japanese side. First, it has aroused an emotional reaction against American "illogical requests." Second, it has encouraged the Japanese to measure individual cases in terms of imports and to dismiss requests because of their negligible effect on the huge macroeconomic imbalance. Of course, the fact that certain imports are under restriction makes impossible an accurate estimation of liberalization. An illogical request encourages an illogical response.

It is important to distinguish between sectoral requests and overall adjustment and to continue persevering in efforts to resolve both issues. Politics in the two countries often betray the economist's expectations. Policy coordination often involves a considerable time lag, required to resolve discrepancies of opinion. Yet there is no royal road to the resolution of the current economic conflict other than maintaining agreement on the basic direction of policy implementation and seeking not to diverge from it.

Impact on the Pacific-Asian Region

The Current Economic Situation

The developing countries of Asia were affected principally by the worldwide depression and fluctuation of commodity prices, but their difficulties have been aggravated by economic conflicts prevalent in the region. The current economic situation differs among them, reflecting their different export structures as well as some ad hoc factors. Both Indonesia and Malaysia were affected most seriously by the drastic decline of petroleum and other primary product prices as well as by a stagnant demand for their products in developed countries. Their export earnings decreased badly because of the decrease of both prices and volumes of their major exports, namely, petroleum and agricultural materials. They had to modify their development programs to slower growth so as to stop current account deficits and avoid the further accumulation of external debts.

The negative growth performances of Singapore and the Philippines were affected more or less by their own ad hoc factors not common to the other three countries. Singapore experienced a −2 percent growth in 1985 after an 8 percent growth in the previous year. Its serious setback resulted generally from the depression of its two neighbors, Malaysia and Indonesia, but it was also hit by the sudden halt in the construction boom and the decrease of exports of petroleum products. The Philippines' growth was decelerated after 1981 because of political instability and was negative in 1985, but it recovered to a small positive growth in 1986 under the new president, Corazon Aquino.

On the other hand, the Thai economy has been performing better, partly because of its small reliance on petroleum exports. Thailand suffered from a reduction of its main export, rice, but its export of manufactured and agroindustrial products has been active and their production has increased.

The South Korean and Taiwanese economies performed much better in 1986, partly because of the decreased import prices of oil and raw material and partly because of the quick resumption of industrial exports after the exchange rate alignment. Both countries achieved over 10 percent growth from continued expansion of exports in 1987, and future prospects are good.

Exchange rate changes (accumulated changes per U.S. dollar) since September 1985 differ among the Asian countries. The Japanese yen and German mark appreciated by 54 and 40 percent, respectively, for the first twelve months. The new Taiwan dollar appreciated by only 10 percent for the same period, and certain other Asian currencies have been virtually pegged to the U.S. dollar; the Korean won appreciated by 1.7 percent, the Thai baht appreciated by 3.8 percent, and the Singaporean dollar appreciated by 2.7 percent. On the other hand, the Chinese yuan, the Indonesian rupiah, the Malaysian ringgit, and the Philippine peso depreciated. South Korean and other Asian NIC exports have benefited from the strengthened competitiveness against Japanese and German products and this certainly contributed to the rapid growth of these countries which resumed in 1986. The better performance of Thai exports resembles that of the East Asian NICs because of its greater reliance on industrial exports than other ASEAN members.

During the recent past, common feature emerged among Asian developing countries, namely, the increasing surplus of their balance of trade with the United States and persistent deficits with Japan. This caused economic conflicts between the Asian developing countries on one hand and the United States and Japan on the other.

U.S.-Asian Conflicts

The United States has provided the largest market for industrial exports from Asian industrializing countries and thus has contributed to their export growth: from Japan since the mid-1950s, from Taiwan and

South Korea since the mid-1960s, and from ASEAN countries since the late 1970s. Asian exports to the U.S. market were accelerated in the boom years of 1983 and 1984. In fact, U.S. imports from Europe and Latin America also expanded rapidly. This overall trend reflects not only the expansion of industrial capacities in developing countries but also the new strategy of American multinationals to relocate their production away from traditional domestic sources to cheaper sources in developing countries. The Pacific-Asian countries have provided a reliable alternative, cheaper but no less inferior in quality.

Another aspect of this import expansion, however, is the enlarged trade deficit of the United States. Table 2 also shows changes in the U.S. trade balance with Asian NICs and ASEAN countries in the 1980s. The U.S. deficits with Taiwan and Indonesia expanded further, and the surpluses with South Korea, Singapore, Thailand, and the Philippines changed to deficits. In 1985, the U.S. deficits with Korea and Taiwan amounted to US$20.9 billion, 41 percent of its deficit with Japan. With these countries, the United States has made requests similar to those it made to Japan. They include, first, protection of American producers against imports from those countries; second, liberalization of those countries' markets for American products; and third, appreciation of their exchange rates against the dollar.

The U.S. request for exchange rate appreciation has been strengthened in the past several years to South Korea and Taiwan on the ground that the small adjustment of their currencies made so far has prevented the strengthening of competitiveness of American products. The South Korea won appreciated against the U.S. dollar by 3.2 percent during 1986 under the deliberate guidance of the Bank of Korea. The increase accelerated further in 1987 to 801 won per dollar (11.4 percent since the first G-5 meeting), apparently in consideration of its increasing trade surplus with the United States. Taiwan has continued to appreciate the NT dollar because it has accumulated a foreign exchange reserve of US$50 billion, almost as much as West Germany and Japan. The NT dollar rate rose to 29.9 per U.S. dollar in 1987. The Thai baht and the Singapore dollar have also appreciated by 8-10 percent.

Furthermore, the Asian NICs have been implementing voluntary restraints on their industrial exports to the United States and have hastened their programs of trade liberalization. A typical example of American protection was the severe restriction of textile imports proposed under the Jenkins Bill. The United States had already restricted its imports of textiles and clothing under the tight framework of the Multi-Fiber Arrangement (MFA) since 1974; the Jenkins Bill provided for the further tightening of this restriction. So far, ASEAN textiles have been less restricted compared with the NICs, but it was reported that 64 percent of Thai exports to the United States would be curtailed by the new bill. Textile workers and college students demonstrated in protest in front of the American embassy in Bangkok. The bill was eventually rejected by President Reagan, but it contributed to the renewal of the MFA in July 1986.

Another example was the Farm Act of 1986, which would promote American exports of farm products by subsidizing the difference between the U.S. domestic price and the world price. Rice exports from Thailand were hardest hit by this act. The price of rice in the world market has decreased and both export and domestic prices of unsubsidized Thai rice are low. Thailand is an active member of the ministerial meeting of Fair Traders in Agriculture (held in Cairns, Australia in August 1986), and the meeting called for a halt to the "predatory trade policies" of the United States.[8]

An additional U.S. request for market liberalization has also been made in the area of trade-related investment and service trade. This area has been subject to various conventional regulations, not only for protection purposes but also on social or cultural grounds, and the American request evoked a protest in Asian countries against interference in their domestic affairs.

The U.S.-Asian conflict, although similar to the U.S.-Japan conflict, has resulted more from the catching-up industrialization of the Asian countries than from policy discrepancies between the United States and Asia. The recent aggravation was of course affected by the expanding U.S. deficit, so that Asian countries cannot avoid the decline of their exports to the United States as part of the resolution of the conflict. Second, more attention should be given not only to the United States' threatened protectionism but also to the acceleration of trade liberalization by Asian countries.

Japan-Asian Conflicts

Although the United States was the biggest importer of industrial products from the Asian NICs and contributed to their growth in the 1960s and 1970s, Japan was the largest importer of primary products from ASEAN and thus contributed to the rapid growth of member countries in the 1970s. In the 1980s, Japanese imports of petroleum and raw materials have been reduced, partly because of the much slower growth of Japan and partly because of reduced consumption of these materials per unit of production. On the other hand, Japanese exports

---

[8]Complaints about American requests from Asian developing countries were occasionally reported in newspapers (*Nihon Keizai Shimbun*, February 17 and April 25, 1986).

of machinery and parts grew rapidly to meet their development demands, and an increasing surplus resulted in bilateral balance with those countries. Thus, there was a change in the bilateral balance of Japan with the Asian NICs and the ASEAN countries. Japan incurred a trade deficit with oil exporters such as Indonesia and Malaysia, and a persistent trade surplus with such industrial exporters as the NICs and Thailand.

Regular trade deficits with Japan have been a major issue raised by the ASEAN representatives at the Japan-ASEAN Forum and on other occasions. Bilateral trade imbalances have also caused economic conflicts and requests similar to those advanced by the United States have been made by ASEAN to Japan. They include improved market access for major ASEAN exports such as boneless chicken, bananas, plywood, and so on, through an improved Generalized System of Preferences (GSP) and simplified standardization and certification procedures. The Action Program includes some official measures responding to these requests.

It should be noted that a new type of request has emerged recently. It is best represented by Thailand's *White Paper on the Structural Adjustment of Thailand-Japan Economic Relations*, authorized by the Thai government in August 1985. The White Paper includes a request for Japanese cooperation in a variety of areas such as trade, private investment, and official development aid; it aims to promote the joint adjustment of the structure of economic relations between the two countries.

Similar ideas appeared in the requests made by Indonesia and Malaysia. Although they maintain a persistent trade surplus with Japan and Japan continues to be the biggest importer of their primary products, they wish to explore new industrial exports to Japan and seek Japan's cooperation in that direction. South Korea and Taiwan, on the other hand, have attempted to diversify their import sources by restricting imports from Japan and promoting import substitution of machinery and parts. They have also requested Japan's cooperation in the provision of sophisticated technology and the transformation of their economies into technology-intensive ones.

The Asia-Japan conflict basically reflects the catching-up industrialization of developing Asian countries, highlighted by the OECD's report on NICs. As the NICs increase their manufactured exports to the OECD countries, they need imports of machinery and parts in turn from the OECD countries. In Pacific Asia, on the other hand, the NICs' products went to the United States and their imports came from Japan. This phenomenon is partly affected by the macroeconomic policy discrepancies between the United States and Japan as well as Japan's catching up in comparison with the United States. The improvement of macroimbalances between the United States and Japan would mitigate this conflict, but coordination of the catching-up process between a developing Asia and Japan is required for any basic resolution.

The Role of Japan in the Pacific-Asian Region

The Pacific-Asian economies have suffered from major fluctuations in growth rates and aggravated economic conflicts. I have identified the three economic conflicts in the Asia Pacific: U.S.-Japan, U.S.-Asia, and Asia-Japan. The U.S.-Japan conflict is of course the most severe and deeply rooted, but the other two are not merely spillovers but are closely interrelated with it.

These structural elements connect these conflicts: policy discrepancies relating to world fluctuations, the catching up of late-industrializing countries, and ongoing integration occurring through multinational firms and financial liberalization. The policy discrepancy between the United States and Japan is most responsible for the aggravation of the conflicts in recent years, but the other two elements should not be neglected if we seek a deep understanding of our difficulties.

The adoption of more austere fiscal policies by the United States seems to be essential for the successful resolution of the conflicts and the maintenance of a viable global economic order. It is widely anticipated among developing Asian countries that U.S. domestic demand will decrease, under which condition both import reduction and increasing protectionism will adversely affect their exports volume to the United States, thereby depressing their economies.

Japan is now expected to play a greater role in the Pacific-Asian region. First, Japan has already implemented its macroeconomic policy for domestic market-oriented growth and has succeeded in reducing exports to the United States. It must continue this policy stance and increase imports, absorbing the exports from developing Asia.

Second, the structural adjustment of the Japanese economy must be promoted as well to enable the successful coordination of changes in trade and production with the rapidly catching-up countries in the region. The strengthening of the GATT system will help keep economic conflicts under control. Domestic adjustment should be promoted in conjunction with trade negotiations, since trade liberalization cannot occur without adjustment assistance during the switchover from incompetent sectors to dynamic ones. In July 1986 and April 1987, using the Maekawa report, the Japanese government announced its promotion of the restructuring of its economy. It should now propose the creation of a Pacific-Asian version of this report, that is, the development of a consensus on the desirable direction for future change in the trade and industrial structure of the region.

Third, because the resolution of economic conflicts will take several years, the continuing imbalance will have to be financed through capital flows. It is imperative for Japan to maintain the recycling of its trade surplus and the smooth functioning of the world financial markets.

10. South Korea-U.S. Economic Conflict and Its Pacific-Asian Regional Impact

HAN SEUNG-SOO

Trade frictions between South Korea and the United States have become the daily items of our news. Soon after the presidential election of December 16, 1987, the pressure on South Korea from the United States intensified.[1] The friction over cigarettes, beef, and insurance services is just the tip of the iceberg. Many more disputes lie ahead. At an earlier stage, South Korea-U.S. trade friction was regarded as part of the spillover effect from the trade disputes between the major trading nations of the world, particularly the United States and Japan, but it is rapidly becoming an internally generated problem between South Korea and the United States. It reflects the changing economic relationship between the two countries.

The economic relationship between South Korea and the United States has gone through roughly three phases since 1945. The first phase (1945–60) can be characterized as the period of South Korea's dependence on the U.S. economy. The first fifteen years saw the liberation of the country from colonial domination, the division of the country, the outbreak of the Korean war, and postwar reconstruction efforts. The division of the nation left South Korea with a negligible industrial base, which was totally destroyed during the war. The economy, then at subsistence level, was heavily dependent on foreign aid, particularly from the United States.

The second phase, a transitional period, lasted roughly from 1961 to 1979, the period of President Park's government. During this period, the outward-looking orientation of Korea's development strategy required a vast foreign market, and the United States offered this market. As domestic savings were meager at the time, South Korea had to rely on foreign savings, and the United States also played an important role as a major source of these funds.

The third period, which started roughly about 1980, can be characterized as the period of increasing interdependence between South Korea and the United States. Although both economies are still asym-

---

[1]*Korea Times,* December 31, 1987. For a detailed, journalistic analysis of the current issues involved, see *Dong-Ah Ilbo,* December 29, 1987.

metric in size, South Korea began consistently to register increasingly larger trade surpluses with the United States during this period, presenting a new dimension with totally different problems between the two countries.[2]

The economic policies pursued by the Korean government in the period after 1980 are relevant to an analysis of the causes of trade friction between South Korea and the United States. Although the recent economic success and trade surplus of South Korea are often ascribed to the realization of the three lows (lower dollar, lower oil price, and lower international interest rate), the fundamental cause is to be found in the pursuit of successful economic policies in Korea in the early 1980s. In that period, South Korea switched the mix of macroeconomic policy from a loose fiscal and high interest rate policy to a tight fiscal and low interest rate one. For example, the government began to curb the growth of public expenditures based on the zero-base budgeting technique in 1982 and completely froze government expenditures for 1984 at the level of 1983 while bringing the lending rate down from 17 percent to 10 percent in 1982.

The major achievement of this policy package was the containment of inflation to a single digit rate since 1982. There had never been a time in the history of the South Korean economy after 1945 when inflation had been kept at a single digit rate for two successive years before that year.

On the other hand, U.S. economic policies, particularly fiscal and monetary ones, seem to have worked against the objective of a balance-of-payments equilibrium. The high interest rate policy of the early 1980s with its consequence of a stronger dollar reduced the competitiveness of U.S. industry, and the expansive fiscal policy resulting in the huge federal budget deficit failed to contain the growth of domestic demand.

The shift in the relative economic power of the United States and the further expansion of U.S. economic openness intensified the process of trade and other economic conflicts initiated by the United States. During the late 1930s and particularly in the course of World War II, the United States began to reorient itself toward participation in interna-

---

[2]For a detailed analysis of South Korea-U.S. economic relations since 1945, see Seung-Soo Han, "Korea-U.S. Economic Relations," in Korean National Committee of Historical Sciences, *Korean-American Relations, 1882–1982* (Seoul, 1982) (in Korean), pp. 498–532; and Utaek Kim, "The Future of Korea-U.S. Relations," paper presented at the Institute of Far Eastern Studies of Kyungnam University (October 1987).

tional affairs.[3] The dominance of the United States in the world economy continued until the 1960s. The unsettling decade of the 1970s with its oil shocks and stagflation was a decade of U.S. decline as a global economic power. West Germany, other Western countries, and Japan began to show resilience in their economies, and the relative decline of the United States can be largely attributed to the relative rise of these countries.[4]

As far as South Korea-U.S. trade and economic frictions are concerned, the increasing openness of the U.S. economy, particularly as the 1980s began, appears to be one of the major determinants. Its increasing internationalization has brought about unforeseen consequences on the U.S. economy, on American citizens' perception of the world, and on the world economy.[5]

How and why do frictions between nations arise? In explaining the trade disputes between Korea and the United States, John Odell hypothesizes that the disputes occurred due to different sectoral market conditions. He argues that the greater the penetration of imports into a market, the greater will be the chance of an international dispute over access to that home market. Odell also feels that frictions may arise because of domestic political structures. The greater the domestic political resources of an import-competing industry, the greater the chance that government policy will tilt in its direction, producing an international trade dispute if the industry seeks protection. Odell's third point concerns international power structures. In situations in which their policies are in conflict, stronger powers will prevail more often and to a greater extent than the weaker, especially in the bilateral bargaining process. Domestic and international structures set only outer limits within which negotiators' abilities and choices make a difference.[6]

---

[3]For the major policy reorientation of the United States and the background leading the United States to take a hegemonic role in the postwar period, see Robert E. Baldwin, *The New Protectionism: A Response to Shifts in National Economic Power,* National Bureau of Economic Research Working Paper, no. 1823 (1986), pp. 2–8.

[4]For the alternative international regime, albeit pluralistic leadership, see Robert O. Keohane, *After Hegemony: Cooperation and Discord in the World Political Economy* (Princeton: Princeton University Press, 1984), pp. 49–63; and Robert Gilpin, *The Political Economy of International Relations* (Princeton: Princeton University Press, 1987), pp. 366–78.

[5]For the impact of this on the United States, see Martin Feldstein, *The American Economy in Transition* (Chicago: Chicago University Press, 1983). For major structural changes in the U.S. economy during the first half of the 1980s, see Lawrence B. Krause, "Changing America and the Economy of the Pacific Basin," ch. 1 in this volume.

[6]For each of these hypotheses, see John S. Odell, "The Outcomes of International Trade Conflicts: The U.S. and South Korea, 1960–1981," *International Studies Quarterly* 29 (1985): 272–76.

Emergence of Trade Conflict

There were many trade disputes between South Korea and the United States during the period from June 1963 to April 1981. Of these disputes, nine were concerned with textiles (three cases of cotton textiles and apparel and six cases of textiles and apparel); two cases involving television receivers; and two cases relating to footwear (one rubber and one nonrubber).[7]

Textiles disputes have a long history and are not unique to the Korea-U.S. economic relationship. The textiles problem became acute when Japan and Hong Kong began to increase their share in the United States and West European countries. The outcome of American concern was the Short-Term Arrangement (STA) in October 1961, which was immediately followed by the Long-Term Arrangement Regarding International Trade in Cotton Textiles (LTA) in October 1962, which lasted until December 1973 after three extensions. South Korea was then at an early stage of textile exports and joined the agreement on December 3, 1964, as the twenty-eighth signatory, to be effective from January 1, 1965.

The Arrangement Regarding International Trade in Textiles, better known as the Multi-Fiber Arrangement I (MFA), effective January 1, 1974, included not only cotton but also wool and other textile apparel. MFA I lasted for three years and was then extended for another three years (January 1978 to December 1981) as MFA II. MFA III was extended for four years and seven months from January 1982 to July 1986, and MFA IV will be in effect from August 1, 1986 to July 1991.[8]

Generally, however, trade friction between South Korea and the United States can be said to have begun in earnest from the 1980s. Until 1986, Korea's overall trade balance was always in deficit and was in marked contrast with such other East Asian countries as Japan and Taiwan, which had already accumulated a vast amount of foreign reserves

---

[7]Ibid., pp. 266–67.

[8]For the details of these agreements, see the Korea Institute for Industrial Economics and Technology, *The Change of International Division of Labor and Policy Response* (Seoul, December 1987) (in Korean), p. 22. See also, Martin Wolf, "Handmaiden Under Harassment: The Multi-Fiber Arrangement as an Obstacle to Development," in *Free Trade in the World Economy: Toward an Opening of Markets*, ed. Herbert Giersch (Tübingen: J. C. B. Mohr, 1987), pp. 253–57. For a brief treatment of U.S.-Japan textiles conflicts, see Yamazawa Ippei, "Textiles Industry," in *Industrial Policy of Japan*, ed. Ryutaro Komiya et al. (Tokyo: Tokyo University Press, 1984) (in Japanese), pp. 354–56.

Table 1

Korea-U.S. Bilateral Trade
(US$ millions)

Year	Export to U.S.	Import from U.S.	Trade Balance
1960	4	144	−140
1970	395	585	−190
1980	4,607	4,890	−283
1981	5,561	6,050	−489
1982	6,119	5,956	163
1983	8,128	6,273	1,855
1984	10,479	6,875	3,604
1985	10,754	6,489	4,265
1986	13,880	6,545	7,335
1987	18,311	8,758	9,553

SOURCE: Korea Foreign Trade Association, *The Trend of Foreign Trade* (Seoul, 1986 and 1987).

by that time.[9] Until 1981, excepting the three years of 1976–78, South Korea's trade balance with the United States had been in deficit (see Table 1.)

Korea's major exportable items were electronics, textiles, footwear, toys, and steel products while agricultural and chemical products, cotton, and machinery were major items imported from the United States. For example, the export of electronics to the United States accounted for 51.0 percent of Korea's total electronics export in 1986, textiles for 33.9 percent, footwear for 71.2 percent, toys for 74.2 percent, and steel products for 29.4 percent. The U.S. market dependence rate was much reduced in 1987, reflecting the diversification of exports owing to various U.S. pressures on Korea. The rate of dependence on the U.S. market for January-October 1987 was 42.4 percent for electronics, 31.5 percent for textiles, 65.0 percent for footwear, 80.2 percent for toys, and 22.7 percent for steel products.

On the other hand, the import of agricultural products from the United States accounted for 36.7 percent of Korea's agricultural imports in 1986, for 30.5 percent of chemical products, for 42.8 percent of cotton, and for 20.8 percent of machinery. The switching of import sources from third countries to the United States has been one of the major

---

[9]For how the Japan-U.S. trade conflict, the first wave of which began in the period of textiles negotiations in 1968 through 1972, became more serious with the second wave of 1976 through 1978, and for how the trade conflict turned into the Japan-U.S. economic conflict in the 1980s, see Ryutaro Komiya and Motoshige Itoh, "International Trade and Trade Policy of Japan: 1955-1984," Discussion Paper No. 85–F-16 (1986), pp. 57-58.

Table 2

Bilateral Trade in Total Trade
(as % of total)

Year	Export	Import	Total
South Korea's dependence on U.S.			
1980	26.3	21.9	23.9
1982	28.3	24.0	26.3
1985	35.5	20.8	28.1
1986	40.0	20.7	30.8
U.S. dependence on South Korea			
1980	2.1	1.7	1.9
1982	2.6	2.4	2.5
1985	2.8	3.0	2.9
1986	2.9	3.5	3.3

SOURCE: Korea Foreign Trade Association, *Changing International Trade Environment and Business Strategy* (Seoul, November 1987), p. 28.

policy efforts of the South Korean government in order to remedy the worsening Korea-U.S. bilateral trade imbalance. The consequence of this effort was the drastic increase of import dependence on the United States of certain products. For example, the import dependence rate of agricultural products in January-October 1987 increased to 42.6 percent, of chemicals to 30.9 percent, of cotton to 61.5 percent, and of machinery to 21.0 percent. It is to be noted that the rapid increase in import dependence occurred in the nonmanufacturing sector while the U.S. manufacturing sector was slow to capitalize on South Korea's sources of import switching policy. But however Korea may try, the asymmetrical nature of the size of the two economies and the differential impact of bilateral trade put limits on the role that South Korea can play in reducing the U.S. trade deficit.[10] The differential impact of bilateral trade can be seen in Table 2.

The marked difference in dependence ratio for exports and imports in the two countries suggests that although South Korea was the fifth largest bilateral trade surplus country vis-à-vis the United States in

---

[10]For the asymmetrical nature of South Korea-U.S. economies, see Seung-Soo Han, "Changing Economic Environment in East Asia and the Korea-U.S. Relations: A Korean Perspective," paper presented at the IFANS-SAIS Conference on "The Changing Security Environment in Northeast Asia: The Impact on Korea-U.S. Relations," Seoul, December 14–15, 1987.

1986, there is not much that it alone can do to remedy the situation.[11] The precise contribution of the Korea-U.S. bilateral trade imbalance to the U.S. trade deficit is shown in Table 3.

South Korea was twenty-third largest contributor to the U.S. trade deficit in 1981, but this changed to ninth in 1985 and to fifth in 1986. As shown in Table 2, Korea-U.S. bilateral trade accounted for almost one-third of Korea's total trade, but it accounted for only about one-thirtieth of U.S. total trade in 1986. The United states was the largest trading partner of South Korea, but it was the seventh largest partner of the United States in 1986. Although Korea is not one of the largest trading partners of the United States, there are a few items where it has had a comparative advantage and made aggressive sales efforts to create concern in the United States. Bilateral trade has been the source of economic expansion and welfare increase in both countries, but the continuing imbalance in bilateral trade has been placing a growing stress on the Korea-U.S. economic relationship.

Issues of Economic Friction

The key areas of economic dispute are goods market access, service market opening, graduation from the Generalized System of Preferences (GSP), exchange rate realignment, and U.S. import restrictions.

Apart from U.S. import restrictions and the friction resulting from them, the recurrent issue that has most concerned both nations is the access of the South Korean market to U.S. products. The U.S. request for liberalization of the Korean market started on the occasion of President Reagan's official visit to Korea in November 1983. Between that time and mid-1987, there were five formal requests for market access. The series of requests and their contents are shown in Table 4.

As shown in Table 4, the U.S. request for market access took the form either of removal of import restrictions or of reduction of tariff rates. By September 1987, there were fifty-seven items for import liberalization (removal of restrictions, that is) and fifty-nine items for tariff reduction.[12]

Imports have been liberalized at a rapid rate in South Korea since the early 1980s. According to the government schedule, the ratio of import liberalization, which was 74.4 percent in 1981, will reach 93.7

---

[11]As in Japan, Korea might have already developed a structural surplus in its trade in manufactures and its bilateral trade with the United States; see Paul Krugman, "Is the Japan Problem Over?" in *Trade Friction and Economic Policy*, ed. R. Sato and P. Wachtel (Cambridge: Cambridge University Press, 1987), pp. 18–19.

[12]For the complete list of detailed items requested for market access, see Korea Foreign Trade Association, *Korea's New Import Policies* (Seoul, November 1987), pp. 10–11.

Table 3

South Korea's Place in the U.S. Trade Deficit
(in US$100 million and %)

	1981			1985			1986		
	Amount	%	Rank	Amount	%	Rank	Amount	%	Rank
Japan	181	45.7	1	497	33.5	1	586	34.5	1
Canada	73	18.4	4	222	14.9	2	233	13.7	2
West Germany	16	4.0	13	122	8.2	4	156	9.2	3
Taiwan	38	9.6	8	131	8.8	3	155	9.1	4
South Korea	4	1.0	23	48	3.2	9	71	4.2	5
Italy	2	0.5	33	58	3.9	7	65	3.8	6
Hong Kong	31	7.8	9	62	4.2	5	64	3.8	7
Mexico	—	—	—	58	3.9	6	52	3.1	8
United Kingdom	9	2.3	17	43	2.9	10	46	2.7	9
France	—	—	—	39	2.6	11	34	2.0	10

SOURCES: Korea Foreign Trade Association, *Changing International Trade Environment and Business Strategy* (Seoul, November 1987), p. 25.

Table 4

U.S. Requests for South Korean Market Access

Occasion	Date	Requests for Market Opening (no. of items)	Requests for Tariff Reduction (no. of items)
President Reagan's visit to Korea	Nov. 1983	38	19
U.S. government official request	Feb. 1984	16	8
Korean-U.S. trade ministers' meeting	Mar. 1984	16	5
Korean special envoy's visit to U.S.	Mar. 1985	25	27
Korean-U.S. GSP meeting	Aug. 1986	19	27
Korean-U.S. trade ministers' meeting	Apr. 1987	5	3

SOURCE: Korea Foreign Trade Association, *Korea's New Import Policies: Expanding Supply Sources, Accelerating Market Liberalization* (Seoul, November 1987), p. 9.

percent by 1987 and 95.4 percent by 1988. The manufactures import liberalization will reach 98.5 percent by 1988. The import liberalization ratio for electric and electronic goods and machine tools, which was 40.9 percent in 1981, will reach 100 percent by 1988.

South Korea's average tariff on manufactures and primary products were 18.7 percent and 27.1 percent, respectively, in 1986. These are being successively lowered to 18.2 percent and 26.3 percent in 1987 and to 16.8 percent and 25.1 percent in 1988.

Of the items that are requested for import liberalization by the United States, 254 out of 379 items (67 percent) will have been liberalized by 1987 and 82.3 percent in 1988. Of the request for tariff reduction by the United States, it is expected that the average tariff rate of 34.0 percent for manufactured products in 1985 will be lowered to an average rate of 25.2 percent in 1988, a decrease by 8.8 percentage points in three years. In the case of primary products, the average tariff rate of 37.7 percent in 1985 will be lowered to 34.5 percent in 1988, a decrease by 3.2 percentage points.[13]

A survey conducted by the Korea Foreign Trade Association reveals that the United States has failed to capitalize on the export of liberalized items for which its government had made unrelenting efforts. The main reasons offered by Korean business circles for this failure were high prices, unsatisfactory delivery conditions, substandard after-sales ser-

---

[13]Ibid., pp. 12–13.

vice, and unfavorable reactions by U.S. companies to small orders. On the other hand, Japan benefited more from the opening of Korea's import market. For example, of 150 items that were liberalized during 1984–86, Japanese exports of US$333 million before liberalization jumped to US$436 million, taking their share of total imports from 38.9 percent to 39.0 percent. On the other hand, U.S. exports of $191 million before liberalization only increased to $215 million after liberalization with the U.S. share in total imports decreasing from 22.3 percent to 19.2 percent.[14]

The recent dispute involving the market opening of insurance services indicates what is involved in the wider context of economic friction between South Korea and the United States. The first indication that the United States was serious about the opening of the service market was when President Reagan directed the U.S. Trade Representative (USTR) on September 7, 1985, to investigate the protection of services in Korea, invoking Article 301 of the Trade Act of 1974.

Since then, the friction over service has become a common phenomenon. For example, on October 9, 1985, the American Association of Movie Exporters petitioned the USTR against South Korea's movie market under Article 301. As a consequence, Korea and the United States agreed on December 13, 1985, on the issue of movie market openings (in which the United States has undoubtedly a comparative advantage), permitting U.S. movie exporters to open branches in South Korea, lowering the deposits for registration, and abolishing the ceiling on import prices.

In the meantime, President Reagan directed the USTR on October 16, 1985, to investigate the violation of intellectual property rights in Korea, once again invoking Article 301. Negotiations followed, and a comprehensive agreement was made on the issue of Korea's service market opening and intellectual property rights on July 21, 1986. The agreement contained five components: insurance, copyrights, software, patents, and trademarks.

Regarding insurance, U.S. participation was allowed in the case of fire insurance by July 1986, and one U.S. company was allowed to operate in the case of life insurance by the end of 1986. It was also agreed that additional participation would be considered for other qualified U.S. insurance companies.

The law governing copyrights was revised in September 1986 and came into effect from July 1987. South Korea joined the universal copyright convention in September 1987, and the protection of copyrights

---

[14]For a summary of the survey, see ibid., pp. 14–15.

was extended from thirty years to fifty years. Retroactivity providing protection of copyrights since 1977 was agreed upon to be made effective through administrative guidance. Software would also be protected similarly to copyrights through the enactment of a new law.

The patent law was also revised to accommodate certain U.S. requests, and the period of patent protection was extended to fifteen years. Retroactivity on the transfer of process patents was agreed upon. In regard to trademarks, conditionality for licensing and limitations on royalty payment was abolished.

South Korea's graduation as a recipient of the GSP was still another thorny issue. It was reported late in 1987 that the U.S. Trade Policy Review Group discussed the possibility of graduating Korea, together with other Asian NICs, from the group of GSP beneficiaries, and shortly thereafter, that was done. This was viewed as a natural progression for any successful developing country, and South Korea, together with other Asian NICs, were approaching that state. Korea's exports to the United States under the GSP provision were US$1.65 billion in 1985 and US$2.22 billion in 1986, accounting for 16.5 percent and 17.4 percent, respectively, of Korea's total exports to the United States. However, as most of these exports originated from small businesses in Korea, the abrupt graduation could cause great difficulties for those medium and small businesses engaged in international trade.

Assistant Treasury Secretary Mulford made a very strong statement regarding Asian NICs on November 17, 1987, asserting, "Tigers live in the jungle, and by the law of the jungle, they are a shrinking population. To survive, tigers—and the NICs—must adapt; and adaptation will require cooperation, not predatory behavior." One of the issues he raised was exchange rate realignment. The reason for U.S. pressure for currency appreciation by the Asian NICs was the slow return of the U.S. balance of payments to equilibrium.

The first U.S. official request on won appreciation was made on July 31, 1986. since then the request has been consistently repeated, with the assertion that the rate of won appreciation was too slow. Treasury Secretary Baker made a similar request in December 1986. Between January and September of 1987, there were six requests for won appreciation from the U.S. government; four times by the Treasury secretary (March 31, April 8, April 9, and September 29), once each by the Secretary of State (May 18) and the U.S. Trade Representative (January 28).

The won-dollar exchange rate was 886.40 won to a dollar at the time of the G-5 meeting on September 20, 1985. By the end of 1985, the won depreciated further to 890.20 won. It was from 1986 that the won began to appreciate against the dollar. During 1986, the exchange rate appreciated by 3.2 percent, being 861.40 won to a dollar. Between September

29, 1985, and October 31, 1987, the won appreciated by 11.3 percent against the dollar. During the same period, major currencies of the world appreciated much further than the Korean won. For example, the Japanese yen appreciated by 71.8 percent, and the West German mark by 64.4 percent.

As there is no immediate likelihood of a drastic decrease in South Korea's trade surplus with the United States or of a restoration in the overall U.S. trade balance, U.S. pressure for exchange rate realignment will continue for some time. By the end of 1987, the won had already broken the 800-won barrier, and it is expected that the rate of appreciation will be faster in 1988.

Even amid various pressures and disputes, South Korea's exports have been increasing. However, Korean exports have been subject to various kinds of import restrictions at destination. There were twenty-one countries that restricted imports from South Korea in 1987. Table 5 shows the country's exports under foreign import restrictions.

Of exports totaling 34,714 million in 1986, those that were subject to foreign import restrictions accounted for 23.4 percent and of the exports to twenty-one advanced countries, 31 percent were exported under import restrictions. Of South Korea's exports to the United States in 1986, 33.3 percent was subject to U.S. import restrictions. Two facts emerge from Table 5. The proportion of exports that is subject to import restriction has decreased, and that of Korea's export to the United States under import restrictions is higher than the average.

As of September 1987, there were nineteen export items that were subject to U.S. import restrictions in one way or other. Of these, ten items were under restrictions by means of intergovernmental agreement, antidumping duties, countervailing duties, global quotas, or patent protection via Article 337 of the Tariff Act of 1930. There were eight items under investigation and one item under petition. There were twenty-seven cases of investigation closed and three cases of restrictions terminated.

U.S. import restrictions on South Korean exports will not disappear soon; on the contrary, they may be intensified in the future. The channel whereby domestic producers and labor unions can petition the U.S. International Trade Commission (USITC) is wide open, and the deindustrialization process of the United States will further aggravate the situation. Although the United States regards the judgment of the USITC as independent and neutral, its positive decisions on the antidumping and countervailing duties, safeguards, and other matters are likely to be perceived by many outside the United States as a strong indication of protectionist policies, which will become a cause for further frictions.

Table 5

South Korea's Export Under Import Restrictions
(US$ million, %)

Country	1985			1986			1987.1–7		
	(1)[c]	(2)	(2)/(1)	(1)	(2)	(2)/(1)	(1)	(2)	(2)/(1)
United States	10,754	4,656	43.3	13,880	4,621	33.3	8,283	2,438	29.4
Japan	4,543	1,454	32.0	5,426	1,065	19.6	3,470	732	21.1
EEC[a]	3,160	933	29.5	4,305	1,538	35.7	2,926	925	31.6
21 countries[b]	20,889	7,649	36.6	26,179	8,117	31.0	16,042	4,605	28.7
Total Export	30,283	7,649	25.3	34,714	8,117	23.4	20,966	4,605	22.0

[a]EEC includes twelve member countries.
[b]The twenty-one countries include the United States, Japan, the EEC countries, Canada, Australia, Finland, Norway, Sweden, Austria, and New Zealand.
[c]Column (1) refers to total exports, column (2) to exports subject to import restrictions.

SOURCE: Korea Foreign Trade Association, *Survey of Import Restrictions of Major Advanced Countries* (Seoul, September 1987) (in Korean), p. 21.

Pacific-Asian Regional Impact

South Korea-U.S. economic friction could have various impacts (political, economic, cultural, and others) on the Pacific-Asian region. Korea is regarded as one of the close allies of the United States in the defense of the free world. U.S. troops are stationed on the peninsula, and there is a security agreement between the two countries. Defense and the two nations' relationship as allies are often used as an excuse for the continuing trade surplus with the United States. However, despite the closeness in political and security relations, South Korea has become one of the target countries for U.S. pressure. Why a close ally like the United States is prepared to pressure it for various economic gains is something most ordinary Koreans cannot comprehend. The economic friction between Korea and the United States is strong enough to reawaken the countries in the region to the political reality of an "animal spirit" displayed by major powers in dealing with smaller partners. They will slowly come to realize that "politics is politics" and "economics is economics."

The economic impact of Korea-U.S. friction on the Pacific-Asian region, coinciding with the rise of income levels in the area, will be a continuous effort to redirect the destination of exports from the United States to other countries, and, perhaps, to switch the source of imports from others to the United States. In the case of South Korea, this strategy is likely to be applied to Japan with great intensity. Korea's diversification policy also implies that the region can assume an increasingly important role as an export market. With a growing intensity of economic friction between the United States and some major trading partners in East Asia (Korea, Japan, Taiwan, Singapore, and Hong Kong), it is most likely that intraregional trade will continuously increase in the Pacific-Asian region. This trend would be further strengthened by the fact that the intraindustry specialization has been under way in the region. The increasing interdependence between the regional economies also indicates a continuous flow of direct investment from capital-abundant countries, such as Japan and, to some extent, Taiwan and Korea, to resource-abundant countries such as the ASEAN states.

South Korean-American economic friction provides the countries closely following the strategy of export orientation as is Korea with a very useful lesson. Korea, as a latecomer, was able to sustain high growth without much cost by learning by doing. Likewise, some of the countries now coming up should also be able to minimize the cost of trial and error involved in trade friction with advanced industrial countries.

Conclusion

South Korea's economic relationship with the United States changed from one of dependence to that of interdependence within the span of one generation. The economic success of the country and the relative decline of the U.S. economy created friction between the two countries. This friction, which started in the early 1980s, has become one of the major political-economic issues facing the Korea-U.S. relationship today.

There is no doubt that the vast U.S. market enabled Korea to succeed in pursuing a growth strategy through export-orientation. It has also undergone drastic changes in its perception of appropriate industrial and trade policies. The Korean domestic market has been rapidly opening to foreign products, and services are rapidly becoming internationally tradeable.

The recognition that government intervention in international trade and industry should be reduced resulted in the establishment of the Korean Trade Commission on July 1, 1987, a Korean equivalent of the U.S International Trade Commission. There is still much to be desired in making the Korean Trade Commission as independent and neutral as the USITC, but a good start has been made. This is just one indication that South Korea has begun to realize that fair and free trade is necessary for the continued success of its economy.

It is hoped that Korea will do its best to minimize economic friction with its trading partners, and with the United States above all. However, as clapping requires two hands, it is not just Korea, the minor partner, that needs to cooperate. The United States as the major partner also needs to accommodate.

11. Trade Frictions and Patterns Among the Pacific-Asian Nations

DJISMAN S. SIMANDJUNTAK

Economic interactions such as trade and investment among the Pacific countries have proved resilient enough to survive the erosion of the trading environment that has accelerated in recent years. It appears reasonable to argue that the coming century will be the century of the Pacific, as many scholars and politicians believe. However, there is also reason to be concerned about the increased obstacles to the implementation of this vision. Though the obstacles may not prove fatal to health and growth within the region, they can be exceedingly painful.

The number of people who find it appropriate to apply war-related metaphors to current events in the Pacific today seems to have grown rapidly. Dennis Encarnation, for example, stated recently: "When contrasted with the Japanese invasion of America, the U.S. counterattack appears less integral to America's export strategy."[1] *Fortune,* a magazine with worldwide circulation, gave the cover story of its August 19, 1985 issue the title: "America's War on Imports." American trade policy vocabulary has recently borrowed such military images as "Trade Strike Force" and "Aggressive Reciprocity."

The increased allusions to war in dealing with trade policy issues—not wholly accurate since war is a zero-sum game and trade is not—is perhaps largely the result of the increased frequency with which the governments of different countries have resorted to economic warfare at a time when the costs, pecuniary and otherwise, of military conflict have become increasingly prohibitive.[2] It is also seemingly irresistible to apply war-related concepts to theories of strategic management. As far as Pacific trade is concerned, however, it is clearly an exaggeration to describe the present situation as an economic war—even though most of the developed countries in the Pacific have imposed an embargo on Vietnam, partly as a response to a request by ASEAN members, who

---

[1]Dennis J. Encarnation, "Cross-Investment: A Second Front of Economic Rivalry," in Thomas K. McCraw, ed., *America Versus Japan* (Cambridge, Mass.: Harvard Business School Press, 1986), p. 141.

[2]See, e.g., Hedley Bull, "Economic Sanctions and Foreign Policy," *World Economy* 7(2) (1984):219.

for their part are actively involved in trade with Vietnam. Nevertheless, the sky over Pacific trade is cloudy with sporadic rainfalls.

Trade frictions among the Pacific countries is by no means a new phenomenon. It can be traced back to the 1950s, when Japan's success as a textile exporter led to the reincarnation of protectionist sentiment and policies in other Pacific countries, especially the United States.[3] Japan's protectionism in agriculture trade has long been a target of trade talks at different levels between Japan on one hand and major food-exporting countries in the Pacific on the other. Though less prominent because it concerns developing rather than developed countries, the phenomenon of protection escalation—in the sense that the level of protection increases as the degree of processing of the product in question increases—has always been prominent in the trade policy agenda of the developing countries of the Pacific. In the 1980s, however, the situation has rapidly worsened. In one way or another, trade disputes have become an issue of *grosspolitik* as sounded, among others, by Walter Mondale during his presidential campaign when he asked the question: "What do we want our kids to do? Sweep up around Japanese computers?"[4]

Trade friction among the Pacific countries has basically centered on U.S.-Japan relations, a natural condition given the sheer size of trade between these two countries. This is not to say, however, that other countries can relax and conduct trade as usual. ASEAN countries, on which this essay focuses its attention, have also been among the targets of trade policy debates of the last few years. Furthermore, this group, which includes some of the least developed countries of the Pacific, has suffered from what may be called the spillover of U.S.-Japan friction. Although the problems faced by ASEAN countries appear much less serious than those confronting the United States and Japan, the solution to these problems is of paramount importance to the future of Pacific economic interactions, given the potential ASEAN market,[5] the importance or even dominance of ASEAN as supplier of some important materials, and the strategic geographical position of ASEAN. The

---

[3]On the evolution of U.S.-Japan economic relations, see Thomas K. McCraw, "From Partners to Competitors: An Overview of the Period Since World War II," in McCraw, *America Versus Japan*, pp. 1–33.

[4]As quoted in Edward A. Olsen, *U.S.-Japan Strategic Reciprocity: A Neo-Internationalist View* (Stanford: Hoover Institution Press, 1986), p. 61.

[5]The importance of solving this problem is appreciated, e.g., by a "group of wise men" asked by the Secretariat of GATT to work out recommendations for the restoration of the trading environment. See *Trade Policies for a Better Future: Proposals for Action* (Geneva: GATT Secretariat, 1985).

nature of the various frictions, the contributing factors, and the accommodative stance taken thus far by ASEAN when responding to the trade policy initiatives of other countries deserve more serious attention from the ASEAN countries' major trading partners in the context of bilateral, regional, and multilateral talks.

Factors Leading to Trade Frictions

Trade frictions and patterns, which are themselves characterized by a mutual relationship—trade frictions are bound to affect trade patterns, and vice versa—can be the result of extremely diverse factors that may or may not reinforce each other. First, worsening economic conditions usually increase the vulnerability of a country to protectionist sentiment. The Great Depression, for instance, was followed by the imposition of what was known as "depression duties," and it was this same depression that led to the enactment of the American Smoot-Hawley Act of 1930 and the immediate retaliation by other major trading countries.[6] To be specific, a weakening growth performance, because it means a less lucrative market[7] and worsening unemployment, together with a widening deficit in the current account can turn out to be very fertile soil for a protectionist trade policy, though the reverse is also possible—namely, that economic difficulties force governments to adjust by reducing rather than increasing barriers to trade.

Economic conditions in the ASEAN countries seriously worsened in the first half of the 1980s compared with the 1970s, when ASEAN was widely known as an association of countries with rapidly growing economies. Largely as a result of a historical low in the prices of primary commodities (on which the ASEAN economies are crucially dependent), growth rates of GDP plunged to as low as 1.9 percent in Indonesia in 1985, compared with an average of 8.2 percent annually in the second half of the 1970s. The situation was even worse in the Philippines though the year 1987 indicated that a strong up turn was underway in terms of the growth performance of all of the ASEAN countries. Previously, their balance-of-payment positions also deteriorated. The combined current account deficit of the ASEAN countries skyrocketed from 1.5 billion special drawing rights (SDR) in 1977 to 15.3 billion SDR

---

[6]See John T. Cuddington and Ronald I. McKinnon, "Free Trade Versus Protectionism: A Perspective," in *Tariffs, Quotas and Trade: The Politics of Protectionism* (San Francisco: Institute for Contemporary Studies, 1979), p. 14.

[7]The problems afflicting international trade in textile and textile products are partly rooted in the increased saturation of the major markets that make domestic producers there highly sensitive to imports. See, e.g., Jose de la Torre, *Clothing Industry Adjustment in Developed Countries*, Thames Essay No. 38 (London: Trade Policy Research Center, 1984).

in 1983. The decline of this deficit to some 4 billion SDR in 1985[8] cannot obscure the fact that the need for credit financing is growing at a time when the international financial market has become averse to state borrowing. The difficult payment position facing the ASEAN countries today is also reflected in the rapid increase of debt service costs— namely, from only U.S.$1 billion in 1975 to U.S.$7.4 billion in 1984—[9], and a decline rather than a growth in the inflow of foreign direct investment. Gross inflow of direct foreign investment in the ASEAN countries in 1985 was only 2.2 billion SDR, or 14 percent lower than in 1984, because of the declining growth performance that made the region less interesting for investors in import-competing industries together with the decline in commodity prices that depressed investment in resource exploration. The recovery now underway may reverse that pattern.

Facing this difficult environment, the ASEAN countries generally succeeded in avoiding an increasingly protectionist course in economic policy, as can be seen in the various steps taken to reduce both tariffs and nontariff barriers.[10] The trade impacts of the adjustment, however, have clearly been felt. Imports declined as a result of contractionary fiscal and monetary policies and exports of manufactured products have been pushed forcefully, notwithstanding the demand of ASEAN's major trading partners for more self-restraint in this area. In other words, even in the absence of additional protectionist measures, an adjustment to worsening economic conditions is very likely to produce trade frictions.

The second important factor that may lead to trade friction relates to the growing tendency among nations to emphasize bilateral trade balances rather than overall balances. The United States, for instance, has clearly directed its campaign for fair trade and reciprocity against all countries that have a "substantial" trade surplus vis-à-vis the United States. The increasing trend to countertrade is also a clear evidence of the tendency to emphasize bilateral balances. Yet all governments are aware of the fact that trade between two countries is seldom in balance and that the world trade regime will collapse if every country insists on a balanced bilateral trade with each of its trading partners. One cannot count upon the dominance of rational arguments in the debate over

---

[8]International Monetary Funds, *Balance of Payments Statistics, Yearbook*, various volumes.
[9]World Bank, *World Debt Tables*, 1985–86.
[10]Nowhere else is this more apparent than in Indonesia, in which repeated steps toward a more open trade policy were initiated by the government as response to the changing environment. See, e.g., the World Bank, *Indonesia*, Economic Report (1987), pp. 72–95. See also J. P. Estanislao, "ASEAN Economies in the Mid-1980s," in *ASEAN Economic Bulletin*, vol. 3 (Singapore: Institute of Southeast Asian Studies, 1986), pp. 1–7.

protectionist policies, however. Even the modest surplus each of the ASEAN countries has achieved vis-à-vis the United States has proved sufficient for the latter to include those countries as targets of its aggressive campaign for fair trade. Little attention is being given to trade in services, which may more than compensate trade balances, in spite of the developed countries' request to address services in the Uruguay Round.

Of no less importance is the trend toward selecting specific trade sectors for emphasis, a third factor that can easily lead to trade friction between countries. This is perhaps one of the worst tendencies in the trade policies of many, if not all countries in the 1980s.[11] Apparel, textiles, footwear, steel products, automobiles, household electronics, not to speak of agricultural products have one after another become targets in this emphasis on specific products, and the list threatens to lengthen.[12]

The weighted average tariff rates imposed by Japan on imports after the Tokyo Round are no higher than 0.5 percent on raw materials, 4.6 percent on semimanufactured products, and 6.0 percent on finished manufactured products.[13] Because of selectivity, however, textiles and clothing are protected by a weighted average tariff rate of 16.7 percent and the categories of leather and rubber footwear, and travel goods enjoys an average of 10.2 percent. Japan may argue incessantly that its market is even more open than those of other developed countries, but it cannot obscure the fact that restrictions are effectively imposed on imports of selected products such as boneless chicken, rice, citrus, and plywood, not to mention products having strategic implications.[14]

Japan is not alone in opting for selectivity in restricting imports. Whereas the United States can repeatedly recite the figures illustrating its large share in the developed countries' total imports of manufactured products from developing countries as evidence of its open trade, the fact remains that a number of products are selectively protected. Relating to this fact, Gary C. Hufbauer and his colleagues have produced an

---

[11]See, among others, Dominick Salvatore, editor's introduction, *Journal of Policy Modeling* (special issue on the new protectionism) 7(1) (1985).

[12]Basically, selectivity means "free trade where we are strong, but protectionism where we are weak." The developing countries had strongly objected to it during the Tokyo Round, but to no avail. The EEC insisted on selectivity as part of a revised Article 19 of GATT, which resulted, therefore, in an end to negotiations.

[13]See GATT as quoted by Leslie Alan Glick, *Multilateral Trade Negotiations: World Trade After the Tokyo Round* (Totowa, N.J.: Rowman & Allanheld, 1984).

[14]See Julian Gresser, *Partners in Prosperity: Strategic Industries for the United States and Japan* (New York: McGraw-Hill, 1984).

interesting report on the victims of the United States' selectivity in its trade policy.[15] In short, it can be easily demonstrated how the Pacific countries, developed and underdeveloped alike, retain harsh restrictions on a selective basis.

Those who believe in an international division of labor based on comparative advantage understand that certain countries are very likely to suffer more than other countries under selectivity. In its extreme form, selectivity means a nullification by the importing country of the comparative advantage of certain countries, which may be limited to a very few products or activities. For instance, it is one of the ironies of the 1980s that the "rapidly" growing exports of textile products from Indonesia to the United States have fallen victim to a "negotiated" protectionism in the form of voluntary export restraint, in spite of the small share in U.S. total imports, namely, 0.9 percent in the case of Standard International Trade Classification (SITC) 65 and 1.4 percent in the case of SITC 84 in 1985.

Failure to appreciate what other countries have initiated in terms of market opening is the fourth contributing factor to trade friction. There is a regular tendency among the governments of developing countries to blame "international protectionism" for the bad performance of their economies, underestimating the importance of a wide range of opportunities that continue to exist despite the increase of barriers to trade in certain areas. On the other hand, some developed countries fail to appreciate the fact that the importation of capital goods to most developing countries, including ASEAN members, is basically free of trade barriers, meaning that the biggest share of imports to developing countries is scarcely subject to protection. The freedom to import capital goods and raw materials is usually granted as part of investment incentives. Yet the Americans, for instance, made no reference to this fact but complained instead about restrictions on the importing of chocolate candies in ASEAN countries.[16]

Of equal importance as a source of friction is a wrong perception of what is happening with respect to one's own country's competitiveness: Overestimating the role of the Sogo Shosha in Japan's export success, countries around the Pacific, both developed and developing, came hurriedly to the conclusion that their lack of competitiveness vis-à-vis Japan was caused by the absence of a similar institution. Accord-

---

[15]Gary C. Hufbauer, Diane T. Berliner, and Kimberly A. Elliott, *Trade Protection in the United States: 31 Cases* (Washington, D.C.: Institute for International Economics, 1986).
[16]See U.S. Trade Representative, *Annual Report on National Trade Estimates 1985*, required by section 303 of the Trade and Tariff Act of 1984.

ingly, they established their own Sogo Shosha, but so far the desired result has failed to appear. Overconfident about the competitiveness of their domestic industries because they have been well equipped with the latest technology, the United States has tended, for instance, to blame other countries' unfair practices for the failure of its products to compete in the international market, ignoring the possibility that the products that American producers try to sell are not the ones for which there is a big market abroad, as Michael Aho asserted recently. Resource-exporting countries, too, can produce friction because of a wrong assessment of the power provided by their resources and the reasons behind their failure to diversify. The temptation is seemingly very great for a resource-producing country to ban the export of unprocessed materials in order to force importing countries to buy processed products. Though there may be cases in which this policy produces the intended result, it provides great incentives for substitution. Had Japan never occupied rubber-producing Southeast Asia and thereby interrupted the export of natural rubber to the United States, the use of synthetic rubber might have grown much more slowly than it has since World War II. Yet both the decision to limit the export of raw materials and the substitution process induced by that decision are bound to lead to friction.

Following the "theory of hegemonic stability," according to which the decline of a hegemony leads to global instability,[17] the perceived decline of the United States as the hegemon of the second half of the twentieth century is accounted by some as another factor that, together with the previous factors, leads to various kinds of friction among the Pacific countries. This theory is highly controversial. It cannot satisfactorily explain the success of the Tokyo Round, which in fact was based on consensus rather than on the hegemony of the United States. Nor is there any a priori reason to worry that the Uruguay Round cannot rely on the mechanism of consensus. Nevertheless, the theory is worthy of further testing since it is frequently advanced by scholars who seek to explain the instability of the trade regime. If the decline of a hegemon is bound to lead to global instability, and if the United States is a declining hegemon, the destabilizing impacts are perhaps likely to be felt most strongly by the Pacific countries.

---

[17]There is extensive literature on this theory, in which Kindleberger, Krasner, and Keohane are among the prominent contributors. See, e.g., Arthur A. Stein, "The Hegemony's Dilemma: Great Britain, the United States, and the International Economic Order," *International Organization* 38 (Spring 1984):355–86.

Trade friction can also rise in anticipation of an international negotiation on trade liberalization. Like Mohammad Ali, who started each match with a campaign to humiliate his challenger, a government tends to dramatize what is happening in the trading environment, or even to increase or to threaten to increase barriers to its domestic market to persuade other governments of the necessity of concessions in order to improve its bargaining position before the negotiatory "round" starts.

Finally, the changing trade structure resulting from shifting comparative advantages is perhaps the most important contributory factor to the problems facing the Pacific countries today and in the foreseeable future. The success of Indonesia in diversifying its exports away from timber toward processed products produced, for instance, a strain in the relations between Indonesia and Japan. That Japan's complaint was formally based on the way in which the government of Indonesia initiated the process of diversification—namely, the reliance on an export ban against timber—is basically immaterial to the conflict; Japan's wood importers know well that Indonesia's wood products would have no chance to penetrate Japan as long as timber was available to Japan in the desired quantity.

This is an example that is likely to be followed by others in the near future, as far as the relations between ASEAN countries and Japan are concerned. Needless to say, it is the resistance to adjustment rather than the changing structure itself that creates friction.[18] The trade friction between Japan on one hand and other countries on the other would have been much lighter had there not been a high degree of commodity concentration in Japan's exports.[19] In view of its importance as a contributing factor to trade friction, the structure of trade in general and that of exports in particular is the focus of the following section. Areas of friction in which ASEAN countries have been involved will be identified and the potential areas of new friction will be explored.

ASEAN's Increased Dependence on the Export of Manufactured Products

The difficult economic conditions of the first half of the 1980s forced the ASEAN countries to intensify their efforts towards increased exports. With the tightening foreign exchange constraints and sluggish domestic demand, increased exports are, indeed, a must if the ASEAN

---

[18]See, e.g., Chung-in Moon and Chull Ho Chang, "Trade Frictions and Industrial Adjustment: The Textile and Apparel Industry in the Pacific Basin," *Pacific Focus: Journal of International Studies* 2 (1987):115.

[19]See Haruko Fukuda, *Japan and World Trade: The Years Ahead* (Westmead: Saxon House Studies, 1973), p. 53.

countries are to regain and maintain high economic growth. Yet such an increase requires improved access to the markets of the major Pacific trading countries. In bilateral and regional as well as global trade talks, ASEAN countries are likely to intensify their demand for better treatment. And the threat of heightening trade tension become apparent if one takes into account the fact that the products the ASEAN countries intend to promote with extra effort are basically limited to those that are treated as sensitive products by Japan, the United States, Canada, Australia, and South Korea, which in turn constitute the core of the present Pacific market. Even if the ASEAN countries' demand is confined to a most favored nation status, the response of the major Pacific trading countries is likely to be less than positive. Yet it is a special, preferential treatment,[20] not merely a most favored nation treatment, that the ASEAN governments are hoping to enjoy in their relations with the developed countries in general and the Pacific countries in particular, even if the actual benefit is small—as in the case of Indonesia.

Table 1 contains ASEAN countries' exports to all OECD countries disaggregated at different SITC levels in 1972, 1984, and 1985. It is apparent from this table that between 1972 and 1985 ASEAN countries' exports to OECD had increased by nearly 20 percent annually in terms of value and that the commodity composition of these exports has rapidly shifted away from raw materials toward processed products. Though the share of food and live animals declined from 16.8 percent in 1972 to 9.9 percent in 1985 and that of inedible crude materials from 35.5 percent to as low as 11.3 percent in the same period, the combined share of SITC 5, 6, 7 and 8 exhibited a rapid increase from 19.7 percent to 33.2 percent. This implies, among other things, a shift in trade policy preoccupation with issues related to commodity trade toward issues of trade in manufactured products. This is not to say, however, that trade in agriculture and primary commodities has become a non-issue for the ASEAN countries. On the contrary, it continues to be of crucial importance to the economies of Indonesia, Malaysia, the Philippines, and Thailand, not only as a foreign exchange earner but also as a contributor to new employment opportunities for the rapidly growing population.

---

[20]"Special" refers to special conditions that justify a differential treatment. This demand for preferential treatment conflicts clearly with the demand of the United States for more reciprocity. Developing countries in general and those of the Asia Pacific in particular will find it the more difficult to justify this demand. In fact, it is time for these countries to scrutinize the empirical content of the hypothesis, saying that developing countries would benefit more from a nondiscriminatory trade regime than from a preferential one. Resistance to the phasing out of the existing preferences is, however, strong, notwithstanding their declining trade importance.

Table 1

Commodity Composition of Imports from the Five Original Members of ASEAN to OECD Countries
(in percentages)

Standard International Trade Classification (SITC)	1972	1984	1985
0 Food and live animals	16.8	9.5	9.9
1 Beverages and tobacco	1.1	0.4	0.4
2 Crude materials, inedible	35.5	12.6	11.3
3 Mineral fuels, etc.	21.2	39.8	40.9
4 Animal and vegetable oils and fats	4.5	3.3	3.2
5 Chemical and related products	0.5	1.2	1.3
6 Manufactured goods	11.5	6.7	7.0
68 Nonferrous metals	(7.26)	(2.65)	(2.4)
63 Cork and wood manufacturers	(2.58)	(1.47)	(1.7)
65 Textile yarns, fabrics related products	(0.77)	(1.13)	(1.2)
7 Machinery and transport equipment	4.26	18.23	17.0
77 Electrical machinery	(2.72)	(10.83)	(9.1)
75 Office machines and ADP equipment	(0.14)	(2.96)	(3.0)
76 Telecommunication and sound-recording equipment	(0.92)	(2.71)	(3.0)
71 Power-generating machinery	(0.03)	(0.63)	(0.4)
74 General industrial machinery and parts	(0.03)	(0.62)	(0.7)
8 Miscellaneous manufactured articles	3.39	7.16	7.9
84 Articles of apparel and accessories	(2.15)	(4.23)	(4.7)
89 Miscellaneous manufactured articles	(0.71)	(1.55)	(1.6)
82 Furniture and parts	(0.05)	(0.50)	(0.5)
88 Photographic apparatus, optical goods, watches	(0.29)	(0.32)	(0.4)
87 Professional and scientific instruments	(0.03)	(0.25)	(0.3)
9 Commodities and transactions, n.e.s.	3.39	7.16	(1.2)
All commodities (US$000)	5,623,874 (100)	47,909,183 (100)	46,715,064 (100)

SOURCE: Organization for Economic Cooperation and Development, *Foreign Trade by Commodities*, series C, *Imports*, various issues.

The ASEAN countries' interest in trade in agriculture is natural. They are among the important exporters of certain agricultural products hardest hit by the present disorder in agricultural trade. Thailand, for example, is an important exporter of rice and is, therefore, highly interested in a freer trade in this commodity. Thailand and other ASEAN countries are particularly interested in the opening of Japan's rice market and in the phasing out of all subsidies enjoyed by agricultural exports from financially strong countries. Sugar, which is also among the products suffering from the severe distortion in international trade, is one of the important exports of the Philippines and Thailand. Coconut oil is of crucial importance to the Philippines, and palm oil is among the major exports of Indonesia, Malaysia, and Thailand. Therefore, ASEAN countries are strongly interested in a more open trade in edible oils and fats as well as in a phasing out of the subsidies granted by various countries to the export of this commodity. Chickens are another product important to Thailand's export trade as are fruits and vegetables.

Second, favorable geographic conditions have led to the belief that each of the ASEAN countries is in the possession of ''latent'' comparative advantages in a very wide range of agricultural production. The success of Indonesia in attaining self-sufficiency in rice and near self-sufficiency in sugar, soybeans, and some other products seems to confirm this belief. The fact that the prices of these products in Indonesia are much higher than the quoted world prices is seen as being irrelevant in view of the extreme distortion of international prices. In other words, agriculture is treated as an infant rather than an aging industry, leading to the imposition of high protective measures even in areas where the comparative advantages are the least apparent, such as with dairy products. It is, therefore, no surprise to find Indonesia and Malaysia among the Cairns Group, even though the present interest of these two countries in agricultural trade is that of a net importer rather than a net exporter.

In spite of their declining share in the total exports of the ASEAN countries to the OECD countries, primary commodities and their by-products are still of great value to ASEAN as earners of foreign exchange and contributors to employment. Coffee and tea are of particular importance to Indonesia's exports. Copra is one of the major export products of the Philippines and, to a lesser extent, also Indonesia. Natural rubber has always been important to the economies of Malaysia and Indonesia and, increasingly, also to that of Thailand. Tropical wood and its by-products are among the most important of the few manufactured products exported by Indonesia, and rattan is important to both the Philippines and Indonesia. The silence prevailing in this area of trade during recent years is deceptive. It is a reflection of helplessness on the side of exporters, who find it inopportune to continue the debate over trade in primary commodities at a time when the market is confronted with an excess of supply rather than scarcities. Beneath the surface, however, ASEAN disappointment over the escalation of protection in the developed countries is clearly present. This escalation is felt in connection with lumber and wood products, natural rubber and its by-products, hide, skin and leather products, metal ingots and by-products.[21] Moreover, the degree of escalation is high in some cases. No one knows precisely the extent to which this escalation has served as a barrier to the export of processed products from the resource-exporting countries.

There are additional problems afflicting commodity trade. The release of general reserves by importing countries is one issue about which the ASEAN countries frequently complain. Finally, there is the relatively new phenomenon of the extensive search for artificial materials facilitated by advances in science and technology, which in turn have enjoyed generous support from governments. Though this support is generally seen as a non-issue in trade talks, it represents one of the important examples of what the United States called "upstream subsidy"; its magnitude is large.[22]

Recognizing their continued dependence on trade in primary commodities and holding a firm belief in the merits of diversification, the ASEAN countries are strongly asking for the inclusion of commodity-related issues into the agenda of trade talks. The way in which these issues should be addressed however, is unclear, apart from the old attempt at phasing out tariff escalation, which is not confined to primary commodities. Nor is it clear to what extent the ASEAN countries would respond positively to the probable demand by importing countries for a better, more stable access to resources, which constitutes the other side of the coin as regards trade in primary commodities. In other words, the potential for friction is abundant in the area of trade in primary commodities.

Mention has already been made of the significant change in the structure of ASEAN exports to the OECD, as shown in Table 1, and the shift in trade policy emphasis as a result of this changed structure.

---

[21]See Alexander Yeats, "The Influence of Trade and Commercial Barriers on the Industrial Processing of Natural Resources," *World Development* 9(5) (1981):485–94. Among the critical writing on this widely known phenomenon of protection escalation, see David Wall, "Industrial Processing of Natural Resources," *World Development* 8 (1980):317–27.

[22]See, e.g., Office of Technology Assessment, *Strategic Materials: Technologies to Reduce U.S. Import Vulnerability* (Washington, D.C., May 1985).

Among the manufactured products in which ASEAN countries have demonstrated remarkable progress are electrical machinery, office machines and automatic data processing (ADP) equipment, telecommunication and sound-recording equipment, and articles of apparel and accessories. The share of electrical machinery in ASEAN countries' exports to the OECD jumped from 2.7 percent in 1972 to 10.8 percent in 1984 but declined to 9.1 percent in 1985; the share of office machines and ADP equipment rose from 0.14 percent to 3 percent in 1985. The share of the tightly controlled apparel trade increased from 2.2 percent in 1972 to 4.7 percent in 1985.

However impressive the performance of ASEAN has been in terms of shift in composition of their combined exports to the OECD, ASEAN's market shares in the import of manufactured products of OECD has remained basically modest. It was 9.3 percent and 7.4 percent for electrical machinery (SITC 77), and 3.3 percent and 3 percent for office machines and ADP equipment (SITC 75) in 1984 and 1985, respectively. Even in the case of apparel (SITC 84), the ASEAN countries' share was not higher than 5.2 percent in 1984 and 1985; it was as low as 1.6 percent in the case of textile yarns and fabrics (SITC 65). Despite their rapid growth, ASEAN exports to the OECD countries are still too small to disrupt the huge markets of these countries. As far as trade in manufactured products is concerned, ASEAN countries have rarely been among the targets of protectionism in the Pacific, the apparel industry being an obvious exception. This is partly the result of the composition of ASEAN countries' export of manufactured products. Chemical and steel products are hardly relevant to the ASEAN exports and it is in these two groups of products that countervailing and anti-dumping investigations and actions have concentrated in recent years.[23]

There is another important aspect to the changes in ASEAN trade in recent years that may have helped heighten the tension between ASEAN and its second largest trading partner, the United States. As Table 2 shows, the ASEAN exports of manufactured products have increasingly been concentrated in the U.S. market. In 1985, the American share in the OECD imports of products belonging to SITC 7 and SITC 8 from ASEAN was as high as 67.6 and 62.7 percent, respectively, whereas Japan's shares were not only as small as 3.8 and 3.6 percent, respectively, but they were declining. The ASEAN countries' dependence on the American market has clearly increased, and it is likely to increase further following their increasing reliance on the export of

---

[23]See U.S. Trade Representative, *Annual Report of the President of the United States on the Trade Agreements Program, 1984–1985*, 28th issue, transmitted to Congress, February 1986.

Table 2

Percentage Shares of Japan, the United States, and the EEC in OECD's Imports from ASEAN

SITC	OECD's Imports from ASEAN (in US$000)		Japan		United States		EEC	
	1981	1985	1981	1985	1981	1985	1981	1985
0	4,369,039	4,630,520	27.6	27.4	23.8	27.0	41.7	35.7
1	214,608	172,377	10.1	7.1	21.8	17.9	45.9	50.3
2	6,706,499	5,277,751	54.8	52.3	14.8	15.7	22.4	23.4
3	22,025,365	19,108,554	78.9	74.3	28.9	21.1	1.2	1.0
4	1,227,134	1,474,537	9.8	10.6	28.0	32.7	50.9	45.4
5	305,346	624,288	63.1	43.1	12.6	21.5	14.3	20.1
6	3,071,127	3,277,103	22.0	28.9	32.7	29.0	35.5	31.2
7	5,007,674	7,939,212	6.1	3.8	64.9	67.6	22.3	23.7
8	2,638,861	3,695,002	5.0	3.6	43.0	62.7	37.1	22.7
All commodities	45,939,915	46,715,064	51.9	43.2	31.3	33.4	16.5	16.6

SOURCE: Organization for Economic Cooperation and Development, *Foreign Trade by Commodities*, series C, *Imports*, various issues.

manufactured products. The Americans are aware of this fact. It is perhaps their awareness of this increased dependence that encouraged the
United States to include countries as poor as Indonesia as a target of its
campaign for aggressive reciprocity. Again, the potential for friction is
apparent.

Trade in services is another important area where friction between
the ASEAN countries and their major trading partners is likely to
worsen in the coming years. Unfortunately, little is known about the
services trade of the ASEAN countries with the Pacific, not to mention a
breakdown according to origins and destinations as well as with respect
to individual services. Nevertheless, the seeds of friction are already
visible. At at time when all ASEAN countries with the exception of
Singapore are net importers of services, the idea of liberalization in
services trade has been introduced into the agenda of trade talks.
Although this is not sufficient reason to resist negotiations on services,
so far countless questions have remained unanswered. The ASEAN
countries' general response to the demands of the United States has, by
and large, been positive. Yet the potential for conflict persists. The
ASEAN countries seem not to have fully understood why the protection
of intellectual properties, for instance, is so important to the United
States. On the other hand, the United States seems to underrate what
the ASEAN countries have done in terms of compliance with the U.S.
demand while exaggerating the involvement of ASEAN countries in the
counterfeiting of American products.

Thus, the areas where friction is likely to heighten are already
numerous. Yet there is another important source of friction—namely,
the different or even opposing positions on the principles underlying
the General Agreement on Tariffs and Trade (GATT) as an international
trade regime to enable more and more developing countries to participate actively. A special and differential treatment is perceived to be
important as an incentive to such participation by ASEAN countries, a
participation that is increasingly important to the global relevance of
GATT. In the words of Gilbert Winham, the greatest problem the world
trading systems faces is how to integrate the developing countries fully
into that system.[24] Yet agreements on the extent to which and the length
of time a country can be granted a treatment other than an MFN treatment without endangering the system are difficult to reach. The same
applies to the principles of reciprocity, the importance of which seems
to have been overemphasized by many observers as one of the factors

---

[24]Gilbert R. Winham, *International Trade and the Tokyo Round Negotiation* (Princeton: Princeton University Press, 1986), p. 375.

behind the success of GATT in achieving tariff reductions.[25] Had the United States insisted on reciprocity in the narrow sense of the word, the war-damaged European countries might have found it harmful to join the various rounds of GATT negotiations. It was perhaps the willingness of the United States in the early days of GATT to extend unilateral concessions that made GATT a viable regime. Should the United States and other developed countries insist on reciprocity, especially aggressive or specific reciprocity in dealing with the developing countries, it will be all the more difficult for negotiations to produce results, as Winham points out.[26]

Equally serious are the differences over the safeguard standards of the GATT. Developing countries' demand for nondiscriminatory safeguard measures may continue to be unacceptable to the developed countries, especially the EEC.

ASEAN's Accommodative Stance

Trade friction can turn out to be very costly. Even if friction is very limited in the beginning in terms of its trade application, it can easily escalate as is clearly reflected today in the ever-growing number of products put into the category of sensitive items. The limited magnitude of trade involved in the early phase of conflict can, moreover, be of crucial importance to certain countries, who may flee to retaliatory actions as their trade is increasingly hurt. The U.S. Smoot-Hawley Act of 1930, for instance, was originally intended to protect agricultural products only, but it quickly spread to include other products as the demand of a growing number of industries for similar protection became irresistible. Retaliation by other countries followed swiftly.

The situation in the Pacific today is certainly not so serious as to be identified as a trade war. Nevertheless, the danger of rapid deterioration is there. The seeds, as have been identified earlier, are abundant, and the costs of a rapid intensification of the problems are likely to be very great. The developing countries in the Pacific, including the ASEAN countries, may continue to be very cautious in advancing trade liberalization, but their interest in a "soft landing" is as strong as that of the developed countries. A trading environment in the Pacific that deteriorates further is likely to impose higher costs on the developing countries than the developed countries. In view of this probability, the ASEAN

---

[25]On these so-called substantive norms of GATT, see Jack Finlayson and Mark Zacher, "The GATT and the Regulation of Trade Barriers: Regime Dynamics and Functions," *International Organization* 35 (1981):561–602.

[26]Winham, *International Trade*, p. 52.

countries' response to the various cases of friction has, by and large, been an accommodative one.

Unilaterally, each of the ASEAN countries has reduced barriers to trade in response to their weakening economic performance in the first half of the 1980s. Increased reliance on exports of manufactured products, which in turn are heavily dependent on imported capital goods and raw materials, makes a more liberal import policy a necessity. The government of Indonesia, for instance, has repeatedly announced import-liberalizing measures with a view to improving the competitiveness of the country's manufactured products in international markets. Through bilateral talks, each of the ASEAN countries has tried to be as accommodative as possible to the U.S. campaign for fair international trade. Although the response of the ASEAN countries may continue to fall short of expectations on the American side, Indonesia's signing of the GATT code on subsidies and the general willingness to address the topic of services trade in the Uruguay Round reflect to some extent this accommodative stance. Even in the area of intellectual property rights, ASEAN countries have agreed to improve the protection of foreign rights in spite of their relative inexperience in dealing with the complicated issues involved and in spite of the fact that most private firms in ASEAN have seemingly complied silently to with the existing norms of intellectual property protection since they are forced to do so by competition for exclusive dealership or similar privileges. Regionally, ASEAN as a group has also increasingly turned out to be a useful vehicle for dealing with trade policy issues. No doubt the differences in trade structure of its member countries, as can be seen from Table 1, have made it very difficult for ASEAN countries to agree on a common agenda. There are areas or issues, however, in which a common ASEAN position is being vigorously sought by member countries, and the willingness is strong to support each other's position wherever possible.

Internally, the Third Summit held in Manila in December 1987 agreed on a substantial improvement of the ASEAN Preferential Trading Agreement (PTA). The heads of government have committed themselves to concrete targets of intra-ASEAN liberalization, something they refused to do during their first summit in Bali in 1976. These concrete targets include: (1) the narrowing of the exclusion list of the ASEAN PTA in such a way as to represent not more than 10 percent of traded items and 50 percent of trade value at the end of a five-year period; (2) the deepening of the margin of preferences to at least 50 percent for items that have already been included in the list of the PTA, whereas newly listed items will be given a margin of preference of at least 25 percent; (3) the lowering of ASEAN content to 35 percent, which implies less stringent conditions for the eligibility of products using non-ASEAN inputs, to the ASEAN PTA; (4) the raising of the margin of preferences to 90 percent for products originating in an ASEAN industrial joint venture; and (5) a standstill and rollback of nontariff barriers. These targets certainly do not amount to the transformation of ASEAN into a common market or other forms of economic integration. Nevertheless, they are substantial and can turn out to be economically meaningful, assuming of course consistent implementation.

The arrangement agreed upon in Manila by the heads of government will probably have a trade-diverting impact. It is very likely, however, to be accompanied by a further reduction in barriers to trade with the rest of the world. Finally, both individually and as a group, the ASEAN countries have actively participated in the preparation and launching of the new round of GATT. Their participation reflects among other things the fact that ASEAN exports have increasingly become "GATT relevant"—that is, increasingly reliant on items to which GATT applies.

It is premature to conclude from the foregoing that, with respect to ASEAN attitudes and policies, there is no need to worry about resistance to trade liberalization. The accommodation to some of the American demands and the endorsement of the new round of GATT cannot obscure the fact that most ASEAN countries are no less protectionist than their trading partners in the Pacific-Asian region. Factors such as unemployment, the need to foster the progress of certain industries for strategic reasons, and the dependence of some areas on economic activities that support the rising protectionist sentiment in the developed countries are also at work in the ASEAN countries. Furthermore, the governments of the ASEAN nations tend to perceive the protection of their economies as less evil than the protection practiced by developed countries. In addition, the experience of the ASEAN countries in dealing with trade liberalization and in coping with its various impacts is very limited. In short, participation of the ASEAN countries in trade liberalization, global and otherwise, is likely to confront various obstacles. Nevertheless, the ASEAN countries are aware of the ever-growing dependence of their economies on exports of manufactured products to the major trading countries of the Pacific. Not only has this awareness led to an increasingly realistic stance on issues that are perceived to be important by ASEAN countries' trading partners;[27] it has also forged a more favorable attitude toward a freer trade.

---

[27]On the diverse issues related to the participation of the ASEAN countries in the GATT, see *ASEAN Trade Policy Options* (Singapore: Institute of Southeast Asian Studies, 1988).

12. Financing Growth and Development in Asia

THOMAS A. LAYMAN

The economic success story of the Pacific-Asian region since the end of World War II is well known to most observers. Over forty years ago, Japan's industrial complex had been devastated, and many other countries in Asia seemed forever doomed to poverty and backwardness. Spurred largely by the opening of international markets for commodity exports of the resource-rich countries and the need to rebuild after the war, Japan and many of the newly independent nation-states of the Pacific-Asian region have been able to realize significant, if not spectacular, improvements in their economic well-being. Home to more than half the world's population, the region accounts for an expanding share of world trade and is expected to produce more than half of all the world's goods and services by the end of the century. The Tokyo stock market, with a total capitalization of $3 trillion at the end of 1987, has overtaken the New York market as the largest in the world. Only a few years ago, such developments would have seemed remote, but they are just a few reminders of the continued and important shift in the balance of world financial, economic, and industrial power.

Though such progress has allowed the countries of Asia and the Pacific to be characterized as the most "dynamic" region in the world, the economic development experiences within the region have varied quite markedly, ranging from declining per capita incomes in Burma, Vietnam, Cambodia, and Bangladesh to extraordinarily high income growth in the newly industrialized countries (NICs) of South Korea, Hong Kong, Taiwan, and Singapore. In recent years, manufactured exports of Malaysia, Thailand, Indonesia, and the Philippines have grown rapidly as well.

The success in Asia during the past two decades occurred mainly because of high and rising investment rates and the judicious manage-

The author wishes to thank Miles Kahler, Lawrence Krause, Robert Scalapino, George Viksnins, Jeff Anderson, Paul Rawkins, and Margaret Shilliday for their help and comments on earlier drafts of this essay. The conclusions and opinions expressed herein are those of the author and do not necessarily represent those of the Institute of International Finance or any of its membership.

ment of domestic policies. Although investment was financed largely by domestic savings, foreign capital also played an important role. In general, foreign inflows of capital can be divided into two broad categories: official and private. Official flows, which traditionally have been restricted to aid and project-related financing, greatly exceeded private capital flows for much of the period since the end of World War II. Beginning in the 1970s, however, fluctuating international oil prices and deteriorating terms of trade for much of the developing world led to widening current account deficits and rising balance-of-payments financing. A majority of this demand was met by syndicated loans and credits arranged through international commercial banks on floating rate terms. The other major source of private finance is direct foreign investment, which in the early 1970s accounted for one-fifth of total capital flows to all developing countries but since then has fallen to around 10 percent of the total.

The development experiences of the Asian countries have amply demonstrated that a country's performance is very much a function of its ability to generate sufficient financing and to utilize this finance in a productive fashion. Some countries relied more than others on external debt to finance their development. Several—namely, South Korea, Taiwan, Malaysia, and Thailand—have reached a stage in their development whereby they have begun to make net repayments of some of these debts. Others, however, still must borrow significant amounts each year, and the accumulation of debt poses a serious bottleneck for the development aspirations of several of these countries. During the coming decade, it is expected that capital flows, especially concessional flows, to the Pacific-Asian region will grow more slowly than they did in the 1960s and 1970s.

It is the purpose of this essay to analyze how various countries in the region have utilized capital (both domestic and foreign) to finance their development. Particular emphasis is placed on the use of foreign capital, both debt and nondebt creating, in this process. The first section reviews the growth performance of selected countries in Asia and how the record has varied across and among groups of countries. The differential rates of economic performance generally reflect differences in the way policymakers managed and utilized financial flows. Next, the patterns of domestic and foreign financial resource flows are identified. Striking differences emerge in the region in the use of official versus private capital to finance the development effort. The final section offers some observations about future financial flows and policy issues that will have to be confronted if the countries of the Pacific-Asian region are to continue to develop and possibly serve as stimuli for economic growth of other countries and regions of the world.

Table 1

Output Growth: Asia
(% per annum)

Country	Real GDP Growth			Per Capita Real GDP Growth		
	1965–73	1973–80	1980–87	1965–73	1973–80	1980–87
Asian 11[a]	6.9	6.5	7.2	4.1	4.5	5.1
NICs[a]	11.2	8.1	7.8	8.7	6.1	6.1
South Korea	11.5	7.6	8.7	9.0	5.9	7.1
Taiwan	11.0	8.3	7.4	8.6	6.2	5.7
Singapore	12.7	8.2	5.8	10.7	6.7	4.1
Hong Kong	9.9	9.0	7.5	7.5	6.2	5.6
Southeast Asia[a]	7.1	7.2	4.2	4.2	4.8	1.8
Indonesia	7.1	7.5	3.8	4.4	5.5	2.0
Thailand	7.5	7.2	5.7	4.2	4.8	3.1
Malaysia	7.3	7.3	4.5	4.7	4.4	1.8
Philippines	5.6	6.1	0.5	2.6	3.3	−2.0
South Asia[a]	3.8	4.1	5.2	1.5	1.9	2.4
India[b]	3.6	3.9	5.0	1.4	1.8	2.3
Pakistan[c]	4.7	5.7	6.4	2.6	2.6	3.4
China	4.4	6.1	9.4	0.9	4.6	8.1

[a]Weighted by 1987 real GDP.
[b]Refers to fiscal year beginning April 1.
[c]Refers to fiscal year ending June 30.

SOURCES: IIF database, IMF, World Bank, and Asian Development Bank.

Financing Asian Development

Growth Performance

Taken as a group, the economic performance of the Pacific-Asian region during the past twenty years has been impressive.[1] Real GDP growth for the countries listed in Table 1 averaged just under 7 percent per annum between 1965 and 1987. Almost all countries experienced a slowdown in their rates of growth during the late 1970s and early 1980s, reflecting wide swings in terms of trade and slower growth in the indus-

---

[1]For an excellent overview of this topic from which much of the following has benefited, see generally Gerald M. Meier, *Financing Asian Development: Performance and Prospects* (New York: The Asia Society, 1986); Michael T. Skully and George J. Viksnins, *Financing East Asia's Success* (New York: St. Martin's Press, 1987); Burnham O. Campbell, "Asian and Pacific Developing Economies: Performance and Issues," *Asian Development Review* 5(1) (1987); and V. G. Bhatia, "Asian and Pacific Developing Economies: Performance and Issues," *Asian Development Review* 6(1) (1988).

trial world. Unfortunately, averages mask important differences in economic performance among the various countries. For example, the poorer countries of South Asia—namely, India and Pakistan—though growing much slower than the average for Asia as a whole, exhibited an improving trend over the entire period. China, which grew rather slowly during the period between 1965 and 1973 by comparison with the Asian average, showed extraordinarily high growth during 1980–87. Not only were the four countries that comprise the NIC group—South Korea, Taiwan, Singapore, and Hong Kong—able to achieve rapid growth during the last twenty years, it was done without experiencing the increasing inequalities and unemployment that have been common to many other developing countries. Real per capita income rose roughly 7 percent per year in these four countries during 1965–87. Given how densely populated these countries are, this was truly a remarkable achievement.

The achievements of the NICs resulted mainly from the emphasis policymakers placed on boosting the level of domestic savings and adopting a development strategy that focused on the importance of earning foreign exchange. Together, these actions allowed the countries to overcome the constraints associated with financing their development. Despite these similarities, each country has had a unique experience driven largely by differences in climate, natural resources, and cultural backgrounds.

The rise and subsequent fall in international oil and commodity prices combined with a recession in the industrial world during the first half of the 1980s to cause a slowdown in growth among the NICs. The effects of these events were much more severe, however, for the commodity-dependent economies of Indonesia, Thailand, Malaysia, and the Philippines. Having posted average rates of just over 7 percent per year between 1965 and 1980, real GDP growth decelerated in these countries to about 4 percent per year during the next seven years (Table 1). Per capita income growth also slowed to under 2 percent annually. The main reason for this slowdown was the significant deterioration in each country's terms of trade. For Indonesia and the Philippines, moreover, exports declined on average during the 1981–85 period. Despite efforts to diversify their export base away from primary products and into manufactured and industrial goods, all of these countries remain vulnerable to fluctuations in international commodity prices.

The countries of South Asia are generally much poorer than other parts of the region, mainly as a result of continued heavy dependence on agriculture. Efforts to improve industrial output have been ongoing for many years, but exports from these sectors are still low relative to other Asian countries. The lower growth rates experienced in India during the 1965–80 period were not, however, the result of low investment. As Table 2 indicates, investment rates in India have been quite high, averaging over 18 percent of GNP each year between 1965 and 1973 and rising to almost 23 percent in the 1973–80 period. Such rates are comparable with those of the countries in Southeast Asia. Domestic savings have also been high, implying that the foreign financing gap has been kept within manageable bounds. Unfortunately, the utilization of capital in India has not been very efficient. India has an extraordinarily high capital/output ratio (6–7) for a country at its stage of development and given the size of its labor force. Pakistan, by comparison, has had more difficulty boosting domestic savings, relying mainly on foreign aid to support investment activity. Growth, however, has been relatively higher, suggesting that investment has been more efficient.[2]

It is encouraging that a number of countries in South Asia have adopted new policies to liberalize their economies and reduce the role of the government. Although these changes are generally too recent for a substantive response, if they are allowed to continue, improved utilization of capital and a more market-oriented economy could result. Given the projected high population growth rates, the problem of labor absorption will intensify the pressure on governments to continue such policies. Because these economies depend less on trade than the NICs or Southeast Asian countries, they were less susceptible to the slowdown in world trade during the 1980s. As a result, per capita real income growth surpassed the average rates of increase experienced in the Southeast Asia group and narrowed the differential of the NIC group. Pakistan was helped during the past five years by its special relationship with Iran, a market that grew for political reasons. India was also somewhat insulated, because of its relatively large share of trade with socialist countries.

In summary, growth in the region slowed during the first half of the 1980s compared with its earlier performance, but important variations across countries have occurred. The improved performance of the poorer countries of South Asia has been particularly noteworthy. Because these countries have traditionally adopted a more inward-looking approach to development, the question immediately arises as to

---

[2]The implied capital-to-output ratio for Pakistan of 2 to 3 is implausibly low, however. Several explanations have been offered to account for this anomaly. One is that over the past decade the country has continually depleted its capital stock, neglecting maintenance and replacement, thus attaining high growth at the expense of slower growth some time in the future. It is also possible that much more investment occurs than is captured in the national accounts data. It is generally recognized that from one-third to over one-half of economic activity goes unrecorded.

Table 2

Investment, Savings and Current Account Balances: Asia
(annual average percentage)

Country	Gross Domestic Investment/GNP			Gross National Savings/GNP			Current Account Balance/GNP		
	1965-73	1973-80	1980-86	1965-73	1973-80	1980-86	1965-73	1973-80	1980-86
NICs									
South Korea	25.1	31.8	30.7	21.5	26.4	26.9	-3.6	-5.4	-3.8
Taiwan	25.1	31.9	25.3	25.6	32.6	32.4	0.5	0.7	7.2
Singapore	30.9	40.2	46.4	18.4	29.9	40.3	-12.5	-10.2	-6.2
Hong Kong	24.7	28.5	31.8	26.0	28.8	27.9	1.3	0.3	-3.9
Southeast Asia									
Indonesia	15.8	24.5	29.4	13.7	24.6	26.6	-2.1	0.1	-2.8
Thailand	23.8	26.6	24.4	22.6	21.5	18.5	-1.2	-5.1	-5.9
Malaysia	22.3	28.7	35.1	21.6	29.3	27.5	-0.7	0.6	-7.6
Philippines	20.6	29.1	25.8	20.6	24.3	20.0	0.0	-4.8	-5.8
South Asia									
India	18.4	22.6	24.4	17.9	22.3	22.6	-0.5	-0.3	-1.8
Pakistan	16.0	16.5	16.2	—	10.5	12.9	—	-6.0	-3.3
China	25.0[a]	—	35.0[b]	25.0[a]	—	33.6[b]	0.0[a]	—	-1.4[b]

[a]1965 only.
[b]1983-86.

SOURCES: IIF database, World Bank, and Asian Development Bank.

whether the opportunities for export promotion that led to the success stories of the NICs of the region are now over. Increased protectionist sentiments in the industrial world fuel this impression. However, a growth path exclusively oriented to inward-looking policies and central planning does not in the long run appear to be the answer. Some of the recent surge in output in the South Asian countries may actually be attributable to the implementation of liberalization programs. There is great potential for export-led growth based on trade between and among the countries of Asia. Already there is an increasing trend among the NICs of the region to exchange goods and services with the lesser developed countries of Asia. A market-oriented development strategy based on export promotion continues to be the model of success. The challenge is to find the right product mix that can be produced efficiently and sold competitively while providing employment opportunities commensurate with the country's resource base.

Domestic Resource Mobilization

Development finance is defined as the "mobilization of real resources—land, labor, and capital—to allow the production of a larger output of goods and services."[3] Besides financial capital, there must be an accumulation of real capital in the form of machines, equipment, factories and the like if output is to be increased. Domestic savings—that is, not consuming—is one way of releasing domestic resources for investment purposes. Such a process can be enhanced by the development of a financial system that can collect funds from a wide range of sources and intermediate them to investors. The government, of course, can provide investable funds by printing money or by creating credit through the country's banking system. Without a concomitant increase in output or in the demand for money, such an increase in money will only result in inflation, however.[4]

It is notable that most Asian countries have succeeded in devoting a growing share of their national output to investment. The high rates of investment in the NICs, Malaysia, and China are especially significant (Table 2). Corresponding to the rise in investment rates for most countries has also been a rise in domestic savings, a large proportion of which has come through a decline in the fraction of national income devoted to private consumption. Singapore is perhaps the most note-

---

[3]This very concise definition was posited in Meier, *Financing Asian Development*, p. 16.
[4]Skully and Viksnins devote two chapters to the relationship between inflation and growth in Asia and in other developing regions of the world. See *Financing East Asia's Success*, pp. 1–55.

worthy in this regard, as domestic savings rose from 18 percent of GNP on average during 1965–73 to almost 30 percent in 1973–80 and to over 40 percent during 1980–86.[5] Taiwan's savings rate recently has been even higher.

Taiwan and until recently Hong Kong had a similar experience: The proportion of GNP devoted to domestic savings was high and relatively stable, whereas that devoted to gross domestic investment declined. The result has been a considerable excess of domestic savings over investment, which for Taiwan, where there are capital controls, resulted in a huge build-up in international reserves.

Among the countries of Southeast Asia, the energy-exporting countries of Indonesia and Malaysia had an excess of domestic savings over investment during the years of high oil prices. Malaysia accomplished this while maintaining a relatively high investment ratio; Indonesia's was more moderate. Nonetheless, both countries continued to borrow from abroad; with the decline in oil prices in the mid-1980s, they had to make structural adjustments to their economies. Thailand and the Philippines are somewhat unique in that their savings ratios have declined since the early 1970s. Thailand, however, was able to maintain its gross domestic investment near past levels, but the Philippines was not.

Not surprisingly, the methods by which Asian countries have encouraged domestic savings have varied considerably. In Taiwan and South Korea, a high real rate of return on time and savings deposits was generally the main factor. Taiwan not only adopted monetary policies beginning in the 1960s that maintained high real interest rates on deposits, but the popular desire to operate small businesses also seems to have had a role in stimulating savings. In Singapore and Malaysia, the government requires a large proportion of earnings—to be deposited into a social security retirement account. Such a requirement has mobilized significant financial resources for the development of the economy, mainly by the public sector. Domestic savings can also be increased through involuntary means, that is, through increased taxes. Indeed, the Central Provident Fund in Singapore and the Employees' Provident Fund in Malaysia are essentially a form of taxation—in contrast to the Japanese Postal Savings System (one of the largest financial

---

[5]Almost all of this increase can be attributed to the private sector, as private savings typically accounts for about two-thirds of total domestic savings. This is mainly due to the existence of the Central Provident Fund (see later), which has been a primary source of funds for public sector investment.

institutions in the world).[6] In recent years, remittances from workers employed overseas, especially in the Middle East, have also helped augment domestic incomes and savings in the Philippines, India, Pakistan, and Bangladesh.

In countries where the savings performance has been good, an improvement in financial incentives was significant not only in raising the real rate of interest on deposits but also in extending the array of financial instruments and institutions, increasing the likelihood that savings will be held in financial forms rather than in nonfinancial assets.[7] Table 3 gives a rough index of financial deepening for selected countries in the Pacific-Asian region by showing recent trends in the ratio of broad money (consisting of demand deposits, currency, and savings accounts) to GDP. This ratio has been rising for most all countries in the region. As one would expect, the NICs show the highest ratio, with Hong Kong and Taiwan having ratios in excess of 100 per cent. Among the countries of Southeast Asia, Malaysia has the highest ratio, in part because of the aforementioned mandatory retirement fund. Thailand has also shown an increasing trend, mainly because of a stable inflationary environment and the expansion of banks into the rural areas of the country. A similar experience has occurred in India as well. China has seen a remarkable rise in this ratio because financial liberalization has been an important component of the overall reform process of the 1980s.

The Role of Foreign Finance

If domestic investment exceeds gross national savings, a gap is created that must be financed ex ante through the country's balance of payments. The amount by which imports exceed exports, often called the "foreign exchange gap," must be accommodated by an inflow of capital

---

[6]As of the end of August 1988, Singaporean workers were required to contribute 24 percent of their wages and employers were required to contribute 12 percent of salaries to the Central Provident Fund (CPF). Similarly, in Malaysia, worker contributions amounted to 9 percent of wages and employer contributions were 11 percent to the Employees' Provident Fund. Beginning in 1986, the Singapore government allowed individuals to mobilize some of their savings in the CPF to purchase equity shares in state enterprises and to purchase private housing.

[7]For an extension and update of the original arguments concerning the role of financial sector development in economic development by R. I. McKinnon, *Money and Capital in Economic Development* (Washington, D.C.: Brookings Institution, 1973), and Edward S. Shaw, *Financial Deepening in Economic Development* (New York: Oxford University Press, 1973), see George J. Viksnins, *Financial Deepening in ASEAN Countries* (Honolulu: University of Hawaii Press, 1980), and Maxwell J. Fry, *Money, Interest, and Banking in Economic Development* (Baltimore: Johns Hopkins University Press, 1988).

Table 3

Broad Money[a]/GDP Ratios: Asia
(percentage)

Country	1980	1982	1984	1986	1987
NICs					
South Korea	48.6	61.0	68.1	82.5	92.2
Taiwan	65.3	76.8	96.2	123.2	139.2
Singapore	65.3	69.9	67.7	81.9	89.4
Hong Kong	70.2	110.9	126.3	177.5	194.3
Southeast Asia					
Indonesia	15.7	17.7	21.0	26.9	28.0
Thailand	36.8	43.0	54.7	61.4	66.7
Malaysia	51.9	60.2	57.7	75.6	73.0
Philippines[b]	25.6	28.0	22.5	24.0	22.5
South Asia					
India[b]	43.4	44.1	47.6	48.0	49.2
Pakistan	39.4	36.2	39.0	39.0	39.5
China	39.2	45.4	58.2	73.8	87.0

[a]Broad money (M2) consists of demand deposits, currency, and saving accounts.
[b]M3, which consists of M2 plus time deposits.

SOURCE: IIF database.

or by a reduction in foreign exchange reserves. Inflows of capital can come from a number of sources, including official transfers, foreign equity and portfolio investments, official loans and grants from multilateral institutions and governments, and commercial bank and other private loans. The capital account of the balance of payments also records other flows that are often not captured in official statistics, including the drawdown or accumulation of foreign assets held by domestic residents.

Beginning in the 1950s, the dominant form of external finance for developing Asia was official aid. The United States government played a major role in providing bilateral assistance to countries in the region where it had military and/or strategic interests, including South Korea, Taiwan, South Vietnam, Pakistan, and the Philippines. Although rapid economic growth in both South Korea and Taiwan ''graduated'' them out of the economic aid flow fairly quickly, sizable military assistance loans were still provided to South Korea until mid-1986 and to Taiwan until 1979. From the mid-1960s to the early 1970s, external financing came primarily from official sources, such as the World Bank and the Asian Development Bank. Most of these funds were targeted for specific investments rather than for general economic assistance. After the

OPEC price shock of 1973, private commercial banks began to play a major role in providing external finance to the developing world in general and to the Pacific-Asian region in particular. More recently, the onset of the LDC debt problem, which has touched Asia through the debt reschedulings of the Philippines, has led to a further shift in the relative shares of foreign financial flows.

Table 4 gives the cumulative breakdown of current account deficits and capital flows for a number of Asian countries during the period 1980 to 1987. Although the accumulated deficits in the current account were nearly US$62 billion, the total net inflow of foreign capital to these ten countries amounted to US$206 billion. The difference, of course, was accounted for by an accumulation of offshore assets by residents (denoted in Table 4 as resident lending), unrecorded outflows (E&O), and increases in reserves. Commercial banks were the largest single supplier of funds to Asia, providing US$88 billion or 43 percent of the total net financing flow. Multilateral institutions, mainly the World Bank and Asian Development Bank (ADB), and governments each provided about US$27 billion net. It should be noted that trade credits from private banks that are guaranteed by official export-credit agencies are included under government lending for purposes of this analysis. During the eight years through 1987, the IMF has provided short-term adjustment loans to almost every country, including a US$5 billion loan to India in 1981. Most of these loans, however, have been repaid or are in the process of being amortized so that the IMF has become a much less important source of net credit to the region. Nondebt capital—made up of official transfers and equity and portfolio investments—contributed net flows of US$41 billion during 1980–87.

Figure 1 shows the relative importance of these sources of net external finance to the Asia region for selected years between 1980 and 1987. Whereas in 1980–82 commercial banks accounted for about 50 percent of total net financial flows to the Pacific-Asian region, that proportion dropped to around 35 percent by 1986–87. Offsetting this relative decline was a significant rise in the proportion of nondebt flows, and in 1987 there was a jump in nonbank private financing, mainly in the form of supplier's credits. One reason for this shift was the reduction in demand for funds associated with reduced aggregate current account deficits, as both South Korea and Taiwan recorded large surpluses. The net flow of capital from official sources also peaked in 1983 in both relative and absolute terms. Flows from the IMF to the Pacific-Asian region actually turned negative in 1985, with net repayments amounting to almost US$500 million in 1986 and rising to US$2.4 billion in 1987.

284   Financing Growth and Development

Table 4

Cumulative Net External Financing flows, 1980–87: Asia
(US$ billion)

Country	Current Account[a]	Nondebt	IMF	MDBs	Govts.	Banks[b]	Other Private[b]	Resident Lending	E&O[c]	Reserve Change[d]
NICs	50.4	11.8	0.3	1.4	-0.6	33.3	5.6	-24.3	3.6	-81.5
South Korea	-2.5	2.1	0.3	1.6	0.8	9.3	0.9	-7.9	-3.9	-0.6
Taiwan	56.8	1.1	0.0	-0.2	-1.6	12.7	3.8	0.1	-0.2	-72.6
Singapore	-3.9	8.6	0.0	0.0	0.2	11.3	0.9	-16.5	7.7	-8.3
Southeast Asia	-60.8	14.7	1.7	10.9	15.9	29.0	5.2	-6.9	-4.8	-4.9
Indonesia	-23.1	3.1	0.7	5.2	6.9	9.4	1.2	-1.7	-1.0	-0.7
Thailand	-13.6	3.6	0.5	2.5	2.2	3.6	1.0	-0.9	2.6	-1.5
Malaysia	-11.8	5.8	0.1	0.5	3.5	8.2	2.3	-1.5	-3.3	-3.8
Philippines	-12.3	2.2	0.4	2.7	3.3	7.8	0.7	-2.8	-3.1	1.1
South Asia	-41.7	6.9	2.4	11.8	5.8	11.4	8.7	0.0	-8.5	3.2
India	-32.7	3.4	2.1	9.7	4.0	9.1	8.5	0.0	-6.9	2.8
Pakistan	-9.0	3.5	0.3	2.1	1.8	2.3	0.2	0.0	-1.6	0.4
China	-9.8	7.5	0.7	2.5	5.6	14.6	-0.6	-3.5	-2.9	-14.1
Total	-61.9	40.9	5.1	26.6	26.7	88.3	18.9	-34.7	-12.6	-97.3

[a]Current account defined to exclude net official transfers that are included under nondebt flows.
[b]Direct credit only. That which is guaranteed by official third parties is included under multilateral development banks (MDBs) or governments.
[c]Unrecorded outflows.
[d]Minus = an increase.

SOURCES: IIF database and IMF.

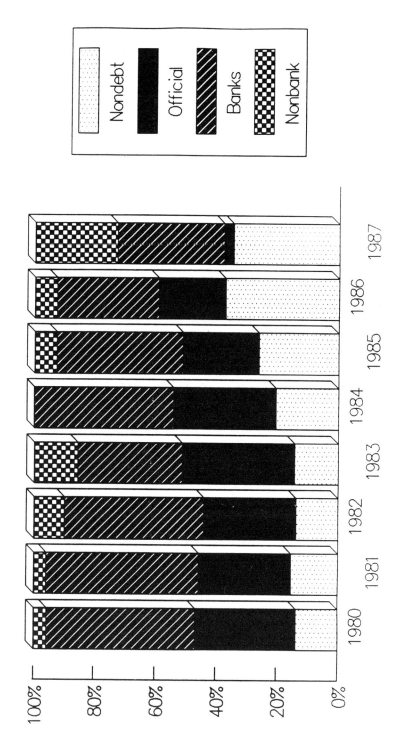

Figure 1. Net Inflows: Asia 1980–87

Official Sources of Finance

Official finance can be categorized into concessional flows, defined as loans or aid provided at below market rates of interest, and nonconcessional flows, usually in the form of loans that carry terms more closely aligned with funds from commercial sources. Most multilateral institutions offer both types of funds to developing countries. This section will give an overview of the lending policies of the multilateral institutions that are primary suppliers of capital to countries in the Pacific-Asian region—the International Monetary Fund, the World Bank, and the Asian Development Bank.

International Monetary Fund. Under the Articles of Agreement governing its activities, the IMF is charged with "making financial resources available to members, on a temporary basis and with adequate safeguards, to permit them to correct payments imbalances without resorting to measures destructive of national and international prosperity."[8] The fund's basic lending policy is referred to as "drawings under credit tranches," with each tranche being the equivalent of 25 percent of a member country's quota. In principle, a member country is limited in its cumulative drawings from the fund to 408–450 percent of quota (net of scheduled repurchases), depending on the severity of the member's balance-of-payments needs and the strength of its adjustment efforts. The most common drawing under these credit tranches is done under a standby arrangement, which allows the member country to draw up to a specified amount during a given period (typically for twelve to eighteen months) as long as it observes the conditionality and other terms included in the arrangement.[9]

The fund also offers loans under other facilities. The extended fund facility (EFF), which can now include loans of up to four years, was set

---

[8]Article 1 (v). For an overview of current lending practices of the IMF, see Anand G. Chandavarkar, *The International Monetary Fund: Its Financial Organization and Activities*, IMF Pamphlet Series no. 42 (Washington, D.C., 1984), and the *International Monetary Fund Annual Report 1988* (Washington, D.C., 1988), pp. 35–58.

[9]Conditionality refers to performance criteria under which a member country must subject itself for drawings under various IMF loan agreements. These usually encompass elements such as budgetary and credit ceilings, appropriate exchange rate and interest rate actions, avoidance of restrictions on current payments and transfers, limits on new external debts, and maintenance of minimum levels of foreign exchange reserves. For a discussion of conditionality, see Joseph Gold, *Conditionality*, IMF Pamphlet Series no. 31 (Washington, D.C., 1979), and Manuel Guitian, *Fund Conditionality: Evolution of Principles and Practices*, IMF Pamphlet Series no. 38 (Washington, D.C., 1981). A comprehensive examination of conditionality was completed in April 1988 by the executive board of the IMF. See *IMF Annual Report 1988*, pp. 47–49.

up in 1974 and is designed to help countries correct structural problems such as production and trading controls that distort relative prices and adversely affect a country's comparative advantage. To supplement the EFF, the structural adjustment facility (SAF) was established in March 1986 to provide concessional resources (the interest rate is only 0.5 percent per year) with repayments beginning five and one-half years after the first drawing. In April 1988, the enhanced structural adjustment facility (ESAF) became operational as a support to the SAF, providing additional three-year concessional financing for strong, growth-oriented adjustment efforts by low-income countries. Although a number of countries in the region are eligible for this new facility, as of September 1988 no Pacific-Asian country had concluded such an arrangement.

Other IMF facilities include the supplementary financing facility set up in 1979 to help recycle the surpluses of oil producers mainly to oil-importing countries already engaged in a standby or EFF. The compensatory financing facility (CFF), begun in 1963, was established to help a country in balance-of-payments difficulty caused by export shortfalls that are both temporary and caused largely by factors beyond the member's control. Given the reasons for extending a CFF loan, conditionality is relatively low. As a supplement to the CFF, an external contingency facility is expected to become operational in late 1988; it will provide additional funds to countries already engaged in support programs that have been thrown off track by adverse exogenous developments. The fund also established a Buffer Stock Financing facility in 1969 to help dampen commodity price fluctuations. Virtually all developing countries in Asia who are members of the IMF have drawn under one or more of these facilities sometime in the past thirty years.[10]

With the exception of the EFF and SAF arrangements, the funding programs of the IMF are short term in nature, designed to offset temporary balance-of-payments shortfalls while macroeconomic policies are implemented to correct the imbalance. Loans are normally classified as nonconcessional financing and are available to developing and developed member countries alike. In addition to the concessional terms provided under the SAF and ESAF loans, the fund has offered on a temporary basis special facilities exclusively to developing countries at subsidized rates. These have included the Oil Facility Subsidy Account (1975–83); the Trust Fund (1980–81), which was funded from windfall

---

[10]In 1987, Indonesia was granted a CFF to help offset a shortfall in export receipts associated with the dramatic decline in commodity prices during the 1985–86 period; it is to be repaid beginning in 1990. See Vaudine England, "IMF Lends Indonesia US$610 million," *Far Eastern Economic Review* (May 14, 1987), p. 5.

profits on gold sales; and a subsidy account for the supplementary financing facility. In 1986 the fund also began to offer enhanced surveillance for countries that have advanced significantly in their process of adjustment and for which a fund arrangement is not envisaged. Although the monitoring agreement does not involve loans from the IMF, the "report card" on the country can be used to stimulate credit flows from private and other sources. In 1987, Yugoslavia and Venezuela came under enhanced surveillance.

World Bank. The sister organizations of the IMF, the International Bank for Reconstruction and Development (IBRD, or simply the World Bank) and the International Development Assistance (IDA), were established explicitly to provide longer-term development assistance. A commercial arm of the World Bank group, called the International Finance Corporation (IFC), was also set up to help countries develop their private sector and domestic capital markets. IDA is primarily responsible for offering concessional funds to its member countries—normally fifty year maturities and no interest. Such loans have been directed to several Asian countries over the years, including Taiwan, South Korea, the Philippines, Thailand, Indonesia, India, Pakistan, and Bangladesh.[11] IBRD loans, which until recently carried lower interest rates than those from commercial sources, traditionally have been directed to project-specific requests.[12] Because these projects are often associated with infrastructural development or some other socially oriented investment, countries have not been able to secure commercial financing for many of these undertakings.

During the 1980s, the World Bank has been constrained in its efforts to boost lending programs to the developing world. Some of the constraint stems from the high level of undrawn commitments for projects that have not been undertaken, usually because of slowdowns in project implementation and a lack of domestic counterpart funds required to

---

[11]See John Lewis, *The Role of Development Assistance in Asian Development* (New York: The Asia Society, 1986).

[12]Loans from the World Bank are denominated in a mix of currencies and at an interest rate reflective of the basket in which the bank raises its funds. These loans must be repaid in the same mix of currencies in which they were borrowed, and for loans committed since July 1982, the interest rate is adjusted every six months in line with changes in the World Bank funding costs. Because of dramatic exchange rate movements and widely varying interest rates during 1986–87, the relative cost of World Bank loans rose. For example, the interest rate for IBRD loans between January 1 and June 30, 1988, was 7.72 percent, whereas the ninety-day U.S. dollar LIBOR (London Inter-Bank Offer Rate), the rate against which many commercial loans are based, averaged only 7.2 percent during that period. See *The World Bank Annual Report 1988* (Washington, D.C., 1988), pp. 49–50.

make the drawing. By its charter, the World Bank is also not allowed to leverage its lending; that is, the total amount outstanding of guarantees, participations in loans, and direct loans cannot exceed the sum of subscribed capital, reserves, and surplus. The majority of this capital is a commitment by donor members. There has not been a general capital increase since January 1980, although in late April 1988 the bank's board of governors authorized a general capital increase of US$74.8 billion that would raise the authorized capital of the World Bank to US$171 billion.[13]

To help offset some of the constraints, the IBRD has engaged in cofinancing programs with commercial banks—called the ''B'' loan scheme—to provide project evaluation assistance as well assume part of the project financing risk.[14] Also, in 1980 the World Bank accelerated a program to extend structural adjustment and policy-related loans (SALs). These loans, which are nonproject related, are given mainly to help countries overcome balance-of-payments difficulties caused in part by domestic structural rigidities and/or inappropriate policies. For example, policy loans have been made for the removal of barriers to international trade or to adjust agricultural pricing strategies to improve productivity. In the seven years to June 1988, thirty-one policy-related loans were granted to twenty-eight countries. In Asia, China, Indonesia, and the Philippines received such loans directed toward trade liberalization and financial sector reforms. A number of other Asian countries could also be eligible for this type of loan in the future.[15]

In surveying World Bank loan commitments to the Pacific-Asian region for the fiscal years 1978 to 1988, agriculture and rural development accounted for the largest share (20 percent) of project loans in East Asia followed by loans for transportation, power, and education facili-

---

[13]As of June 30, 1988, a total of 142 member countries had voted to approve the general capital increase (GCI), representing 70.1 percent of shareholder power. The paid-in portion of the GCI is only 3 percent, with 97 percent callable. Member governments have until September 30, 1993, to complete their new subscriptions. As of August 1988, the U.S. Congress had not authorized its commitment. If all subscriptions are approved, the new capital will allow the World Bank and its affiliates to achieve nominal growth in lending of about 10 percent per year over the period through 1995. See *World Bank Annual Report 1988*, pp. 32–33.

[14]The ''B'' loan scheme does not allow the World Bank to guarantee any portion of the commercial bank underwriting. The bank serves only as project adviser, administrator, and co-lender.

[15]A 1986 study of adjustment loans by the World Bank indicated that many of the reforms for which loans were made had not been completely implemented. As a result, the bank has begun to monitor more carefully the implementation of reform through agreed indicators of success with the member country. See *World Bank Annual Report 1988*, pp. 64–68.

ties.[16] Given the level of development of the countries involved, it is not too surprising that the majority of finance (88 percent) was made available by the IBRD on nonconcessional terms. In South Asia, by comparison, IDA funds predominated until 1984. The primary sectors receiving World Bank assistance during this period were again agriculture, energy, and transportation projects. Unfortunately, the data do not reflect the amounts actually disbursed, which for the South Asia group are only a small proportion of the total committed.

Asian Development Bank. Regional development banks are another important source of official finance to the developing world. The ADB has become increasingly active in the region since it began operations in the mid-1960s.[17] Between 1968 and 1987, total commitments by the ADB reached US$22 billion, reflecting loans for roughly 800 projects.[18] Almost 55 percent of these loans were energy and agriculture related. Nonconcessional loans from the ADB carry an interest rate close to commercial rates (in 1987 it was fixed at 7.36 percent for January through June and 7.03 percent for July through December), and the maturity for loans varies from 10 to 30 years with a grace period of two to seven years. Concessional loans, by comparison, carry a fixed interest rate of 1 percent, with repayment spread over forty years, including a ten-year grace period.

Like the World Bank, the ADB has also been hindered in recent years by a high level of committed funds but few disbursements. The Bank has been active in soliciting cofinancing loans with commercial banks and increasingly with official export/import credit agencies of industrial countries. Unlike the World Bank, the ADB remains solely oriented to providing development finance through specific-project loans almost exclusively to the government sector. A suggested change in this policy stance by the United States to grant structural adjustment and private sector loans caused increased tensions in 1987 and 1988 between that country and Japan over the future direction of ADB lending.[19]

---

[16]Figures derived from *World Bank Annual Report 1988*, pp. 90–96.

[17]For an overview of the operations of the Asian Development Bank, see *ADB Questions and Answers* (Manila: ADB, 1988), and the *Asian Development Bank Annual Report 1987* (Manila: ADB, 1987).

[18]Figures derived from *Asian Development Bank Annual Report 1987*.

[19]Cheah Cheng Hye, "ADB's Policy on Lending May Hinge on Japan-U.S. Conflict over Influence," *Wall Street Journal*, May 1, 1987, p. 17; and "ADB Bows to No Line Pressure, Boosts Lending to Private Enterprises," *Asian Wall Street Journal Weekly*, May 9, 1988, p. 26.

Table 5 provides a breakdown of total commitments and disbursements by member country between 1968 and 1987. The proportion of funds committed that have been disbursed varies quite widely from a low of only 1.8 percent for India (China received its first loan approval for US$133 million in 1987) to a high of 93.1 percent for Hong Kong. Out of US$22 billion in loans approved for all member developing countries, US$9.7 billion had been disbursed as of the end of 1987.

Bilateral Flows. Government financing on a bilateral basis has also been an important source of funds for developing Asia. The motivation to provide aid and concessional loans to developing countries is largely politically based, but can often be humanitarian and economically oriented as well. As noted, the United States played an important role in the years immediately after World War II and continues to be an important source of both economic and military assistance to the region.

Increasingly, Japan has taken on a larger role in providing official funds to the Third World in general and to Asian countries in particular. In 1986, Japan became the world's second largest development-assistance donor after the United States, disbursing US$5.6 billion to the developing world. In January 1987, it pledged an additional US$10 billion over three years in funding to the international agencies; in May, a further US$20 billion three-year commitment was made to the Third World, mainly through Japanese international banks. Of the latter, a significant portion is expected to be devoted to the Pacific-Asian region and the ADB. For example, in March 1987, US$1 billion in untied funds was allocated to Indonesia to provide local cost financing for World Bank projects; the following December, Prime Minister Noboru Takeshita pledged US$2 billion to the six-nation Association of Southeast Asian Nations.[20]

The massive build-up in international reserves and the interest in creating international good will has led the government of Taiwan also to set up a US$1 billion tied-aid program for developing countries in 1988.[21] Although Taiwan was a founding member of the ADB in 1966

---

[20]Most of these loans will be untied in the sense that the borrowers are not required to use the money to purchase the lender's products and will be distributed mainly through the Overseas Economic Cooperation Fund and the Export-Import Bank of Japan. For a good overview of the difficulties the Japanese government is confronting in its new role as the world's largest creditor, see Elisabeth Rubinfien, "Japan Tries to Find a Foreign-Aid Policy to Match Its Multibillion-Dollar Pledges," *Wall Street Journal*, December 15, 1987, p. 29; and James Clad, "Something for Everyone," *Far Eastern Economic Review*, December 31, 1987, pp. 42–43.

[21]Jonathan Moore, "Aid Begins at Home," *Far Eastern Economic Review*, September 10, 1987, p. 69.

Table 5

Asian Development Bank Loan Approvals
and Disbursements, 1968–87
(US$ million)

Country	Noncon- cessional	Con- cessional	Total Approvals	%	Disburse- ments	As % of Approvals
Afghanistan	—	95.1	95.1	0.4	27.9	29.3
Bangladesh	11.4	2,181.3	2,192.7	10.0	843.7	38.5
Bhutan	—	28.0	28.0	0.1	6.3	22.5
Burma	6.6	524.3	530.9	2.4	311.0	58.6
Cambodia	—	1.7	1.7	—	0.6	35.3
China, People's Republic of	133.3	—	133.3	0.6	—	0.0
Cook Islands	—	5.2	5.2	—	2.5	48.1
Fiji	60.5	—	60.5	0.3	48.1	79.5
Hong Kong	101.5	—	101.1	0.5	94.5	93.1
India	643.6	—	643.6	3.0	11.6	1.8
Indonesia	4,051.8	297.3	4,349.1	19.9	1,508.8	34.7
Kiribati	—	3.0	3.0	—	1.6	53.3
Laos	—	106.6	106.6	0.5	37.7	35.4
Malaysia	1,361.6	3.3	1,364.9	6.2	599.3	43.9
Maldives	—	9.5	9.5	—	2.4	25.3
Nepal	2.0	638.9	640.9	2.9	258.4	40.3
Pakistan	1,689.2	2,080.4	3,769.6	17.3	1,326.3	35.2
Papua New Guinea	142.2	140.3	282.6	1.3	120.1	42.5
Philippines	2,342.0	129.3	2,471.3	11.3	1,375.7	55.7
Singapore	178.1	3.0	181.1	0.8	144.4	79.7
Solomon Islands	—	38.1	38.1	0.2	19.8	52.0
South Korea	2,199.0[a]	3.7	2,202.7	10.1	1,462.9	66.4
Sri Lanka	14.1	660.6	674.8	3.0	286.1	42.4
Taipei, China	100.4	—	100.4	0.5	91.1	90.7
Thailand	1,656.2	72.1	1,728.3	7.9	1,056.4	61.1
Tonga	—	11.2	11.2	0.1	8.0	71.4
Vanuatu	—	10.8	10.8	0.1	1.9	17.6
Vietnam	3.9	40.7	44.6	0.2	25.4	57.0
Western Samoa	—	50.4	50.4	0.2	35.5	70.4
Total	14,697.6	7,134.9	21,832.5	100.0	9,707.8	44.5

[a]Adjusted to reflect withdrawal of US$100 million loan to the Sixth Korea Long-Term Credit Bank, which was approved in 1985.

Source: ABD, *Annual Report 1987*.

Table 6

Net Direct Private Investment Flows[a]: Asia
(US$ million)

Country	1971–75	1976–80	1981–85
NICs			
South Korea	327	255	1,875
Taiwan	254	563	1,030
Singapore	1,178	2,335	7,615
Hong Kong	n.a.[b]	4,058[c]	n.a.
Southeast Asia			
Indonesia	694	1,035	1,749
Thailand	385	441	2,568
Malaysia	1,113	2,239	3,684
Philippines	118	298	643
South Asia			
India	–23	412[c]	805
Pakistan	38	135	612
China	n.a.	n.a.	6,375

[a]Includes equity capital and portfolio investment flows.
[b]Not available.
[c]1977–83.

SOURCES: IIF database, ADB, World Bank, and national sources.

and a contributing member since the early 1980s, this represents the first major commitment to official overseas lending. The fund is open ended and presumably will grow over time. Initially targeted are three countries in Southeast Asia—Indonesia, Thailand, and the Philippines—to receive loans for industrial development. Similarly, the South Korean government set up a W90 billion (US$118 million) Economic Development Cooperation Fund in June 1987 to strengthen diplomatic relations and to increase accessibility to export markets in developing countries.[22] Although this fund is not concentrated on Asian countries, Indonesia received one of the first loans during 1987.

Private Sources of Finance

Nondebt Financing. The primary source of nondebt-creating capital is private equity capital and portfolio investment. Net private foreign investment inflows to the Pacific-Asian region have risen in recent years, as shown in Table 6. Although a majority of these flows have traditionally

---

[22]Mark Clifford, "Overseas Attractions," *Far Eastern Economic Review,* May 5, 1988, p. 119.

gone to the NICs, especially to Singapore and Hong Kong, an increasing proportion has gone to Southeast Asia, especially to Malaysia and Thailand. Much of this investment has been in the form of direct investment, rather than through the purchase of securities and bonds (portfolio investment), in manufacturing and processing plants, producing for both the domestic and overseas market.

This is especially true for U.S. and Japanese investments. Historically, the United States accounted for the majority of direct foreign investment in developing Asia; in the early 1980s, however, Japanese investors became much more aggressive. By the end of 1983, total Japanese investment in developing Asia had reached US$14.6 billion, surpassing that of the United States by over US$1 billion. As Table 7 reveals, the stock of Japanese investments grew US$4.9 billion in the fiscal year ending March 1988 to reach a cumulative total of US$27 billion. By comparison, U.S. investments in the region at the end of 1987 were US$18 billion. The rapid depreciation in the U.S. dollar vis-à-vis the yen, of course, contributed to the surge in Japanese investments during 1986 and 1987. Japanese investors have been particularly interested in the resource-rich countries of Southeast Asia, with Indonesia being the largest recipient of equity funds. The potential manufacturing base of Hong Kong made it the second largest host of Japanese investments, followed closely by South Korea and Singapore. For the United States, Hong Kong topped the list, with Indonesia also strongly represented because of oil company investments there.

Over the years, U.S. and Japanese direct investments have become more concentrated in skill-intensive, high-technology industries. As relative labor costs in the East Asian NICs have increased, the labor-intensive, low-technology industries originally located there have tended to relocate in labor-abundant China as well as Southeast and South Asia. This transfer of resources has also been stimulated by efforts to find export production centers that are still eligible for preferential tariff treatment in industrial country markets. The major realignment of exchange rates during 1986 and 1987 also contributed greatly to increased net outflows of foreign direct investment by Japanese and Taiwanese investors to the countries of Southeast Asia.

Because many of the countries in developing Asia align their currencies with the U.S. dollar, production for export to the United States and

Table 7

U.S. and Japanese Direct Equity Investments[a] in Developing Asia
(US$ million)

Country	Investment Flows			Investment Position	
	1985	1986	1987	1986	1987
South Korea					
United States	36	51	184	792	976
Japan	134	436	647	2,118	2,765
Taiwan					
United States	–2	86	401	860	1,261
Japan	114	291	367	1,051	1,419
Singapore					
United States	–58	253	129	2,291	2,420
Japan	339	302	494	2,571	3,065
Hong Kong					
United States	–38	198	1,143	3,580	4,723
Japan	131	502	1,072	3,433	4,505
Indonesia					
United States	165	–149	–115	4,305	4,190
Japan	408	250	545	8,673	9,218
Thailand					
United States	–49	–8	149	1,048	1,197
Japan	48	124	250	884	1,134
Malaysia					
United States	43	–69	72	1,074	1,146
Japan	79	158	163	1,283	1,446
Philippines					
United States	–258	109	–15	1,117	1,102
Japan	61	21	72	913	985
India					
United States	52	65	108	450	558
Japan	13	11	21	103	124
China					
United States	172	–98	112	213	325
Japan	100	226	1,226	513	1,740
Other Asia					
United States	–8	–33	44	292	336
Japan	8	6	11	248	257
Total Developing Asia					
United States	55	405	2,212	16,022	18,234
Japan	1,435	2,327	4,868	21,790	26,658

[a]For the United States, flow data reflect calendar year, investment position as of December 31. Foreign investment is defined as equity investments reflecting 10 percent or greater ownership by U.S. residents and corporations. For Japan, flow data reflect fiscal year beginning April 1, investment position cumulative from fiscal 1951 to year ending March 31. Foreign investment is defined as equity investment and loans with maturities longer than one year reflecting 10 percent or greater ownership by Japanese residents and corporations.

SOURCES: U.S. Department of Commerce and Ministry of Finance, Japan.

even to Japan has become much more cost effective.[23] Rising domestic labor costs and further appreciation of the South Korean won may also stimulate businesses there to produce more of their products overseas. During 1987, for example, overseas investments by South Korean companies rose to almost US$400 million, double the amount of the previous year. Although the majority of these funds were directed to the United States and Canada, an increasing amount went to developing countries, especially Southeast Asia.[24] Should the authorities decide to decouple the Hong Kong dollar from the U.S. dollar, a similar reaction could occur there as well.

To encourage foreign direct investment inflows, a number of countries in the region have liberalized and/or otherwise enhanced the domestic environment for investors. In 1987, Thailand, Indonesia, and Malaysia relaxed a number of restrictions on equity investments in manufacturing, high technology, and agri-related industries. To attract increased portfolio investment, several countries—namely, South Korea, India, Taiwan, Thailand, and Malaysia—also have established trust funds exclusively for foreign investors, and prospects are that several other countries will soon set up funds as well. One advantage of such funds is that they avoid issues of national patrimony. Opportunities for greatly expanding capital inflows by this means are limited, however.

Despite the October 1987 global stock market collapse, which reduced the general attractiveness of equity investments throughout the world, many equity markets in Asia have grown markedly. Most notably, by mid-1988, the stock markets in Japan, Taiwan, South Korea, Malaysia, and Thailand had reached and even surpassed the peaks prior to the October crash. For other developing countries in the region, however, the size of domestic equity markets remains quite small, suggesting that significant foreign investor interest could easily swamp the amount of domestic investments.[25]

---

[23]For the first time, Asia, including China, became the top exporter of manufactured goods to Japan in the fiscal year ending March 1988, accounting for 28.2 percent of the total versus 26.8 percent from the United States. See "Asian Manufactured Goods Tops Japan's Imports List," *Asian Wall Street Journal*, April 28, 1988, p. 6. For an overview of how Japanese firms are coping with the rise in the yen, see Karl Schoenberger, "Japan's Manufacturers Confront Painful Future," *Asian Wall Street Journal Weekly*, June 1, 1987, pp. 1, 24.

[24]Clifford, "Overseas Attractions," p. 118.

[25]To get an overview of developing country equity markets, see International Finance Corporation, *Emerging Market Database 1988 Fact Book* (Washington, D.C., 1988); and Robert Dickie and Thomas Layman, *Foreign Investment and Government Policy in the Third World* (London: Macmillan, 1988).

Table 8

Total External Debt and International Reserves, End 1987
(percentage shares)

Country	US$billion	Total Debt	Official	Banks	Other Private	Official Reserves[a]
NICs	77.3	100.0	20.7	68.8	10.5	123.0
South Korea	35.5	100.0	37.6	59.6	2.8	10.1
Taiwan	22.8	100.0	5.9	72.3	21.8	336.9
Singapore	19.0	100.0	6.8	81.7	11.5	77.9
Southeast Asia	125.5	100.0	49.0	43.3	7.6	14.7
Indonesia	53.9	100.0	60.3	32.4	7.5	12.1
Thailand	20.5	100.0	49.3	42.9	7.8	19.5
Malaysia	22.4	100.0	30.6	55.9	13.5	31.9
Philippines	28.7	100.0	43.7	52.6	4.0	3.3
South Asia	76.1	100.0	68.3	17.4	14.3	10.5
India[b]	57.6	100.0	64.7	17.4	17.7	11.8
Pakistan[c]	18.5	100.0	81.3	17.4	1.9	5.8
China	35.9	100.0	44.0	46.5	9.5	45.4
Total	314.8	100.0	46.2	43.6	10.2	43.8

[a]Official international reserves excluding gold, as percentage of total external debt.
[b]Refers to fiscal year beginning April 1 and includes deposit liabilities of nonresident Indians.
[c]Refers to fiscal year ending June 30.

SOURCE: IIF database.

Commercial Sources of Finance and Debt Strategies. As Table 8 shows, total external debt for the ten Asian countries reached US$315 billion by the end of 1987, with commercial banks and other private creditors accounting for over half of the total. The reliance on commercial sources has been the heaviest by the NIC group and China, followed closely by the countries of Southeast Asia, and least by South Asia. With the exception of China, this tendency reflects the relative stage of development and ability to attract concessional and official credits.

Within the NIC group, the relatively high proportion of bank credit (82 percent) to Singapore is associated with its role as an international financial center and is mainly in the form of short-term liabilities of domestic financial institutions to nonresident banks. Much of this debt is offset by holdings of foreign assets by domestic banks. As a result, only a very small proportion of Singapore's external liabilities would be regarded as sovereign debt. Hong Kong, also a major financial center, has had a similar experience, with the government borrowing quite rarely, mainly to help finance the building of the mass transit system.

South Korea, in contrast, has depended heavily on commercial bank credit to finance the rapid expansion of its economy. During the late 1960s and early 1970s, the government encouraged external borrowings by the large domestic business groups, called *chaebol*, and various government entities to supplement the massive capital expenditures required to develop a range of heavy, medium, and light industries. Subsequently, the two OPEC price shocks and persistent current account deficits caused South Korea's external debt to grow rapidly through the 1970s and early 1980s. Despite this increase, continued access to commercial funds was maintained because of a rapid growth in exports, with the outward orientation of the country's industrialization strategy allowing for the production of high quality and competitively priced products. By 1985, South Korea's external debt peaked at US$47 billion or 140 percent of exports of goods and services. Since then, current account surpluses have allowed a reduction of over US$11 billion in external debts through the end of 1987, and further reductions are expected. Moreover, lower debt levels and improved credit conditions have permitted South Korea to refinance high-cost external liabilities arranged in early years with cheaper credits.

In the early stages of its development, Taiwan relied mainly on bilateral aid flows from the United States. Later, this aid was replaced with increased private financing, especially from commercial banks. During the 1970s, however, domestically generated capital increasingly satisfied the needs of the growing economy, based mainly on exports, first of agricultural products, then moving into light manufactured goods such as textiles, processed foods, and electrical products and machinery. With exports expanding rapidly, the current account moved into surplus in 1980 and reserves began to accumulate. By the end of 1987, official reserves amounted to over 336 percent of total external liabilities (Table 8). Taiwan's external debt rose almost US$10 billion during 1987 as residents borrowed large amounts of U.S. dollars from banks to speculate against the appreciating New Taiwan dollar.

The developing countries of Southeast Asia have relied heavily on commercial credits to offset the effects of fluctuating commodity prices and periodic slowdowns in the industrial world. Indonesia, the only member of OPEC in Asia, reaped huge benefits from the run-up in international oil prices between 1974 and 1981, registering current account surpluses during much of the period. Despite these inflows, the government continued to borrow heavily, from both commercial and official sources, in order to finance heavy industrial and infrastructural projects to reduce the country's dependence on oil. Bilateral and official credits were greatly facilitated by an aid consortium made up of the multilateral institutions and government donors called the Inter-Governmental Group for Indonesia (IGGI).

Unfortunately, many of the investments were inefficiently managed and yielded very poor returns. A commercial rescheduling of credits to the state-owned oil company, Pertamina, also occurred during the mid-1970s. With the decline in oil revenues in the early 1980s, the government scaled back or canceled many of the projects and has increasingly provided incentives for the private sector to help diversify the economy. Increased commitments by official creditors through the IGGI, however, have not allowed Indonesia to reduce its heavy dependence on commercial borrowings. During the mid-1980s, the Japanese government and banks began to play a larger role, offsetting some reduction in exposures by U.S. banks. By the end of 1987, Indonesia's total external debt had risen to US$54 billion, of which 32 percent was from commercial banks and 35–40 percent denominated in yen. It is encouraging that nonoil exports have begun to grow rapidly, aided in part by a large devaluation in September 1986 and the implementation of a number of trade liberalization measures since then. The uncertain future for oil prices, however, and the increasingly large debt servicing burden in dollar terms underscore the need for the continued diversification of exports and creating a more competitive domestic market.

The Philippines has suffered the most, being the only country in Asia to reschedule the majority of its outstanding external debt. Although government policies were generally successful during the 1950s in boosting the level of income, mainly through increased agricultural production, it was done at the expense of creating a highly protected and regulated manufacturing sector associated with the general policy of import substitution. Falling terms of trade during most of the 1970s and an overreliance on imported energy compounded the problems. The excess of investment over domestic savings was financed primarily through foreign borrowings, especially from commercial banks. By 1983, an unsustainably large level of external debt had been amassed. In the ensuing several years, policy performance was further weakened by political unrest. The situation remains uncertain, with little likelihood that the Philippines will return to the international commercial market on a voluntary basis in the near future. Policy changes and a resumption of growth in 1987 are encouraging, but creating an environment for sustained investment flows from both foreign and domestic sources is a key to continued economic revival and improved creditworthiness.

Malaysia and Thailand have been much more successful in balancing the need for external financing against their economic development goals. Malaysia benefited during the 1970s from increased oil prices and did not borrow heavily to support its development objectives. With the decline in oil prices and subsequent recession in the industrial world in the early 1980s, however, the government adopted expansionary policies to maintain domestic growth, resulting in a deterioration in the current account balance. The foreign exchange shortfall was offset by a significant jump in commercial borrowings. As a result, total external debt tripled between 1980 and 1984, reaching US$18 billion, of which bank credits accounted for over 61 percent. In an effort to reverse this trend, the government adopted a more cautious policy approach, and with the external environment improving in late 1986 and 1987, domestic growth resumed and the current account moved into surplus. As a result, the accumulation of external debt slowed considerably, with the government engaging in a number of prepayments and refinancings of existing loans to take advantage of improved credit conditions.

Thailand, in contrast, had to increase its borrowings quite markedly during the 1970s to offset its rising bill for imported energy. Cautious policies designed to improve on and diversify from the country's strong agricultural base began to pay off by the mid-1980s, however. Domestic real growth has stabilized at an annual rate of 5–7 percent, the current account deficit has been reduced to manageable levels, and increased inflows of direct investment are satisfying a larger share of each year's foreign capital requirement.

Only in recent years have India and Pakistan begun to tap commercial sources for their external financing needs. India more than Pakistan has increasingly looked to private creditors as the availability of concessional loans diminished and the cost of nonconcessional official funds increased. As of March 1988, India's total debt reached an estimated US$57.6 billion,[26] making it the largest debtor in Asia on an absolute basis and close to Indonesia and the Philippines relative to exports of goods and services (Table 8). Although Pakistan's total debt is much smaller, so is the economy and its capacity to generate foreign exchange. As a result, heavy reliance on official financing flows are expected to continue. Such figures suggest that both countries will have to reinforce their efforts to boost exports and improve the efficiency of investment in their economies.

Since the opening of relations with the People's Republic of China, there has been a steady increase in commitments of official and commercial bank credit. Given the potential size of China's borrowings from official sources, much concern has been expressed by other heavily pop-

---

[26]This figure includes estimates for both public and private external liabilities, inclusive of foreign exchange deposits by nonresident Indians.

ulated countries, like India, over the impact such borrowings might have on their share. Despite large commitments by both official and private creditors, the authorities have managed to keep outstanding debt within manageable levels. When the current account deficit widened in 1985 and 1986, commercial borrowings increased dramatically. Since then, more restrictive policy actions by the authorities have reduced the need for external financing. Nonetheless, during 1987 total external liabilities rose almost US$10 billion to reach US$36 billion, with commercial and private creditors accounting for almost 60 percent of the total. China has been particularly active in floating bonds and other securities in recent years to take advantage of its good credit standing in the international commercial market.

Issues and Future Prospects of Financing Flows to the Pacific-Asian Region

From the foregoing it should be apparent that the Pacific-Asian region in general has been able to garner sufficient financial resources from both domestic and foreign sources to finance its growth and development. Had there not been sufficient finance, growth in per capita income would certainly not have been as robust. The main reason for this success stems from the implementation of generally appropriate policies which boosted domestic savings as well as exports. Where domestic resources and export growth were not sufficient, countries have been able to obtain funds from commercial and/or official sources to maintain their growth momentum. One indicator is the fact that between 1980 and 1987 the region was able to add almost US$100 billion to official reserves (Table 4). Although Taiwan accounted for US$73 billion of this net addition, only a few countries drew down their reserve positions—namely, the Philippines, with its debt rescheduling, and India and Pakistan which used their reserves by small amounts to offset their external financing shortages.

Given this historical record, one is tempted to assume that sufficient finance will be available in the future as well. There are a number of factors that might suggest otherwise, however. These include concerns over the ability of these countries to continue generating high levels of savings, the desirability of continuing to base development strategies on export-led growth in an environment of increasing protectionism around the world, the constraints in the growth of official finance, and the increased unwillingness of commercial banks to lend internationally, largely as a result of the ongoing debt problem in the developing world.

Domestic Resource Mobilization

Although savings rates in most countries of the Asia Pacific region are high, there are still a number of instances where governments could foster increased savings. The Philippines and Thailand, for example, by reforming their domestic financial system, could enhance the environment for savers, raise the efficiency of intermediation, and bring more savings into the formal monetary system. Also, tax reforms could be implemented to raise the level of resources available for investment purposes. It is encouraging that changes to address these areas are presently underway in both countries.

For other countries in the region, the issue is not necessarily to raise the level of savings further, but rather to improve the efficiency with which those savings are used. In India, for example, the government has been the primary user of private savings. Stimulation of the private sector, through liberalization and the adoption of market-oriented policies, could enhance the use of domestic savings there. Improving the efficiency of the state enterprises through rationalization and modernization could lead to a more productive use of invested capital. Although reliance on the private sector and market forces to guide investment decisions is expected to increase in all countries of the region, government control will remain dominant, especially in the more socialist-oriented societies of India and China.[27]

Development Strategies

The opportunities for export-led growth in the region are still quite high. But ensuring market access requires that industrial country policies maintain the momentum of domestic growth to provide for increased employment and thereby mitigate pressures for increased protectionism. Traditional trade relations between many of the countries in Asia and the industrial world, especially between the NICs and the United States and Japan, will have to evolve. Traditionally, Japan has restricted its purchases of products from developing Asia to raw materials and primary commodities and has exported to the region finished manufactured goods and capital equipment. It is encouraging that Japan is opening its domestic market to manufactured goods from the NICs and the Southeast Asian countries. The significant appreciation of the yen since 1986 is forcing this change to occur. A further opening will hopefully be achieved in the not too distant future. Similarly, with South Korea and Taiwan now moving into a surplus position in their

---

[27]See Robert Scalapino, "Asia's Future," *Foreign Affairs* 66(1) (Fall 1987):89, for an excellent overview of the political and social tendencies in the Pacific-Asian region.

external accounts, pressures are intensifying for an opening of their domestic economies to foreign imports and competition. Increased trade between the NICs and the lesser developed countries of the region will therefore provide further opportunities for export-led growth. Exports can continue to grow, provided appropriate domestic policies accommodate a commensurate rise in import demand. Also, export potential lies not only with merchandise trade, but also with trade in services.

Flows from Official Sources

Only moderate increases in net new financial flows from the multilateral banks and official agencies can be expected as long as capital resources are constrained. The aforementioned efforts to increase the World Bank's capital and those by the Japanese government to increase bilateral flows are noteworthy, but additional commitments may be necessary. The World Bank has been particularly constrained by the sharp appreciation of nondollar currencies, which has resulted in a larger dollar value increase in the commitment of its capital than would otherwise have been the case. To offset capital shortages, both the World Bank and the Asian Development Bank should expand their cofinancing schemes. One way to increase leverage would be for these institutions to assume a partial guarantee of the principal rather than simply participate in the commercial loan. This could encourage increased mobilization of private capital by reducing the risk.

As a general solution to the capital constraint, the World Bank and the ADB could consider freeing up existing capital by selling a portion of their portfolio with certain types of repurchase agreements.[28] The ADB would also be wise to consider altering its current lending policies to provide credits for structural adjustment and policy changes. Finally, setting up of aid consortia for certain developing countries, similar to the IGGI for Indonesia, might help in the coordination of additional resources to these countries. Such a facility has been mentioned with regard to the Philippines to provide increased resources, especially for investment purposes.

As for the IMF, the decline in net lending to the Pacific-Asian region is perhaps a reflection of good policy management by these countries, but it also reflects a general downturn in lending by the fund. The

---

[28]For a more complete description of how the roles of various financing institutions are expected to evolve in the future with regard to solving the LDC debt problem, see *Restoring Market Access: New Directions in Bank Lending,* a report by the Board of Directors of the Institute of International Finance, Washington, D.C., June 1987.

expansion of the SAF could help a number of the poorer countries in the region, such as Pakistan and Bangladesh. It is encouraging that the Japanese and Taiwanese governments, mainly through their export/ import banks, are set to play a more significant role in recycling their surplus of savings. Asia and the Pacific are likely to receive a large portion of those funds.

Finance from Private Sources

In general, it can be said that the Pacific-Asian region remains quite creditworthy and most countries should be able to borrow whatever is needed from commercial sources. The constraint, therefore, is not one of supply, but rather, the cost of obtaining such loans as well as the desirability of adding, in some cases, to an already large debt burden. Large syndicated loans for balance-of-payments purposes from commercial banks will continue in Asia, but at a decreasing rate. The trend is increasingly toward the use of securities as an alternative financing technique. The use of bonds, floating rate notes, swaps, and the like reflect a general disenchantment with syndicated Eurocurrency lending, in the wake of the developing country debt problem and the growing preference by banks for acquiring tradable assets and issuing longer-term liabilities. Those banks that have chosen to maintain an international presence have generally sought to become more flexible in their response to borrowers' requirements.

This flexibility is perhaps most apparent from the wave of new financial instruments that have been introduced in the securities markets to supplement more traditional bond issues. Many of these instruments seek to blend the features of bank lending with bonds while enhancing their marketability and liquidity and reducing risk. A parallel development has been the exponential growth in interest rate and currency swaps.

Thus far, most developing countries have remained on the periphery of the international securities markets. The main exception has been the countries of East Asia, which accounted for the majority of developing country bond issues during 1985–87. Most of these issues have taken the conventional fixed or floating rate form, and many were denominated in yen and issued in the increasingly important Tokyo market. As Table 9 shows, China, India, Malaysia, and South Korea have grasped the advantages of some of these newer instruments, suggesting that there may be considerable growth potential for the future. In late 1987, for example, India negotiated a deal that linked a Euro-commercial paper program with one of the most complex interest/ currency swap facilities yet arranged. The proceeds were used to prepay a World Bank loan.

Table 9

International Borrowing by Country/Instrument
(US$ billions)

Country		Total	Fixed Rate Bonds	Floating Rate Notes	Euronotes	Syndicated Bank Credits[a]
China	1985	1.3	0.8	0.2	—	0.3[b]
	1986	3.4	1.0	0.3	0.2	1.9
	1987	4.3	0.7	0.4	—	3.2
India	1985	0.8	0.1	0.3	0.2	0.2
	1986	1.8	0.2	0.1	0.3	1.2
	1987	2.1	0.3	—	—	1.8
Indonesia	1985	0.6	—	—	0.4	0.2
	1986	1.5	—	0.3	—	1.2
	1987	1.8	—	—	—	1.8
Malaysia	1985	2.3	0.3	1.7	0.1	0.2
	1986	1.2	—	—	—	1.2
	1987	0.4	0.2	—	—	0.2[b]
Pakistan	1985	0.3	—	—	—	0.3
	1986	0.2	—	—	—	0.2
	1987	0.1	—	—	—	0.1
Philippines	1985	0.9	—	—	—	0.9
	1986	0.0	—	—	—	—
	1987	0.0	—	—	—	—
South Korea	1985	5.9	0.4	1.3	0.5	3.7
	1986	3.2	0.4	0.3	1.0	1.5
	1987	1.4	—	0.2	0.5	0.7[b]
Thailand	1985	1.8	0.1	0.8	0.2	0.7
	1986	1.7	—	0.1	0.5	1.1
	1987	0.5	—	—	—	0.5

[a]Includes loans granted by a syndicate of banks of the same nationality in their domestic currency to a non-resident borrower. Totals reflect commitments basis.
[b]Excludes renegotiations.

SOURCE: OECD, *Financial Market Trends.*

Increased use of these instruments raises some issues, however. Less attention has been devoted to the risks inherent in the new forms of borrowing, not the least of which is the more distant relationship between creditor and debtor that is evolving. The presumed superior liquidity of securitized assets has also yet to be tested. In addition, the demarcation between "junk" sovereign bonds and creditworthy borrowers may become less clear, increasing the uncertainty for lenders as competition may keep returns from adequately reflecting the risk.

There is also evidence of a dramatic shift in the role of U.S.-based banks in providing finance to the Pacific-Asian region. As U.S. banks have slowly withdrawn from international lending in general since 1985, an increasing proportion has been provided by large Japanese banks and to a lesser extent by Australian and Western European banks. Relaxation of capital controls since 1980 in Japan and Australia has contributed to this trend. The huge excess of savings in Japan promises to allow banks and increasingly nonbank financial institutions, such as insurance companies, leasing companies, and pension funds, to provide even greater flows over time, although the cost of such finance may become more burdensome for the borrower.[29] Furthermore, banks from Taiwan, Hong Kong, Singapore, South Korea, and Thailand are likely to play an increasing role in financing trade and project-related investments in the Pacific-Asian region over the coming decade.

Finally, there are ample opportunities for most Asian countries to attract nondebt-creating financial flows, mainly in the form of direct equity and portfolio investment. The shift from a heavy reliance on foreign borrowing to greater use of portfolio and equity investment by nonresidents is apparent across the region. To be attractive, policies regarding nonresident direct investment must be clearly articulated and remain stable. Only then can foreign businesses make the appropriate calculations to determine whether an adequate rate of return on investment can be made. This usually requires that the environment for domestic investment be conducive as well. Bouts of capital flight by domestic investors is usually a good indicator of a lack of appropriate policy. This may explain why the Philippines did not experience the same rise in equity capital inflows from Japan and the United States that was enjoyed by Singapore, Malaysia, and Thailand during 1987 (Table 7). Portfolio investment opportunities will remain limited by the size of most domestic equity markets. As they become more important as a source of funds for domestic companies, however, consideration should be given to allowing foreign investors to contribute as well.

---

[29]April 1, 1988, tax law changes in Japan on earnings from time deposits are expected to cause increased competition by banks for such deposits, raising the cost of funds for loan purposes. Also, increased capital requirements are expected by the end of 1992, suggesting that Japanese banks may become more profit-oriented in their approach to business. Combined, there may be a tendency for loan rates from Japanese banks to shift upward. With many countries in Asia also borrowing more heavily in yen, the servicing burden has also increased because of exchange rate valuation adjustments. For an excellent overview of changes in banking across the Pacific-Asian region, see ''Banking 88,'' *Far Eastern Economic Review,* May 5, 1988, pp. 55–102.

In sum, the outlook for continued growth and development in the Pacific-Asian region is bright. The rise in economic well-being of the past twenty-five years has led to the growth of an important middle class, supported by trained managers and skilled workers in both the private and public sectors. With a continuation of pragmatic policies, most countries of the region should be able to combine sufficient financial resources with an abundance of human and physical resources to provide for a rising standard of living. More fundamentally, the Pacific-Asian region has now reached a stage of economic development whereby an increasing share of financial capital for investment and growth will come from the region rather than from outside.

13. Prospects for Pacific-Asian Regional Trade Structures

M. HADI SOESASTRO

Ideas of Pacific economic cooperation need to be assessed from at least two angles: the rationale for such cooperation and the proposed institutional arrangement that derives from that rationale. The first conceptualization promoting cooperation among Pacific countries, as formulated in the early 1960s, was based on a recognition of the global trend toward "regional solidarity through mutual cooperation" resulting from "the ever-increasing progress of science and technology."[1] Its aim was to create a Pan-Pacific organization or movement.[2]

During the subsequent quarter century, many other proposals for Pacific regional economic cooperation have been developed.[3] Therefore, it is neither relevant—nor possible—to speak of *the* idea of Pacific economic cooperation. Furthermore, even though a given rationale in support of promoting regional economic cooperation may seem acceptable, its proposed institutional design may not be feasible.

Among the more concrete institutional designs that have been put forward, Kiyoshi Kojima's Pacific Area Free Trade Association (PAFTA)—originally presented in 1965—was the first.[4] Kojima proposed the inclusion of only the five developed Pacific countries—the United States, Japan, Canada, Australia, and New Zealand—primarily as a reaction to the establishment of the European Economic Community (EEC). Global developments strengthened the rationale for PAFTA, particularly in view of the conclusion of the Kennedy Round of multilateral trade negotiations (MTN). Kojima thought that another round of significant global tariff reductions was probably not feasible within the next

---

[1]See Morinosuke Kajima, *The Road to Pan-Asia* (Tokyo: Japan Times, 1973), as described in the preface.

[2]Tessa Morris-Suzuki, "Japan and the Pacific Basin Community," *World Today*, December 1981, pp. 454–61.

[3]For a review of the history of Pacific cooperation ideas, see M. Hadi Soesastro, "Institutional Aspects of Pacific Economic Cooperation," in M. Hadi Soesastro and Sung-joo Han, eds., *Pacific Economic Cooperation: The Next Phase* (Jakarta: Center for Strategic and International Studies, 1983), pp. 3–52.

[4]On this proposal, see Kiyoshi Kojima, *Japan and Pacific Free Trade Area* (Berkeley and Los Angeles: University of California Press, 1971).

decade; therefore, he argued, complete regional trade liberalization would have considerable advantages over partial trade liberalization in world markets.[5]

A number of factors worked against the PAFTA proposal. They will not be reviewed here. Various assessments followed however, together with many proposed institutional arrangements. These took into account new factors and realities, both globally and in the Pacific, and led to the phenomena of diffusion and fragmentation in the development of Pacific economic cooperation ideas.[6] The diffusion phenomenon was a move away from a strict EEC-type institutional organization to a more loosely structured consultative body; from institutional integration to functional cooperation; from a preoccupation with trade to the inclusion of a wider range of areas for cooperation, including the sociocultural field.

The fragmentation phenomenon refers to proposals to create a series of separate, subregional groups as an alternative approach to a single, regionwide organization. Both diffusion and fragmentation seem to have sprung from one and the same reason—namely, the inclusion of greater numbers of participants. Having more participants would make the objectives of cooperation much more diverse. This requirement appears unavoidable in view of the diversity of the Pacific region, economically and otherwise. Nonetheless, it was argued that the creation of a Pan-Pacific cooperation arrangement should focus on a clearcut objective. This view led to the conclusion that, at least at the outset, it was more realistic to emphasize "an approach toward sub-regional issues rather than towards the complex affairs of the entire Pacific region."[7]

Indeed, the concept of fragmentation does have a greater appeal in some parts of the Pacific, notably among the members of ASEAN, who are still preoccupied with efforts to strengthen their own regional organization and are gravely concerned that a wider regional focus would dilute ASEAN. Indonesian leaders were known to have harbored the idea that the development of subregional groups could eventually be transformed into a full-fledged regional organization.[8]

---

[5]In fact, another round of multilateral trade negotiations (MTN), the Tokyo Round, did take place in the 1970s.

[6]For a discussion of this issue, see Soesastro, "Institutional Aspects of Pacific Economic Cooperation."

[7]See Kiyoshi Kojima, "Economic Cooperation in a Pacific Community," *Asia Pacific Community,* Spring 1981, pp. 1–10.

[8]This was revealed to the author by Jusuf Wanandi.

In addition, despite the recognition that a host of less sensitive "functional" areas—energy, fishery, forestry, and other resources, including human resources—lend themselves more readily to serving as a basis for Pan-Pacific cooperation, the most relevant, and highest-priority item in the region's current agenda is trade.

Today, then, a trend toward the development of subregional trade structures can be clearly observed. In addition to trade cooperation within ASEAN, the southwest Pacific region has seen the establishment of a free trade agreement between Australia and New Zealand. As recently as late 1987, the North American subregion entered the picture with the signing of a free trade agreement between the United States and Canada. There are various current proposals for the establishment of trade cooperation arrangements in the South Pacific region involving various island countries, Papua-New Guinea, Australia, and New Zealand.

Conspicuously missing in the emerging picture of Pacific trade cooperation is the Northeast Asian region, Japan in particular. Some have taken the view that in fact some kind of "soft regionalism" has been developing in Northeast Asia, as manifested in growing and intensive trade among Japan, South Korea, and Taiwan, as well as China.[9] The establishment of a formal subregional trade structure in Northeast Asia, however, appears quite remote in view of the complex political or psychological relations between Japan and Taiwan on one hand and between Japan and South Korea on the other. It has been suggested that South Korea might profitably form a free trade arrangement with Australia and New Zealand.[10]

In fact, the trend in the region is not only toward subregional trade structures but also toward bilateral trade agreements. The latter trend has resulted mainly from continued deterioration in the international trading system over the past few years, as shown in the proliferation of so-called "grey area" measures—voluntary export restraints (VERs) and orderly marketing arrangements (OMAs). This development has undermined the fundamental trade rules of the GATT, which among other duties have the following functions: (1) to ensure *equality* or nondiscrimination in trading conditions between countries; and (2) to ensure *stability* in trading conditions, namely, the avoidance of sudden changes in conditions of market access.

The principle of market access equality can be upheld only with the restoration of a generally applicable system of norms, rules, and proce-

---

[9]The author thanks Robert Scalapino for pointing out this development.
[10]See the discussion in the following sections.

dures. The development of such a system is currently being attempted globally in the new round of multilateral trade negotiation, the Uruguay Round. In fact, many Pacific countries are actively engaged in such efforts through a variety of regional conferences, such as the series of Trade Policy Forums of the Pacific Economic Cooperation Conference (PECC), the Cairns Group, and the informal meetings of Western Pacific senior trade officials. Equality of market access now appears, however, to receive less attention than stability of market access. Many countries are now much more ready to enter into bilateral trade agreements for the sake of stability of market access even at the cost of sacrificing the principle of equality (of market access for others). A system (or the lack of it) in which stability becomes the name of the game while equality is disregarded is what *managed* trade is all about.

The U.S.-Canada Free Trade Agreement can be seen either as a subregional trade structure or as a bilateral agreement of the type just discussed. It may indeed set into motion the development of a managed trade system as an alternative to the GATT system. Following the successful conclusion of the U.S.-Canada bilateral negotiations, recent reports indicate that Taiwan is also interested in negotiating the establishment of a similar free trade pact with the United States.[11] There is also a growing interest in both Japan and the United States in exploring the desirability and feasibility of a U.S.-Japan free-trade agreement.

The various subregional and bilateral trade agreements in the Pacific differ from one another in nature. The main question here is whether this fragmented development can produce a more integrated structure in the future. It is not quite clear in this regard whether bilateral agreements of the type previously discussed should be treated differently from other subregional trade structures.

The general proposition advanced here is that the respective subgroups must be "outward oriented" as a condition for integration. However, this is a necessary, but not a sufficient condition. Developments in the international trading environment and trading system will greatly influence any transformation. Further deterioration or a failure to restore the international trading system are not likely to bring the various subregional trade structures to a more integrated regional structure. There could develop instead a complex network of bilateral trade agreements, each aimed at ensuring stable access to each other's market. In such an event, the Pacific region might experience a greater degree of stability in intratrade relations. It is questionable, however,

---

[11]*Indonesia Times*, November 20, 1987.

whether such a fragmented but managed regional trade structure could last, in view of its complexity and the high costs of managing it.

The following section briefly reviews the development of subregional trade structures in the Pacific. This review will be followed by an examination of the various models that have been proposed to link those subregional structures to the broader Pacific region.

Development of Subregional Trade Structures

In the ASEAN subregion, the ten-year-old Preferential Trading Arrangement (PTA) has received a new stimulus from the ASEAN economic ministers who met in Singapore in July 1987; it was subsequently endorsed by the heads of government in their Third Summit in Manila in December 1987. The decision to further promote intra-ASEAN selective trade liberalization through the PTA fell short of the more far-reaching schemes of a free trade area or a customs union for ASEAN—or a combination of the two, as entailed in the so-called Rieger proposal.[12] The recent measures agreed on are still not sufficient to bring about even a limited free trade area by the 1990s, as originally intended in the 1977 agreement.[13] Nonetheless, the determination of the ASEAN heads of government to give another try at trade cooperation can be regarded, in fact, as a breakthrough. The wisdom that previously prevailed, resulting from an analysis of the poor record of ASEAN economic cooperation, especially in trade, suggested that ASEAN should concentrate on cooperative efforts of a "resource-pooling" rather than a "market-sharing" nature.

The political sensitivity of trade cooperation is well recognized, but, as suggested elsewhere, "intra-ASEAN trade has a central role in any scheme of ASEAN economic cooperation because it both creates additional income and measures the success of cooperation measures."[14]

---

[12]See Hans Christoph Rieger, "ASEAN Trade Direction: Trends and Prospects," in Karl D. Jackson and M. Hadi Soesastro, eds., *ASEAN Security and Economic Development* (Berkeley: Institute of East Asian Studies, University of California, 1984).

[13]A Preferential Trading Agreement (PTA) entails a reduction of internal (intra-ASEAN) tariffs on selected commodity items, but the individual (ASEAN member) external (with non-ASEAN) tariffs are maintained. In an ASEAN limited free trade area, the internal tariffs are reduced to zero for *selected* commodity items and individual external tariffs are maintained. In a full-fledged free trade area, *all* internal tariffs are reduced to zero whereas each participating country maintains its own specific external tariffs. A customs union entails both a reduction of internal tariffs to zero and harmonization of external tariffs to a common level. A common market is a customs union with free mobility of capital and labor within the regional group.

[14]Institute of Southeast Asian Studies, *ASEAN—the Tasks Ahead* (Singapore, 1987), p. 67.

Although the sensitivity and complexity of the problem often led to a tendency to shift the focus of ASEAN cooperation measures to other arenas, it is likely that trade cooperation will be given greater and more consistent attention in the future. Developments in the global trading system as well as the challenges of the Pacific region trading environment have exerted equally strong pressures for the ASEAN countries to do so.

This being the case, it should not be unreasonable to expect further moves in the area of ASEAN trade cooperation. But the question is: To where should such cooperation lead? The ideal—as generally accepted in ASEAN—is to create an outward-looking economic area. This entails and, in fact, requires continuous efforts to liberalize trade, both among ASEAN member states and with the rest of the world. Even if undertaken vigorously, a reduction of internal tariffs alone, without due attention to external tariffs, may become counterproductive.

Both conceptually and in terms of policy, it is important to inject an outward-looking orientation as early as possible into the process of ASEAN economic cooperation. By the very nature of current and future patterns of ASEAN's overall economic relations, its outward-looking orientation must be both global (multilateral) and regional (Pacific).[15] In line with its multilateral orientation, ASEAN has only recently stepped up its interest and involvement in strengthening the GATT framework. ASEAN's "Pacific focus" is also of recent origin and is still confined to consultations. In the matter of overall economic development in the Pacific region, the vehicle for government-to-government dialogues between ASEAN and its Pacific OECD trading partners (Australia, Canada, Japan, New Zealand, and the United States) is the annual post-ministerial six-plus-five meetings, the so-called ASEAN-Pacific Forum.

In the area of trade, a series of informal meetings of Western Pacific senior trade officials have taken place over the past four years or so, but they also are only of a consultative nature. Within the tripartite (government-business-academic) PECC process, policy consultation on trade has received considerable prominence. The focus of these regional exercises has been largely on multilateral trade policy issues and on the possibility of developing a Pacific regional consensus, both in the launching of, and in subsequent negotiations in, the Uruguay Round.

---

[15]A discussion of this issue can be found in M. Hadi Soesastro, "ASEAN and Pacific Basin Cooperation: Where Do We Go from Here?" paper presented at the Second Meeting of ASEAN Institutes of Strategic and International Studies on "Regional Security and Development: The Ties That Bind Us," Kuala Lumpur, January 12–16, 1986.

The search for structure in ASEAN's trade relations with its Pacific partners indeed may become one of ASEAN's priority items in its future agenda. The possibility of establishing such a structure between ASEAN and the United States has been proposed since 1982, but only recently has it gained more serious consideration, with announcements on both sides to examine carefully the so-called ASEAN-U.S. Initiatives (AUI).

Despite ASEAN's efforts to relate itself more closely to the broader Pacific region, it is not immediately clear whether its fragmented, perhaps piecemeal, approach to regional trade cooperation is the best under present circumstances. But the basis for such an approach perhaps rests with the arguments that led to the inclusion of what became Article 24 of the GATT: so long as a regional arrangement brings about the elimination of trade barriers within a multilateral area, it is acceptable.[16] Article 24 allows countries to grant special treatment to each other by establishing a free trade area or a customs union, provided that: (1) duties and other trade restrictions are "eliminated on substantially all the trade" among the participants; (2) the elimination of internal barriers is scheduled to occur "within a reasonable length of time"; and (3) duties and other barriers to imports from nonmember countries "shall not on the whole be higher or more restrictive" than those preceding the formation of the customs union or the free trade area.

The Australia–New Zealand Closer Economic Relations Trade Agreement (ANZCERTA), more popularly known as the Closer Economic Relations Agreement (CER), which came into force in 1983, is one subregional grouping in the Pacific based on the free trade area provisions of Article 24 of the GATT. Its preamble declares that the member states have a "commitment to an outward-looking approach to trade." The CER is seen to increase the capacity of the member states to contribute to the "development of the region through closer economic and trading links with other countries, particularly those of the South Pacific and South East Asia."[17]

In fact, the first post-GATT agreement between Australia and New Zealand, known as the New Zealand–Australia Free Trade Agreement (NAFTA), which came into effect in 1966, was a rather limited agreement. Although its declared goal was complete free trade, the agreement had no timetable for arriving at that destination. Many safeguards

---

[16]See Kenneth W. Dam, *The GATT: Law and the International Economic Organization* (Chicago: University of Chicago Press, 1970).

[17]Most of the information on CER is taken from Sir Frank Holmes et al., *Closer Economic Relations with Australia: Agenda for Progress* (Wellington: Victoria University Press, for the Institute of Policy Studies, 1986).

were also written into the agreement. NAFTA was replaced by the CER Agreement for reasons not associated with the GATT. This agreement, however, provides a firm framework for the removal of all import barriers between the two countries. As such, it represents a full-fledged free trade area, in complete conformity with the GATT requirements. It is more comprehensive than many other free trade arrangements in existence.[18]

In another corner of the Pacific Basin, negotiations on a comprehensive free trade agreement between the United States and Canada were concluded in October 1987. The series of trade negotiations that began in May 1986 had their origin in the agreement reached between President Reagan and Prime Minister Mulroney in March 1985.

The issue of free trade between the two countries, however, dated back to the middle of the nineteenth century and indeed had a long history of ''go and no-go'' situations.[19] Because of the great importance of trade between these two countries, bilateral free trade issues have never died. The 1965 Auto Pact, providing duty-free trade in new cars and original equipment parts, which led to a rapid increase in two-way trade, did not originate, however, in any grand free trade design. It was only later, on the basis of the Trade Agreement Act of 1979—when reporting to the Congress in 1981 on the integration and rationalization that had occurred in the automotive industry since the 1965 Pact—that the U.S. trade representative recommended exploration of further opportunities to rationalize industries through freer trade.

That report also concluded that the United States should pursue separate trade discussions with Canada and Mexico rather than on a broad regional basis. At first, the prospects for negotiating a more comprehensive U.S.-Canada free trade agreement did not seem encouraging. In 1983, the Trudeau government in Canada proposed negotiations for additional bilateral sectoral agreements. Initially, both governments agreed upon four sectors for negotiations: surface transportation procurement, informatics, agricultural equipment, and steel. Negotiations never actually began because the United States preferred a broader

---

[18]See P. Jenkins, ''Australia–New Zealand Closer Economic Relations Trade Agreement,'' paper presented at the First ASEAN Economic Congress, Kuala Lumpur, March 13–23, 1987.

[19]A very elaborate review of the history and an in-depth examination of issues for current negotiations are given in Paul Wonnacott, *The United States and Canada: The Quest for Free Trade—an Examination of Selected Issues,* Institute for International Economics Policy Analyses in *International Economics,* no. 16, March 1987.

agreement.[20] The proposed sectoral approach had a number of drawbacks, including among others the proliferation of specific industry safeguards such as those accompanying the Auto Pact. Although this approach would result in a very slow reduction in trade barriers, it would essentially be inconsistent with the commitments of the two countries under Article 24 of the GATT.

Indeed, as with all other bilateral arrangements, at issue during the Canada-U.S. negotiations were the implications of departures from the most-favored-nation (MFN) principle. Despite the drawbacks of the MFN principle, most notably the "free rider" and "convoy" problems, this principle remains at the heart of the GATT system.[21] For the U.S.-Canada agreement to meet the test of their obligations under the GATT, it must also conform to Article 24 of the GATT. Both countries have expressed such a commitment. The United States further hopes that by negotiating agreements with its neighbors it can demonstrate that progress is possible and set the stage for broader multilateral negotiations, particularly in new areas such as services and the protection of intellectual property.

These subregional or bilateral trade agreements appear to have given due consideration to the participant countries' obligations under the GATT, which is a necessary condition they need to fulfill. It is not immediately clear, however, whether this condition is sufficient to make such subregional or bilateral trade agreements function as building blocks toward a regionwide trade structure in the Pacific. The question is: How to bring the current fragmented structures into a more integrated regional trade structure in the future?

From Fragmentation to Integration

After only four years of operation, it is perhaps premature to attempt an in-depth analysis of the full implications of the CER Agreement between Australia and New Zealand. It appears, however, that the agreement has already produced worthwhile results. From New Zealand's perspective, the agreement has been a crucial steppingstone in moving away from a highly protective system of quantitative restric-

---

[20]See William A. Niskanen, "Stumbling Toward a U.S.-Canada Free Trade Agreement," *Cato Institute Policy Analysis*, no. 88, June 18, 1987.

[21]The "free rider" problem refers to one country's inclination to sit back and let other countries negotiate lower tariffs that, under the MFN principle, will unconditionally be extended to its exports; the "convoy" problem emerges when a country participates in multilateral negotiations, but holds back and agrees only to minimal concessions. Other countries either hold back to the speed of the slowest ship in the convoy, or proceed ahead at a faster pace and thus give the slower participants a free ride.

tions (import licensing) and tariffs not only on imports from Australia, but also unilaterally on imports from the rest of the world.

As elaborated elsewhere, the important factors that have enabled New Zealand to make the transition from a highly protected national economy to a member of a much more outward-looking free trade area included, among others: (1) growing public discussion of the costs of insulation and protection; (2) the enthusiasm for a closer relationship by a few key ministers and influential officials in the two countries; (3) a political will to proceed and a clear exposition of the aims of the agreement by political leaders; (4) Australia's willingness to allow New Zealand considerable time to phase out its main form of protection (import licensing), while insisting that it must ultimately be eliminated on trade between the two countries; (5) concentration in the original agreement on issues regarded as basic to full liberalization of trade in goods, leaving other issues for later "second-generation" treatment.[22]

In contrast to its predecessor, NAFTA, which was signed in 1965 and resulted in only a limited free trade area, the CER Agreement provides for the elimination of tariffs and quantitative restrictions on all goods traded bilaterally. With very few exceptions ("modified arrangements"), New Zealand tariffs were to be eliminated by 1988 and all quantitative restrictions by 1995. The elimination of tariffs and export incentives is taking place on schedule, and quantitative restrictions are likely to be gone in 1988 or 1989—ahead of the original schedule. More important, this is not only in relation to Australia but in relation to imports generally.

Trade between Australia and New Zealand had grown to about US$2 billion by 1985. New Zealand's exports to Australia have risen much faster than its corresponding imports so that their bilateral trade has become approximately in balance now, compared with large imbalances in Australia's favor previously. Bilateral trade balances do not appear to be an issue; rather, New Zealand's international competitiveness is of much greater relevance: if it can compete in the Australian market, it has greater chances to compete in the international market.

Neither Australia nor New Zealand is greatly dependent on trade with each other. In 1985, about 16 percent of total New Zealand exports went to Australia and only 5 percent of total Australian exports went to New Zealand. Therefore, it is not surprising to see their emphasis on, and commitment to, an outward-looking approach to trade. Nonetheless, it needs to be acknowledged that liberalization either on a bilateral

---

[22]Sir Frank Holmes, "New Zealand, ANZCERTA and ASEAN," First ASEAN Economic Congress, March 13–24, 1987.

or on a regional (subregional) basis is certainly easier to "sell" politically than a unilateral reduction of protection.

The CER Agreement is due for review in 1988, and both sides are currently exploring further developments that might be in their mutual interest. An important question that needs to be posed is: How will CER attempt to relate itself to the broader Pacific region in the future? The freeing of trade, which the CER has made possible thus far, definitely has a broader regional effect since both New Zealand and Australia trade heavily with the Pacific region.

In terms of the development of a broader regional trade structure, Article 24 of the CER Agreement provides for accession or association by other countries with the agreement. Currently, serious considerations are being given to the possibility of some form of association with CER by the South Pacific Forum (SPF) island countries. On an individual basis, both Australia and New Zealand already accord—within the South Pacific Regional Trade and Economic Co-operation Agreement (SPARTECA)—nonreciprocal free trade treatment to most goods from the SPF countries. A separate Papua-New Guinea–Australia Trade and Commercial Relations Agreement (PATCRA) also exists. A formal association with CER, therefore, would not automatically bring additional gains in trade for the SPF states. Such an association, however, could strengthen their commitment to keep their own protective regimes under control in relation to each other and to the CER member countries, and eventually to reduce their own barriers.

As reported in a New Zealand study,[23] the idea is also circulating of either incorporating the SPF states into CER or creating a new zone of economic cooperation and trade in the South Pacific region. These two options would involve the development of free trade among SPF members and the application of eventual reciprocity between the SPF and Australia and New Zealand. An extended trade structure of this kind would require some flexibility in dealing with countries at different stages of development and with different impacts of freer trade on their economies. This may prove to be too difficult to achieve given the nature of the SPF economies, most of which have very narrowly based economic structures and often depend on only a few export crops.

Another option, involving a more gradual process, is to link the existing arrangements—CER, PATCRA, and SPARTECA—under a broader Economic Cooperation Agreement (ECA). Such an agreement could first concentrate on removing existing restrictions under PATCRA and SPARTECA and would involve only the larger island economies.

---

[23]This refers to Holmes et al., *Closer Economic Relations with Australia*, pp. 122–24.

This process, however, needs to be accompanied by specific targeted development assistance programs from Australia and New Zealand in a variety of areas.

Development of closer relations between CER and ASEAN has also been suggested. Others have suggested that a free trade arrangement with South Korea could be feasible and desirable, or that Canada or Japan or Singapore could be interested in negotiating some arrangement with CER.[24] It was also noted that the United States has sounded out Australia on its possible interest in forging a free trade arrangement. In Australia, in fact, a study has been commissioned to examine such possibilities.

The various approaches suggested for CER in its attempt to develop links with its immediate neighbors, the SPF states as well as with ASEAN, some Northeast Asian countries, and eventually also with the United States deserve further studies. They could provide some useful models for the Pacific region.

Similarly, the agreement in principle concluded between the United States and Canada on the establishment of a free trade area could provide a model for possible future bilateral agreements between the United States and other countries.[25] It should be noted, however, that the U.S.-Canada Agreement may be a unique case in view of very special trade relations between these two countries, particularly for Canada. In 1985, for example, the United States took approximately 75 percent of total Canadian exports. Canada was the single largest market for U.S. exports, taking about 22 percent of its total exports in 1985. Today, most of the trade between the two countries is already duty free. Approximately 80 percent of U.S. imports from and 65 percent of its exports to Canada are free of duty. The completion of the Tokyo Round tariff cuts in 1987 adds another 15 percent of U.S. imports from and 25 percent of its exports to Canada that face tariffs of 5 percent or less. Of the remaining, double-digit tariffs are still in existence; Canadian tariffs on clothing and footwear are still above 20 percent and the U.S. tariff on clothing is close to 20 percent. It can be expected that besides the issue of tariffs, a comprehensive agreement between the two countries will also address other—and more important—issues such as nontariff barriers, the so-called "trade remedy laws" (antidumping and countervailing duty laws), as well as services, investment, and exchange rates.

---

[24]Ibid.

[25]The U.S.-Israel Free Trade Agreement of March 1985 has been described as another model of a successful conclusion of a bilateral arrangement that also included the so-called new areas such as services.

Canadian interests in negotiating a bilateral agreement were quite obvious and to a large extent originated with the growing protectionist sentiment in the United States that led to what they perceive as "variability, unpredictability, and apparent arbitrariness of the implementation of U.S. trade laws." What are seen in the United States as remedy laws are described in Canada as "contingent protection" by the United States.[26]

The interests on the U.S. side in entering into bilateral trade agreements are linked to its concern with the perceived proliferation of "unfair" trade practices by its trading partners as well as to the GATT Round. With regard to the latter, bilateral agreements appear to be used both as a bargaining chip (to get the negotiation going) and as a fallback (in case of failure to reach a satisfactory agreement). Aggressive reciprocity as currently demanded by various sectors in the United States finds its expression in bilateral deals, either on an ad hoc basis or of a more formal nature. The concern over such a development is that it will lead to a proliferation of conditional MFN arrangements. Such bilateral free trade agreements were aggressively promoted by the U.S. trade representative, William Brock, some three years ago, in part as pressure to reluctant governments to initiate a new GATT Round. Now, with the Uruguay Round in progress, it may well be that the U.S. interest in bilateral trade agreements will not subside but will be continuously pursued as a fallback, especially with countries with which it has a large bilateral trade deficit. This trend, however, will depend to a large extent on the development of overall U.S. trade deficit.

A bilateral trade agreement between the United States and ASEAN, for example, would certainly be different in nature from that between the United States and Canada. It is not immediately obvious whether a bilateral agreement between the United States and ASEAN should be largely a nonreciprocal, partial preferential arrangement or essentially a reciprocal arrangement. When Brock first proposed a free trade agreement with ASEAN in 1982, the ASEAN side was not enthusiastic because it was fearful that such an agreement might lead to a flooding of U.S. goods into the region. At the fifth ASEAN-U.S. Dialogue in December 1983, however, it was the ASEAN side that—after recognizing that relations with the United States have reached a plateau—expressed the desire to have some kind of a more structured and comprehensive

---

[26]See Niskanen, "Stumbling Toward a U.S.-Canada Free Trade Agreement."

trade and economic cooperation program to enhance economic relations between ASEAN and the United States.[27]

ASEAN then made a counterproposal along the lines of the U.S. Caribbean Basin Initiative (CBI), which essentially is a preferential trading arrangement and thus nonreciprocal in nature. As such, it was rejected by the United States. Later, in a 1985 meeting with ASEAN economic ministers, Brock suggested a third idea, namely, that the two sides adopt a two-stage approach. In the first stage, the two sides would enter into a broad agreement on economic issues. The second, and more important, stage would see individual ASEAN members negotiating bilateral trade agreements with the United States, each at its own pace and taking into account its own respective interests. With the departure of Brock from the USTR Office, the proposal was not pursued further. At the postministerial ASEAN-U.S. Dialogue in June 1987, Singapore's foreign minister suggested that the two sides should take a closer and higher-level look at the ASEAN-U.S. Initiative (AUI) that originated with Brock's proposal. Prime Minister Lee Kuan Yew reiterated this suggestion in his opening address to the ASEAN economic ministers' meeting in July 1987. Indeed, a special meeting of the ASEAN economic ministers with the deputy U.S. trade representative, Michael Smith, took place, but the substance of this talk was not disclosed.

There are many reasons why a CBI-type arrangement between ASEAN and the United States would not be feasible. First, such an arrangement—as with the original—could only be supported in the United States on the basis of a strong politico-security concern,[28] which is not present in relation to ASEAN. Second, the CBI, which entails more than just trade—tax incentives, development assistance, and bilateral investment treaty negotiations—is feasible from a U.S. budgetary standpoint only when the total amount of aid (plus private resources) involved is not substantial.

---

[27]See M. Hadi Soesastro, "ASEAN-U.S. Economic Relations: An Update," in Karl D. Jackson, Sukhumbhand Paribatra, J. Soedjati Djiwandono, *ASEAN in Regional and Global Context* (Berkeley: Institute of East Asian Studies, University of California, 1986). A discussion of this subject can also be found in Ow Chin Hock, "ASEAN-U.S. Economic Relations: Problems and Prospects," in Ray S. Cline, ed., *U.S.-ASEAN Relations: Prospects for the 1990s* (Washington, D.C.: United States Global Strategy Council, 1987).
[28]A survey of conflicting views on the CBI can be found in the series of articles contained in *Foreign Policy* 47 (Summer 1982), under the heading "The Caribbean Basin Initiative."

Such an essentially Lome-type arrangement has long been found undesirable for ASEAN.[29] Lately, empirical evidence has shown that the group of sixty-six African, Caribbean, and Pacific (ACP) countries, granted preferential access to EEC markets, has not done better under the Lome Convention. EEC shares of ACP exports, in fact, have declined since 1975.[30]

The Generalized System of Preferences (GSP), which is a limited one-way trade preference, is found to have meager results as well. The developing countries as a group have gained little from the GSP. For example, U.S. imports from the developing countries amounted to US$120 billion in 1981. From GSP beneficiaries, the total was US$69 billion, and of this only US$8 billion actually entered duty free. In the case of the European Economic Community's GSP, studies have shown that imports from nonbeneficiaries were growing at a faster rate than those from countries covered by the GSP.[31]

Nonetheless, the developing countries as a whole, ASEAN countries included, continue to attach great importance to the GSP—if largely as a symbol of "special and differential treatment"—and ignore calls for the incorporation of the graduation principle. The two-stage approach towards an ASEAN-U.S. trade structure we examined earlier is likely to be obliged to make room for graduation, particularly when a separate bilateral agreement with Singapore is being negotiated. Thus, ASEAN as a group needs to come to terms with a new set of principles governing trade relations with the developed countries.[32]

The two-stage approach may also wind up in a "variable preferential trading arrangement" analogous to the set of EEC-Mediterranean agreements, involving reverse preferences (reciprocity). In this model, each respective Mediterranean country has a PTA with the EEC, but they vary in coverage and degree of concessions so that the overall result is "a complex system of sectorally and country-wise differentiated preferentialism."[33] In addition, the respective Mediterranean countries do not have PTAs among themselves. The lesson that can be drawn

---

[29]See Narongchai Akrasanee, "ASEAN and the New International Economic Order: A View from Thailand," in B. A. R. Mokhzani, Khong Kim Hoong, and R. J. G. Wells, *ASEAN Economic Cooperation and the New International Economic Order* (Kuala Lumpur: Malaysian Economic Association, 1980).

[30]See World Bank, *World Development Report 1987* (Washington, D.C., 1987), pp. 158–59.

[31]Ibid.

[32]For a discussion of this issue, see M. Hadi Soesastro, "ASEAN's Participation in the GATT," *Indonesian Quarterly* 15(1) (January 1987):107–27.

[33]Richard Pomfret, "Variable Preferential Trade: The E.C.-Mediterranean Agreements as an Example for intra-ASEAN Liberalization," First ASEAN Economic Congress, Kuala Lumpur, March 13–23, 1987.

from the Mediterranean experience is the high administrative and negotiating costs that arise from complexity and the tendency to generate
political friction both among the countries involved and from outside.[34]

Beyond the ideas of bilateral ASEAN-U.S. trade structures, a broader,
Pan-Pacific scheme was proposed—the so-called Pacific Basin Initiative,
along the lines of the CBI but involving essentially ASEAN and other
Pacific LDCs on one hand and all Pacific OECD countries on the other.[35]
This modified CBI would allow all products from Pacific LDCs to freely
enter Pacific OECD markets provided that: (1) at least 75 percent of the
f.o.b. export value of the products represents value sourced from the
industrialized country admitting the product plus value added by the
exporting country or economic grouping (such as ASEAN); for example,
if the free entry market country is the United States, at least 75 percent of
the f.o.b. ASEAN port value of the product should be U.S.-sourced value
or ASEAN value added; and, (2) at least 30 percent initially and rising to
50 percent in five years of the production of products claiming free entry
privilege should be consumed in the producing country or sold to third
countries. Provision 1 is meant to allow Pacific OECD countries to benefit
also from the arrangement, whereas provision 2 is meant to prevent a
Pacific LDC from becoming an overnight export processing zone with a
single target market country.

In view of the enhanced momentum in the ASEAN region in its
search for new trade structures, including other countries or entities, all
these proposals will have to be examined carefully. The foregoing
review, however, also suggests the importance of trading arrangements
within ASEAN itself.

The past few years saw highly critical evaluations of ASEAN's PTA.
This scheme, adopted in 1977, proposes liberalization of trade among
the member countries through the implementation of five measures.
These are: (1) the granting of tariff preferences; (2) long-term quantity
contracts; (3) preferential terms for the financing of imports; (4) preferential procurement by government agencies; and (5) the liberalization of
NTB's in intraregional trade. Out of these five instruments, the granting
of tariff preferences has been the most widely used.

In the initial stages of the scheme, tariff preferences were granted by
employing a voluntary approach (discontinued in 1983) and a matrix
approach (discontinued in 1986). Under the voluntary approach, each

---

[34]Ibid.

[35]This idea has been aired over the years by David Sycip; the outline of such a proposal
can be found in *Pacific Economic Cooperation: Issues and Opportunities*, Report of the Fourth
Pacific Economic Cooperation Conference (Seoul: KDI, 1985).

country volunteers a list of products for preferential treatment at each round of negotiations. Under the matrix approach, a country makes a specific request to, and may get a response from, another country. The concessions exchanged at the bilateral negotiations are subsequently "multilateralized" to include the other ASEAN countries.

At the end of 1982, a total of more than 8,000 items were granted tariff preferences under the voluntary approach, but this was not a very meaningful figure since the majority of the products could not be imported from ASEAN sources anyway. The matrix approach only led to the granting of preferences for 378 items and later was abandoned because it was too restrictive.

Paralleling the "product-by-product" approach, since 1980 "across-the-board" tariff reductions were introduced to speed up the process. Indeed, since then, over 10,000 items have been included in the scheme under this approach. Initially, all items with an annual import value of less than US$50,000 each in 1978 trade statistics will qualify for tariff reductions of 20 percent across the board. The cutoff ceiling was raised to US$500,000 in May 1981, to US$1 million in January 1982, and further to US$10 million in November 1982. This US$10 million cutoff limit represents about 10 percent of all intra-ASEAN trade.

The introduction of the across-the-board approach was subjected to the exclusion of "sensitive items" and provided for the suspension of preferential tariffs where they threaten "serious injury" to domestic industries or adversely affect the balance of payments. In fact, the exclusion list has undermined efforts to broaden the coverage of the scheme. To date, Thailand has excluded 2,257 items or 63 percent of the total from across-the-board tariff cuts. The respective figures for Indonesia are 1,284 items or 54 percent; Malaysia, 1,436 items or 37 percent; the Philippines, 890 items or 25 percent; and, Singapore, 83 items or 2 percent of the total.[36]

Efforts were made in 1985 to review the exclusion lists, and sensitive items were classified into three categories: (1) nonsensitive items, to be withdrawn from the list; (2) semisensitive items, which are subject to negotiation; and (3) sensitive items, which are not subject to negotiation. It was proposed that semisensitive items qualify for preferential tariff treatment under the ASEAN Preferential Tariff Quota (APTQ). Under this scheme, the quota for each product would be based on a percentage of the moving average of an ASEAN country's total imports of that product during the three years preceding the completion of the

---

[36]See Ooi-Guat Tin, "The ASEAN Preferential Trading Arrangements," First ASEAN Economic Congress, Kuala Lumpur, March 13–23, 1987.

negotiations. The quota would be set at a minimum of 30 percent, and the results of bilateral negotiations would be multilateralized.

Despite those measures, the PTA scheme remains the object of great skepticism. In addition, empirical studies have shown that the effect of PTA was very small, and that today it covers at most only 5 percent of intra-ASEAN trade.[37] Intra-ASEAN trade as a proportion of ASEAN's total trade has increased steadily from 13 percent in 1973 to 21 percent in 1983. About 75 percent of intra-ASEAN trade flows, however, are between Singapore and Malaysia and between Singapore and Indonesia. In addition, about 65 percent consists of fuel trade. Therefore, the proportion of intra-ASEAN trade has dropped back to 16 percent since 1985. This decline led to many proposals aimed at giving a boost to ASEAN trade cooperation. A free trade area, a customs union, or a combination of the two—the ASEAN Trade Area, also known as the Rieger proposal—were all considered. They have been rejected, however, on the basis of the prevailing ''gap'' that exists in stages of economic development among ASEAN members. Others saw the rejection as an indication of the lack of political will on the part of ASEAN governments.

The Third ASEAN Summit in December 1987 agreed to liberalize the PTA in a more substantial way than ever before. The agreement stipulates that within the next five years: (1) each member can exclude from the PTA no more than 10 percent of items traded within ASEAN; (2) each member is to have at least 50 percent of its intra-ASEAN trade volume in the PTA; (3) tariff preferences for existing PTA products, or the margins of preferences, are to be increased from 25 percent to at least 50 percent; (4) products with a minimum of 35 percent ASEAN content, instead of 50 percent as previously, can qualify for PTA. In addition, the economic ministers agreed to erect no more NTBs against other member countries (standstill) and to negotiate removal of existing ones (rollback).

So far, ASEAN has made no concrete suggestions about how it would relate itself to the broader Pacific regional concern. It may be that ASEAN wants first to see how the agreements reached in the Third Summit would be implemented before it is ready to discuss concrete steps toward realizing ideas along the AUI proposal and other extrare-

---

[37]See Gerald Tan, ''ASEAN Preferential Trading Arrangements: An Overview,'' First ASEAN Economic Congress, Kuala Lumpur, March 13–23, 1987.

gional or any other region-broadening schemes. Nonetheless, ASEAN
has clearly recognized the importance of the broader Pacific region to its
development. As stated in the joint press statement at the end of the
Third ASEAN Summit:

> The Heads of Government noted certain changes around ASEAN that
> open up opportunities and challenges for their countries, including the
> modernization programme of China, the rise of the Newly Industrializ-
> ing Countries of East Asia, the increased involvement of the Soviet
> Union and the other Eastern European countries in global economic
> issues, Japan's emergence as the leading supplier of capital, and the
> growing perception of the Pacific rim as the "region of the future."

Beyond Trade: Some Tentative Conclusions

The examination presented here suggests a few interesting conclusions. First, subregional structures and arrangements in the Pacific
region are being seriously pursued and developed. Such a fragmentation effect is most pronounced in the area of trade, and may largely
reflect: (1) the different stages of economic development among the
Pacific economies that led to a natural subgrouping at the subregional
level, although bilateral trade agreements (such as one between the
United States and ASEAN, or between the United States and Taiwan)
could overcome such natural tendencies; (2) continued uncertainty in
the global trading environment resulting from deterioration in the international trading system.

Second, these various subregional trade structures do recognize the
need to maintain an outward orientation and the need to relate themselves to the broader Pacific region. What is not clear, however, is how
such objectives can translate themselves into measures toward integration. It is likely that the region may end up with a set of subregional
trade structures that cannot easily be integrated. Perhaps only a restoration of the international trading system can provide a framework for
such subregional structures to develop into a more integrated structure
through their determination and ability to pursue open and outward-
oriented trade policies.

Third, a subregional structure involving Japan is conspicuously
missing. This may suggest a role for Japan in a more integrated regional
structure in the Pacific. It seems, however, that such a role can be performed more readily by Japan when the regional structure so conceived
involves more than just trade. In fact, it may be necessary to go beyond
trade when an integrated regional structure is the matter at issue.

ASEAN-Japan relations may provide an example. Throughout 1987,
ASEAN has discussed and seriously examined Japan's offer to set up an

ASEAN Special Fund. The proposal was first announced by Japanese Foreign Minister Tadashi Kuranari at the ASEAN foreign ministers' meeting in June 1987. The fund would be different from the aid package announced by Takeo Fukuda in 1977, which was meant to help finance five big industrial projects initiated and backed by the respective ASEAN governments. Instead, the Special Fund would be designed for private sector projects. Either directly or indirectly, this fund needs to be seen in light of efforts to "recycle" the Japanese surplus, including the proposal of Okita Saburo for a "Japanese version of the Marshall Plan." Foreign Minister Kuranari stressed that the proposed ASEAN Special Fund was suggested before the announcement of a US$30 billion Japanese "aid" package for LDCs.[38] Nonetheless, the use of the fund could be designed to help strengthen ASEAN outward-oriented economic cooperation programs.

It should be noted that the value of the Marshall Plan was not just in the U.S. aid flows, but also in its consultative and negotiating machinery. ASEAN should also note that the recycling of the Japanese surplus would require the development of appropriate mechanisms; essentially, the surplus lies in private hands. The need to improve the investment climate in the ASEAN region to accommodate greater flows of such resources has been duly recognized.

Perhaps the breakthrough for ASEAN were the decisions of the Third Summit in the area of investment. These include: (1) a joint Investment Guarantee Agreement to protect investments against nationalization, etc.; and, perhaps most important, (2) the agreement to improve the ASEAN Industrial Joint Venture scheme (AIJV). These improvements consist, among other factors, of an increase in margin of preference from 75 percent to 90 percent for AIJV products and a stipulation that foreign (non-ASEAN) participation in AIJV projects can be increased to 60 percent, compared to 49 percent previously. It is hoped that this new scheme can contribute to the creation of a more dynamic investment climate—involving a stepped-up Japanese participation— and at the same time stimulate greater ASEAN cooperation, the way the Marshall Plan contributed to economic cooperation in Europe.

In the same way that trade cooperation could help stimulate cooperation in other fields, cooperation in the field of investment, for example, could have a positive effect on trade structures. Thus, although trade cooperation is important, trade issue concerns should not overwhelm other potential areas for cooperation. The CER, in reviewing its progress and directions for the future, is seriously examining cooperation in

---

[38] *Straits Times* (Singapore), June 20, 1987.

terms of policy harmonization in many fields other than merchandise trade such as the removal of restrictions on investment or in services trade. Although trade remains at the heart of CER, its member states discover the potentials for CER to develop into a comprehensive economic relationship. The U.S.-Canadian free trade agreement is also aimed at a comprehensive agreement to cover investment and services as well.

Further examination is merited to determine whether more comprehensive subregional structures can better accommodate or accelerate the transition from fragmentation to integration in the Pacific Basin.

14. Organizing the Pacific

MILES KAHLER

Any observer of the progress of regional economic organizations in the Pacific is immediately confronted with a major anomaly: despite an enormous investment in research and discussion, despite periodic obeisance to the concept of Pacific cooperation by politicians, despite economic success during more than a decade of mediocre world economic performance, very little has been accomplished in constructing an intergovernmental organization at the regional level. In the words of W. W. Rostow, "rarely has a concept been so intensively and systematically studied with so little result."[1] Although many international organizations dedicated to economic cooperation exist within the region, a Pacific regional economic organization is not among them. One task, then, is explaining this negative outcome.

As Han Sung-joo has noted, this first task, of explaining the feasibility of organization, past and future, must be separated from the question of desirability.[2] In addressing the question of what level of institutionalization would be optimal for the Pacific region, past discussion has left many questions unanswered. Models have been drawn from other regional and international contexts; they have been endorsed or dismissed largely on grounds of political feasibility rather than being evaluated according to the cooperative ends they are meant to serve.

This second, normative task is clearly related to the first: the optimal level of organization in the Pacific may not match the political realities that must underpin it. Although the study of international cooperation within political science is still in its infancy (an infant, paradoxically, with a lengthy lineage), the insights it has generated can be applied to both of these questions: What is the optimal political organi-

---

[1] W. W. Rostow, *The United States and the Regional Organization of Asia and the Pacific, 1965–1985* (Austin: University of Texas Press, 1986), p. 95. In attempting yet another analysis of this subject, I am cautioned by an observation made in 1980 that the concept had "been studied to death by the academic community" (Lester L. Wolff, *Asia-Pacific in the 1980s* (Jakarta: Center for Strategic and International Studies, 1980), p. 160.

[2] Sung-joo Han, "Political Conditions of Pacific Regional Cooperation: Theoretical and Practical Considerations," in M. Hadi Soesastro and Sung-joo Han, ed., *Pacific Economic Cooperation: The Next Phase* (Jakarta: Center for Strategic and International Studies, 1983), p. 53.

zation that will further economic cooperation in the Pacific? Is that organization likely, given present international economic and political realities?

A Surfeit of Models for a Late Starter

Existing accounts of the efforts to construct a Pacific economic organization usually omit one important explanation for the halting progress toward an economic organization for the Pacific: the Pacific is a relative latecomer in the organizational space of the overall Pacific-Asian region. In his analysis of successive waves of international organization in Asia, James N. Schubert discovered three phases: the 1950s, when broadly political and macroregional organizations, often led by India, attempted to organize the developing countries of the region; a brief period in the early 1960s, when Japan took more of a leadership role in organizing "Western" allies in the region; and finally, the growth of Southeast Asian organizations, and particularly ASEAN, from the 1960s on.[3] The first economic organizations to encompass the Pacific were proposed during the second of these periods, but from the start the concept had to compete with subregional groupings such as ASEAN and with preexisting economic organizations such as ESCAP. Thus, the particular niche of any new organization became an immediate issue.

A second feature of proposals for a Pacific organization is their debt to external models and external changes in the international system. Unlike ASEAN, which seemed to evolve, haltingly, in response to internal dynamics *and* the pressures presented by changes in the Asian system, the internal impetus toward Pacific institutions has seemed weak.

Given excellent existing analyses and chronologies of Pacific regionalism, a detailed discussion is hardly necessary here.[4] The first plan was, ironically, the most ambitious: Kiyoshi Kojima's Pacific Area Free Trade Association (PAFTA), which was modeled on the European Economic Community and the European Free Trade Association. Kojima's proposal reflected the then-current widespread emulation of the Euro-

---

[3]James N. Schubert, "Toward a 'Working Peace System' in Asia: Organizational Growth and State Participation in Asian Regionalism," *International Organization* 32(2) (Spring 1978):425–62.

[4]Among the surveys to which the author is indebted are M. Hadi Soesastro, "Institutional Aspects of ASEAN-Pacific Economic Cooperation," in *ASEAN and Pacific Economic Cooperation* (Bangkok: Economic and Social Commission for Asia and the Pacific, 1983), pp. 272–307; Michael West Oborne and Nicolas Fourt, *Pacific Basin Economic Cooperation* (Paris: Organization for Economic Cooperation and Development, 1983); M. Mark Earle, Jr., and Eric A. Trigg, *Pacific Economic Cooperation and an Overview of the Canberra Process* (Pacific Basin Economic Council Papers, 1985); W. W. Rostow, *The United States and the Regional Organization of Asia and the Pacific, 1965–1985* (Austin: University of Texas Press, 1986).

pean model of integration as well as a particularly Japanese concern over its own place in an international economy that seemed destined for domination by the Atlantic economies. In its original formulation, however, Kojima's blueprint seemed too ambitious, and its limitation to the industrialized economies of the region did not take into account the accomplishments of the Asian NICs already apparent by the late 1960s. Japanese governmental interest waned with the formation of ASEAN, and further elaboration of the concept was carried forward by two key groups: academics (in the Pacific Trade and Development Conferences, or PAFTAD) and businessmen (through the Pacific Basin Economic Council).[5]

The late 1970s brought a second wave of interest in organizing the Pacific, drawing strength from the economic success of the region (and the conflicts that it spawned) and from the uncertainties resulting from the American withdrawal from Southeast Asia. The emphasis during this period was no longer on schemes for regional economic integration, but rather on countering the negative political spillover from growing economic interdependence.[6] In addition, Japan and other Asian nations also saw organization of the Pacific as reinforcing a continuing American role in the Pacific in the post-Vietnam era.

Discussion took place on several tracks. National politicians were more supportive during this period than before or since: Prime Minister Ohira of Japan established a study group on Pacific cooperation (chaired by Okita Saburo), and he and Prime Minister Fraser of Australia endorsed the conference that would give birth to the ''Canberra process.'' Senator John Glenn focused interest in the U.S. Congress through hearings at which Hugh Patrick and Peter Drysdale presented the principal institutional initiative of this phase: the Organization for Pacific Trade and Development (OPTAD).

If Kojima's suggestion followed one overambitious external model—the European Economic Community—OPTAD was also modeled on an existing international organization, the OECD. This model was intended to demonstrate declining ambitions for organizing the Pacific; the organization, however,

> would attempt to improve intergovernmental economic relations and intentionally not attempt to replace them or in any sense become a

---

[5]Soesastro, ''Institutional Aspects,'' pp. 283–85; Oborne and Fourt, *Pacific Basin Economic Cooperation*, pp. 8–9.

[6]For a particularly clear statement of this rationale, see Lawrence B. Krause and Sueo Sekiguchi, eds., *Economic Interaction in the Pacific Basin* (Washington, D.C.: Brookings Institution, 1980), ch. 9.

supranational government. Nor would such an organization . . . try to evolve into a common market.[7]

Apart from frequent use of the OECD analogy (without careful examination of the usefulness of the OECD) and the award to this limited Pacific institution of an impressive array of tasks, the means by which an OPTAD would accomplish those tasks were equally impressive in their vagueness. Trade was the centerpiece (as it was in defining economic interdependence in the region), but foreign direct investment, structural adjustment, energy and resources, and trade with the Soviet bloc were also included on the institutional agenda.[8] Improved economic cooperation was to result from the somewhat magical process of "consultation"; Lawrence Krause alone gave concrete meaning to this elusive term.[9]

Lack of precision in the means of intergovernmental cooperation was combined with (and may have caused) persistent ambiguity over membership in the organization. With the heterogeneous region no longer limited to the industrialized countries of the region, difficulties in defining boundaries became acute.

Even the reduced scale of an OPTAD proved too grandiose for the states of the region, however. In a series of seminars and conferences during 1979–80, and particularly at the Canberra seminar of September 1980, movement toward an intergovernmental organization was effectively shelved, and the pace slowed further; indeed, the new catchword became "hasten slowly." Haltingly, the "Canberra process" emerged: tripartite (government representatives acting in their private capacities, businessmen, and academics) national committees, regular Pacific Economic Cooperation Conferences (PECCs), and the organization of functional international task forces to deal with issues of particular concern to the region.[10] Given the reticence of governments in the region toward the looser framework of an OPTAD, construction of an intergovernmental organization has been set aside; all that remains at the intergov-

---

[7]Lawrence B. Krause, in Sir John Crawford, *Pacific Economic Cooperation: Suggestions for Action* (Petaling Jaya: Heinemann Educational Books [Asia], 1981), p. 136.

[8]U.S. Congress, Senate, Committee on Foreign Relations, *An Asian-Pacific Regional Economic Organization: An Exploratory Concept Paper* (Washington, D.C.: U.S. Government Printing Office, 1979), p. 25. An even more daunting set of tasks are given in Krause and Sekiguchi, *Economic Interaction in the Pacific Basin*, p. 260.

[9]Krause, in Crawford, *Pacific Economic Cooperation*, p. 136.

[10]The second Pacific Economic Cooperation Conference, to "restart" the process after Canberra, was held in Bangkok in 1982; the fifth conference was held in Vancouver in November 1986. Task forces have dealt with trade, minerals and energy, fisheries, and livestock, and feedgrains.

ernmental level is the "6 plus 5" dialogue between ASEAN and the industrialized countries of the Pacific (instituted in 1984). After repeated initiatives and lengthy discussion, what remains is an effort to organize economic cooperation in the Pacific "from the ground up," through a process of "socialization" of elites.[11]

Obstacles to Pacific Institutionalization

The organization of economic cooperation in the Pacific has moved from a goal of integration to consultation to the current "process," which seems to have no teleology save discussion. Governments are only peripherally involved after twenty years of intermittent discussion. It is worth exploring, before addressing the more difficult question of the optimal political organization of economic cooperation in the region, the reasons for the record thus far. Explanations for this peculiar translation of ideas into political realities can be offered at four levels: the international system, national aims, the attitudes of key domestic elites, and the conceptual ambiguities within the successive proposals for Pacific economic cooperation.

International Environment

Other experiments in regional organization have been highly dependent on the international environment for their success. One drawback for Pacific organizations has already been noted: the crowded organizational space in the region when this latecomer first appeared. Equally significant was the security setting in the region, which, as Rostow has noted, was a constant backdrop to proposals for economic organization.[12] Unlike the EEC, which took shape in the shadow of the cold war, the cold war in Asia was dissolving by the time that Pacific organizations were proposed. The Sino-Soviet split in particular made the security calculations in the region particularly ambiguous: there was no common external threat to cement an organization.

Perhaps the most important feature of the international setting was the structure of economic power in the region. Political scientists have devoted a great deal of attention to the implications of power distribution for the organization of the international political economy. Following Charles Kindleberger, some have argued that a single, hegemonic power is necessary for international economic stability; others have dis-

---

[11]The rationale for the Canberra process is given in the "Summary Report of Proceedings and Main Recommendations" of the Canberra Seminar, in Crawford, *Pacific Economic Cooperation*, pp. 27–32. A useful summary of the steps in the process is given in Earle and Trigg, *Pacific Economic Cooperation*, pp. 7–12.

[12]Rostow, *United States and Regional Organization*, p. 29.

puted this finding, pointing to the far from disastrous record of a more pluralistic world economy in the 1970s and 1980s. Without expounding the intricacies of what has become known as hegemonic stability theory, one hypothesis pertains directly to the construction of a Pacific economic organization: although existing "rules of the game" (or regimes) may not require a hegemonic power to persist, the construction of new structures of cooperation may require such a power, willing to incur the start-up costs.[13]

Efforts to construct institutions for the Pacific regional economy have foundered in part on the absence of a leader (or hegemonic power) to play the role regionally that the United States (some would argue) played globally after 1945. Pacific regional initiatives began *after* (and in part because of) the decline of American influence in the region and the rise of Japan's economic weight. In the 1980s, defining the respective roles of the United States and Japan has become even more contentious, as recent conflicts within the Asian Development Bank demonstrate.[14] The United States has viewed Pacific regional organizations at times as a way to devolve more international responsibility onto Japan, yet it has also hesitated to participate in structures that could seem to designate the region as a Japanese lake. Japan has seen the Pacific as a means of organizing an international role for itself that would diminish the sensitivity of its bilateral relations in the region, yet it has avoided assuming a leadership role that might appear too dominant. Both the United States and Japan must also weigh the benefits and costs of regional leadership against their existing global interests.

Discussions of Pacific regional organizations have also been bedeviled by ambiguity in their relationship to hegemonic power. Patrick and Drysdale argued that an OPTAD would promote the "revitalization of U.S. economic leadership in the Asian-Pacific region."[15] Krause and Sekiguchi, on the other hand, argued quite explicitly that such an organization is one means to "find a surrogate for hegemonial power," that international economic policymaking must attempt "to

---

[13]For review of the arguments surrounding hegemonic stability theory and a revision along these lines, see Robert O. Keohane, *After Hegemony* (Princeton: Princeton University Press, 1984). Duncan Snidal has distinguished among bargaining situations in evaluating hegemonic stability theory; see "Coordination versus Prisoners' Dilemma: Implications for International Cooperation and Regimes," *American Political Science Review* 79(4) (December 1985):940–41.

[14]Only part of the recent conflict within the Asian Development Bank concerns the issue of leadership, but as *The Economist* recently noted, "If Japan is to fulfill American calls to take on more of the responsibilities that its economic strength demands, then this will often be at the expense of the United States' own influence" (May 2, 1987, p. 90).

[15]*Asian-Pacific Regional Economic Organization*, p. 20.

create a system that can operate efficiently without a single or hegemonial country at its center."[16] This view, that American hegemony should be replaced, not by Japanese hegemony, but by collective leadership, was strongly supported by the developing countries of the region, particularly the members of ASEAN. In effect, a consensus emerged by the early 1980s that "leadership for an eventual community should not be assumed by an industrial power of the region."[17] The question that lingers is whether any degree of institutionalization can be accomplished without such leadership.

National Interests

The structure of power in the Pacific region has had a decided effect on national attitudes toward institutionalizing economic cooperation. For somewhat different reasons, the governments that have demonstrated at least sporadic enthusiasm for greater organization of the Pacific region have been Japan and Australia. For Japan, as noted earlier, a Pacific regional organization offered a role between, on one hand, global organizations that appeared dominated by Europe and the United States and, on the other, specifically Asian organizations that might recall imperial structures such as the Co-Prosperity Sphere. A regional organization would also serve to deflect the tensions from bilateral relations—with the United States, with ASEAN—into a multilateral forum.[18] Despite its support for Pacific initiatives, however, Japan's enthusiasm fluctuated over time, probably reaching its peak under Prime Minister Ohira. For Australia, the Pacific also provided an escape from sticky bilateral ties—the overwhelming economic presence of Japan—and a means to adjust to a new niche in the international economy, as ties to Britain and the Commonwealth faded.[19]

The United States, though rhetorically supportive of Pacific economic cooperation, has had mixed motives in constructing institutions for the region. As Patrick and Drysdale suggested, one attraction of organizing the Pacific was to provide a means of reasserting American leadership during a time of doubt following the Vietnam War. Against that benefit, however, had to be weighed the possibility that such an organization would simply provide American support for de facto economic dominance by Japan in the region. And other strategies were

---

[16]Krause and Sekiguchi, *Economic Interaction*, pp. 260, 244.

[17]Oborne and Fourt, *Pacific Basin Economic Cooperation*, p. 17.

[18]On Japanese dissatisfaction with ASEAN relations, see Bernard K. Gordon, "Japan and the Pacific Basin Proposal," in Soesastro and Han, *Pacific Economic Cooperation*, p. 249.

[19]Sung-joo Han, "The Pacific Community Proposal: An Appraisal," in Crawford, *Pacific Economic Cooperation*, p. 104.

possible for the United States: on one hand, continued commitment to global economic institutions; on the other, the increasing appeal of bilateral bargaining or unilateral *faits accompli* that seemed to award the United States more leverage than a multilateral approach. Other factors inhibited the United States during the Reagan administration: an intense ideological distaste for international economic organizations that conflicted with the usefulness of the Pacific as a (misperceived) "free market" economic model and a stick to wave at recalcitrant Europeans. Growing protectionist pressure in Congress—much of it directed against Pacific economies—also made the task of institution building politically sensitive for any American government.[20]

If the industrialized countries were at least sporadically supportive of organizing the Pacific economy, the developing countries of the region, and particularly the ASEAN states, were far less enthusiastic, and their skepticism was a major determinant of the slow and informal trajectory of Pacific economic organization after 1980. ASEAN was born in the same era as the first Pacific initiatives; its institutional development responded to the same international pressures as those surrounding Pacific regional proposals, particularly the fall of South Vietnam. As a result, Pacific organizational proposals were frequently seen as rivals, rather than complements, to ASEAN.

Concern that Pacific loyalties might weaken a fragile ASEAN was only one of the objections voiced by ASEAN. Given that the Pacific proposals emanated from the industrialized countries of the region, there was also concern that they might cloak a renewed neocolonial economic domination to replace the colonial ties so recently overturned. Nonalignment also could be threatened, if the Pacific regional organizations became instruments of a new policy of containment (even though each of the proposals hewed to a strictly economic agenda). It became clear from Canberra onward that any intensified institutionalization of Pacific economic cooperation would move only as quickly as ASEAN would permit.[21]

---

[20]On American attitudes, see Han, "Pacific Community Proposal," pp. 101–2; Charles E. Morrison, "American Interests in the Concept of a Pacific Basin Community," in Crawford, *Pacific Economic Cooperation*, pp. 114–17; Mark Borthwick, "U.S. Governmental Responses to the Pacific Community Idea," in Soesastro and Han, *Pacific Economic Cooperation*, pp. 278–89.

[21]ASEAN views of Pacific regional cooperation have been set forth in a host of articles and speeches, among them: Tan Sri M. Ghazli Shafie, "Towards a Pacific Basin Community: A Malaysian Perception," in Crawford, *Pacific Economic Cooperation*, pp. 96–100; Russel H.

Elite Attitudes

In this sketch of national attitudes toward Pacific institutionaliza-tion, countries have been reified and portrayed as unified actors, a stan-dard analytical shorthand. Nevertheless, it is worth examining the attitudes of the three elite networks that have been incorporated in the Canberra process since 1980 and have been influential in Pacific discus-sions for two decades: governments, private corporations, and academ-ics. Though government attitudes are often equated with the national stances already outlined, it is important to note that the occasional enthusiasm expressed by some of the regional governments has come from politicians, not from bureaucrats. A major weakness of projects for Pacific organization has been the failure to enlist any powerful national bureaucracies in the cause. This failure suggests the difficulty in institu-tional innovation when the organizational space is well filled: most bureaucracies have ties to existing international organizations that could be threatened by new institutional demands.

In the case of corporations, the key question is how many view their organizational interests and strategy in Pacific terms: most of the largest multinationals are global in outlook; many smaller firms define their overseas interests in terms of one or two markets or fields for invest-ment. Is there any intermediate group of corporations that are essen-tially regional in outlook? Despite the support given to the Pacific Basin Economic Councils, the answer remains unclear.

Academics from university or policy research settings have served as one of the most influential lobbies in support of Pacific regional orga-nization, and economists have been particularly prominent. Their enthusiasms have been influenced by prevailing academic fashions, however, and the cause of Pacific regionalism in the 1980s has undoubt-edly suffered from two contemporary trends. One, mentioned earlier, is particularly clear on the right of the political spectrum and within the economics profession: skepticism about the value of any international organizations, which are assigned the same negative role as govern-

Fifield, "ASEAN and the Pacific Community," and Noordin Sopiee, "ASEAN and the Pacific Basin Concept: Questions and Imperatives," in Soesastro and Han, *Pacific Economic Cooperation*, pp. 189–214; Rhondda M. Nicholas, "ASEAN and the Pacific Community Debate: Much Ado About Something?" *Asian Survey* 21(12) (December 1981):1197–1210; M. Hadi Soesastro, "ASEAN and the Political Economy of Pacific Cooperation," *Asian Survey* 23(12) (December 1983):1255–70.

ments in the domestic sphere.[22] Regionalism itself has also declined in academic esteem since the 1960s, when the EEC was viewed as a model of international cooperation by industrialized and developing countries alike. Now the obstacles to regional economic organization and its potentially negative consequences are given far greater attention.[23]

Conceptual Cloudiness

The decline in regionalism as an academic fashion points to the fourth and final explanation for the record of Pacific institution building thus far: a progressive decline in any certainty about what cooperative ends the informal or formal processes are to serve and in what way they are to serve these ends. Lack of specificity in defining cooperative arrangements has been particularly troublesome in three areas: *boundaries, alternatives,* and *modalities.*

The boundaries of the region have remained vague, a circumstance that has made the potential membership vary from a club of industrialized countries to (potentially) all states from Pakistan to Brazil. Although the rapidly growing weight of the Pacific region in the world economy is clear, the degree to which it has become more of a region in terms of economic transactions is less certain.[24] Some of the apparent intensification of economic exchange in the region may be an artifact of features specific to the 1980s: the Latin American debt crisis (diminishing the relative economic importance of Latin America as a market and site of investment for both the United States and Japan) and the sharp decline in oil prices since 1981, reducing the importance of the Middle East/OPEC for Japan and other Asian exporters.

Regional definition may be given by other than purely economic criteria, but here as well the boundaries have been poorly specified. If the Pacific region is to be characterized by a set of regimes governing relations among the states of the region, the normative content of those

---

[22]Particularly significant in this regard has been the public choice perspective on intervention by governments (and international organizations). See John A. C. Conybeare, "International Organization and the Theory of Property Rights," *International Organization* 34(3) (Summer 1980):307–34; Bruno S. Frey, "The Public Choice View of International Political Economy," *International Organization* 38(1) (Winter 1984):220–21.

[23]To cite only one example, see the survey of African efforts at regional integration in Domenico Mazzeo, ed., *African Regional Organizations* (Cambridge: Cambridge University Press, 1984).

[24]For one analysis, mixed in its implications, of data from the 1970s, see Oborne and Fourt, *Pacific Basin Economic Cooperation,* pp. 22–29.

regimes could provide an alternative definition of the region.[25] Unfortunately, the heterogeneity of the region has made it difficult to specify such norms. Some conservative observers have attempted to use the Pacific region as a proxy for free market economies, an appellation that, save for Hong Kong, hardly matches reality.[26] The recent Vancouver Declaration of the PECC used the criteria of "free and open economic exchanges" (also far from reality, though perhaps a reasonable statement of intent) and "extensive economic activities in the Pacific." Using such norms to define boundaries for the region may well conflict with at least one of the tasks for Pacific organization—integrating reformminded socialist economies, such as China, into the regional economy.

Political norms have served to reinforce the integration of other regions: democracy was used as a necessary ticket of admission to the EEC. Such similarity in political norms served not only as a value in itself; it also increased the symmetry in bargaining within the EEC and permitted a level of openness that may be a prerequisite for higher levels of international collaboration. In the Pacific region, political heterogeneity is even greater than heterogeneity in economic practices. The region includes established democracies, consistently or sporadically authoritarian regimes, and countries that have adamantly rejected movement toward democratization.

The alternatives to Pacific regional organizations have provided the most powerful ammunition for skeptics from the start. Two alternatives seem particularly compelling: other multilateral and bilateral negotiating forums or simply "muddling through" with ad hoc negotiations to facilitate a successful market-based economy. In an early comment on the Drysdale-Patrick OPTAD proposal, Alfred Reifman argued that "these five countries do not need another forum to talk to one another."

---

[25]In introducing the concept of regimes here, I am employing a term developed by political scientists to describe "sets of implicit or explicit principles, norms, rules and decision-making procedures around which actors' expectations converge in a given area of international relations." Although I remain skeptical of long-run usefulness of regimes in research, given the lack of precision in specifying boundary conditions, the concept is useful in describing a particular international ordering—" injunctions of greater or lesser specificity," in Keohane's words—without implying the necessity of a formal international organization. See Stephen D. Krasner, *International Regimes* (Ithaca: Cornell University Press, 1983); Keohane, *After Hegemony* and "The Study of International Regimes and the Classical Tradition in International Relations," paper presented at 1986 annual meeting of the American Political Science Association; on difficulties in employing the concept, see Friedrich Kratochwil and John Gerard Ruggie, "IO as an Art of the State: A Regime Critique," *International Organization* 40(4) (Autumn 1986):753–75.

[26]While offering certain disclaimers, Staffan Burenstam Linder makes this argument in *The Pacific Century* (Stanford: Stanford University Press, 1986).

Regional issues were adequately addressed by ESCAP, he claimed; broader functional issues were more effectively discussed in global multilateral organizations that may go beyond consultation. A Pacific organization might be more than superfluous, undermining the nondiscriminatory norms of global postwar economic organizations. On this point, proponents of regional economic organizations have always had a difficult case: a wholly nondiscriminatory organization with open admission is likely to be ineffective, whereas a discriminatory organization could produce yet another club of successful economies turned away from global issues and responsibilities.

The second alternative is not so clearcut, but it underlies the viewpoint of many who are skeptical of the need for multilateral economic organizations to facilitate market transactions. The Pacific regional idea has been propounded in an atmosphere not of regional economic crisis, but of considerable economic success. In the eyes of many, an American aphorism seems appropriate: "If it ain't broke, don't fix it." The Pacific economy seems less in need of an overhaul than a little peripheral tinkering, and that should not require more than case-by-case negotiation.

The final conceptual shortcoming in many proposals to organize the Pacific economy is an unwillingness to specify the *modalities* that will lead to resolving economic conflicts in the region. As noted, the use of the OECD model and the phrase "consultation" are hardly adequate: conflict is presumably caused by government policies, and "consultation" may not produce the adjustment in policies necessary to resolve the conflict.

An Agenda and Its Dilemmas

The conceptual shortcomings described here help to highlight several criteria that can be employed in determining whether a higher degree of institutionalization would be desirable in the Pacific; obstacles in elite attitudes and the international environment suggest one means of estimating its feasibility. Beginning with the question of institutional design, it is worth asking what areas of economic conflict are widely perceived within the region, or, put differently, in what areas could economic performance be improved by changes in government policies and which of these could be better dealt with by new regional institutions than by existing global or regional organizations or regimes. Merely establishing that agenda, however, is not enough: the means by which the adjustment of government policies might be accomplished must also be stipulated.

Four functional issue areas—trade, direct foreign investment, natural resources/commodities, and finance—have received the most attention in discussions of Pacific institutions. Each, it will be argued, requires different modalities and a different level of institutionalization to adjust state policies. To this list could be added coordination of macroeconomic and exchange rate policies. Although past proposals and the existing Canberra process have held that functional specialization within a Pacific organization is optimal, one advantage of a regional organization (as compared to most global economic organizations) is that it need not be compartmentalized on functional lines. One shortcoming of postwar economic organizations is their fairly rigid functional divisions, a phenomenon that has hindered adaptation to new issues (such as the debt crisis) or the linkage of issues (trade and finance, for example). It has also produced unseemly turf battles. Even though functional organization may be effective in the regional setting as well, a regional organization might contribute most at the boundaries of issue areas.[27]

Finance and Economic Policy Coordination:
Information Sharing and Consultation

International financial issues, particularly those dealing with private capital flows, should assume a prominent place on any agenda of Pacific discussions in the 1980s. The rapid internationalization of the Tokyo capital market and its implications for other financial centers in the region, from Singapore to Los Angeles, presents in itself a substantial agenda. More broadly, however, the region is home to a major source of capital exports (in Japan) and also a large number of middle-income developing countries that increasingly rely on private financial markets for their international borrowing.

Although a number of other international organizations—the International Monetary Fund, the World Bank, regional development banks, the Bank for International Settlements—deal with portions of private financial issues, they have often been preoccupied with resolving the debt crisis rather than looking beyond it to encouraging future private financial intermediation and preventing future debt shocks. In a region barely brushed by the debt crisis, but with members (including the United States) heavily dependent on continuing financial flows, a Pacific organization could play an innovative role that would not duplicate other entities. The means necessary for raising the probability of cooperative solutions in this area would also be relatively modest: in this instance, simply sharing information (though it would be sensitive

---

[27]Krause and Sekiguchi noted this valuable dimension of a regional organization in *Economic Interaction*, p. 260.

information) and consultation on future policies would be an improvement over current outcomes.

Consultation on macroeconomic and exchange rate policies is another issue area that could benefit from similar processes. Although the IMF and the Group of Seven (G-7) have begun to focus attention on improving multilateral surveillance, the coordinating process has remained restricted to the industrialized countries. In the Pacific region, the bargaining between Japan and the United States in this issue area has an enormous impact on the smaller economies of the region. Given their interest in the outcome, could the two economic superpowers be convinced to include these affected parties in an informal process of consultation? Probably not, but the smaller economies do have a few bargaining chips: two at least (Taiwan and South Korea), given their large trade surpluses, have already received intense scrutiny from the United States. Both the United States and the surplus economies might find a multilateral regional forum more congenial than a bilateral context for bargaining over adjustment strategies. (Such a regional forum could also include Taiwan, which is no longer a member of the IMF.)

Even in these cases, where simple consultation and provision of information would improve existing levels of cooperation, an intergovernmental organization of some sort would appear to be desirable, though it need not be a massive bureaucracy: confidence in the information shared would be enhanced, and such an organization could also propose alternative alternatives for member states, if desired.

Trade: Regime Enhancement and Insurance

Trade interdependence and the conflict it produces has been a major element in the rationale for Pacific regional cooperation. In the case of trade, however, unlike finance or even macroeconomic policy adjustment, a Pacific institution is in danger of duplicating the global GATT regime or undermining it. A Pacific trade regime could avoid duplicating the GATT through two linked strategies, which have already been suggested in light of the new Uruguay round of trade negotiations. Should those negotiations become stalled—presumably because of the obstruction of the EEC—the Pacific economies could move ahead on their own toward greater trade liberalization: they would not deviate from the GATT norms but would offer an island of additional liberalization within the existing trade regime. The insurance (or threat) that the Pacific states would move ahead on their own could serve as a useful prod in the global negotiations.[28]

Such a Pacific trade strategy assumes that liberalization would be easier within the region than at a global level, though for certain items on the agenda, such as agriculture, that seems unlikely. The question of discrimination would also have to be confronted, since the deeply engrained norm of reciprocity makes it unlikely that the states of the region would extend any liberalization on a most-favored-nation basis to others outside. Krause suggests "only minimum differentiation . . . to protect the region from free riders," but the wide consensus up to this point has been that any Pacific trade arrangements must be nondiscriminatory. Given the binding character of the commitments that would be necessary—since trade bargaining is a game of assistance rather than coordination—a far higher level of institutionalization would be required for a regional organization to be effective in facilitating the movement toward trade liberalization.[29]

Regime Creation and Foreign Direct Investment

The industrialized countries of the region have long sought a code governing direct foreign investment as part of their agenda for Pacific economic cooperation. Given the competitive (and pointless) character of investment incentives offered by many developing countries in the region and their desire to attract more foreign investment, the developing countries in the Pacific region might also have an interest in such an arrangement.

Unlike the trade regime, however, no comparable authoritative global regime exists in this area: the countries in question would be creating a regime rather than adapting an existing one, and the level of institutional commitment would presumably go up. Given the competition for foreign investment and the possibilities for deviation from agreed norms in particular instances, considerable powers of surveillance and even arbitration might be required.

North-South Cooperation and Commodities

Each of the foregoing issue areas has a North-South facet, and one of the principal rationales for a Pacific regional organization is that it provides a means for innovation in North-South economic relations distinct from arrangements based on previous colonial ties (such as the EEC's Lome Agreements) or the failed arena of global negotiations.

---

[28]See the comments by Peter Drysdale and Lawrence Krause in James W. Morley, ed., *The Pacific Basin: New Challenges for the United States* (New York: Academy of Political Science, 1986), pp. 19–20, 159–60. Alternative regional trade strategies are described by M. Hadi Soesastro in ch. 13 of this volume.

[29]Duncan Snidal describes the different institutional requirements of these two games in "Coordination versus Prisoners' Dilemma: Implications for International Cooperation and Regimes," *American Political Science Review* 79(4) (December 1985):923–41.

In no area of North-South relations is such innovation more necessary, or more important to the region, than in commodities. The 1980s have been a dismal decade for commodity producers, and by the middle of the decade the slump in commodity prices had severely affected the Southeast Asian economies. Although the Soviet Union's stated intention to participate in the Common Fund may revive that moribund scheme, few, following the collapse of the Tin Agreement in 1985, expect an efficacious global solution.

In this sphere, a Pacific regional organization would not duplicate existing organizations and could conceivably serve as a useful model for innovation at the global level. But the task here is even more daunting than in the other issue areas: policy innovation would be necessary, given the exhaustion of existing solutions, as well as a substantial measure of positive cooperation.[30] Presumably this would require the most highly developed institutional structure; it would also raise a question of commitment of resources more directly than any of the other issue areas. And with resources come the contentious issues of leadership and discrimination.

Before summarizing the model of Pacific organization implied by this policy agenda, we must examine the question of membership, since it is affected by and affects the question of discrimination and also the norms that may underpin Pacific institutions.

Who Should Belong: Latin America, China, the Soviet Union?

For those who view the Pacific region as defined by market-oriented economies, Latin American membership does not pose a dilemma. Despite a growing level of economic interaction with the Pacific (and Japan in particular), however, Latin American interest in Pacific regional organization has been minimal.[31] Should that indifference change, Latin American membership would bring a number of benefits. Already connected to Japanese and American financial institutions, Latin American countries should be involved in discussion of Pacific financial flows. Membership would also jog the Latin states out of their fixation on hemispheric affairs and the United States, placing them in a setting with another group of middle-income developing countries that are con-

---

[30]Jacques Pelkmans has distinguished between negative cooperation, "removing discriminatory treatment against goods and factors flows from abroad," and positive cooperation, "the construction of institutions and agreements for *common* policy making," in Robert J. Gordon and Jacques Pelkmans, *Challenges to Interdependent Economies* (New York: McGraw-Hill, 1979), p. 97.

[31]Chile has recently applied for membership in the PECC.

fronting similar economic problems but have dealt with them more successfully and pragmatically.

Latin American membership would raise a serious question of membership size, however. Even though some comments on potential Pacific organizations have blithely proposed completely open admissions, such a broad membership would dilute the cooperative ends of such an organization. A large membership is likely to hinder bargaining and increase both the costs of reaching agreement and the costs (in terms of resources) of implementing any schemes of positive cooperation.[32] A larger organization would also risk extensive freeriding by its smaller members.

The membership of China in a Pacific regional organization poses once again the importance of norms in organizing the region. The fact that China's reforms have hardly made it an open or even market-oriented economy would call into question the incorporation of those norms in any regional institutions. On the other hand, the common characteristics of the other Pacific economies are also difficult to discern, and there are considerable benefits to Chinese membership. Indeed, one additional task such an organization should undertake is the integration of such economies into the region—an integration that might otherwise, in the case of China, be disruptive.[33]

The last potential member, the Soviet Union, presents not only the problem of a centrally planned economy just embarking on a course of reform, but also the issues of international security that Pacific regional organizations have resolutely sidestepped up to this point. Concerns over security have long cast a shadow over efforts to construct regional institutions. Given the sensitivities of both Japan and the developing countries in the region, however, security issues have been banished from the agenda of any Pacific initiative.

The interest of the Soviet Union in the Pacific economy necessarily resurrects the issue: excluding the Soviet Union while accepting China would give the impression that an anti-Soviet bloc was being con-

---

[32]Snidal notes that the negative effects of group size are more serious for certain collective action problems than for others: For coordination, organization may be impeded, but the stability of any arrangement reached might be enhanced. In prisoners' dilemma situations, the possibility of exclusion may be an important sanction (in some cases the only real sanction) in maintaining the regime (Snidal, "Coordination versus Prisoners' Dilemma," p. 936).

[33]China's external economic relations are clearly concentrated in the Pacific region. How problematic China's entry into the world economy will become is the subject of some debate: see, e.g., comments by McCulloch and Dernberger in Bruce Dickson and Harry Harding, eds., *Economic Relations in the Asian-Pacific Region* (Washington, D.C.: Brookings Institution, 1987), pp. 74–76.

structed, despite assurances to the contrary.[34] The possibilities for increased Soviet economic involvement in the region have been viewed with justifiable skepticism.[35] Fears that the Soviets might disrupt a fledgling institution have also been voiced. Rather than regarding Soviet interest as a dangerous dilemma for Pacific organization, we should view it as a double opportunity. Soviet involvement would be beneficial in certain economic issues, in which it is a key player (fisheries is a major example). Other regional players should take the risk that the cooptation effect of Soviet participation will outweigh any possible future disruptive behavior. Soviet interest also permits a reopening of the taboo security agenda. Although that may offend some of the non-aligned states, the opportunity to reopen security issues as part of an informal dialogue with the Soviet Union while keeping those issues on a separate track from economic ones might well meet with their approval. In any case, some economic issues already touch on national security—in particular, security of supply for energy and other mineral resources.

The Model and Its Prospects

An examination of the economic agenda for the Pacific region confirms that an important niche for regional economic cooperation does exist, namely, in bridging issue areas that are separated at the global level and in addressing aspects of other issues in which global solutions are doubtful (trade) or nonexistent (commodities).

A careful examination of the regional economic agenda also confirms, however, that the institutions designed to deal with this agenda must match the cooperative problems. Throughout this discussion, the mutual adjustment of government policies has been used as the test of successful international economic cooperation. Evaluating Pacific institutions, existing and prospective, by the same standard may be too demanding a test in the short run; in the longer term, it remains the most useful yardstick. Simple reliance on "consultation" as a cureall for failures of cooperation is not enough, and consultation without the involvement of governments, characteristic of the present Canberra process, is even less likely to succeed.

The Canberra process may have been designed as a stopgap when the lack of momentum for an intergovernmental organization became

---

[34]Of course, exclusion could be based on an argument that the Soviet Union is not deeply involved in the regional economy; like Latin America, it has faced Europe, not the Pacific, in its economic relations.

[35]Soviet economic policies and their impact on the Pacific-Asian region are described by Robert Campbell in ch. 4 of this volume.

apparent, but it risks becoming accepted as a permanent solution. The drawbacks to the current approach are already apparent. Participation by government representatives in their private capacities is in many ways the worst of both worlds, constraining the agenda of the PECC within fairly narrow bounds while avoiding government commitment. The process is also excessively elitist: its incorporation of government, business, and academics resembles the old stereotype of "Japan, Inc.," and has decided limits in building political support for Pacific economic cooperation. Little attention has been paid the groups—labor in particular—that bear most of the costs of increasing interdependence, even though it is their political resistance that often shapes government policy.

Finally, using the yardstick of change in national policies, the influence of the Canberra process is likely to remain limited. The Canberra process provides at best two routes to mutual adjustment of policy and attainment of more cooperative solutions: shifting government policies through provision of improved information and research or through the informal consultation that takes place among the "private" governmental representatives involved in the process. Although proponents of the Canberra process already detect some effects on international agenda-setting, the success of either of these routes—given the proliferation of alternatives—remains unproven. Another assumption—that such "socialization" will ultimately lead to structures of governmental cooperation—seems a misreading of neofunctionalist arguments about international organization. Often the intergovernmental structure comes first and is then reinforced by interest group activity.

For even the most modest consultative processes described here, an intergovernmental organization (IGO) is probably necessary; for those issue areas requiring regime enhancement or creation, or positive cooperation, an IGO is essential. An IGO could perform research and information-gathering functions more effectively (by gathering information denied to private researchers); it could also assist in agenda-setting and innovation in the uncharted areas that such a regional organization might enter. Two stumbling blocks that have often been cited—membership and relationship to existing multilateral organizations—could be dealt with in the design of the institution or institutions. Given costs to the level of cooperation in a completely open membership, membership could be available on a "two-track" (or "three-track") basis.[36] Those members with less involvement in the region (or conceivably less attachment to organizational norms) could assume fewer obligations (and receive fewer benefits). Relations with multilateral organizations could be eased by finding niches for the Pacific organization that are not occupied by existing organizations (the strategy outlined here) or by making explicit the connections to global regimes (by involving the IMF staff in regional macroeconomic policy consultations, for example).

The aim would be an organization that complemented broader multilateral organizations rather than undermining or competing with them. Although the involvement of private individuals and groups with such an organization (as in the present Canberra process) would be important to its political success, that involvement would have to be broadened beyond the present pattern. Such activation of private individuals and groups, however, should not be viewed as a substitute for intergovernmental action.

Probabilities and Conditions for Cooperation

This sketch of an argument for renewed interest in a Pacific intergovernmental organization should remain simply that, since at present the political feasibility of such a proposal is virtually nil. Until some of the obstacles and conditions described earlier change, no Pacific regional economic organization is on the horizon. The region does not face economic crisis, which might stimulate an organizational leap. Any future crisis is likely to originate in one of the two economic powers of the region. Japan's economic adjustment in the face of a rising yen could result in persistent high unemployment (by historical standards) and declining economic growth. Protectionism in the United States could become a divisive political issue directed at Asian countries in particular. Though the probability of these outcomes is not zero, it is fairly low. Even in the event of such crisis scenarios, a cooperative international solution seems a highly unlikely result.

A more persistent hindrance concerns the question of Pacific leadership. Can more cooperative economic solutions or a new organizational structure be devised when two leading economic powers must share in their creation? The experience of the Asian Development Bank is not encouraging as a microcosm. There also does not seem to be any domestic political payoff for a political leader in Japan or the United

---

[36]The idea of two-track or "two-speed" membership was mooted for the EEC at a time when British recalcitrance seemed to threaten cooperative momentum. It was later set aside.

States who endorses an organizational initiative of this sort, and there could be political costs.

Finally, nearly all observers have pointed to ASEAN hesitation as a major barrier to further organizational initiatives in the Pacific.[37] Although ASEAN concern for its own institution-building is understandable, its lack of enthusiasm remains puzzling: increased multilateralism could only increase ASEAN's bargaining weight in negotiations with Japan and the United States, particularly when the two economic giants are often at odds. Indeed, the diplomatic skills of ASEAN should give it a decided advantage in such a setting, and formulating a joint negotiating position could well strengthen ASEAN institutionally.

ASEAN represents a final alternative to Pacific regional organization: not global multilateralism, but more restrictive groupings within the region. Despite the enormous number of fans that ASEAN has accumulated in the United States and Japan (not to speak of ASEAN itself), its accomplishments have been mixed: quite striking in the security and diplomatic sphere, limited in the economic sphere. ASEAN has managed to create a de facto security community among a group of states that were, in some cases, at war twenty-five years ago. It has managed to build a joint diplomatic position toward the Vietnamese occupation of Cambodia and has mobilized support for that position internationally. It has not significantly increased regional economic integration, however, and given the distinctly different preferences and economic structures of its members—free-trading Singapore in particular—it seems unlikely that large-scale advance in this area will occur.[38] In addition, political trends in the region, particularly widened participation, might well give added weight to nationalist and inward-looking concerns.

The strategic choices for developing countries—whether NICs of the first or second generation—are highly constrained. Regional integration among developing countries, whatever its benefits in underpinning diplomatic cooperation, is no longer viewed as the panacea for Third World

---

[37]Of course, even without the convenience of ASEAN reluctance, other obstacles could easily be found.

[38]Rieger's analysis of intra-ASEAN trade suggests a striking increase over ten years, but closer analysis reveals its dependence on trade in petroleum products among Indonesia, Malaysia, and Singapore, which, as he notes, has already begun to decline with the opening of new refinery capacity by Malaysia and Indonesia (Hans Christoph Rieger, *ASEAN Cooperation and Intra-ASEAN Trade* (Institute for Southeast Asian Studies, ASEAN Economic Research Unit, Research Notes and Discussion Paper, no. 57, 1985). On the modest achievements in finance, see Michael T. Skully, *ASEAN Financial Cooperation* (London: Macmillan, 1985).

economic development that inspired such enthusiasm in the 1960s.[39] The UNCTAD strategy of global negotiations appears bankrupt. North-South negotiation and collaboration within a regional context may well provide the best hope for shifting the rules of the game in a more favorable direction. The success or failure of any future Pacific regional organization would clearly depend on whether it can fill the need for a new instrument of North-South collaboration. Integration of one successful newly industrializing economy (Japan) was a task that the regional economy failed to accomplish in the 1930s, and it remains an arena in which Pacific economic organization could make its greatest contribution. Given the political landscape, internationally and domestically, that need is likely to remain unfilled.

---

[39]For an interesting comparison of ASEAN with another model of regional integration in the developing countries, see *Regional Industrial Cooperation: Experiences and Perspectives of ASEAN and the Andean Pact* (United Nations Industrial Development Organization, 1983).

Contributors

Robert W. Campbell is Distinguished Professor of economics at Indiana University, Bloomington.

Dante B. Canlas is professor of economics at the University of the Philippines, Quezon City.

Seung-Soo Han is a professor of economics at Seoul National University, a member of the National Assembly, and recently appointed trade minister.

Sung-joo Han is professor of political science at the Asiatic Research Center, Korea University, Seoul.

Miles Kahler is a professor of international relations in the Graduate School of International Relations and Pacific Studies at the University of California, San Diego.

Mingsarn Santikarn Kaosa-ard is associate professor of economics at Chiangmai University, Chiangmai, Thailand.

Lawrence B. Krause is professor of international relations and Pacific studies in the Graduate School of International Relations and Pacific Studies at the University of California, San Diego.

Thomas A. Layman is director for Asia and the Pacific at the Institute of International Finance, Washington, D.C.

Yukio Noguchi is professor of economics at Hitotsubashi University, Tokyo.

Gustav F. Papanek is professor of economics and director of the Center for Asian Development Studies, Boston University.

Seizaburo Sato is professor of political science at the University of Tokyo (Komaba) and a member of the board of directors of the Asia Pacific Association of Japan.

Robert A. Scalapino is Robson Research Professor of Government and director of the Institute of East Asian Studies, University of California, Berkeley.

Sueo Sekiguchi is professor of economics at Seikei University, Tokyo.

Djisman S. Simandjuntak is chair of the department of economics at the Centre for Strategic and International Studies, Jakarta.

M. Hadi Soesastro is Director of Studies at the Centre for Strategic and International Studies, Jakarta.

Jusuf Wanandi is executive director of the Centre for Strategic and International Studies, Jakarta.

John Wong is professor of economics and statistics at the National University of Singapore, Kent Ridge.

Ippei Yamazawa is professor of economics at Hitotsubashi University, Tokyo, and visiting professor at the University of Sheffield, England.